Es gibt wenig noch zu erzählen: was nachher
kommt, ist bloß Nachklang, Echo, Zittern der Nerven.
Nach diesem Erlebnis hat unser Dasein, immer am
Rand des Todes, eine sehr einfache Form bekommen
sich auf das unbedingt Notwendige eingeschränkt.
Wir leben, — sagen die einen — weil wir unser Leben
auf das primitivste eingestellt haben.
Wir leben — sagen die anderen — weil die
Gefühle für das Grosse, Gerechte, Zukünftige ~~immer~~
von uns immer noch wachgehalten werden.
Wir leben — sagen die einen — weil alles nur der
Erhaltung des Lebens zu dienen hat.
Wir leben — sagen d. a. — weil wir auch noch Sinn
haben für das Metaphysische. — Wir haben
uns an das Gegenwärtige angepasst, aber im Innern
bereit für das Zukünftige.
Man hat für uns bereit: Gewehr, Typhus, Galgen, —

—

Es ist Spätherbst. Es ist Winter. 2½ Jahre Getto,
ein Jahr Einsiedelung.....
Werden wir jemals das G. [illegible] überwinden? —
Mit dieser Frage begeben wir uns auf d. Weg.

—

./.

In the Beginning Was the Ghetto

IN THE BEGINNING WAS THE GHETTO

Notebooks from Łódź

OSKAR ROSENFELD

Edited and with an introduction by Hanno Loewy

Translated from the German by Brigitte M. Goldstein

NORTHWESTERN UNIVERSITY PRESS
Evanston, Illinois

Northwestern University Press
Evanston, Illinois 60208-4210

Printed in the United States of America

10 9 8 7 6 5 4 3 2 1

ISBN 0-8101-1488-7 (cloth)

Library of Congress Cataloging-in-Publication Data

Rosenfeld, Oskar, 1884–1944.
[Wozu noch Welt. English]
In the beginning was the ghetto : notebooks from Łódź / Oskar Rosenfeld ; edited and with an introduction by Hanno Loewy ; translated from the German by Brigitte M. Goldstein.
p. cm.
ISBN 0-8101-1488-7 (cloth : alk. paper)
1. Rosenfeld, Oskar, 1884–1944—Diaries. 2. Jews—Poland—Łódź—Diaries. 3. Holocaust, Jewish (1939–1945)—Poland—Łódź—Personal narratives. 4. Łódź (Poland)—Ethnic relations. I. Loewy, Hanno, 1961– II. Goldstein, Brigitte. III. Title.
DS135.P63 R67813 2002
940.53'18'094384—dc21 2001006691

The paper used in this publication meets the minimum requirements of the American National Standard for Information Sciences—Permanence of Paper for Printed Library Materials, ANSI Z39.48-1984.

Endpapers: Facsimiles from Notebooks E and 11 of Oskar Rosenfeld's diary. Courtesy of Yad Vashem Archives.

Contents

Editor's Introduction

In the course of preparations for an exhibition at the Frankfurt Jewish Museum[1] about the ghetto of Łódź, we discovered a diary in Israel that burst all our previous notions. It was a fragmentary text, handwritten in twenty-one Polish school notebooks in the ghetto of Łódź between February 17, 1942, and July 28, 1944.

The notebooks are kept in the archives of Yad Vashem, the Israeli memorial in Jerusalem. In addition there is a five-hundred-two-page transcription of fifteen of the notebooks as well as eighty pages from six notebooks that have not yet been transcribed. The author of the diary is Oskar Rosenfeld, a writer from Vienna.

Rosenfeld was known to us as a contributor to the daily ghetto chronicle. But even more than his articles in the chronicle, which was under supervision of the Jewish Council, his private notebooks lay bare the profound contradictions of the ghetto, as subtle measures alternating with violent excesses slowly squeezed the life out of the captive Jewish community.

These notebooks contain a microcosm of daily, very personal notes, drafts, sketches, and themes for a planned literary account as well as notes for a history of the ghetto. Several pages of the diary are illustrated with drawings, among them several sketched self-portraits. In addition to those texts that were, in part, printed in the official ghetto chronicle, the diary is filled with unembellished descriptions of everyday life and the internal conflicts of the ghetto: hunger, forced labor, and deportations; endeavors to maintain a cultural, social, and religious life; the struggle for the preservation of human dignity despite the ceaseless assault on it. But we also find discussions of the ways in which the victims gradually became mired in a pattern of cynical behavior that served their own destruction, at the center of which stood the Eldest of the Jews, Mordechai Chaim Rumkowski.[2] Beyond such observations, the writings contain philosophical and theological reflections about what is now called the Shoah, in which all the questions that since then have been debated concerning whether civilization is possible after Auschwitz are already touched on.

The language of presentation has been condensed to the absolutely necessary and derives from a consciously concise, radical form of expression rather than Rosenfeld's own formal style. At the beginning of one of the notebooks we find the motto: "Completely factual, short sentences, eliminating anything sentimental, reading of the self far from the world, without a thought of the surroundings, alone in space, not meant for others . . . as remembrances for future days. . . ."

Writing the Destruction?

For many of the imprisoned in the ghettos, bearing witness was the last remaining possibility of transcending reality and of establishing a link with another world, the world "outside" or a "future" world. The writers regarded their diaries as a sort of message in a bottle without being sure where it would land or who would read it.

The act of keeping diaries, of which only a fraction have been published to this day and many have been lost, as an act of bearing witness was considered by some an existential mission or even a religious duty.

In this sense, the group around Emanuel Ringelblum in the Warsaw ghetto, which sought to collect every bit of information available about the ghetto and camp, called itself Oneg Shabbat, "the Joy of Shabbat,"[3] designating not only the day on which the group met but also the "sacredness" of their mission. Not only collective undertakings, like the Ringelblum archive, but also individual, Jewish diarists were imbued with a sense of the need to faithfully transmit to the world the events they were witnessing, as a lasting vestige and a saving power for that future of which they themselves had been deprived. Many of the notebooks were hidden and buried in bottles, tin cans, milk cans, and canning jars. Part of the Ringelblum archive was discovered in tin boxes and milk cans in the ruins of Warsaw after the war. It often took years for buried documents to be found in the areas that had comprised the ghettos and camps. In one instance, a former inmate led a search party to the ruins of Crematorium III in Auschwitz-Birkenau where notes about the ghetto by deportees from Łódź had been hidden. These notes had been buried in a cooking tin in August 1944 by Zelman Lewental, a member of the Jewish Special Division. Since he did not believe that he would ever have a chance himself to tell the story of what had happened, Zelman Lewental attached a comment of his own: "That's why I regard it as my duty to hide this package of papers, filled with writings, which I found, so that it will last for a long time. If not for anything else, so at least that his work will not have been in vain."[4]

Some writers consciously assumed the role of *sofer,* Torah scribe. Emanuel Ringelblum remarked: "The sofer picks up the pen with a trembling heart, for the slightest mistake in writing would mean the annulment of his entire work. It was with this same feeling that I began this work."[5] Elie Wiesel describes the role of the sofer as an "instrument of events," quoting from the Talmudic Rabbi Ishmael who tells the sofer: "Take care. Should you omit or add a single word, you might destroy the world."[6]

However, the traditional sofer's work was not to record positive, historical knowledge, but God's word as it is revealed in history, and its interpretation in Scripture. This strict delimiting is basically true in a narrower sense for all Jewish historical writing. David Roskies and Yosef Hayim Yerushalmi, and after them James E. Young, have pointed out that "even though catastrophic events occupy an enormous amount of Jewish historiography, the specific 'facts' of destruction are never really the aim of early Jewish historical writing."[7] Or, as Yerushalmi describes the function of subsuming history under traditional categories of exegesis: "There is a pronounced tendency to subsume even major new events to familiar archetypes, for even the most terrible events are somehow less terrifying when viewed within old patterns rather than in their bewildering specificity."[8]

Only with the Enlightenment did Jewish historical writing begin to focus, as Yerushalmi shows, on details of factual history. Thus we find an unsolvable paradox between historical testimony and the Jewish tradition of divine revelation in history. By seeing themselves as faithful "instruments of events," the [diarists of the Shoah] prevent the destruction of the world by giving testimony of their own destruction. By recording the complete senselessness, they try to interpret even this abyss as the revelation of the divine will in order to make some sense of history. Oskar Rosenfeld has articulated the aporia of this paradox better than anybody.

"In the Beginning Was the Ghetto"

As we were reading Rosenfeld's diary, our view that presentation of the ghetto is only possible through language was confirmed, more than ever. This is, of course, a language whose theme is its own undoing, which through its own destruction approaches that fateful connection between terror and endurance, normality and monstrosity, that characterized the ghetto. Maybe language is best suited to tracing the expansion of these shock waves through an endless expanse of time, this catastrophe that, in open or hidden form of erosion, abrades all meaning. Conscious abrogation and progressive deterioration of linguistic forms under outside pressure and inner anguish are inextricably intertwined in Rosenfeld's writings. Not only did Rosenfeld dismantle his own language in the ghetto; the language virtually burst in his hands, as of itself, into disparate fragments of a rich and formerly integrated body of knowledge that now appeared like a foreign object, like incoherent ballast. At the same time it represents, in the breathless succession of the diary entries, the counterworld to civilization on the eve of its destruction.

Whether purposely or not, Rosenfeld achieved a radical expression of the noncontemporaneous, of that which is irreconcilable. Rather than being directed toward the future as a construction of that which is unfinished, through the act of remembering and of halting the passage of time, by insisting on the wealth of the intellectual legacy, it becomes a paradoxical form of memory. Biblical citations, encyclopedia articles, passages from literature and philosophy: The author of these writings belongs to a different world, a cultural sphere whose echo becomes an ever more surreal, saving anchor of his existence. What remains is speaking, a language like a landscape of ruins in which the hope for a world to come wanders about like a flickering light and is again and again halted and twisted by a prescience of the extent of the catastrophe.

"If something like this is possible, what else can there be? Wherefore still war? Wherefore still hunger? Wherefore still world? [. . .]

There is little left to be said," wrote Oskar Rosenfeld after the deportation of the children in September 1942; "whatever comes after is merely reiteration, echo, a trembling of nerves. After this experience, our existence, always at the edge of death, has taken on a very simple form, to limit oneself to what is absolutely necessary. [. . .] What they have in store for us are rifles, typhus, gallows, death."

Oskar Rosenfeld wrote down his observations not only from the "waiting room of death," of which Jean Améry spoke in connection with the ghetto, but with prescience of what would follow this "prehell." Thus he jotted down on April 17, 1943, the following "rumor" that was making the rounds in the ghetto: "A small town. Five hundred to six hundred Jews are coming from the province. Disrobed in a big building. SS says: 'Nothing will happen to you. Just a bath. Cleaning, delousing, etc.' They move on. Slanted wet surface. They start sliding. They slither down. A sort of basin. Steam. Suffocating. Terrible screams. Dead."

As if he were obeying an impulse for self-preservation, Rosenfeld, like others, lived and wrote against this premonition of the full extent of the truth, dreaming of redemption, which he was awaiting in a state of powerlessness.

In a world turned upside down, a world in which any attempt at resistance was not only condemned to fail but would itself be turned into an instrument of destruction, categories no longer had any values by which resistance and acquiescence are traditionally distinguished.

"Within this monstrous machinery of death organization, which death makes so horrifying that it becomes impossible to integrate it into a culture and to think of it merely as a negation of a dialectic, death no longer matters; it becomes banal, anonymous, and public. In this world, the most abject humiliation does not lie in being unable to survive in the attempt, the only possible course, of resisting and refusing."[9]

Oskar Rosenfeld describes in minute detail this form of daily resistance in the naked struggle for survival as well as its insurmountable odds: "The tragedy is tremendous. The ghetto inhabitants cannot grasp it. For it does not produce greatness as in the Middle Ages. There are no heroes in this tragedy. And why tragedy? Because the pain does not touch on something human, on a strange heart, but on something incomprehensible that touches on the cosmos, an event in nature like the creation of the world. In the beginning God created the ghetto."

Rosenfeld's reflections end in an affirmation of Kiddush HaChaim, the sanctification of life, which increasingly came to oppose the traditional conception of Kiddush HaShem, the sanctification of the Holy Name.

No longer was it possible to give one's own life in order to escape forced conversion, forced baptism, and, with it, a betrayal of the covenant with God. On the contrary, what the enemies wanted was this life and nothing else. In the ghettos, even many rabbis declared survival to be the highest duty. For a deeply religious man, as Rosenfeld had apparently become in the ghetto, this theological discourse became the last attempt to give meaning to the suffering in face of the unfolding destruction.

In this sense, Rosenfeld also basically endorsed the efforts of the controversial Eldest of the Jews of Łódź, Mordechai Chaim Rumkowski, who tried to keep the ghetto alive through a policy of accommodation to the presumed economic interests of the Nazis with the slogan "Redemption through Work."

However, in the ghetto, any form of conventional resistance as well as any attempt at individual action to influence the course of events was subject to the arbitrary rule of the Nazis. Any open act of resistance could result in the immediate liquidation of the entire ghetto—the attempt of the Jewish Council to make the ghetto indispensable through work and perfect bureaucratic organization actually facilitated the Germans' task of deportation. The attempts on the part of communists in the ghetto to sabotage forced labor through work slowdowns endangered the continuance of the ghetto. But all attempts to give the ghetto economic significance lost all value once the Nazi authorities had decreed its liquidation. Not all deportations, from which many tried desperately, mostly in vain, to escape, ended in the extermination camps. Some people, albeit few, were ultimately saved by the invading Allied troops because they had actually been deployed for forced labor elsewhere.

In the turmoil of these events, Rosenfeld himself clung to a faint hope, to the moment after, to rescue from outside. He wrote for posterity, a future world, a world that was not his own.

In August 1944, during the final liquidation of the ghetto, he was deported, together with sixty-five thousand fellow Jews, to Auschwitz, where he was murdered in the gas chambers of Birkenau.

But who was Oskar Rosenfeld, whose diary was left behind in the ghetto? The diary gives hints of the most important stages of his life. The same data can be found in the "Encyclopedia of the Ghetto," to which he was a contributor, which had been compiled under the auspices of the archive set up by the Eldest of the Jews.[10] As far as can be determined, the list of Oskar Rosenfeld's publications and journalistic works is by and large complete.

Through Lucian Dobroszycki[11] at the YIVO Institute for Jewish Research in New York, I was able to contact Lia Mann, the widow of Rosenfeld's nephew Erich Mann (1902–1967), in Switzerland. She had met the actor and later travel writer Erich Mandl, who had adopted the name Mann in about 1920, in 1944 in New York, and they got married in 1950. The families on both sides had known each other previously. However, Lia got to know Oskar Rosenfeld only through Erich's stories. The frequency with which Erich's name appears in Rosenfeld's diary confirms that he must have been Rosenfeld's (Uncle Posi's) favorite nephew. So, the little that we know about Rosenfeld's family comes from Lia Mann. She was also responsible for maintaining the grave in Vienna of Frieda Mandl, who was her mother-in-law and Rosenfeld's sister, as well as the graves of other members of the family. Frieda's headstone also bears an inscription in memory of Oskar Rosenfeld.

"Wearing Jewish Is Very Fashionable Nowadays!"

Oskar Rosenfeld was born on May 13, 1884, in Koryčany, Moravia. His mother, Jeanette Rosenfeld, née Jellinek, was distantly related to those Jellineks whose financial support (and whose daughter's name was Mercedes), at the beginning of the century, gave a decisive boost to the prospects of a German automobile manufacturer.

Oskar Rosenfeld, whose mother had moved her business manufacturing ladies' lingerie and trousseaux from Koryčany to Kohlmarkt 5 in Vienna, completed his studies in 1908 with a doctoral thesis about Philipp Otto Runge and Romanticism, and thereafter devoted himself primarily to his literary interests. Rosenfeld was active in various Zionist organizations and wrote commentaries and critiques about art, literature, and theater for Jewish newspapers and magazines like *Die*

Welt (*The World*) and *Jüdische Volksstimme* (*Jewish Folk Voice*). As a young student in 1903, he had been introduced to the Zionist press by Theodor Herzl and belonged to the Association of University Students. In 1904, he was among the founders of the Jewish youth and student newspaper *Unsere Hoffnung* (*Our Hope*). The debates that took place then concerning specific forms of Jewish art and literature may seem today anachronistic and outright dogmatic. In several of his essays, Rosenfeld made his contribution to the then prevalent discussion about "race soul" and national art without being able initially to give these concepts a more specific definition except to hint at Lesser Ury's description of the essence of art as a struggle between man and nature: "Faced with the ruins of mutability, humble people acquiesce in their fate: It is always a struggle between the possible and the impossible, a contest between opposing forces, which is exactly what takes place in the soul of the artist: the wait for the flames of genius."[12]

In 1909, Oskar Rosenfeld, together with Hugo Zuckermann, founded the Jewish Stage, the first Jewish theater in Vienna. Here too we find the pathos of a pioneering spirit, hope for Jewish self-expression, and part of a profound sense of dissipation among his generation which saw this period, the eve of the First World War, as eroding all traditional conditions: "They live in the consciousness of having experienced the moment when Jewishness is for the first time able to lift its head up high with pride within the Austrian—I might say international—camp of antisemitism."[13]

However, Rosenfeld's literary talent does not find its expression in a philosophy of life euphoria, which was part of the temper of the time, but rather in his Viennese novel *Die vierte Galerie* (*The Fourth Gallery*), published in 1910.[14] The narrative, set in a student milieu, unfolds in a confusion of voices between Germans, Jews, and Russian revolutionary emigrants and ends largely in a vacuum. The fourth gallery, the mount Olympus of the opera, with its teeming youthful masses in pursuit of romantic dreams, becomes the symbol of the wait for a redemptive event. Michael Irrgang, a young Jewish student, is as much at a loss as his friends are about where to direct his sweeping aesthetic energies as well as his erotic longings.

So feels Agnes, who confesses to her mother: "I am in love with someone and don't know which one."[15] Some phrases are as pathetic as they are helpless and are thus an authentic mirror of expectations without aim. Hanna, another "girlfriend" of the ambivalent hero, expresses it: "Love—that's the spring of peoples" and "When will what is in them reach maturity?"[16] "You must get yourself together and begin something serious."[17] Each character has a premonition of things to come; they are all circling around each other in search of identity and the meaning of existence; and, in any case, they are affirming their Jewishness, which remains a vague notion, as does everything in this book. "There's only one Judaism, and that means being noble and having a desire to help. . . ."[18] Irrgang is not satisfied with this either. The novel ends with a scene in which he parts from Hanna, neither of them speaking the decisive words. Passing the opera house, where a collapsed horse is being mistreated, a sense of indifference toward all life overcomes him. "Mahler's parting, he thought. He lit a cigar and hurried to the Café Central."[19]

According to Lia Mann, Rosenfeld spent much time at that coffeehouse. During the war, he ended up in Bulgaria where he worked for the Austro-Bulgarian chamber of commerce in Sofia. From 1916 to 1918, he was editor-in-chief of a Bulgarian trade newspaper.

In 1920 appeared a collection of six novellas by Rosenfeld with the title *Tage und Nächte* (*Days and Nights*). Here, too, as in his novella *Mendel Ruhig,* published in 1914 and reprinted several times, Rosenfeld's narrative does not focus on a hero who represents the national Jewish cause but on a lone figure whose solitary path leads inevitably to a laconic, open end. His characters are strangers wherever they may be: A train stationmaster, who ended up somehow in Moravia and wears his uniform like a burden, performs his duties and waits for whatever may come. At some point he becomes deranged and sets the tracks the wrong way so the trains are likely to collide. Or the lodger of a sublet room who listens to the sounds in the room next door: the whimpering of a child, the moaning of an ailing woman, the buzzing of a fly circling the lamp. At some point, the woman in the room next door kills herself, and he has to look for new lodgings.[20]

Mendel Ruhig is about a mysterious loner, the beadle of the Jewish community of Rosenfeld's childhood whose sudden disappearance had intrigued him as a child. The story begins when the fourteen-year-old Mendel wants to say the blessing over rain one night. As he reaches for the prayerbook, the bookshelf collapses, burying his mother and father. "This night cut deep furrows into Mendel's soul. It seemed to him that his real life had ended and what came after were only fatuous episodes in which he played the part of a stranger."[21]

Mendel Ruhig from then on becomes the charge of the community and is housed in an unused women's bath, the mikvah, furnished with straw. One day, after many years, Mendel gets up to climb a nearby mountain "to view the big city." He never returns. Maybe he fell off a cliff or maybe he killed himself.

Oskar Rosenfeld had for the time being won out in his own struggle against loneliness. It seems that the time of self-doubt was gone after the war. He became active in a group of Zionist revisionists, the Jewish State Party [Judenstaatspartei]. It was this party that, in contrast to the moderate General Zionists [Allgemeine Zionisten] and the socialist Worker Zionists, advocated in the 1920s an uncompromising fight, if necessary by force, for the establishment of a Jewish state in Palestine that would include Transjordan. Rosenfeld was not only proud of having known Herzl, who had introduced him personally to the Zionist movement, but also of his relationship to Ze'ev Jabotinsky, the leader of the radical revisionists.

Rosenfeld used the contacts he had made during the war while traveling through the Balkan countries as Zionist propagandist and organizer. From 1923 to 1927, he was also active as the editor of the Zionist *Wiener Morgenzeitung* (*Viennese Morning Gazette*). However, his first love belonged to furthering the Jewish theater in Austria and Germany. In 1926, he sponsored the first performance in Vienna by the Moscow Jewish theater Habima before it moved permanently to Palestine. In 1927, he founded a new Jewish theater in Vienna, the Jüdische Künstlerspiele (Jewish Artists' Theater), and organized guest appearances by various Jewish theatrical groups, like the Vilna Troupe and the ensemble of Morris Schwarz. In addition, he translated classical and contemporary Yiddish literature, from Mendele Sforim and Sholem Aleichem to Yitzhak Leib Peretz and Joshua Singer.

In 1929 he became coeditor of the illustrated Zionist revisionist weekly *Die Neue Welt* (*The New World*). Until 1938, he regularly contributed lead articles, reports, and commentaries.

One of his first biting critiques was directed at Granowsky's touring Moscow Jewish-Academic Theater. Rosenfeld considered the troupe's attempt to connect the humoresque world of Sholem Aleichem with a modern mechanistic, revolutionary theater as an "eradication of the Jewish soul." He turned a sharp pen against any manifestation of "assimilationism"—even any kind of assimilation with the contemporary revolutionary movements.

Under the headline "Wearing Jewish Is Very Fashionable Nowadays," Rosenfeld wrote: "The Bishop of Paris concerns himself with questions of Palestine, the great minds of France gather at the Pro-Palestine Committee, and novels about Jews are as widespread as antisemitic excesses in Hungary. Indeed, it is de rigueur to speak of Jews even if one first has to slay them oneself!

"Things Jewish are very fashionable these days: Thomas Mann left his magic mountain to descend into the land of our fathers, where he got acquainted with Joseph and his brothers. Berlin tips its hat to the new fashion [. . .], with an association of friends of Habima to which even superior-court judges belong. And Richard Beer-Hofmann reads from his latest creation, 'Young David.'

"Assimilationists run the danger of having to assimilate with the creators of this new Jewish fashion. How is this—I almost said nebbish—supposed to end?"[22]

Rosenfeld's lead articles show him as a keen observer of the dramatic political developments in Germany. Early on he rejects the notion that the Nazis would be satisfied with merely segregating and ghettoizing the Jews. On the "possibility of a lessening of the contrasts once the separation of the Jews is complete," Rosenfeld wrote in 1936, in an article with the title "We Are Taking up the Fight!" "such optimism no longer has any basis in reality."[23]

Rosenfeld's work in Vienna ended with the Anschluss of Austria to the German Reich in 1938. He had gotten married only in 1937 and now he had to flee with his wife, Henriette, to Prague, where he worked as a correspondent for the *Jewish Chronicle,* based in London. And he became active in anti-Nazi efforts, such as boycotts against German films. In a memorandum to President Edvard Beneš he even outlined a program of systematic anti-Nazi propaganda he wanted to organize from Prague. [This information is from Sascha Feuchert, Gießen. The document is kept by Archiv Bibliographia Judaica, Frankfurt.] In 1939, Oskar and Henriette Rosenfeld prepared to emigrate to Great Britain. Henriette went ahead and Oskar was to follow shortly. At the end of August, Erich Mann spoke with "Uncle Posi" on the telephone and discussed his imminent journey to London. However, with the outbreak of the war on September 1, 1939, his route to Great Britain was blocked.

Two years later, in November 1941, Oskar Rosenfeld, together with five thousand Jews from Prague, was deported to the Polish industrial city of Łódź, which, since April 11, 1940, had been renamed "Litzmannstadt" after a German Nazi general.[24]

The Ghetto of Łódź

Before the war, Łódź was not only the center of the Polish textile industry, but one of the largest Jewish communities in the world. Of a population of seven hundred thousand, about two hundred thirty-three thousand were Jews.

Within days of the attack on Poland, on September 8, 1939, Łódź is occupied by German troops. And beginning in the first weeks of the occupation, an endless series of decrees excludes the Jews from the life of the city and destroys their economic basis. Their bank accounts are confiscated, their businesses "aryanized," any kind of trade and the use of public transportation are prohibited, and curfews are put in force. Finally, on November 14, comes the "obligatory badge"; in December, the yellow Jewish star is introduced. Violent raids, mistreatment, and abductions to fill forced labor quotas are becoming the order of the day. On September 21, by order of Reinhard Heydrich, a "Jewish Council" is formed in Łódź under German auspices. In October, Mordechai Chaim Rumkowski becomes the Eldest of the Jews. He had already played a role in the Jewish life of the city before the war as an insurance agent and director of an orphanage.

Łódź becomes part of the newly created *Reichsgau* (German province) Wartheland (or Warthegau), and is thus annexed to the Reich. A German administration is installed. The authorities launch resettlement programs with the aim of Germanizing the city. The aim of the plan is first and foremost to make the city of Łódź *judenfrei* (Germ., free of Jews), to pack them off to the "Generalgouvernement," as the rest of Poland under German occupation had been renamed. In the fall several thousand Jews flee from Łódź to Warsaw where they hope to find support from relatives and friends. Until February, forced deportations to the southern part of Generalgouvernement are also carried out. However, the governor of the area, Hans Frank, succeeds in stopping these deportations since he, too, wants a *judenfrei* domain.

By December, the Warthegau authorities seem to have come to terms with the fact that they will not be rid of "their Jews" so soon. On December 10, a secret letter from governing president Uebelhoer in Kalisz informs the various agencies of plans for the establishment of a ghetto. The concept describes in great detail the tasks of the Jewish Council and envisages concentration of able-bodied Jews in workers' barracks. The part of the city being apportioned to the Jews as a ghetto is the old town, the poverty district Baluty and the suburb Marysin, where a large Jewish cemetery is located. Only about 725 of the approximately 30,000 apartments and rooms in this part of town have running water; sewers are nonexistent, and many of the structures are wooden houses.

Beginning on February 8, 1940, the Jews are driven into the marked-off area. Non-Jews are ordered to leave the area.

One hundred sixty thousand Jews are now living in the ghetto, which is hermetically sealed on April 30. It is the first ghetto in Poland that is completely cut off from the outside world. Neither in Warsaw nor in Cracow, Lublin, or Vilna is the isolation of the ghetto achieved so completely. Houses around the ghetto are demolished, the Polish inhabitants of adjacent areas are resettled and replaced by Germans. At no time in the entire history of the ghetto, which is to last until late summer 1944, are the ghetto residents able to establish any significant contact with the Polish resistance. No weapons make their way into the ghetto. Even the smuggling of foodstuff fails to attain even symbolic significance. The ghetto is enclosed by a wire fence and a tightly woven net of Protection Police (Schupo), who shoot at anybody coming near it. In the four years of its existence, the only contacts the ghetto is able to establish with the outside world come from homemade radio receivers.

The line of communication between the locked-in Jews and the German authorities runs through the Jewish Council. Since the ghetto is completely dependent on German deliveries, Rumkowski concentrates his efforts on preserving the ghetto through work. By April 5, he submits to the mayor of Łódź a plan outlining the reorganization of the textile industry.

The Germans, for their part, try to determine how to minimize the cost of the ghettoization of the Jewish population. Uebelhoer's order to concentrate able-bodied Jews in workers' barracks has to be rejected for obvious administrative problems.

On May 1, 1940, Hans Biebow, a coffee merchant from Bremen, assumes the directorship of the German ghetto administration. He furthers the plan of transforming the entire ghetto into a production workshop of goods for the army and for civilian enterprises. In the summer of 1940, all food supplies in the ghetto are rationed by a centralized agency. The food allowance is set at thirty pennies, below that of prison inmates. Later it is lowered to nineteen pennies.

A criminal police (Kripo) and Gestapo precinct are established in the ghetto. Random looting of Jewish property continues after the ghetto is sealed. Rumkowski tries to bring confiscation of valuables under his jurisdiction to use them as bargaining chips for foodstuffs. After lengthy negotiations and conflicts between the ghetto administration and the Kripo, all confiscations are signed over and credited to the account of Biebow's ghetto administration for investment in the expansion of production and, at the same time, for relieving the municipal budget of the burden of feeding the ghetto inhabitants.

The Eldest of the Jews creates, step by step, an elaborate ghetto bureaucracy. From the registration office, which assigns housing, to the health department, which sets up numerous hospitals and first-aid stations in the ghetto, from the education department to a banking system with its own currency, from centrally organized grocery shops to nursery schools, old-age homes, a court system, and a special Jewish police force, from the "Order Service" to the prison and the cultural center, where concerts take place regularly—a complete microcosm, a pretense of a normal, routine life. A desperately maintained atmosphere of normality that not only serves physical survival but becomes more and more a psychological refuge. The flight into this self-nourished illusion becomes the only protection still in existence. "This illusion of a normal life, being maintained over a period of more than two years, gave support to the immunological system of the psyche of the sequestered human beings."[25]

Even the growing resistance in the ghetto, directed against the charismatic Eldest of the Jews, his autocratic regime, and his self-overevaluation, is part of this illusion. Strikes and hunger demonstrations are being staged repeatedly. Opposition in the ghetto is organized by all political parties, from the socialist Bund to the Worker Zionists, from the religious to the communists, under slogans like "Work and Bread." But Rumkowski can obtain either one only from the Germans.

The opposition fights for bigger food rations, but Rumkowski cannot distribute more than he gets. It fights against the privileges of the Jewish Council. However, in the end, thirteen thousand people find a place in the bureaucracy of the Jewish Council, all believing that they are safe from being deported.

"Frequently, they behaved," remembers Arnold Mostowicz, a young physician and communist who lived in the ghetto, "as if, by comparison with the prewar period, only the enemy had changed."[26] For many, the name of the enemy is now: Rumkowski. Many people in the ghetto find sustenance, giving them inner strength to go on living, in plans for a political struggle, in the unity of political groups, and in their psychological resistance.

Rumkowski's policy, by contrast, centers on the slogan "Our Only Way Is Work." And this means: "Peace in the Ghetto!"

Besides the bureaucracy of the Eldest of the Jews and its departments, called "ressorts," are the countless factories which produce supplies for the German army or products for private firms like the department store Neckermann or Alsterhaus in Hamburg, items like textiles and shoes, bullet shells, and furniture.

Like other Elders of the Jews in various ghettos, such as Białystok, Vilna, Sosnowiec, and Bendzin, Rumkowski places his bet on German interests with which the survival of the ghetto community is presumed to coincide at least for some time—the interest in the most efficient way of exploiting Jewish labor.

That the exploitation of work was in the end only a function rather than a cause of the German "Jewish policy," that it was merely meant to smooth the execution of the policy of extermination, in order to rob those already condemned to death of the very last that still made them cling to life, namely, their physical strength to work, still lay beyond the imagination in 1941.[27]

From the beginning, the food supply situation in the ghetto was problematic and led to the progressive physical decline of the ghetto inhabitants. In the first two years, thousands died of hunger and weakness, of tuberculosis and dysentery.

On July 16, 1941, a few weeks after the assault on the Soviet

Union and the beginning of mass shootings behind the front, SS-Sturmbannführer Höppner reports to Adolf Eichmann about discussions in the Reichs Government [Reichsstatthalterei] of the Warthegau in Poznan. "In view of the danger that not all Jews can be fed this winter, serious consideration should be given to the most humane solution to finish off those Jews who are unable to work by some means that will have a quick effect."[28] All those who are still able-bodied would be taken to a camp, all women sterilized, "so that the Jewish problem will be solved once and for all with this generation." Höppner, who calls these suggestions "fantastic in part" but "quite feasible," does not forget to mention that the governing president in Kalisz, Uebelhoer, apparently wants to maintain the ghetto for economic self-interests.

In the fall of 1941, the situation in the ghetto suddenly takes a turn for the worse. In the course of the forced deportation ordered by Himmler, twenty thousand Jews from Berlin, Vienna, Prague, Frankfurt, Cologne, Hamburg, Düsseldorf, and Luxemburg are deported to Łódź. In addition, five thousand Roma from Burgenland in Austria are transported to Łódź and sequestered in a separate "gypsy camp" at the edge of the ghetto area. All this takes place in spite of furious protests from the German authorities of the Warthegau who, with support of the army, fear a decrease in productivity in the ghetto. In the ghetto proper, the transfer of German Jews precipitates a violent conflict, pitting the old ghetto inhabitants against the newcomers and bringing to the fore age-old internal Jewish resentments between Western and Eastern European Jews.

The last of twenty transports reaches Łódź on November 4, 1941, from Prague. On one of them is Oskar Rosenfeld.

Oskar Rosenfeld and the "Statistics Department"

Among the many branches of the bureaucratic apparatus set up by the Eldest of the Jews is also the ressort for population statistics, which has a multitude of tasks. The "statistic" assumes the function of a population registry and thus a central position in the ghetto, in which each individual depends on central provisioning for the anyway always insufficient food supply, lodgings, and medications. At the same time, the statistics department keeps an acribic book of all demographic data in the ghetto as if the increasing decline of the population could be halted by an appeal to numbers. The statistics department also produces countless more-or-less elaborate scrapbooks documenting the activities of the Eldest of the Jews with regard to his "ressorts" in health care, education, vocational training, and most of all, of course, the productivity of the ghetto enterprises, which the captives created practically out of nothing.

At the end of 1940, an archive is set up with the task of collecting all available information and documents about the history of the ghetto. Unlike the secretly recorded chronicle of Ringelblum in Warsaw, Rumkowski's archive works with the knowledge of the German authorities, although, it seems, they never seriously interfered in this particular department of the Eldest of the Jews. From January 12, 1941, on, the archive keeps a daily chronicle of events in the ghetto.[29] Recorded here are not only population statistical data but also suicides, diseases, food rationing, production reports, decrees and actions of the Eldest of the Jews, strikes and protests, cultural performances, and the actions of the Kripo and Gestapo.

For two years the chronicle is kept in Polish by the well-known journalist and publicist Julian Cukier (pseudonym Stanyslaw Cerski), with participation of Abraham Kamieniecki, Szmuel Hecht, Bernard Ostrowski, and Józef Zelkowicz. However, in the course of 1942, several intellectuals, who had been deported to Łódź in the fall of 1941, are employed by the archive. Oskar Rosenfeld too finds work here on June 4, 1942. Until September 1, the reports continue to be written in Polish; after that, until December 1942, they are written in both German and Polish. By January 1943 at the latest—Julian Cukier is by now seriously ill and weakened—Oskar Singer, a Jew from Vienna like Rosenfeld, takes over the editorship of the chronicle. Next to Singer, Oskar Rosenfeld becomes the most important contributor. In addition, Alicja de Bunom, Bernhard Heilig, and Peter Wertheimer are regular contributors to the chronicle, which is now written exclusively in German.

Unlike most Jews deported from the German Reich or from Vienna, and unlike his colleagues at the chronicle, Rosenfeld seeks out contact with the Polish Jews in the ghetto. His experience as translator of Yiddish literature, his longtime love for Eastern European Jewish culture, and his emergent interest in religious questions move him in that direction. Not only his entries in the chronicles, his diaries too are free of all conceit so characteristic of many Jews from the West toward Eastern European Jewry and for which the "natives" in the ghetto would at times take revenge.

The entries in the *Daily Chronicle* are markedly cautious; Rumkowski especially is exempt from all criticism. This remains true even when the entries become more elaborate and include commentaries and finally even short stories based on daily life in the ghetto. Even though the writers of the chronicles have to keep in mind that the German authorities might get hold of their articles and thus are guarded in their formulations, the reports contain, nevertheless, compelling descriptions—disguised, of course, in a deliberately light, even humorous, tone, which stands in outright grotesque contrast to Rosenfeld's personal notes. And yet this tone too belongs to the daily life of the ghetto and to efforts for "normality." Thus Rosenfeld notes in the chronicle of Sunday, August 1, 1943: "Sunday in the ghetto is only a day of rest for the dying. A look into the windows behind which, unobstructed by curtains, one sees the dying—half sick, half starved—rather alone on fly-ridden beds. The family members are busy with fetching food, with washing and cleaning. Those lucky enough to be buried on Sunday will not be honored with a numerously attended burial. For Sunday in the ghetto is only a day of rest for the dead."[30]

The *Daily Chronicle* continues publication until the final liquidation of the ghetto in August 1944. The last preserved and presumably very last issue of the chronicle is dated July 30, 1944. "The present Sunday too," so it reads, "passed quietly. The Praeses held various council meetings. All in all, however, the ghetto is quiet and orderly." The entry concludes with the words: "Cause of death of today's mortality cases: suicide 1."[31]

The End of the Ghetto

A few weeks after the settlement of German and Prague Jews into the ghetto, on December 6, 1941, Rumkowski receives the order to make available twenty thousand persons for use as a "work detail outside the ghetto." Even before, it had occurred again and again that groups of people were picked up for forced labor, in one instance as many as one thousand. They were primarily employed in the construction of the Reichsbahn (railroad) and Reichsautobahn (motorway) near Poznan. Murderous labor. But now the demand is suddenly for twenty thousand. Rumkowski negotiates the number down to ten thousand, he seeks counsel with the rabbis in the ghetto and with political parties, but all he gets is the advice to do the Germans' bidding and the names of people who should be exempt from the list.

Unbeknownst to anybody in the ghetto is the fact that the Sonderkommando Lange (special commando), later the Sonderkommando Bothmann, has set up an extermination camp near the village of Chełmno. Beginning on December 7, 1941, Jews from the rural communities of the Warthegau are suffocated in mobile gas trucks. At the beginning of January, the Roma who had been deported to Łódź from Burgenland are likewise murdered at "Extermination Camp Kulmhof." January 16, 1942, marks the beginning of the deportations of the Jews from Łódź to Chełmno. By January 29, 1942, 10,103 human beings from the ghetto have been gassed in Chełmno. Less than a month later begins the second wave of deportations, lasting until April 2, to which 34,073 people fall victim. Meanwhile the mortality rate among the Jews from the German Reich and Prague in the ghetto rises dramatically. Without the possibility of becoming gradually accustomed to the privations and the heavy physical work, and forced into the role of pariahs among pariahs in the ghetto, the Jews from the West succumb with frightening speed to hunger and disease. Few documents attest to their struggle for survival, their struggle with death. Irene Hauser, a woman from Vienna, whose diary has only recently been discovered, describes this routine at death's door: "July 16 [1942]: God help me and my child, for I cannot go on, a miracle has to happen. [. . .] Erich is sweating in bed of weakness, eerie to look at, flies sit in his eyes and mouth, as intrusive as the populace in this place, terrible people. [. . .] August 15: [. . .] From today on I am living in filth. I can't clean anymore. I am just taking things as they come. Don't want to fight anymore, as far as I am concerned we can all suffocate. August 19: One way or other, why don't I just put an end to it? Out of the window. But I can't leave my child and he still wants to live. He begs me to stay with him and the heat drives me out of my mind. Dear Siblings, I wanted to see you once more, and you, dear Father. Where are you all? I am completely forsaken. Ten months of bitter torment and the end is still not near, I cannot comprehend that something like this is humanly possible, it would be best if they came and shot us, that would be for us the most beautiful moment."[32]

Between May 4 and 15, 1942, 10,161 of those who had been settled in the ghetto are deported to Chełmno. In May, large amounts of clothing with bloodstains and Jewish stars reach the ghetto, along with many personal objects reminiscent of those deported from the ghetto. The first rumors begin to circulate that the deported were murdered. While, during the summer of 1942, more than fourteen thousand human beings are brought to the ghetto in Łódź from various communities in the Warthegau, one hundred fifty thousand human beings are murdered in Chełmno. The Jewish communities of Kalisz, Zgierż, Sieradz, Główno, Wieruszów, Praszka, Pabianice, Włocławek, Żelów, Koźminek, Lask, Wieluń, Zduńska Wola, Warta, Sulmierzyce, Dąbie, Kowale Pánskie, Lututów, Sempolno, Kłodawa, Kutno, Brześć Kujawski, Chodecz, Kowal, Lubraniec, Ozorków, Bełchatów, Brzeziny, and Stryków, among many others, are wiped out.

While reports and rumors about the fate of the deportees intensify, Rumkowski still gambles on the conflicting interests among German bureaucrats. Even as the step-by-step deportations from the ghetto continue together with the self-selection of victims connected with them, forced labor remains the only possible way of communicating with the persecutors, the last remaining means: stalling for time. However, the Nazis, writes Dan Diner regarding the dilemma of the Jewish Councils, "remained the masters of time, and the result was the sacrifice of the many for the few."[33]

In September 1942 follows the next mass deportation from the ghetto. Sixteen thousand human beings, including all children under ten and many old and sick people, are forcibly deported. Rumkowski appeals to parents to give up their children to save the rest of the ghetto. However, many try to hide their children or themselves. The Jewish police are unable to round up the required number. The Gestapo takes over the action, and the terror in the ghetto exceeds anything seen heretofore. At least six people are murdered outright; babies and children are thrown out of windows onto waiting trucks.

From this point on, the entire ghetto is designated as a work camp. And in contrast to other towns of occupied Poland, the ghetto of Łódź is for the time being preserved. For two years, the ghetto produces goods for the German army, garment shops, and furniture stores, and finally also temporary housing for Germans who are bombed out. All the ghetto inhabitants can do is hope for the front to move ever closer, their only chance for survival.

In the winter of 1943–44, the tug-of-war between various German bureaucracies and the ghetto intensifies. The SS Chief Economic Administration Bureau tries to pull one over on the authorities in the Warthegau and the Wehrmacht (German army) and turn the ghetto into a bona fide concentration camp. In the end, Himmler and Governor Greiser come to an agreement to gradually "reduce" the size of the ghetto. Sonderkommando Bothmann, which had been transferred to the Balkan area, is to reactivate the installations at Chełmno for this purpose. At this point, more than forty thousand Jews have died inside the ghetto itself of hunger and disease.

In view of the approaching Red Army and the Allied invasion of Normandy, Himmler orders the evacuation of the entire ghetto in June 1944. News of the Allied landing in France reaches the ghetto through clandestine radio receivers. The next day, June 7, 1944, most of the clandestine radio listeners are arrested and executed. Oskar Rosenfeld could have been among the arrested. A few days before he had been listening to Allied broadcasts with the Wechsler brothers who were now being arrested.

The final liquidation of the ghetto is again announced as "outsettlement for work." From June 23 to July 14, 1944, more than seven thousand people are murdered at Chełmno. However, at this point the SS in Chełmno begins to erase the traces of the mass murder as the front moved closer. The deportations are temporarily halted.

Rosenfeld's last entry is dated July 28, 1944. Under the heading "Apocalypse or Redemption," he describes the hope for liberation during the last days of the ghetto: "We are facing either apocalypse or redemption. The chest already dares breathe more freely. People look at each other with a glance that says: We understand each other, right! The Eldest knows that such glances are dangerous. [. . .] The eye of the sentry is still awake. A laugh can betray us, a cheerful face can endanger the ghetto. [. . .] The heart is marred with scars, the brain encrusted in dashed hopes. And if at long last the day of 'redemption' should be at the doorstep, it is better to let oneself be surprised rather than experience another disappointment."

In August, a new place is found for the murder of the Jews of Łódź. It is called Auschwitz-Birkenau. In August 1944, sixty-five thousand human souls, among them Rumkowski, are taken to Birkenau and subjected to the "selection." An estimated twenty thousand are designated for "extermination through work" and taken from Auschwitz to various satellite camps. However, most of them are directly taken from the ramp to the gas chambers and murdered.

In the end, six hundred Jews remain in the ghetto of Łódź as a "cleanup squad." They are joined by about two hundred seventy who escaped deportation in hiding. In January 1945, the SS orders them to dig ditches in the cemetery. However, the members of the "cleanup squad" are able to disappear into previously set-up hiding places and thereby avoid certain death by firing squad.

On January 19, 1945, Łódź is liberated by the Red Army.

A few days later, the survivors begin salvaging buried documents, diaries, photographs, and files in the ghetto. Nachman Zonabend and other members of the "cleanup squad" manage to hide a large stash of the documents so that today many documents of the history of the ghetto can be found not only in the Polish State Archive in Łódź and Warsaw, but also in numerous archives in the United States and Israel.

The Diary

Oskar Rosenfeld's diary came into possession of Yad Vashem in 1973. It was donated to the memorial, so we were told, by a Mr. Zikert from Australia, without documentation of the circumstances under which the notebooks had been salvaged. In 1989 we could only presume that Oskar Rosenfeld's notebooks remained in Łódź during the liquidation of the ghetto in August 1944 and that they were taken into safekeeping by a member of the "cleanup squad," or else that they had been found in the area of the ghetto after the liberation. Nothing indicated that Rosenfeld had been able to take the notebooks with him to Auschwitz. Although, as mentioned, documents from the ghetto of Łódź had been buried on the campgrounds of Birkenau by members of the special inmate squads, who were employed in the crematoria, and others had been smuggled out through channels of the Polish resistance, nothing indicated that Rosenfeld's notebooks might have taken such a route.[34]

It was only after the German publication in 1994 of Oskar Rosenfeld's diaries that light was shed on the history of their retrieval.

The diaries came into the hands of Abraham Cykiert [Zikert], a writer and journalist living in Australia, in 1970. They were among the papers left by his friend Moishe Lewkowicz who had often spoken about his friendship with Oskar Rosenfeld in the ghetto. Lewkowicz had apparently buried the notebooks for Rosenfeld in early August 1944 and retrieved them in the summer of 1945. In 1973, Abraham Cykiert finally sent the diary to the then director of Yad Vashem, Yosef Kermisz. It was bound in a leather cover with a silver plaque and a dedication that had been given to Oskar Rosenfeld by his friends in the ghetto on May 13, 1944, for his sixtieth birthday.[35]

Altogether there were twenty-one notebooks, sequentially numbered by Rosenfeld himself and with numerous cross-references to each other. Notebooks 18 and 19 are missing, however—and an unnumbered notebook entitled "Varia" has been preserved.

The dating shows that Rosenfeld made simultaneous entries in several notebooks. Parallel with entries into his personal diary, he jotted down information and short sketches with the intent of using them later in planned writings and examinations of the ghetto history. As the diary shows, even in the ghetto he worked on several literary projects from which the narrative "My Two Neighbors" has been preserved. However, the narrative "The Secret of the Ghetto," which is frequently alluded to in the diary, and with which he apparently entertained his friends, is missing.

Notebooks A through K comprise Rosenfeld's diary, written between February 17, 1942, and June 6, 1944. For the last two months of his stay in the ghetto, no daily notes have been found. Whether he took the last notebook with him to Auschwitz is not known. Notebook K ends with a reference to a notebook begun on June 1, 1944, which, however, is missing. The remaining extant notebooks are filled with studies and notes. Notebook 11, written in mid-1942, contains, among other things, a sketch for a cultural history of the ghetto. In Notebook 12 (starting date, June 5, 1942) are notes for a cultural essay, critiques of concerts and revues, and notes about language and artists in the ghetto. Notebook 13 (likewise from June 1942) lists, among other things, questions for a fellow ghetto resident, Dr. Josef Lamm. Notebook 14 (beginning July 4, 1942) recounts a few brief episodes, but mostly contains jotted-down quotations from the Bible with which Rosenfeld was apparently much preoccupied. Notebook 15 (April 1943) describes brief episodes, especially deportations and a Passover Seder. In Notebook 16 (August 4, 1943) is the story "My Two Neighbors." Notebook 17 (1943) contains various episodes and a collection of Yiddish proverbs. The unnumbered notebook, entitled "Varia" (December 1, 1943, to March 8, 1944), contains the preface for an encyclopedia of the ghetto and a series of articles that were apparently meant for the archive. Two of them can be found in the *Daily Chronicle* as well. In Notebook 20 (March 8 to July 27, 1944) are more articles written for the archive; some of them can be found in the *Daily Chronicle.* Notebook 21 is only three pages long, listing keywords. Notebook 22, a rough version of literary reflections on hunger in the ghetto and several sketches on various subjects, apparently drawn from various time periods, is likewise undated. The diary ends with a Yiddish song deriding the impractical Jews from the West, written in the ghetto and set to the tune of a Polish military march:

Es geyt a yeke
mit a teke
er zikcht piter margarin
beshum oyfm
nishtu tsi koyfn
nemt er a vize
nokh Maryshin

A German Jew
goes around with his briefcase,
looking for butter or margarine,
nowhere, nowhere,
nothing to buy,
he takes a visa
to Marysin [the site of the ghetto cemetery].[36]

Editorial Note

Editing the preserved notebooks posed a series of problems, the solutions of which will certainly not be without controversy.

Rosenfeld's notes contain many repetitive descriptions of the same events, keywords for a future documentation, clean copies of decrees, biblical quotations, and other literary allusions as well as repetitive enumerations of food rations and statistics.

In the interest of readability, several cuts were made, indicated with ellipses in brackets. Care was taken not to change the character of the writing. Notebooks 12, 14, and 21 were left out altogether, with the exception of a few short passages which were incorporated into the annotations. The sequence of the notebooks follows the author's dating. The texts found in both Notebook 20 and "Varia," and the daily ghetto chronicle, were chronologically inserted into the diary and marked with special emphasis.

In the interest of making the texts understandable, important cross-references between the various notebooks that Rosenfeld made himself have been specially marked. In some cases, the respective texts were placed in the endnotes.

Emphases in the original appear in italics. The same goes for headings in the margins of the diary. Other marginal notes were integrated into the running text. Obvious spelling mistakes were silently corrected. In the brief English-language paragraphs (with which Rosenfeld apparently practiced his language skills in hopes of emigration to England, where his wife was living) no corrections were made. Retained were contemporary usages and places where Rosenfeld purposely departed from regular syntax and grammar. The same holds true for the Ashkenazic spelling of Hebrew expressions as well as variations in the text of the spelling of names and place-names, for example, Marysin (Polish), Maryshin (Yiddish), Marischin (German).

Where necessary for better understanding, abbreviations were spelled out, and the change was noted in the endnotes. Stenographic passages in the original were silently written out. Only when the use of stenographic writing was obviously used to guard against discovery by the Germans, a note to that effect was added. For this reason, Rosenfeld spells almost throughout the words "Kripo" and "Gestapo" in Greek letters. As far as possible, Rosenfeld's numerous code words—for example, for the Germans or the Red Army—have been explained.

Most of the diaries were transcribed several years ago by Dr. Ruven Shatkai, who had been commissioned by Yad Vashem, and whose work made in large part the publication of this volume possible. Thanks go

17. Ibid., 108.
18. Ibid., 154.
19. Ibid., 155.
20. Oskar Rosenfeld, *Tage und Nächte* (Leipzig-Vienna-Zurich: Ilf-Verlag, 1920).
21. *Mendl Ruhig* was first published in 1914 by Saturn Verlag in Heidelberg. The citation here is from the magazine *Menorah,* Vienna-Frankfurt, 1, 2/3 (1923): 17.
22. *Die Neue Welt,* no. 59, November 2, 1928, 7.
23. *Die Neue Welt,* no. 537, February 14, 1936, 1.
24. Long before his rise in the Nazi Party, General Litzmann had commanded a decisive battle in the First World War near Łódź.
25. Arnold Mostowicz, "Alltagsleben im Getto. Die Perspektive der Eingeschlossenen," in *"Wer zum Leben, wer zum Tod. . ." Strategien jüdischen Überlebens im Getto,* edited by Doron Kiesel et al. (Frankfurt am Main and New York: Campus, 1992, 45).
26. Ibid., 46. Compare Isaiah Trunk, *Judenrat: The Jewish Councils in Eastern Europe under Nazi Occupation* (New York: Macmillan, 1972); also in Yiddish, *Łódź her getto* (New York: Yad Vashem, YIVO Institute for Jewish Research, 1962).
27. Zelman Lewental's commentary concerning the writings from Łódź buried in Auschwitz also contains the sentence: "I cannot hide this without adding a few words concerning the great delusion to which we all fell prey when we talked ourselves into believing that he [Hitler, the Nazis] needs people to work; it is true, he needs them, but the destruction of the Jews is his primary aim" (*Briefe aus Litzmannstadt,* 91).
28. An original carbon copy of the document is in the archive of Chief Commission for the Investigation of Crimes against the Polish People in Warsaw, in the dossier of the trial against Arthur Greiser.
29. The original chronicle is in the Polish State Archive. An abbreviated version of the chronicle was edited by Lucian Dobroszycki in *The Chronicle of the Łódź Ghetto 1941–1944* (New Haven, Conn.: Yale University Press, 1984).
30. *Tageschronik* [*Daily Chronicle*], August 1, 1943; in the Polish State Archive, file of the Eldest of the Jews.
31. *Tageschronik,* July 30, 1944.
32. "Nicht einmal zum Sterben habe ich Protektion . . ." in *Tagebuch*

von Irene Hauser (*Diary of Irene Hauser*). Arbeitsstelle Fritz Bauer Institut, Materialien no. 2. Frankfurt am Main, no page.

33. Dan Diner, "Die Perspektive des 'Judenrats.' Zur universellen Bedeutung einer partikularen Erfahrung," in *"Wer zum Leben, wer zum Tod. . . ." Strategien jüdischen Überlebens im Getto,* 31.
34. A diary from Łódź, written in Polish, Yiddish, English, and Hebrew in the margins of a French novel—likewise in the holdings of Yad Vashem—apparently made its way to Auschwitz with its author and ended up in the safekeeping of a survivor; it is available in German translation. *"Les Vrais Riches"—Notizen am Rand. Ein Tagebuch aus dem Ghetto Łódź (Mai bis August 1944),* edited by Hanno Loewy and Andrzej Bodek (Leipzig: Reclam, 1997).
35. Abraham Cykiert lives near Melbourne in Australia. As a young man in 1939, he published his first poems in Poland. After the liberation and a few years' stint with a refugee aid organization in Geneva, he emigrated to Australia in 1948. There he worked for Yiddish newspapers and radio broadcasts as writer and editor. His experiences in the ghetto and his reflections on Mordechai Chaim Rumkowski found expression in the play *The Emperor of the Ghetto.* Cykiert did not know Rosenfeld closely in the ghetto, but he remembered very well that Rosenfeld was regarded by the "natives" in the ghetto as "one of us," that is, as *amcho* (our people) and not as *Yekke* (German Jew).
36. The version of the song cited here follows the research of Gila Flam. See Gila Flam, *Singing for Survival: Songs of the Łódź Ghetto, 1940–1945* (Urbana: University of Illinois Press, 1992).

❁

Translator's Note

Much of Oskar Rosenfeld's notes are rendered in fragmentary style, jotted down for his later use. I have resisted the temptation to fill in missing verbs, pronouns, and the like. Rather, it has been my goal to preserve the tone and feeling of the original work and the intensifying undercurrent of urgency that runs through it. Only in a few places did I feel compelled to fill in a word if required for sake of clarity. The same goes for punctuation: I introduced a comma or semicolon on occasion. By and large, I have sought to produce a translation as faithful as possible to Rosenfeld's style.

A few remarks about word choices: I have retained all expressions in Yiddish, Hebrew, or Polish in the text followed by translations in brackets. To render them only into English would destroy the atmosphere of the milieu Rosenfeld was attempting to project for posterity. By the same token, I retained words like "ressorts" for "workshops" or "factories," which seems to have been a ghetto-specific expression, and "Praeses," one of the designations for Rumkowski, the Eldest of the Jews. The German words *Aussiedlung* and *Einsiedlung* I translated as "outsettlement" and "insettlement," respectively, as these to me reflect most closely the irony of the German bureaucratic euphemisms. Wherever Rosenfeld used the term "Deportation" or "Evakuierung," and on occasion "Emigration," I have rendered it as "deportation," "evacuation," or "emigration," respectively. I have also retained Rosenfeld's name for the German oppressors, "Ashkenes," a word derived from "Ashkenazim," which generally designates Eastern European and German Jews. (When he speaks of "Germans," he means German Jews.)

Another word that occurs frequently is the English word "talkie"—it always precedes the description of a scene Rosenfeld has observed or something he heard people say. He apparently imagined himself to be a camera or a documentary film director capturing the sights and sounds of life in the ghetto.

The passages that Rosenfeld wrote in English have not been edited. They are marked in the text by italics.

BRIGITTE M. GOLDSTEIN

In the Beginning Was the Ghetto

Say it descriptively: completely factual, short sentences, eliminate all that is sentimental, reading oneself far from the entire world, without thinking of the surroundings, alone in space, not meant for other human beings . . . as memory for *time to come . . .*

NOTEBOOK A

February 17, 1942—Private Diary

About Moods to Keep in Memory — Public

What the doctor says: It makes no sense to give in to moods that oppress the mind. A cheerful disposition is as valuable as good health and good health is what's most important. We must preserve our nerves, avoid anything that might weaken the organism. For we have only *one* goal before us: to outlast the crisis and to live. We must live and see the moment when we can say: It was all worthwhile, having endured all the hardship and suffering. . . . We wanted to be witnesses of a new era and that's what we are. If it weren't for this moment, then everything that happened (misery, humiliation, hunger, cold, sickness) would have been in vain. The purpose of our life, of which they wanted to rob us, is: to live this moment. Everything else pales next to it, is meaningless, ephemeral. This moment even makes up for the death of hundreds of thousands, who died before being redeemed. In place of all those things that we cannot give you, patients, you must replace with fortitude of mind, endurance of suffering, daily pride, and the consciousness of being blameless. Somehow, sometime, liberation will come. This is attested by our history and the eternal maxim that has reigned in the world up to now: Justice triumphs over iniquity. It is therefore wise to remain silent, to bite the teeth together, to suffer, and to be ready for the moment. . . . Mood: a bleak, gray sky behind yellow, dirty-blue huts and barracks, completely covered with snow, the paltry trees stretching their paltry branches, covered with snow crystals, upward. . . . Question of detail: Which groups or individuals are against the Eldest?[1] How do they plan to seize power? What are these people doing? Are there political groups? Will we have food to eat during the interregnum (part Prague)?

Like all cruel, perfidious, and base surprises that the Prague Jewish community[2] stages, the invitations for the collective transport were passed out at night. The Jewish couriers were handed the addresses of those who had been selected and rushed through the darkened streets to their houses, up the dark staircases with their flashlights in order to wake the sleeping unawares, and to hand each individual personally the marching order. Since the registration of all Jews shortly before had been whispered about as preparation for the confiscation of property, meaning something harmless, even something legitimate, the call-up was all the more a surprise. Each candidate received a transport number that was to accompany him from the place of departure to the place of destination. Each one had to fill out a detailed form listing his entire possessions, from house to shirt button; it was prohibited to tell anybody, not even one's own brother, anything about the content of this list. The Gestapo was so bashful that they wanted to keep the total robbery of the Jews a secret for as long as possible. Or did they have other reasons for the prohibition?—The city was in a state of excitement. There was much talk, whispering, speculating, and paralyzing fear. Suddenly people remembered the so-called Viennese-Polish action in March 1941 in the course of which hundreds of Jews in Vienna (the fearful question in the night: Will it be my turn or not?) were caught and kept in a camp for a few days before being transported to a forsaken, starving place (Opole)[3] and left to their fate. People recalled letters from these deported Jews to their relatives, stating that they were on the verge of starvation if somebody didn't send bread; they also asked for warm clothing and other articles for their daily needs. That was it. A similar fate seemed to be planned for these newly registered. Nothing positive was known. The Jewish community either didn't dare tell the truth or else didn't know what the truth was. The fifty-seven thousand Jews who were living in Prague in the fall of 1941 had to be prepared for the worst, the unexpected, that which the human mind was unable to grasp. In the taverns that were open to us Jews, stories were told of the Łódź ghetto and its council of elders, which had offered to take in the Jews transported there and to take care of them to the best of their ability. It was even said that the Jews who were fit for work would be assigned work in Łódź, according to their skills and training, against pay. A gentle ray of light in the darkness of the deportations. . . . Outside the Jewish center, Beth Ha'am, groups of Jews mingled who claimed to have heard that five transports of one thousand Jews each would leave Prague either for the Pyrenees near the Spanish border or the camps where refugees from Spain were once housed. Hopes were attached to both areas—one held the possibility of a better climate and the French nearby, the other receiving food packages and money, and possibly the Russians nearby. All these considerations couldn't prevent the Jewish families from being seized by panic, especially since it was impossible to determine which place of destination it would be. The mood among the Prague Jews was worsened by rumors making the rounds that the present decrees for the Jews would be stiffened. The fear was justified, for the lives of Jews had already been constricted by about fifty decrees, and there was still room for ostracizing them some more. For instance, Reich Protector Neurath established in a decree concerning the registration of citizens of Bohemia and Moravia this order: Germans, Czechs, Gypsies, Jews.

On September 18, the Jews' star was added. This was a decree from Berlin, effective for Germany and the Czechoslovak Republic. Early Friday morning, September 18, all Jews appeared in the street with the yellow Jews' star on the left side of the chest. The star was inscribed with the word *Jude* in German lettering that was to imitate Hebrew script, which made this mark appear even more ghostly, crass, antisemitic, and provocative. However, the Czech people did not react in the expected manner. On the contrary. They all averted their eyes, and their expression of contempt could clearly be seen in gestures and signs of goodwill. With the Jews' star pinned to their chest, the Jews were unable to merge with the crowd. The presence in Prague of thousands of Jews from the provinces created the impression that Prague was overrun with Jews so that the Czechs too would welcome a massive sweep of "dejudification." The Jews wandered through the streets of Prague like vestiges from the Middle Ages, who owed their existence solely to the apathy of the local population but who were rife for disappearance. People looked at each other without sympathy, they all had been cut down to the same level; even more, they burdened each other, seeing themselves in the other: each holding the other responsible for the specter *Jude.* Now the distinction between Jew and non-Jew became clearly visible on the outside as well. This was the situation at the time when the call to come to the collection point Messepalast went out. Nobody was spared. Bedridden patients were taken from the hospitals, the old, the infirm, the lame, the blind, the dying, arrived from the nursing homes; before the rise of day, still in the dark, Jews (men, women, children) with suitcases and backpacks crowded the streetcars. The use of taxis had long been prohibited. Apartments, filled with household goods, were abandoned. The beds were still warm, the table set, china and books remained in boxes, in the foyers and rooms were clothes, blankets . . . rugs, pictures—and the hyenas, the strangers and the locals who had been notified of the departure of the Jews, were already lying in wait for the possessions. Four transports went rolling. Still nothing definite was known about the destination of the evacuees. Direct news had still not been received. When, at the beginning of November, the fifth and last transport was called up, nobody knew for sure what country was the final destination. This time the participants arrived at the Messepalast in the daytime. It was no longer necessary to keep the deportation of the Jews, nor the methods and techniques employed, a secret. Prague had already become reconciled to these measures. The sight of Jews with backpacks, suitcases, sacks, bundles, bedding, crowding the streetcar stops for the last, mostly overcrowded car—occupation of the other cars by Jews was prohibited—was no longer anything out of the ordinary. Among them were people who had emigrated already three times—from Berlin to Vienna, from Vienna to the Sudeten area, from the Sudeten area to Prague—every time starting a new life, quietly hoping to finally find peace and be satisfied with the most modest nook.

But this nook was granted them for only a short time. There was no mercy. The war against the Jews knew no peaceful conclusion. The machine that had been put in charge of taking care of the Jews worked relentlessly, for any pause would have been dangerous, would have demonstrated the superfluousness of this machine. The Jews had been expelled from every profession, their houses were being administered by a trust, their money in the banks was frozen, any dealings with non-Jews had reached its nadir, they were not allowed to be seen in any park or garden or theater or movie house or bath or railway station or even any tavern . . . now it had been decreed that even their physical presence was to disappear from the scenery of towns and cities. The protectors promised the Czechs that the country would be made *judenrein* and then went about that task in a systematic, thorough, circumscribed, but legal—it's called legal—way. The deportations began.

Families were destroyed, marriages smashed, friends torn apart, bonds that had been formed during a lifetime were broken, products of the mind were wiped out in a moment's time, everything that had been gathered and carefully guarded in the course of centuries with diligence and love and devotion was shattered by a kick of the foot. Countless [human] values, created with knowledge and reverence, were irreparably lost. The condemnation of a spiritual heritage, literary and artistic, was given free rein by those in power. The authorities now made good on their promises to their followers and sympathizers—the risk-free destruction of all hitherto relished Jewish cultural treasures. Collections were demolished, libraries were collapsed, scientific instruments were scattered, solid homes were left in shambles. With tears in their eyes and a broken heart, the Jews marked for deportation took leave of all they had to leave behind. Dogs, cats, and other pets were gently being stroked . . . often under the derisive gaze of the officials who oversaw the departure. (This laying waste will be reported separately in a special section.)

So it was goodbye. Goodbye forever? Or perhaps only a brief separation, followed by a happy reunion? Who can tell with complete certainty! No matter how the preparations for the departure into the unknown were being made, they all had the mark of being improvised and provisionary. Nobody said a final goodbye, nobody gave up everything without reservation. There wasn't a single Jew who was resigned once and for all to the loss of his life. In the heart of each traveler remained a spark of hope for restitution, a kernel of faith in the return. All kinds of cherished objects, even those without value, were placed with good friends and reliable neighbors, and the many objects that were left behind and given away did not thereby lose their significance. . . . The possessions were disposed of in no time, and only then, at the moment of parting, did they realize, when faced with saying goodbye, how easily common possessions collected over the years (a household) can dissolve and how attached they were to them. But time was pressing and no tear had enough power to bring alleviation or relief. Too much was lost, hundreds sat in their apartments, unable to comprehend "all this," as they called it. Thousands flung themselves into the turmoil of packing, of cleaning up, choosing objects, attempting to assume a casual attitude, putting on airs toward their surroundings as if everything happened according to the laws of the world order and, therefore, all lamenting and criticizing was a misplaced exercise. More urgent were practical questions. Since the word was out that each person was allowed to carry only 50 kg of belongings, including 5 kg of foodstuff, thousands of Prague Jews were faced with the problem of equipping themselves with lightweight luggage that could easily be carried. Everywhere in town, especially the Jewish quarter, Jews were seen hunting for backpacks, hats, caps, suitcases, tableware, and nonperishable provisions. The city was in turmoil. Something unthought-of, something profoundly disturbing, was felt to be happening. A new epoch in the handling of the Jews, the solution of the Jewish question, had begun. Five thousand Jews, whose forebears had resided in the old "golden" city of Prague, their homeland, left the city on order of the Germans. The Central Authority for Jewish Emigration selected the candidates, but the principles of this selection were not obvious, unless it was all put into effect the way it had been done now, that is, in a haphazard, random way. Among the deportees were poor Jews, supported by the Jewish community, next to the rich, those who, before the occupation of the country, had owned real estate, bank accounts, pensions, apartments, collections, and other valuables, citizens of diverse rank and station in life, young and old, people with foreign visas. There also was a Nobel transport, the "A" group: physicians, lawyers, engineers, scholars, teachers, professors, writers, actors, musicians, and other Jews suspected of concerning themselves with things cultural. This is how the plan worked, by tearing old bonds, atomizing families, emptying countless apartments and homes for newly immigrant families. The dejudaization of Prague was in progress. The selected Jews, many of whom were remote from Judaism, even with a hostile attitude toward it, were ordered to report for the collective transport. The authorities had chosen the Messepalast, a building that was temporarily vacant. Once a year it served as a tradeshow facility and had now been made available for the Jews who were to be transported. Those who entered this building could say a final goodbye to their homeland. Here is where the ghetto began. Only a handful were lucky enough to be sent back home as unfit, and these few, too, were not safe from a later call-up. The number of each individual was checked off by Jewish community officials—he had been thrown out on the dung heap. The Messepalast was a warehouse where, instead of goods and wares, people were exhibited, closely pressed together in bunks, resting on backpacks and mattresses, with bundles, suitcases, packages, stuffed to bursting, and cots that served as sleeping places. Three days and three nights they lingered here, more than a thousand in the drafty, filthy warehouse, slowly consuming their stores of food since the provisions from the Jewish community were inadequate.

Connections were made, friendships began here, people who once had renowned names were dozing on rags and coats, happy to be able to stretch out their emaciated limbs somewhere. At times there was singing and laughter to be heard, for many young people were called up as well, and the casual observer could gain the impression that the authorities had decided to favor the Jews too with an excursion of "Strength through Joy" ["Kraft durch Freude," a Nazi holiday program, trans.]. For—and this must be stated here once and for all—the loss of existence, of possessions, of a homeland, of a peaceful life without care for tomorrow, was not able to break the soul of the Jews. Accustomed to suffering and strengthened through suffering, the Jews here remained unshaken in their trust in their eventual liberation, in their redemption, as so often in earlier centuries. No tears were to be seen, no breakdowns. And still nobody knew where the journey would take them.

The functionaries were silent, not even revealing the hour of departure. The German director responsible—an outwardly likeable young man—was in charge of the Jews, holding total power over the Jews' fate. When he appeared with his entourage, a movement went through the call-ups, and the poor, weak, partly already famished Jews suddenly turned into recruits, lining up before their commander. On several occasions there were inspections. Everything had to be in order. These Jews had the good fortune, shortly before being transported, to be taken care of and to enjoy discipline. Not even the Jewish stooge from the Central Authority for Jewish Emigration is allowed to be disregarded or belittled. It was to him that the deportees owed their discipline, with which all orders concerning the transport were being carried out. Wrapped in a leather . . . [illegible], equipped with a huge dark lantern, he was up early in the morning, before sunrise, drilling masses of Jews, while he himself—for the time being, at least—was safe from having to leave the Protectorate inasmuch as he carried out his job of slave driver with great skill and equally great pleasure. This kind of character existed, by the way, in other districts of Jewish life as well, those who carried out the will of the German authorities and benefited for a certain time from their privileged position.

The blind, the lame, the dying, were lined up. From the hospitals, the infirm in a state of high fever were taken, the old were taken from the nursing homes. They all lined up now, accepting the sentence without a word. At the same time, the official made sure that everything went without a problem at the Messepalast. Mrs. [illegible] wants to commit suicide, Veronal, the Gestapo, demands: "You will guarantee that *all* of them leave here alive. . . ." There were no complaints. All male participants of the transport had their heads shaven—as a precaution against infections (lice, etc.) there in that faraway place—and looked like prison inmates who were being transferred. In this connection, it should be noted that many participants would have been only too happy to assume the role of prison inmate if the judge and executor had not been an official of the Third Republic [*sic,* Third Reich]. Siberia and Cayenne seemed to us not the worst of all evils, for these land areas were geographically delimited, their climate known, whereas we traveled into the unknown or at least the inhospitable.

Shortly before the departure, everybody had to appear at the conveyor belt of the Jewish community officials, which had been made available at the Messepalast for the dispatch of the transport, with their money, papers, apartment keys. The penultimate act of the drama began.

The order went like this:

1. (Say it directly, more graphic!) Surrender of apartment keys. The home was thus handed over to the protectors. None of those departing betrayed a single trace of pain over the loss. Here, take it, you, who took away our honor and belongings and existence and all purpose of life. Most of the keys were passed on the same day to the German speculators. Trucks pulled up and then loaded up with furniture and small household items of those who had been robbed.
2. Surrender of all legitimations, personal documents, certificates with photographs, or other identity papers.
3. Surrender of all money and gold without a receipt (hand over because of robbery of the German people).
4. Signing of a form without being permitted to read what it said,

that is, they remained ignorant of its content. The signature authorized the Jewish community of Prague, that is, the Gestapo, to dispose freely of all assets left behind.

5. Receipt of a police declaration with a stamp "evacuated on . . ." (in order to separate out the parasites).

With this the complete pilfering and depersonalization was complete. Nothing remained to the "evacuees" except for the rucksack or the suitcase they were carrying. It also happened that, shortly before the departure, several pieces of luggage were taken away by Gestapo officials. Books, musical instruments, things close to the individual's heart, pleasurable memorabilia, heirlooms, safeguarded by the family for centuries, had to be left behind or handed over to the Gestapo. Dirt poor, outlawed, delivered to a blind fate, this is how five times one thousand Jews each reported to the Messepalast for their journeys into the unknown.—It wasn't human beings who departed; rather, it was "transports" that were being dispatched.—They had to line up. They marched, the young and old, the infirm, the blind, the dying, the children, to somewhere, to some railway station. Along the way, behind the windows of the houses, the faces of the Czechs were visible, here and there Czech passersby, without exception serious faces, some sad, pensive, disturbed. A train was waiting. Doors were pulled open, they entered the cars by number, which each one had to display clearly visible on clothing and luggage. All this took place very quickly, the soldiers pushed, bayonets blinked, pushing and shoving, but no sound was heard. The compartment doors were slammed shut, windows closed, nobody was permitted to appear at the window. A transport of sheared, intimidated sheep—this was the "evacuation" of the Jews from Prague. The train rolled along the periphery of the town into the open countryside. Whereto? West, toward Germany, past Breslau—that's what they said—further and further. Evening descended. Thirst. When the train stopped in the middle of the night and one of the Jewish transport guards wanted to get water, the accompanying soldiers would beat him, shouting and cursing. No water. . . . The night was long. Suddenly a steel helmet opened the door of one car after another and ordered in a menacing tone: Every man was to shave and to polish his shoes. . . . It seemed they were supposed to arrive nice, neat, well groomed, even soigné, in Łódź—the place were they would end up was finally known. It was more intuition than knowledge, for the journey went through the desolate Polish landscape, through autumnal potato fields, which stretched along a horizon without the slightest elevation. Hungover, hungry, sleepy, hundreds of men began to polish their shoes in the dark coupé and to shave with a shaver . . . water from the toilet. From time to time a Gestapo man with a flashlight appeared and had some of them line up, cursing when an evacuee didn't seem elegant enough for him.

So it was Łódź, into the ghetto of Litzmannstadt, where they reportedly had a council of elders, who were glad to receive guests, had made everything ready: apartments, food, work, even joy of life. For—and this was being said already before the departure—the Jews there will live in freedom, will pursue their work, will be amongst themselves, and will finally find peace, a rare good fortune for which one had to be thankful to the dear Gestapo. . . .

The train came to a halt in an open field. The coupé doors were flung open. Tired, weary, suitcase in hand, rucksack on their backs, a bundle under their arms, more than a thousand human beings dragged themselves down the running board, stepping into deep sewage, morass, water. It was autumn, a Polish-Russian autumn. Gestapo in field-gray uniforms drove them on. "Move! Run! Run!" the blond, well-nourished boys shouted. Unforgettable was the one with a reddish stubble beard and reddish eyebrows, stinging eyes, a rattling voice. He yelled at the new arrivals: "Run, you Jew swine," pushed the women who didn't know where to turn. Where had they ended up? To whom did they belong? Where was the hand helpfully extended? Who took over the thousand who had been tossed into the wasteland of Łódź? Nothing, nothing. Unable to gain consciousness. The brain was empty, they even forgot that they had almost nothing to eat for a day and a night.

A line formed. Through dung and morass, the march went to somewhere. Curiosity seekers lined the streets of a rundown, sparsely developed area, impossible to say whether it was a city or village. . . . A few carriages, an emaciated horse tied to each, received the old and the sick. The coachmen cursed, whipped the poor horses. A taste of their own future suffering, perhaps. Carts, small carriages, drawn by young and old people rather than by animals, were met along the way. Dreary mud huts. . . . Helpless trees and shrubbery . . . pools of sewage . . .

stinking refuse . . . countless tired, crooked creatures. . . . Amidst them faces that had already overcome all misery, in which was written: We'll persevere, we'll survive you, you cannot destroy us . . . shabby sundry stores, taverns, coffeehouses, cigarette vendors, young girls and children who were selling something or other, the smell of things unknown in the West, young people in uniform with Zion stars on their arms, screams amidst the silence, above it all a fog-gray sky, traversed by ravenlike birds. This was the criminal quarter of Łódź, the ghetto of Litzmannstadt. . . .

(Ghetto = to mark the Jews with a yellow star as a piece out of the Middle Ages.)

The Camp in the Schoolhouse

Thus the thousand marched on, automatically—nobody guided them, the so-called transport leaders, the confidants of the evacuees, had run ahead to somewhere without telling the human train what to do. We were in an unknown country, a foreign terrain. . . . Our hearts did not beat for the sight of human beings, streets, and houses, even though each one of us knew that we were dependent on the goodwill of this unknown district. We walked as in a trance. Our consciousness was not awake enough to grasp the peculiar situation in all its abhorrence. . . .

Without knowing how they got there, about a thousand people arrived in front of a gate that led to what seemed to be a schoolhouse. The entranceway was filled with sewage and water, and it was very difficult to enter with heavy luggage, to cross the courtyard, and to squeeze through the dark, narrow hallways.

Now they pushed and shoved, shuffling from the hallways into the classrooms, which again had to house a thousand people. The hallways had already been converted into sleeping quarters. Wooden cots were lined up on the side by the window, two people to one cot, 75 cm in width, and a length that made the feet extend beyond the wooden ledge. In this narrow, small room each person also had to store the luggage, rucksack usually at the head, suitcase and bundle at the foot of the cot, if one didn't prefer to unpack right away the meager possessions, clothes, shoes, underwear, and eating bowls, and place them somewhere along the wall while awaiting how life was going to unfold here. Each room held about sixty people, fewer in the hallways. On the upper floor, a medical clinic was set up: the doctor, who had been on the transport, and some assistants, as well as a few common types of medications. The rooms were kept warm by the human bodily secretions, keeping us from freezing even during the most biting winter days.

The first days passed without a care. Nobody thought as yet of tomorrow. Everybody received a loaf of bread to last for one week. In the morning, black coffee like tepid brown water. For lunch a thousand people lined up with their bowls. Young local women brought buckets of soup from the kitchen: warm water swimming with some green stuff, carrots, and turnips. People fell over this meal, their lunch. The only meal of the day. Toward evening, again a small bowl of coffee, that is, tepid brown water. But since most of the evacuees still had provisions, white bread, preserves, artificial honey, canned meat, baked goods, chocolate, cakes, among other things, they did not feel the want as all that crass. Very difficult was washing. We had to go out into the courtyard to the well since the running water in the pipes was not enough. Only the sick and children benefited from it. Furthermore: queuing up at the latrines. In snow and freezing temperatures. Toilet paper—a rarity. Toilets only for the sick.

Gradually the stock of food ran out. Money from back home was sparse. Besides, the Jewish mail service takes a huge deduction. Ten percent for handling mail, about 60 percent for collecting. Out of 10 marks usually no more than 4 are left. Meanwhile the prices are rising. Clothing and shoes are being sold to the locals for next to nothing. The prices for these items are much less than those for food. One pair of shoes = one loaf of bread. By contrast, services are at a premium; a pair of leather soles = 40 marks.

The physical and social decline has begun. Greedily they fall over the lunch soup. Those who have a few marks in their pockets supplement the meal with a lump of chopped meat, called a *klops* [Germ., dumpling], weighing about 40 grams and costing 30 or 50 pennies, or with margarine or sugar. A few cook their own soup on a spirit stove they had brought along. Side dishes like baked goods, carrots, meat, sugar, etc., are not yet available for us. Back home they had assured us that every evacuee would receive 100 marks as a onetime subvention once we arrived at the final destination. Only 40 marks were paid out, which were already partly spent. Now concern about daily nutritional supplements. Everything is centered on the Eldest of the Jews in the

Litzmannstadt ghetto. (About him earlier in connection with the establishment of the ghetto.) But still a film drama. Children lounge around the schools where we are housed. Take some soup from us. For the stomachs of many of the evacuees don't tolerate that much water. Children are waiting for hours in the courtyards by the windows collecting the warm soup in bowls or pots they carry with them. A slice of bread is for them the biggest treat, an event. Deprivation screams from their eyes. Once they get something, they come back again and again—like gypsies who attach themselves to the big hearts that disseminate alms among them. Impossible to get rid of them. Not a flicker of shame left in them. No longer creatures with a soul. They don't speak, they only stare at you. It's impossible to resist the gaze. A gnawing, rumbling in the pit of the stomach, the palate demands to be whetted. You still have an appetite. But here in the eyes of the children you see for the first time in your life the word that had been an empty concept to you and was only known as a legend. The word: "Hunger." We used to read: Famine in Russia, in China millions died of hunger . . . newspaper headlines, sensations for indulged European readers. Now, at last, in its brutal, inescapable nakedness: Hunger! But hunger of the others. We'll help ourselves. Tomorrow will be better again. Those here, the Poles, our Jewish brethren, have endured "this" already for two years. They have better nerves. But we must help each other and we'll find a solution. How much longer? Day after tomorrow it's all over, all is well . . . That's how the days pass. The nights have a different face (night, describe in mass quarters . . . the sound, the first little fantasies). What happens during the nights at first makes one wish they were over. They frighten the hungry, who long for the morning although it brings nothing but uproar, noise, scurrying back and forth, and that certain "black coffee." [. . .] Only later, only gradually, one longs for the nights, the long nights, the darkness, during which one can ponder, mull things over, mumble, sigh, and whisper words that nobody understands, except the whisperer alone.

Painting of the First Hunger in the Camp, That Is, the Newly Arrived (See Earlier, Should Be Summarized)

Numbed by idleness, harried, the thin, tepid coffee in the empty stomach, a thousand beings crawl into their hard wooden cots. At first they must find a place somewhere to store their clothing, luggage, rags, pots, and pans, so that those in need of sleep have enough room. Around some of the sleeping places, strings have been strung on which wet clothing has been hung out. Only that generosity is lacking. Everybody is moving as close together as possible, children are babbling, crying, whining, and many of the sick give off the sounds of their illness. Coughing, hissing, snarling, moaning, groaning, sobbing, tossing and turning, more moaning, creaking of wooden planks, and animal noises fill the emptiness of the night. The excretions of hundreds of people produce so much warmth that even on the bitterest winter night one isn't cold. One has to run in the middle of the night into the yard where the latrines are, which couldn't be cleaned since they are overflowing from too much use.

A slight uneasiness seizes the body. The abdomen gets loose and eventually sags. Hesitant, almost fearful, the hand feels the restless body, finds bones, ribs, finds limbs, and discovers the self, suddenly becoming aware that not so long ago one was fatter, meatier, and one is surprised how quickly the body decays. . . . The abdomen has been sagging, giving the feeling of directly encountering the bowels. Below the bulging abdomen—the bulge has already disappeared—something heretofore unknown is stirring, an inexplicable pulsating of nerves and muscles. Gradually this condition is felt as pain, as a gentle, even mild, pain, which suddenly appears in the back of the head and spreads over the forehead and eyes. How many of us wondered about this pain, which they even loved in the beginning (because it gave the illusion of eventual redemption), until sometime, again at night, this gentle pain turned into something bad for which there was no remedy? We remembered from a previous time that such discomfort could be alleviated with bread and butter or an apple or some sweets, but this memory had very little effectiveness left at this time. At the moment of such considerations, the word "ghetto" spread over us and settled on our brain, forcing it to forget about inventing any remedies. Here and there a hand would appear from under the blanket, searching the rucksack for something edible. One had to be careful, frugal, with oneself, weighing carefully the purpose and the hour. Though it is true, hardship and duress gave the weak strength, the reckless, consideration, the careless, a sense for rationing. Lined up in opposition to these virtues were the hardships and especially the dictates of the stomach.

The nights flew, the days went by. In the morning there was still only tepid water, at noon the ghetto guests crowded as before with their bowls around the soup, which never changed its bland taste. Some kind of vegetable was swimming on top giving off an odor that pervaded the camp from top to bottom. The odor persisted into the night. It literally clung to the walls. But the urge to get rid of the discomfort in the stomach area and the pain around the forehead remained.

The weakness in the limbs was increasing. Many were in great pain climbing the stairs from the first to the second floor. They didn't know where the weakness came from. They presumed that the monotony of their existence had made them apathetic toward their surroundings and that it served no purpose to put any energy into physical things. Only when they noticed that their clothes were getting looser, the shirts around the neck became wider, skirts, blouses, hung loose around the body, they began to turn their attention to this phenomenon—at first with cheerful, laconic laughter, showing off to each other the lack of fat and flesh; they even made fun of their bodily deformity, which had resulted from the lack of nourishment.

One still kept oneself erect. It was a matter of pride to endure. The children's cheeks became hollow, thin little legs, their faces and eyes sullen. Their mouths were being stuffed with hoarded pieces of food. When there was no other way, then one would get sick. Stretched out it was possible to recuperate. They advised each other to "lie down" for a few days. A few days of rest and then they could go on again. But one evening a man collapsed in the stairwell. A man of sixty-eight years, a physician, a renowned professor from Germany. He was carried to his bed. The doctor came, felt his heart and pulse, shrugged his shoulders, left, came back, gave the sick man an injection. Arsenic to give him strength, or something like that. It didn't help. The professor died. His legs were swollen, crusts of blood were visible on his arms and thighs. Commonly it is called "famine edema." Here it was called "enfeeblement."

This case gave the camp inmates cause for thought. When night fell, they became restless, tossing and turning, whispering from bed to bed. . . . Now, a lot became clearer. Several weeks of malnutrition had already caused devastation outside the stomach linings. They began to hold human beings and things, what was done and not done, responsible for the misery, all that was remote from this misery, the famished did each other injustice, each read in the eyes of the other his own fate, saw the other wasting away without recognizing himself, for there were no mirrors and one had to rely on the sense of touch. . . .

Some savored pleasures of the past, tasting all kinds of flavors with a parched palate, regretting that they had not indulged themselves with more gusto in years gone by and that they had denied themselves this or that—be it indifference, be it foolish culinary reticence, they were mortified by the word "diet," which had back then made their lives dismal; finally they made up their mind that they would catch up on all the pleasures they had forgone as soon as the opportunity should present itself in a happier time. . . .

This was, of course, dream, illusion, self-deception. But whatever it was, it helped them overcome the moments of most profound mental depression, overcome the moments of mortification and self-humiliation! What an idiot you were that you didn't save yourself in time, didn't recognize in time the threat, that you weren't determined enough to leave everything behind and go somewhere far away where there are no ghettos and no field grays! [Soldiers; field gray was the color of the German uniform.] Regret sometimes overwhelmed even the pangs of hunger and the inability to sleep. But after the regret, hunger again made itself felt, overriding all considerations about the past. . . . Somehow help had to be found or they would waste away, go to the dogs, succumb, somehow, sometime. . . . This is how it was when winter came. In the camps and in the ghetto.

Idleness

Since there are neither chairs nor tables nor benches—except for a few small tables that were found here and there in the hallway—everybody is just lounging around all day, getting into each other's way, knocking against each other. People walk up and down the stairs, crowd around the kitchen door, go in and out of the doors, stand around in the courtyards . . . not knowing what to do with themselves. There are no books. No musical instruments except for a few harmonicas. No gramophone, no radio. No place to gather for a friendly conversation. Constant movement. Scurrying, running, pushing, shouting, bawling, more pushing . . . here and there some light work for those asked to sweep the morass away from in front of the doors, to clean the hallways, to carry the soup kettle, and similar housekeeping chores. But division of the day, as everybody had when they were free, diversion that reflects the rhythm of one's own will, all this did not exist. It wasn't that they had been laid off or were unwilling to work. In the ghetto all existence was outside the laws of the universe.

Dogs are barking, horses neighing, birds twittering, *slaves are toiling,* but we, here in the ghetto, are vegetating, a burden to ourselves. Our lives have lost all purpose. We needn't be thrown onto a dung heap, we have been lying there from the moment we entered the ghetto. Idleness has eaten into our bones, suffusing us with a sense of aversion against everything. Life out there rustles and sings and swings, there is an up and a down, a high and a low, those who hold power and those who are subject to power. Here, we are all dirt-poor, idle bums.

Only doctors, experts in some field or trade, and strong young men are working; their day is filled, they are not parasites. (Above this, separately, add: ressort, hospital, the sick, etc.)

They must make up for what we, the others, have to endure through no fault of our own. There are several thousand of them and they feel that they are the bearers of a responsibility loaded on their weak, malnourished bodies by a higher power. Lawyers, engineers, writers, teachers, artists, musicians, workers of the mind, guard the entrance doors, clean latrines, carry excrement if they didn't have the good fortune to be employed as doctors, judges, policemen, officials in the service of the ghetto administration. But however the fate of the individual may have turned out here—almost twenty-five thousand human beings are going hungry, leaning against the walls of the hallways and the doors, in the courtyards; they wander aimlessly from cot to cot, talking to themselves . . . for not all that is being said has any real meaning, it is hanging in the air . . . not to be taken seriously—honor does not exist, neither does responsibility nor keeping one's word, the days and nights have no hours, nothing exists through which one might become guilty. There is only one word, one concept, one symbol that floats before everybody's eyes: bread! For the sake of bread, people turn into hypocrites, fanatics, boasters, miserable wretches. Give me bread and you're my friend. Hunger and idleness go together here. But idleness does not spare the individual from noise, restlessness, being drawn into disputes and strife. In peacetime, back home, inactivity was part of resting. Inactivity was connected with solitude, tied to solitude. Those who didn't want to do anything lost themselves in solitude. Such a condition calmed the nerves, refreshed the spirit for work later on, provided the time for thinking of something beautiful and great, or even for being creative. Inactivity was sweet in this state of solitude, liberating, stimulating. The founders of religions were steeped in inactivity while they had their grandiose visions before embarking on their realization. So once more: solitude. Here inactivity is a bane, no relaxation, nothing but loafing, which doesn't turn into vice only because in the Jewish ghetto there is no room for vice. In the realm of high culture, of morality, of order, and of the superior race, idleness leads to theft, burglary, deceit, sexual excess—to criminality. The ghetto stays removed from such crimes despite the fact that it is forcibly embedded within the enclaves of the Łódź criminal element. They are selling their shoes, their last pieces of clothing, their last shirt, but nobody sinks to the level of those who, through their crimes, bear the blame for this ghetto. Even if on occasion, driven by immense misery, a small theft occurs, a quick reach for somebody else's possessions, the ghetto is, nevertheless, free from violence or incrimination. On Shabbat the poorest of the Jews are found in prayer, ragged, famished, wretched figures crowd the houses of worship on High Holy Days, and the fervor of their praying has not been lessened under the pressure from hunger and the cold. . . .

Hunger (Second Stage), Camp

Lying around on cots, every flavor in the mouth, exotic dishes, since even the more common ones are unattainable. Tearing away of bread, stealing, letting die, professor—child—clothing sold (pulling up the coat collar), faces changed, unrecognizable. Exchange: a piece of soap for liver paté, coffee in the morning, soup at noon; this describes the eternal monotony.

December 1941 had come. In the camps the twenty-five thousand "evacuees" were waiting daily for the lunch soup that never arrives on time but is usually carried in about three in the afternoon in huge tin vessels. The smell of the soup is wafting from far away. . . . Frequently it is unclear what the smell is. . . . It isn't cabbage that exudes the well-known poor-people's aroma, not bad meat as found in second-rate restaurants. The smell is indescribable. The people had gotten used to this smell the way one gets used to the smell in a prison cell. A few suffered from light nausea when the soup approached. But it had to be suppressed if one wanted to fill one's stomach, if one didn't want to suffer the disdain of the neighbors. The black morning coffee served as tooth polish, for it was warm, and warm water was otherwise not available; in the evening people poured down the coffee to fill the stomach with something warm, with it they ate a little bit of bread. Bread is carefully rationed. Those who are particularly prudent divide the loaf of bread into seven parts, one part a day. This part is then again divided into day portions. Woe to him who eats more. However, some consume a whole pound in one fell swoop, which cannot be made good, impossible to catch up.

(Carlyle: *French Revolution.* Kubin: *The Other Side.*)

Those who consume more than their ration of bread get hungry sooner. Those who don't apportion well are the first victims of famine edema. He wanders around the hallways, between cots, trying to exchange some item for bread. He is rarely successful. They all guard their loaves of bread jealously. At the beginning of winter, the price of a loaf of bread on the bread exchange, on the black market, is already 20 marks. From autumn to the beginning of winter it rose from 8 to 20. But the selling prices for textiles, clothing, shoes, leather bags, did not keep up with bread prices, so the owners of the wares they had brought along sank daily into greater poverty. There were no controls. No authority that would put a stop to it. Resentment among the consumers against those suspected of forcing up prices as well as against black marketeers was useless. For the ghetto market did not permit other sources. It was dependent on the good graces of the city administration. [On the margin: "Bread expensive? Clothing, underwear, for bread! Saving bread and in its stead finally sewing a suit for the coming years—carry it out!"] Otherwise there were considerations whose results didn't condemn the bread sellers all that sharply, that even almost excused them. This question gave rise to daily, heated debates, discussions in the camps and the "private apartments" where some of the evacuees had been housed.

"Outrageous prices, that this should be allowed in the ghetto where almost everybody is a beggar. . . ."

"Why are you buying?" the critic is being asked.

"Because I am hungry, I have to buy."

"And he, the man from Łódź, sells on his part because he is hungry. . . . So what you have is hunger versus hunger. . . ."

"But he shouldn't be allowed to demand such high prices."

"You are doing the vendor an injustice. . . . Those who sell their bread have to go hungry for a few days. After all, he doesn't buy the bread in the market in order to sell it again for usurious prices. He sells what he has saved, going hungry himself, rather than leftovers from the table. He sells bread that was part of his ration, for which he pays the regular price of 80 pennies. This then is a matter of bread that he has taken from his own mouth. And how much he charges for his frugality, for his abstinence, his heroism, that's his own business. He puts a price on his hunger."

"That may very well be so. But don't forget that the proceeds allow him to buy the official ration of food quite comfortably. For a few marks he gets sugar, vegetables, preserves, detergent, flour . . . even if only in small quantities. . . . So he pays the official allotment and has some money left in his pocket. . . ."

"That may be. But would you sell your ration of bread, and, if so, for what price?"

The critic fell silent. He simply mumbled, "Hunger." He didn't know what to say. This kind of debate was taking place everywhere.

Uncleanliness (Medical Questions)

About nutrition: ration (food card, private). April 12, for three weeks: three loaves of bread, 50 dkg flour, 50 dkg sugar, 20 dkg margarine, 6 kg potatoes, 2 kg vegetables—a little more than usual.

People had changed in the three months of hunger. Almost everybody walked with a stooped back, had twitching legs. Illnesses of all sorts had crept in. Even young people had pneumonia. Thousands tossed and turned on their cots in the prostrate position, since their bones were hurting, and daydreamed of foodstuff like potatoes, apples, sausages, baked goods, of beer and wine and coffee. Their palates broke out in sweat and contracted sweet and bitter. . . . The smell of soup increased the weakness of the famished, but their hands reached automatically for the tin into which the soup was poured every day. Again and again soup . . . thin soup, thinning soup, thicker soup, but soup. . . . It was no longer eating per se that was important, rather it was a matter of postponing the hour of the inevitable breakdown. Every day somebody died here and there in his bed, sometimes there were three, sometimes seven. Nobody gave a damn about the corpses. Complete indifference toward the fate of the dead or dying neighbor, whose presence did not inhibit any gaiety, laughing, trilling. A pretty young girl puts on her lipstick and gives signs of displeasure when she is disturbed by the removal of a body. Some individuals have already lost all constraints. . . . The human beast seeks to satisfy its greed. But there are still some who have preserved a spark of dignity and self-respect, a modicum of respect for the past and for family reputation; those who once held high positions still preserve restraint and decorum, but that remnant threatens to dwindle. Hunger, cold, illness, and disconsolateness (hopelessness) work together to undermine the last bit of self-possession. Death walks up to every cot, to every broken windowpane, and asks: "When may I come?"

The weather is unstable. It is snowing and raining. Water cannot be pumped, the well fails. The latrines are swamped. Attempts are made to clean up. A woman knocks against the latrine wall with her soup pot and spills the soup. A crippled child next to her throws itself on the floor and laps up the soup together with the dirty snow. Airplanes are thundering overhead. Suddenly somebody darts into the yard where a dozen people are relieving themselves: "The bread ration is being cut." Despair in the faces. Two pregnant women get into an argument, without knowing what about. . . .

A piece of rag is missing, a dust rag. One man wants to clean up, the other fights against him because it will whirl up dust. Both good people. Senseless hatred. . . . Both from good Jewish homes. A blind rabbi nearby hears their curses and profanities. He is groping his way toward them. His entire body is trembling. O how hunger has reduced my poor fellow Jews. A piece of bread, a few grams of fat, could help you. And somehow here they are, pitted against each other, father against son, brother against brother, friend against friend. . . . Is it because we turned away from the commandments of our teaching? . . .

Yes, yes. . . . If we had remained the holy people, we would be in a different situation now. . . . O my beloved Jewish people, how bitterly did you disappoint me. . . .

Behind the rabbi, a woman takes a little piece of margarine from a dirty brown paper, gets a knife from her cot, and starts to spread it on a slice of bread. It's not eating time. It's afternoon. An older woman stands next to her. Her stomach growls loudly. When she sees the margarine, she bursts into screams, staggers. A fit of hysteria. She has to be calmed down. The transport doctor is called; he gives her a harmless injection. The woman is so weak she falls asleep. The body is in uproar, the nerves tense, the ears become keener. This is told by somebody who was saved shortly before he was going to starve to death. A rare case. Those from Vienna and Frankfurt are falling victim in quick succession. The deportees from Prague are holding firmer. They are hardier, more resilient, due to their constitution and due to their optimism. They also know better how to adjust quickly to the pace and organization. They could be called privileged. Hospitals, precincts, ressorts [workshops or factories] swarm with Czech Jews providing their services as doctors, policemen, workers. . . . The Slavic landscape is more congenial to those from Prague. . . .

"Today I saw three eggs, about 50 marks. . . ." Nobody wants to believe it. Nobody has seen a chicken egg since entering the ghetto. Tales, fiction, fantasy. . . .

Illnesses are increasing. . . . We hear of typhoid fever and that several camps have been put under quarantine. Nothing specific. Symptoms of illnesses are abounding enough. After decades of practicing medicine, the doctors finally have the opportunity to confront cases of mass famine edema. Three months of malnutrition endangered the lives of thousands of people in the ghetto. . . . Many collapsed after they had survived an acute illness since the damage to the blood circulation had progressed too far.

About "hunger." "We don't talk about eating," one of the many famished women said once. Such a conversation stimulates the stomach, gives off secretions, thereby weakening the organism. It happened frequently that people who talked themselves into the illusion that they were eating foods from which they had long abstained displayed severe nervous disorders and turned outright wild during the night. We tell each other stories about clothing one evening, another time about travels, then again we talk about books we once read. . . . We also avoid any kind of physical exertion. Every step must be weighed. . . . Otherwise one gets tired very quickly. The body is no longer up to longer walks. . . . Pain in the shoulder blades and limbs. . . . Many who are kept awake at night by hunger reach for sleeping pills they have brought along from home, like Shanodorny, Sedomit, Quadronok, Luminal, and Bromoral . . . on occasion even Veronal. . . . But these are no cure for hunger or illness caused by hunger. The morning weighs all the heavier on the minds of these "happy ones" who gained a night. . . .

What a sensation: From the street, through the window, a woman is visible cooking beans on a spirit stove. People queue up, children crowd the window . . . the police have to interfere, so that the traffic won't be disrupted.

Beans—that was something different, not like the vegetables that were allotted to the one hundred twenty thousand inhabitants of the ghetto. A diabolic method of slowly killing people by feeding them worthless grass rather than nutritious legumes; indeed, an outright scientific process of bringing about, with clock in hand, the complete debilitation of an entire community under the guise of charitable food allocation! In combination with cold weather, being forced to relieve oneself in open latrines, pulling like draft animals the carts and wagons with arms that have lost their musculature, sleeping on a damp ground, the organism had to fail, the heart had to cease servicing. Water and vegetables—the ingredients of the soup, the basis of nutrition! About two hundred thousand portions of soup were dispensed daily in the ghetto! What a wonderful word is "soup"! Here it was a curse, for no prison inmate would be satisfied with such contemptible stuff, no prison inmate would endure a protracted imprisonment on such a soup, for the three most important elements were missing: carbohydrates, fat, and albumen. Carrots, water beets, red beets, a few kernels of barley swimming around in the warm water—that was called soup. This caricature of a soup was the major cause of the hunger symptoms, the famine edema that became matter-of-fact in the ghetto rather than a phenomenon. People were drinking, eating, slurping, gobbling the soup, brutally suppressing thereby with it the subjectively unpleasant feeling of hunger. The stomach was full for a short while. The main goal of nutrition, the essential character of nutrition: the ingestion of valuable elements, was not served by it. The provider, the Ashkenazic authorities [reference to the Germans], the field-gray power, was satisfied with filling our stomachs with yellow and red feed so we would be able to work in the ressorts and so that the illusion of being sated would be awakened . . . like a careless doctor who suppresses the symptoms of headaches or fever with narcotics or antipyretics instead of eliminating the actual sickness through causal means.

Time does not stand still, the days and nights are fleeting, the stomach must be filled. The immigrants—we are also called "evacuees" or "new settlers"—have long spent the 40 marks they received immediately upon arriving in the ghetto as an allowance. There was a need for soap, toilet paper, bread, or even fat. . . . Since February 1942 they can be seen roaming the streets, carrying shirts, trousers, clothing, shoes. . . . They must sell their clothing in order to be able to garner food or soap or lice salve or even a clothes brush. . . . The cramped living in the camps and mass quarters, the lack of water and soap, the impossibility of keeping clean and of changing the undergarments more often, the various forms of malnutrition of the skin, and the numb apathy of older people with regard to caring for their body all led to the first outbreak of skin diseases, mostly caused by parasites. The doctors—without the means for a radical cure—diagnose these illnesses, various kinds of eczema, boils that infect the surrounding tissue, which often kill these parts and are sometimes even lethal. Regeneration of the affected parts was not possible. Watery soup is not an adequate regenerator. Above and beyond all this, there was a lack of necessary medications—bandaging material was a rarity.

NOTEBOOK B

Mailbox for Jews' Mail

Remembrances for the Future (Jotted-Down Notes, Etc.)

About the Prehistory of the Ghetto

Remembrances of one who had died in the hospital. Even the criminal district in the ghetto area was cleared out before the drive into the ghetto from Litzmannstadt. Those who were driven into the ghetto had even their rucksacks mercilessly taken away from them.

1. The old farmer had a little house, cows, horses, geese. . . . All gone in fifteen minutes. . . . Go! . . . Came without slippers. . . .
2. In the course of being ousted immediately at the beginning of the *milchome* [Yidd., war], Ivri [Yidd./Hebr., Jews] herded together, brutally shot, immediately covered with dirt. "Why are you burying us? After all, we are still alive."
3. Ashkenes [O. R.'s code word for Germans] come into the ghetto. "Come here, show yourself, hit me? Hit? Go!" He turns around and is gunned down.
4. Four Ivri tied to a cart . . . Ashkenes—"Sit down. Let's go!" Whip! As in ancient Rome quadriga.
5. Near Częstochowa, Poland, at the beginning of the war the civilian population runs, runs along . . . caught by the victor, about three hundred Jewish men in a cellar for three nights and three days, with food, their own refuse. Two brothers walk up to the lattice of the cellar hole: Shoot us! We can't stand it any longer. . . . "No, you'll have to croak down there." Then they get out, filthy, with swollen legs, being chased . . . under a hail of bullets. . . .

6. A block of houses in Litzmannstadt[1] was cordoned off. The ghetto had already been set up but was not yet sealed off with a wire fence. Everybody was removed from this block, men, women, children, into the streetcar, then into railroad cars and to various places, Lublin, Rzeszów, Tarnów. . . .[2]
7. In Litzmannstadt (the ghetto already created) = a city where at three in the afternoon all streets are blocked off by the police; every Jew stopped in the street, children, women; groups being formed, these chased through town, exercises: squads and then chased off. Other groups locked up in factories. (With 150 marks, a day of freedom could be bought!?) Several groups expelled to various other cities, others taken to an empty jail, some of them shot dead. Even some of those who (shortly after the beginning of the war) paid 150 marks were shot.
8. Springels (nice how they are robbing us [about Prague]).
9. Łódź: Ashkenes lawyer confiscates apartment, tells woman who lives there: "Take only personal underwear." She wants to sneak in a towel. He: "We don't permit stealing."
10. Officer comes to the apartment after five o'clock (curfew for Jews), demands furs, tears out the inner lining, comes back the next day; sometimes he gives money for the articles, demands it back the next day; holds conversations, has tea, gives cigarettes, dances with the daughter of the house.
11. Łódź: Rabbi Menachem Mendel arrested. His shammes [beadle] is forced to hit him in the mouth and vice versa. Set free after a few weeks (terribly beaten, kicked at), Sefer Tojre [Yidd., Torah scroll] torn out, trampled on, burned. . . . Ivri afraid to go out into the street since Ashkenes take them away on the spot to hard labor. . . .
12. Ivri flee in civilian clothing from the invading field-gray troops in 1939, taking the road to Warsaw, many turn back, airplanes above are bombing and machine gunning the masses below, furthermore in several places mass executions, freezing to death, starving to death, that's approximately a quarter million people by July 1942. Outside by the fence an unknown man tells stories (cannot be verified) . . . (every time a dead body is taken from the house, even though it is something commonplace, terrible screams from the women).

Friday, February 20. A fantastic red streak across the sky. People in Marysin (part of the ghetto with summer cottages)[3] are standing still.

Violet-gray even in the latest dusk. People tremble. What will happen to us? Intimations of the apocalypse?

Jewish police make known: Members of the transport from Vienna, Berlin, Frankfurt, Hamburg, Cologne, Prague, all have to report the next morning at nine o'clock to the big market square, only very old people and the sick are exempt. . . . Why? Rumor has it that the Eldest will address the crowd. . . . People go there, a gallows! The sight of the gallows, indication of what was lying ahead. Suddenly a man of about fifty is led into the square, which is blocked off by soldiers with machine guns. The field grays lead the man to the gallows. Jewish policemen force him to mount the stool. Seeing the gallows he calls out: "Let me live, I didn't do anything wrong . . ." Then he murmurs something incomprehensible. The Jewish policeman places the rope around his neck. The crowd trembles. A field-gray Kripo asks: Maybe the rope is too tight? The drama lasts fifteen minutes. But the crowd must remain there from ten to twelve (Shabbat!). Many get sick, their knees shake. The scene is being photographed and filmed. The whole thing as "deterrence." The dead man remained hanging until five in the afternoon, life in the ghetto continued, then he was tossed into an open pit. About all this no indignation, only shock. For a few hours it was the main topic of conversation, by evening all was forgotten . . . Talk turned to the price of bread, of margarine, sugar . . . The dead man: a book printer named Herz from Cologne. Had wife and daughter. Mentally disturbed. Made a desperate attempt to flee the ghetto . . . Was already at the train station. Railway car. When he opened his wallet, a German passenger noticed the yellow star which he had removed from his jacket and hidden inside. Arrested. Locked up for two weeks. Death penalty incomprehensible, since leaving the ghetto was not planned.[4]

Bleak and barren roads, partly snowed in and partly covered with mud, stretch between houses dotting the landscape. Stunted trees and bushes extend their meager, trembling branches toward the sky. Throngs of children in rags cross the streets, their yellow, weatherworn faces furrowed, weary. At times a fleeting smile appears on one of those faces, sometimes one of those bloodless lips begins to sing. At times these children throw snowballs like children everywhere in freedom. Nobody can tell what the morrow will bring. What the future will bring. What will happen with all of us? What is this all for? Why the ghetto? Is there a tomorrow? A day after tomorrow? Is it worth thinking about it? We are beggars, lepers, pariahs, parasites, people without music, without a piece of soil, without a bed, without a world. The likes of this city does not exist anywhere. Come here, people over there where workdays and holidays alternate, where there are dreams and purpose and resistance. Come quickly. For when it is all over, our numbers will have been so thinned, so downcast, that we will be unable to enjoy our reunion . . . And yet, everybody wants to live, "to live it," to know that this life was not completely senseless after all.

Face of the Ghetto

The snow is filthy. Nobody knows from what. After all, the soot from the chimneys could not possibly be swept over here . . . A cart rolls down the street. Instead of a horse, human beings are reined to it, three to the pole up front, several in the back. Alongside little boys. The bodies are clad in tatters, yellow, black, gray rags sewn together, wooden shoes filled with straw, the hands wrapped in old, torn pieces of cloth, everywhere ropes that had to keep it all together. Faces are not visible, the eyes hardly peer out from under the dirty mufflers, it is hard to see what they are made of, cloth or hide or whatever . . . One gets the suspicion that the dead had been wrapped in clothing and, as a gag, had been sent out into the street in order to show all the more blatantly the senseless obtuseness of this ghetto. (Brueghel gives an indication . . .)

Here and there uniformed Jewish policemen with their billy clubs, placed there as toys, as if it were desirable from an visual standpoint to place next to gray-black specters a few colorful dots: a little yellow and a little orange . . . (more on *Face of the Ghetto*). Conclusion: More than sixty thousand skeletons in tatters.

Evacuation (To Perceive the Legend of Ahasver)

What day is today? Nobody knows. They argue about it. Hardly anybody has a clue, for the days pass one like the other. Month after month, they all wear almost the same clothing, one and the same wrapping around the emaciated body. Saturday is recognizable since the shops are closed, and Sundays from the smokeless chimneys in the nearby, and yet unattainable, German city Litzmannstadt. So, today is Tuesday. What a meaningless fact . . . More important, more exciting and evoking alarm, is the news that preparations are being made for the outsettlement of, for the time being, ten thousand ghetto residents (natives). Whose turn will it be? Answer: convicts, those receiving assistance, those unwilling to work, and other "inconvenient" people. Among the convicts are primarily those who had been incarcerated a few weeks for selling the food rations allocated to them. It began on December 26.[5]—Into the midst of the preparations came the Eldest's order to exchange all male sport and ski shoes for 10 marks and a pair of wooden shoes. This was followed by raids of the camps and private dwellings for those shoes. Thus began the year 1942. The cold weather intensified, which didn't keep the Jewish policemen from collecting the demanded shoes to hunt for the oldest and most worn furs, valuables, and precious metals.—The saying went: The evacuees would be transported to Polish villages for agricultural work. But that was merely a rumor. The only thing the ghetto knew and saw was that seven hundred to eight hundred Jews a day were driven from their huts, their holes, and their rooms. The temperature had dropped to 15 degrees [all temperatures in Celsius, trans.] below freezing. Jews were also caught in the streets and taken directly to the railway station. These were people who some time ago in Łódź lost all their assets, their homes, their furnishings, their clothing, and had at last, in the course of two years of privation, been able to gather a few household items and clothing only to be deprived of these last possessions, and now, totally destitute, were being forced to embark on the road to an unknown country. The police stormed the lodgings of the Jews marked for evacuation. Not infrequently they found the corpses of children who had starved to death or of old people who had frozen to death. A shock had gone through the ghetto. Only 12½ kg of luggage and 10 marks in money were allowed to be taken along. Therefore the order to the ghetto to deliver all currency in reichsmarks. People sold, squandered, the little they had to supply themselves with food, especially bread. The temperature dropped to 19 degrees below. Keys froze in the keyholes. In the rooms lay frozen mice next to shoes and refuse, too weak (like the human beings) to tear them with their teeth. One kilogram garlic was 10 marks, 1 kg potatoes 3½. A good shirt could buy

1 kg of potatoes. The evacuees were driven to the railway station amidst a terrible snowstorm, children and old people. The price of bread rose to 35 marks a loaf, potatoes to 6 marks, then to 10 marks, per kg, bread rose further to 70 marks. The bundles of the evacuees contained slices of bread, potatoes, margarine . . . They had better not get sick. No doctor accompanied them, no medications. In the collection camps, people were wild with hunger before they were transported. (Those next to them knew no mercy.) Police bludgeoned those who impatiently pushed themselves toward the coffee (water). Eastern winds rattled the broken windowpanes. Giant black crows ate the bark from the bare trees. Thus it went, day after day. One loaf of bread 100 marks, 1 kg margarine 100 marks. That was at the end of February 1942. The shock lasted. For it was said that the evacuation would continue.[6] Nobody was safe anymore from being deported; at least eight hundred people had to be delivered every day. Some thought they would be able to save themselves: chronically ill old people and those with frozen limbs—not even that helped. The surgeons in the hospital were very busy. They amputated hands and feet of the poor "patients" and discharged them as cripples. The cripples too were taken away. On March 7, nine people froze to death at the railway station where they had to wait nine hours for the departure of the train. In the collection places (open schools and prisons),[7] people keeled over from hunger. They too were dragged to the trains and handed over to the German Kripo. An old woman had inadvertently been forgotten in her room—on March 11 (five days later!), she was found starved to death. About this time, there were already more than twenty thousand candidates for deportation. Deportation? Without blankets, without warm clothing, without hope for a place to sleep? "We'll take you from the ghetto to somewhere in the countryside . . . You can go wherever you want . . . go to work for the Polish peasants, if there are any left in the surroundings of Łódź . . ." Thus speaks Ashkenes. Bread was no longer offered in loaves but in quarter loaves.

It continues. Since it was prohibited to carry clothing, some women put on several layers one above the other. A few Jewish policemen try to treat the evacuees "humanely." An Ashkenes beats a Jewish policeman with a whip because he treated the evacuees too well. The Jewish policeman doesn't care about the beating, happy that he had suffered for the Jewish cause.

One kilogram water turnips costs 12 marks.

On the first day of spring in the year 1942, a new winter arrived. Such a winter had not been recorded for decades. When they ran short of the required numbers of deportees, the Jewish police randomly hunted down people in the streets and herded them to the collection camp. Many were hiding in huts and on abandoned farms, many spent the nights away from their own domicile. When they were caught, they were carried off, loaded onto a cart, and people, human beings like themselves, pulled the cart to the railway station. Many of the hapless no longer had the strength to sit upright. They were lying flat on the floor. When spoken to, they didn't answer. Despondency filled their eyes. They no longer needed consolation since they no longer understood the words that were meant to console. Most people did not even carry a bundle for fear that the Ashkenes would take it away at the station.

Mothers searched for their children in the collection camps, children for their mothers. Children who had fled the hospital with feet in a cast came to say goodbye to their parents. People with prostheses hobbled along, fell over, remained lying until they were somehow gotten rid of, those who didn't want to part from their families. The dying were dragged along. Children fled the orphanages at night presuming that one relative or another was about to be put on the transport. Then others, torn from their beds, were rubbing their eyes, unable to determine what was happening to them. Children and old people cried and sobbed, but most of them just had a hopeless gaze. In the midst of the turmoil, the heavy steps of the Jewish police, threats with the bludgeon, the coughing and moaning of the seriously ill . . . The black coffee came . . . Crowding around the hot water, sometimes not even that, distribution of bread for the road . . . 1½ reichsmarks in coins permitted per person. Not a single tenpenny piece can be found in the ghetto. One and a half marks buys 1 dkg of bread in the ghetto, in other areas outside the ghetto 10 dkg. . . . By the end of March the story made the rounds in the ghetto that the deportees are taken off the train about 150 km from Łódź, are checked for their fitness to work, and are "employed." The workers are to support those who don't work . . . Furthermore, so it was said in the ghetto (according to a public declaration), the doctors should volunteer to accompany the evacuees to the villages and take care of them there. April 2 was a cutoff day. The evacuees who were gathered at the railway station were sent back home since all evacuations were presumably being halted. The hapless people were caught in the greatest misery since they had already sold their few belongings to buy foodstuff at the highest price for the new home (and now returned to empty dwellings). At that time, bread was 150 marks a loaf, margarine 130 marks.

Entire rows of houses had remained empty, many hundreds of those people registered for evacuation died before the departure, families were torn apart, children were made orphans, the healthy were crippled. Thirty-five thousand Jews lingered in limbo somewhere near Colm? Or Lublin? Or Warsaw? The deportation was temporarily concluded. The price of bread fell from 160 marks to 80 marks. This was the only benefit of the halt of the deportations . . . for a few days. However, nobody trusted in the future. It was the Christian feast of Easter. Is it possible that the field-gray Ashkenes were overcome with a Christian Easter sentiment and exercised compassion under the impression of the legend of resurrection? Nature continued to rage. Snowstorms on April 3 . . . A major event in the camps: potato soup. Sensation! Finally! This continued until the end of the month. But April 19 (Sunday) brought a surprise: On order of the authorities, all unemployed persons in the ghetto—men and women—from age ten on must report for a medical exam. Submit: identification papers, and perhaps bread card. To appear in washed and clean condition! The bedridden are to be registered with their respective Order Service[8] and will be picked up for examination by the orderlies.—All names will be checked during the examination, and those who do not appear will be punished. Exempt from the medical exam are:

1. All those employed.
2. All those in possession of a work assignment as well as those from a work detail and the personnel department.
3. New settlers from the German Reich, Luxemburg, Vienna, and Prague.—Examination taking place April 20–23, Mühlgasse 32. Division by place of residence. All further plans for medical examinations will follow.

Fear seizes the entire ghetto. Again, deportation? What will happen to us? What new calamity? Work in the countryside? The excitement grows, since no upper age limit . . .

The examination of the candidates takes place under supervision of a German commission, doctors, and SS men. Everybody, ten-year-olds and seventy-year-olds, belongs to the same category. They are being examined (looked over) for how much work they can still perform, how much work energy is left in them after two years of hunger, misery, moaning, fear of death, and waiting . . . They receive a stamp on the chest like animals at an exhibition . . . ten-year-old orphans with stamps on their chest. The Ashkenes commission is "surprised" about the dilapidated condition of those being paraded to be mustered for work . . . Malnutrition . . . famished figures . . . as if the ghetto in and of itself could be held responsible for this condition. Yes, the ghetto is the cause of hunger and its consequences . . . Women among those being mustered have supposedly already been assigned for work in Germany while the men who had previously been employed in the ghetto will stay behind. Irony of fate: The gentlemen of the examination commission saw only the acute condition of many thousands of Jews in the ghetto, but the process that had led to this condition is unknown to them, that is, it remains concealed from them. The ghetto inhabitants lost 1 million kg in weight in the course of one year. Wrinkled faces, and folds around the neck and under the chin and the abdomen, are the visible symptoms of malnutrition, that is, of constant hunger. A quick death, the increase of stomach and colon diseases, diseases of the skeletal apparatus, constant weariness in the limbs, are due to chronic lack of nourishment. The pulse slows, blood pressure decreases. Apathy is for many the onset of dying. The chronic malnutrition has a catastrophic effect on the metabolism.

Calories! According to German scientific findings, the consumption of calories in normal times was 3,640 calories with 93 grams of albumen per person. The allocated ration in the fall of 1941 was 1,300 calories and 36 grams of albumen. Since the fall of 1941, the ghetto—with the minor exception of the workers in the factories—received a mere 900 calories and 25 grams of albumen per person. Not taking into account the lack of vitamins. This was no longer nutrition, this was a prescription for a slow death. Added to this was the mental depression, the condition of hopelessness and powerlessness, the recognition of an inescapable fate. They remembered the late fall of 1939 when Poland was conquered! At that time, about forty-five hundred Jews from Łódź had been sent to a prisoner-of-war camp near Nuremberg. After a short while twenty-five hundred of them were dead. Those who survived were allowed twenty-four hours to get foodstuff for themselves. The Jews were taken in sealed railway cars from Nuremberg to Cracow. The journey took six days. The provisions the Jews carried were one loaf of bread and one tin of canned food . . . A bad memory! And the words of the Eldest still rang in their ears: "If I told you everything I knew, you wouldn't be able to sleep. This way, I am the only one who doesn't sleep . . ." And also these words of the Eldest: "The ghetto too is part of the war . . ."

Face of the Ghetto (Early April)

In the gutters, piles of snow and excrement. Filthy water splashes the clothing. People wade through the puddles. The horses almost sink into the mud, people try to help, everywhere wagons and carts that are being pulled and pushed by weakened, downtrodden figures, now and then they call out, horses stomp their hoofs . . . The passersby hug the walls of the houses. Sometimes a cold rain mixed with snow showers falls on them . . . The houses seem abandoned. Nobody at the windows, nothing green behind the panes, no curtains . . . The city has no promenade, no boulevard. There are no residential areas that are better or worse. . . . Everywhere the same low buildings of the petite bourgeoisie with their unadorned, drab façades, smokeless chimneys reaching into the sky . . . And scurrying, rushing, starving, quick-stepping people . . . Most of them carrying some load, steering a cart, or lugging bundles, buckets, troughs. Vessels for soup: plates or bowls or cups of tin, pewter, or china, tied to their body with a string. Hardly if ever do they stop to talk to each other. Now and then a policeman calls out something or passersby get into a loud argument that turns into fisticuffs over some childish matter . . . sometimes the call of street vendors can be heard, hawking cigarettes or knitwear or food ration cards . . . gray-black dressed in rags . . . except for those in uniform caps and armbands. Those are the privileged: policemen, doctors, people in service to the ghetto community.

But everybody, those who are rushing and lugging and pulling and trotting, those who work and those who watch, those who take care and those who are being taken care of, people and horses . . . everything and anything that moves through the streets, all without purpose, like puppets on a stage . . . and the more one observes the scene the more senseless appears the whole thing. For whom? For what? Why? For how long? None of these questions has an answer. There was no purpose in the beginning and there is no purpose at the end. . . . Maybe it's like a silent movie unrolling, to which we have long become unaccustomed and which therefore seems grotesque to us . . . The face of the ghetto? Nobody can paint it, nobody can describe it more naturally.

Face of the Ghetto. Beautiful children, blond, but with rickets and tuberculosis. If you are lucky, you'll encounter on occasion hordes of laughing children, blue-eyed girls with blond curls and reddish blond boys . . . very attractive, lovely, who even in the midst of these bleak surroundings, amidst the misery and excrement, have preserved the cheerfulness of a child's soul. Orphans, guided by their teachers, are singing in the streets, some chorus in Polish, whereas their daily language is Yiddish, which seems to slowly disappear even in the Jewish ghetto of Łódź. The children's faces are cheerful, their color even rosy at times, but the doctors know better: The majority suffer from rickets and tuberculosis, the majority are candidates for death. The color and song are misleading. The children are confined to their own area in the ghetto. Nobody can escape the fate that awaits the prisoners of the ghetto . . .

Gazing at the horizon while walking through the desolate alleys, one felt the endless Russian-Polish steppe . . . Something foreign touched us . . . those of us who were captivated by mountains, black-blue fir forests, and deep-green meadows in our sense of beauty, we were disquieted by the character of the landscape around Łódź, which was apparently suited to the Slavic soul, but not to the Westerner who was alienated from nature. We fought against the sight of starlings starving with us, flapping their wings here and there during the frosty winter days. There were no breadcrumbs out in the open in the ghetto that they might pick. Every crumb of bread was being guarded carefully. Neither were there any dogs nor any feed for them.

At the same time, a terrible loneliness spread over the newcomers, despite the cramped quarters. People of all categories slept, breathed, vegetated next to each other, strangers to each other despite the common suffering and same prospects for the future. . . . Any kind of intimate life had been squashed, living together became painful . . .

families torn apart. . . . Where are my children now? My brother? My friends? My books? And suddenly, despite hunger and cold, out into the cold courtyards, to the frozen boards of the latrines . . . And suddenly again screams for bread, for water, for potatoes. Yes, slowly it dawned on all of us, the merciless truth of the words with which the brownshirts [storm troopers, SA] had described the ghetto of Łódź: *the croaking hole of Europe* [*der Krepierwinkel Europas*].

Death statistics. As a doctor with practical experience reports, in his town fifteen people per one thousand would die on average in a year (in places with good hygiene, twelve); that is, 1.5 percent. According to these figures, the mortality in the Litzmannstadt ghetto, with a population of one hundred fifty thousand (until the fall of 1941, before the mass evacuations), from spring 1941 to spring 1942, would have been two thousand two hundred fifty; per half year, about one thousand one hundred. Reality looked very different. The great dying began on December 26, 1941. Of the new arrivals, the twenty-three thousand Jews who had been brought to Łódź from Luxemburg, Frankfurt, Cologne, Hamburg, Berlin, Vienna, and Prague, about five thousand died between October 1941 and April 1942, that is, more than 20 percent. If this death rate was to hold for the whole year, about 45 percent. This number, however, does not hold up as typical since the severe winter (1941–42) contributed considerably to the rate of death. Of the one hundred thirty thousand local inhabitants, about fifteen thousand died in the course of 1941–42, that is, an annual rate of 12 percent. From this we can conclude the following: The mortality of the local population is ten times greater than that in normal countries; among the newly settled, twenty times higher than the normal death rate. One must, however, take into account special contributing factors like constant malnutrition and the large number of old people.

Face of the Ghetto, April 6. An order went out for the thorough cleaning of the ghetto in anticipation of the imminent "spring" that was expected to bring a new, better mood. Hygiene is regarded as necessary. The courtyards and streets are to be polished. The entire ghetto is being mobilized for this task, everybody, even the officials and factory workers, from the age of eighteen to fifty, is being drafted. Refuse, broken household goods, rags, broken beds, excrement and excrement mixed with snow, and animal and human filth were loaded up and taken somewhere. Whereto? There is no river nearby that could swallow up the refuse, which instead is being dumped into nearby brackish ponds, and, despite the cold, the excretions can be felt.

Face of the Ghetto, **April 17.** On March 22, 1942, a declaration by the Eldest was posted according to which ghetto ground would be rented out for planting. Seeds available at an official place. This squashes the rumor that the ghetto was to be dissolved. On April 17 began the planting of the small plots, corners, gardens, front gardens. Among the things being planted were especially radishes, chives, onions, and various kinds of salad greens. People planted without knowing whether they would be able to enjoy the fruits of their labor. Young and old worked in front of their houses, next to the gutter, adjacent to the puddles, the sun was warming the ghetto air, but people were still wrapped up in their winter rags since they did not trust the first spring . . . Jews from Łódź, Frankfurt, Vienna, Prague, calling out in German, Polish, Yiddish, as they busied themselves with unaccustomed work. . . . Lower-middle-class people, children, boys from the prayer chambers and from the taverns, doctors, chemists, virtuoso pianists, scholars, know how to handle nature. Though malnourished, they till eagerly while, overhead, airplanes are heading toward the East . . .

Face of the Ghetto, **May 4, 1942.** *Evacuation of the newly settled. Outsettlement of the newly settled.*[9] A terrible shock: Declaration concerning "emigration" of the newly settled. (At first, exemption of holders of Iron Cross First Class and of those who were wounded, then this was no longer listed.) Text on hard red-gray paper on a duplicating machine:

Emigration Order

Mr.—Mrs.—are herewith ordered to appear on . . . at . . . [time] in Trödlergasse 7 for the purpose of emigration from Ghetto Litzmannstadt. Each person is allowed 12 kg of baggage.

Should the above-named persons fail to follow this order and fail to appear on time at the time indicated, then the family will be forcibly expelled without the possibility of taking any belongings.

Ch. Rumkowski, Eldest of the Jews in Ghetto Litzmannstadt

Stamp: Deportation Commission

So it reads *emigration* above and *deportation* below!!

The "outsettlement" of the newly settled from Berlin, Cologne, Düsseldorf, Hamburg, Frankfurt, Vienna, Prague, and Luxemburg began on May 4, 1942. A bleak, rainy day, intermittent snow flurries. Impression of a November day . . . The street has changed. No more aimless scurrying about, no more bundled-up faces of corpses . . . Something new. From everywhere people with bundles and sacks on their backs, bags and baskets, knapsacks and little bread sacks, rushing toward some destination . . . all around, people who are accompanying those who are in a hurry, supporting them or guiding them . . . old people and children . . . carts loaded with bundles, the streetcar carries the human masses . . . Bundles in all colors, from gray-white to black-green . . . Suddenly they arrive in front of the central prison. The deportees who had already been "drafted" pass over the wire fence clothing, overcoats, blankets, and other meager belongings, which they don't dare take along, to their relatives and friends, attempting to exchange these items for a few grams of sausage or bread or margarine . . . The human chains are mostly soundless, all are prepared. . . . Some fall dead to the ground . . . others put an end to their lives before embarking on the journey by hanging themselves . . . But the street hears little about this. It does not care about individual fates. It belongs to everybody. It is just. Those who fall remain lying there. We have no time. Hunger pushes us on, death awaits.

Behind the local figures who are rushing along—men and women who circle around the swarm of deportees like scavenger birds cunningly attempting to lift from them for a few marks those meager belongings that will have to be left behind . . . They disappear into courtyards and building passages where the business is concluded. . . .

These human figures appear fat and heavy from wearing several layers of undergarments, clothing, overcoats, since not even the authorized 12 kg will be tolerated at the train station . . . Other women are at the beauty parlor getting their hair done before the deportation, eagerly embracing life. Then they eat their gallows meal—a thin cabbage soup from a tin cup with a few grams of bread—while a few of the select enjoy their meal in a heated room, gas, leather club chair, smoking fine French or Yugoslav cigarettes even though they too are evacuees from Germany.

Seder and Discussion about Judaism, and Mood in the Ghetto

The date is March 31. The criminal police is said to have taken the Torah scrolls and sacred objects (breastplates, finials, Kiddush cups, etc.), presumably also from the hall at the cemetery where a service had been held on the High Holy Days. (On the same day, bread was only available in slices on the free market.) In the home, preparations for the Seder. Rabbi Dr. Krakauer[10] tries hard to get the necessary ingredients together. Will it be possible to organize the Seder? Will there be wine? Wine in the ghetto?

April 1. Preparations are being made. Finally. The Eldest sends wine, four bottles, while the ghetto drinks grape wine. The rabbi leads the Seder, gives a sermon. Festive mood. *Ato bochartonu* [Hebr., You have chosen us] and *Secher l'tzias Mizrajim* [Hebr., Remember the exodus from Egypt]. Wonderful is the strength to believe in the coming of the Messiah amidst this misery. He will lead us out. . . . "This is the bread of affliction, which we eat . . ." [Hebr., *Hu lachmu anyu*] matzot [unleavened bread] made of dark flour, so stiff it's hard to chew and won't even soften when dipped in a hot liquid. . . . Sermon about *Erez* [Hebr., the land; Israel/Palestine] Israel where we will all end up (Dr. Wilczek, Krefeld)[11]. . . . The next day a few boys are pulling a cart with junk. A few older Jews are looking on. One of the boys says, without moving a face muscle, so to speak, in remembrance of the reading of the Haggada [story of the exodus read at the Seder] the night before: "Not one rose against us, but in every generation [Hebr., *dor*] they rose to destroy us, and he, the Blessed One, saved us each time with an outstretched arm."

One of the Jews, a redhead, says: "Had he left us in Mizrayim [Egypt], we would now be sitting in a hotel in Cairo drinking Turkish coffee." He laughs. So does the man next to him. Then that one, a gray-haired man, says: "Moshe knew what he was doing. Had we stayed in Mizrayim, we wouldn't have been blessed with receiving the Torah . . ." "And what did the Torah get us? Nothing but unpleasantness. Suffering. Persecution." "But also a pleasant time. The most beautiful time. Without Torah, no life. I never care about the fleshpots of Egypt and so I don't miss them as much as so many here. Hunger? So one goes hungry. Getting beaten? So one gets beaten. We are, like it or not, the *am s'gulo* [Hebr., chosen people], nothing can be done about it. We are chosen . . . we took the task upon ourselves. And when we are called up to fight, we will fight. For the time being, it is not possible. For the time being, we have not received the call . . ." "What are we to fight with? With our knapsacks? With our weak arms? And where is the strong arm, the strong hand, that leads us? I don't see it . . ." "Just look at the boys, how patiently they are pulling the cart. Not one of them is willing to give up what he received at birth. Tell any of them to go and change, to merge with another people, and he will answer: No! He holds fast to the *bris* [Yidd./Hebr., covenant]! For the Eternal made the covenant not only with our fathers' fathers, he made it with us, too, and will make it with the next generation, and so on, into all eternity. Do you want to exclude yourself? Should we want to be smarter than our ancestors? They went into the fire. For us, for us who are alive today. And our children here won't want to be smarter than us, their fathers . . . This is how it will go from generation to generation . . ."

A car with field-gray Ashkenes races by. A cart, loaded with red beets, pulled by a horse. A few beets slip through bars. A few boys run over and pick them up off the dirty ground, bite into them with burning hunger. The oldsters look on. One of them cites a passage from the Talmud. The other one nods. Suddenly Jewish police appears. Chases them to work: People are needed to clear away excrement. Everybody has to pitch in. "You'll get an extra bread ration, maybe even 5 dkg sausage . . ." The Jews scurry. Extra bread ration! Maybe it will be possible to save some bread for the little children . . . A ray of hope. "He didn't forget us, sends us bread," says the gray one.

Suddenly the red one: "I knew it . . . He is just and all-powerful." And with a gesture toward Litzmannstadt . . . "He will punish the wicked over there . . ." And the first one (again) cites the *Yizkor* prayer [Yidd., prayer for remembrance of the dead]: *"Lu chochmu yaskilu, tsaus yovinu, l'acharisom . . ."* "O if only they would wise up, think it over, that they would think of the end." "What use is all this talk? Will they think it over? Maybe when it is too late? By that time we'll all be *nifter* [Yidd., dead] . . . Don't you think so too?" They turn toward the wall of the cemetery. "Much work over there . . . business is booming . . . The angel of death is busy . . . and the creator of the world looks on . . ." "Hush!" The two fall silent. Children's noise. Orphans singing Polish songs with their teacher. A stream of *cheder* [Hebr., religious school] boys issues from one house. Hebrew books are in the window. A piece of traditional Judaism. Opposite the window a cross with the man on the cross, erected in 1934, and a few hundred meters away, a modern church in cubist style . . .

"Dampness." Dampness was creeping in through the windows, the walls, the attic. There was no basement beneath the floors of the apartments, crystals were forming on the walls. Water was running under the beds. Paper goods were disintegrating, wood was swelling so that cabinets and drawers wouldn't close. Things that had been glued together were loosening, opening. Clothing, suit-cases, mattresses, were molding, food was rotting. Cabinets were bending out of shape. Dust was creeping up from the floor into noses and eyes . . . chronic infections . . . a specific ghetto illness as nowhere in the world. Added to that was the fact that the one hundred fifty thousand inhabitants of the ghetto had to live without drinking water. Fearing an outbreak of an epidemic, the doctors prohibited drinking water from the well. The only way was either to borrow a pitcher of boiled water from a neighbor who had a handful of coals for heating or to heat a meager meal in one of those little, miserable kitchen facilities. This lasted for three winters. It is a miracle that illnesses, wasting away, and death did not rage more severely than they did . . . Hunger, cold, dampness, illness, nervous breakdown, despair . . . The components of death, of *Juda verrecke* [Germ., Judah, go to the dogs; Nazi slogan] . . .

***Face of the Ghetto,* June 1942.** Despite deepest summer, the sun's rays burned only mildly on the dusty, bumpy streets. People hobbled between the loosened cobblestones, the mortar, holes, gusts of wind whirling up shreds of paper, all kinds of stuff, foul-smelling grass. At the street corners, barefoot boys and girls, almost children, offered Sacharina [sugar substitute] original for sale, six pieces for 1 mark . . . They had their own melody, their singsong, their *nigun* [Hebr., melody] not only for saccharine but for other wares as well, like candy . . . not candy in the European sense. These were sugar cubes molded in the kitchen by inventive minds from coffee or the juice of turnips or . . . addition, wrapped in a bright little piece of paper with holes, and there were plenty of passersby who would spend half a mark for such candy . . . Nearby loitered young boys and men, mostly barefoot, their filthy, sticky toes wrapped in old, malodorous shreds, brown like hamals, the burden carriers in the Balkans, with ropes over their shoulders. Those were the servicemen of Łódź, waiting for a job; they carried briquettes, pulled little carts, directed "resettlements." They were not recognizable as Jews, they could have been taken for gypsies. Everybody was in a hurry, who knows what for. From kitchen facility to kitchen facility, or to avail themselves of a few leaves of lettuce somewhere, or to push themselves into a cooperative. The shops, which used to have Polish owners, shut down, bolted up, one next to another, signs torn down . . . Behind broken windowpanes in the dark rooms, through which one can look in as one passes by, a dying middle-aged man . . . or a woman . . . is lying on an old broken-down bed in broad daylight—pillow and blanket covered with the excrement of flies and cockroaches . . . such scenes can be observed by the dozens even in the main streets . . . An old woman leaned near a street corner, saying out loud to herself, without attracting attention, "Oy, veh is mir." Nobody rallied around her moaning. Young girls were sitting nearby, by the open window at their sewing machines (or they were sewing by hand): ressort. They were working for "over there," light and heavy work. . . . They embroidered the finest embroideries for dirndl dresses that went to Ashkenes, to Vienna, Berlin, Hamburg . . . Other young girls made the rounds of the streets like prostitutes, painted their lips, using dirty windowpanes as mirrors—beautiful figures among the refuse of the street and the wretched beggars, blue-eyed blondes alluringly decked out, with coquettish little hats, hair curled, nails manicured, pedicured, the painted toes were visible in the open summer sandals—and were one to follow one of them, one would soon arrive at vegetable beds where radishes, lettuce, were being grown, among other things, even directly adjacent to the open latrines, attractive little vegetable gardens created by hand and the proceeds of which did not go to the planter and harvester but to the ghetto, the Eldest . . . All men without exception were wearing caps of any shape and all types of material. Even in the summer heat, one saw fur hats and thick wool wrappings around the legs, night asylum . . . Rotting sheepskins, sticking out from under short jackets. . . . At the beautiful Gothic church with its tall fresh green maple trees, father and son, leaning against the fence, shining shoes . . . There were still Jews in the ghetto who didn't want to do without polished shoes even if the soles and heels were long gone. Brave people. Their fee was 25 pennies, and since fivepenny coins didn't exist, they forced one customer to sign a coupon for 25 pennies, a little brown piece of paper that entitled him to a second polish. The shoeshine man too issued emergency currency, not only the Eldest with his chaimki.[12] . . .

How does one die in the ghetto? With hard cots and beds that have to be shared with other people. The doctor was met with imploring glances and despair when he was about to order the end of treatment and discharge from the hospital. But here too dying was swift and easy . . . Nobody made much of a fuss. A sick man is brought in on a stretcher:

Hospital—pneumonia . . . weakness . . . swollen hands and legs. His breathing is heavy. Delirium. He is given something hot to drink, injection . . . Not much care is applied in such cases. Doctors, nurses, patients, don't treat him with the usual care. A case like any other. Night falls. He screams and moans: "O woe is me, o woe is me! Damn it! Damn it! Mother, Father, give me . . . give me bread . . . May choke, croak . . . that miscreant, that enemy of Israel . . . May his name be blotted out . . . bread, bread . . ." He rattles, he sings, he stretches his thin yellow hands toward the heavens. "Ah, the bread is good, Father, Mother . . ." The hands drop. Not one of the patients deems it necessary to even glance at the bed of the man in agony—he is barely forty years old. The nurse comes by on her night rounds. Points her flashlight at him. She turns away, goes back down the aisle, without the slightest sign of emotion. A few minutes later, three men arrive in the dimly lit sick hall, carrying a stretcher. They are young, strong, robust, their gaze firm like that of handymen whose daily routine never changes. No muscle moves in their faces. The yellow star on chest and back becomes visible. Several of the sick, disturbed by the heavy steps of the men in wooden shoes, turn angry in their beds, demanding quiet. Most are asleep, dozing. With a few skilled maneuvers, the men load the dead man on the stretcher, wrap him in sheets, and dispatch him out the door. Only a few of those in adjacent beds noticed what was going on. Again quiet. One man, who had been taken for seriously ill, jumps up, goes to the bed of his neighbor, and calls out heatedly—in the middle of the night: "Yesterday . . . the Jewish police came to me at two in the morning . . . house search . . . my wife's old fur, an heirloom from my mother-in-law, taken away, supposedly on orders from higher up . . . for the Deutsche [Germans] . . ." Every night there are scenes like this. Some of the sick who come in are, however, in the last stage of their illness. The patients don't recognize this. The doctor says one word: "Screen." Whereupon a divider is put up on both sides of the bed, separating the patient from the neighbors. He is given up. Nobody cares about him anymore. He is lost. Expenses and medications have to be used for those who can be saved. The lost one gets only the prescribed food and injections. His death rattle is heard. Sometimes it takes a day and a night. Yes, "screen" is a dangerous, but enlightening, word . . .

The old saying "Die and become" was also given short shrift. The Jewish concept of *ovaus ovousaynu* [Hebr., *avot avotenu;* our forefathers] was likewise lost in the face of the daily events. While in the past, generation followed generation in a natural sequence, in accordance with the historical consciousness, with Jewish tradition, with the biblical worldview. "He returned to his fathers," now everything is mixed up: the son before the father, the grandchild before the grandfather, the young before the old. Absurd, ludicrous, unharmonious—therefore the chaotic states of mind, therefore that which is called "godless." Dying has lost its celestial beauty, its wondrous secret felt as sacrosanct. The mystery of death is desecrated hourly by the brutality of its earthly cause—hunger, which desecrates. The framed bulletin boards list the names of the recently deceased, that is, those who had been brought here, requesting close relatives and friends to report. It's a matter of inheritance . . . A few pieces of old clothes, shoes, shirts, since most had already either been sold or wasted. These remains too—any form of reverence has been wiped out by hardship—wander into the hands of the dealer in exchange for bread and margarine. The inheritance from a deceased brings a few days' supplementary foodstuff, not more . . . For he alone was also unable to save us from starvation.

Dying in the ghetto. The Kripo[13] goes to the apartment of an orthodox Jew. Denunciation. He has an old fur he would like to keep. Beating. Thrown against the wall, kicked in the stomach. Heels in the face, whipped across the forehead. Bloody. Dead. The family is looking on. "He is dead already." The Kripo continues beating—the corpse.—Many people coming from the Kripo station half dead died later.

Jewish living places, later. *Old-age home.*

Old people, mostly over seventy to over eighty, are being housed in a school-like building. Five to six lying in a room on wooden cots.

Without consideration, the ghetto was envious of these people who are being cared for by doctors and nurses—it was considered a stroke of good luck to be housed there. Earlier there was coffee twice daily, 2 dkg of fat, and three soups. Starting in April 1942, only ½ dkg of fat and one soup. The consequence followed immediately. The old people visibly lost weight. Skeletons on the wooden cots. They screamed and moaned, it was the hunger. "Shoot me, I can't take it any longer . . . ," a wife of a renowned university professor was heard saying shortly before she died from the symptoms of famine edema. The doctors were surprised that these old, sick people, totally exhausted and close to death, became mentally completely normal, even prescient and alert, and were exactly aware of their situation . . . The medical staff stimulated them with medications; they were agitated, animated, and developed surprisingly strong nervous energy . . . However, it didn't help much. The energy dissipated. Within a week they aged by many years, often becoming unrecognizable even to close friends—that's how much they changed. On April 24—that is, in *one* day—*twenty* people died there. The corpse of one six-foot-tall man weighed 37 kg.

Cemetery dying: A long, extended field surrounded by a high wall that had been erected recently in the fall of 1941 and adjoins the rear of the Łódź cottage Marysin[14] . . . There, where one believed to encounter only cheerful rest, there in the mansion district, at the end of the ghetto, far from the actual ghetto city, the "green lawn" for the dead is located. No green lawn. Brown, rancid, muddy earth, already dotted with thousands of gravestones . . . The corpses are carried in endless procession from the hall of the dead to various parts of the cemetery. The kind of activity that goes on here resembles that at the market. Every day there are a dozen interments, all at the same time. On Friday it's even more hectic since everything has to be done before the beginning of Shabbat. The graves are small, even smaller than the wooden cots in the camps and lodgings, about 60 cm wide. Ritual washing of the bodies is prohibited by order of the Ashkenes. Coffins are nonexistent. The body rests between two wooden planks and is wrapped in shreds of old paper. Biers are likewise nonexistent. Like dead fish, the bodies are carried in a net attached to two poles (slats), which is emptied of the dead at the graveside. Here and there sobbing and lamenting. Again and again the tin carts carrying the dead arrive at the hall, and again and again they are carried out in a net. The earth fills with the dead. These are the people condemned to the ghetto of Łódź, that is, to a quick death. The starved, the frozen, the condemned, and those who commit suicide. Like the sand at the sea, like the stars in the heavens—this is how numerous the dying are . . . Eighteen percent of the transport from Frankfurt died within six months (October 1941 to April 1942). Mass dying in the croaking hole of Europe! By the end of December a thousand graves dug in advance; ditches 70 cm deep! Corpse will be piled on corpse.

(Turning on the memory.) How much courage all the dead victims had! At home mothers save small bites for their sons, sisters for sisters, even for distant relatives. Storing bread even though they are plagued by hunger. The husband has hunger cramps, makes his wife believe he is full, and vice versa.

May 3.—Price of bread reaches fantastic heights. People sell in exchange for foodstuff, that is, the newly evacuated! Whereto? Guessing game. Who comes next? Supposedly thirty thousand locals. Bread more than 300 marks, margarine 600 marks, 1 dkg of garlic 5 marks, a pair of good shoes = a loaf of bread, 3 strings of chives = 1 mark. One hundred thousand people in the ghetto are asking each other: "Did you have a thick soup? Maybe with potatoes in it?"

A new epoch of hunger since not even the allocation of 6 kg of vegetables has been distributed so far. One cigarette = 3 marks, 1 reichsmark = . . . [illegible]. One kg potatoes = 60 marks, 5 dkg of bad horse sausage = 12 marks.

May 7.[15] Ashkenes cut off the rucksacks because of the leather straps, put on a truck and carried away. As a result, people sell everything. Enormous market, low prices. At the same time, food prices are falling because there are not enough buyers. Heavy hand luggage only partially confiscated; however, Ashkenes took away the wedding bands. Some people take only a sack with bread since they know that everything will be taken from them. From the central prison, Jews are like the [illegible] . . . knapsacks in their hands. RM: 4 M = 10:1. When the criminals leave the prison, they are allowed to take their baggage. Bread 450, margarine 600. With "hands up" into the compartment so that people can't carry anything in their hands. They save turnips and potatoes, taking them along in small glass jars as bread spread. Some even save a single potato. Tremendous trade, shoes are in demand; everybody wants to have shoes.

May 9. Children are playing soccer, pale, running on thin little legs, nearby are wagons that bring back the baggage of the evacuees since these are things the Ashkenes would take away at the station and this way they can be salvaged. Soup (water) in two shops 6 marks. [. . .] Tremendous hunger as never before. Flour, fat, vegetables, sugar not distributed for days as punishment (!), whatever is available has been bought from the evacuees. One hundred thousand volunteer, telling themselves it cannot get any worse. Main thing is that we get there, if only they won't kill us at the station. Out there, we'll find a way to make it through. The peasant will give us food, breadcrumbs, fat rinds, pig's trough. All else doesn't interest us. That's how far they have come . . . [illegible] the ghost workers.—Soup in the store—15 marks.

Dandelion leaves torn off in the open field, cooked, eaten as vegetables, what a business, paid for harvesting, prepared as salad.

"And ten women will be cooking on one stove."

Bread, Bible, *tauchocho* [Hebr., *tochacha;* reprimand, rebuke] = reprimand on Shabbat, 22 Iyar (May 9, 1942).

Leviticus 26:23–26. "And if in spite of these things ye will not be corrected unto me; (verse 26) then I will break your staff of bread, ten women shall bake your bread in one oven, and they shall deliver your bread again by weight; and ye shall eat, and not be satisfied."[16]

May 10. Railway car with baptized [Jews] departs.—A field near the road is being ploughed with a pair of oxen by a doctor, many academicians are tilling, planting. One kilogram garlic 500 marks. Everywhere women are sitting and sewing pockets into the coats to keep things in. Extraordinary quiet, but in various corners weeping and sobbing. Petroleum is nowhere to be had. A spirit stove 50 marks = 1 liter fuel. An old woman says: "Every stitch is wetted with tears."—Tears . . .

Wire. The victors have put up a barbed wire between the conquered city of Łódź and the artificially created ghetto. On the Łódź side, always field-gray guards. Anybody on the ghetto side, of course, who lingers around the wire fence for a few minutes is called on by the guard.[17] Any gesture, any attempt to explain, fails, is useless. Even if a ghetto Jew lives near the wire fence, he has to be careful, has to duck when he enters the gate, has to flee, so to say. The guard aims, shoots, a bang—over. Nobody pays attention to the dead man. Sometimes he is removed on orders from the Ashkenes, bullets are as cheap as beans—there is a war on. On November 17, a young girl left the camp, the living quarters of her collective. "Unhappy love." . . . Since there are no guns in the ghetto and no poison nor a river nor strong enough rope, and since one could easily be disturbed in the process of committing suicide—everywhere are people, rushing about, lounging, sitting around—the girl decided to go to the wire. There she stood lost in a dream, disregarded the guard's warning, acted as if it didn't concern her. The guard didn't like the scene, he had no understanding of sentimentalities, he aimed, shot. The girl fell. It was the first suicide of an evacuee in the ghetto.—This experience with the benefactor "wire" benefited many unhappy people. The natives, used to the category "ghetto" for two years, did not avail themselves of it, their callousness and religious faith did not permit them to go there. Others, however, mainly deported "Germans," used the area near the wire as a suicide terrain. "I am going to the wire" became a standard saying. It meant something like "I have taken my leave from life."

On February 24, a man from Prague went to the wire. He was told three times to move, then was shot. Farewell letter: "I cannot bear life any longer." In addition, a few shootings just for the fun of it. Whoever wanted to threaten, blackmail, arouse sympathy, just spoke the words: "To the wire." How many people made good on their threat and fell there, victims of their own courage or an outside compelling force, is so far not known.

Ghetto: curiosity. Every community will breathe, flourish, grow, create. It wants to grow. It's part of the animal instinct, the law of nature. To come into being, to grow, to pass away, ever renewing life, parallel to nature . . . ghetto the exception. People are locked in decaying buildings, granted just enough air to vegetate. They don't plant crops, don't have cattle, no poultry, no vegetables, no fish, no milk, no fat, no bread that they bake themselves. When the neighbor pulls back his hand, the slogan "Judah, croak!" is fulfilled. It is the purpose of human existence to give free rein to animal functions as much as possible and thereby slowly, gradually, wilt away . . . The numbers are getting ever smaller. There is no fabric, no leather, no metal, and so on. You cannot produce. When the suit becomes worn, you have to walk in rags . . . when the shoes are torn, you can wrap them with rags so water, snow, and dirt cannot seep in . . . The bolts get rusty, the colors fade, the shirts get frayed, the garments disintegrate . . . There are no shops, no available goods, goods in the sense of objects from which to chose . . . There are no cameras, no radios, no books, no artist's paint, no clocks . . . The things you find in shops are the leftover goods no European anywhere would want to buy, a broken-down object that, once sold, cannot be replaced since there is no replenishment, no new production, no wholesalers. The natural process of production and distribution, of buying and selling, is absent. Nobody knows where the junk (trash) comes from, where it goes . . . Broken drinking glasses and pots, torn pieces of cloth, damaged kitchen equipment . . . nobody knows, for example, where the craftsmen get their raw material: leather, linen, nails, tin . . . a divine miracle, a secret . . . Beautiful prayerbooks, Polish, Yiddish, German, and Russian novels, are being sold as damaged goods, things which the Jews of Łódź, who were pressed into the ghetto, had salvaged somehow . . . But . . . there is no growth, everything falls apart step by step. . . .

And without work, starving here are engineers, chemists, mathematicians, botanists, zoologists, pharmacologists, physicians, architects, teachers, writers, actors, directors, musicians, linguists, administrative officials, bankers, pharmacists, handicraftsmen like electricians, woodworkers, carpenters, metal experts, upholsterers, house painters, furriers, tailors, shoemakers, textile manufacturers, turners, watchmakers . . . The talent is available. Just put the means into their hands and they'll build houses, mansions, apartments, streets, canals, water pipes, railway stations, railway tracks, for you; they'll clear forests, saw boards, erect institutes, hospitals, universities, laboratories, libraries, schools, observatories, kitchens and laundries, workshops . . . They will build you cities and colonies with every possibility of growth and beauty . . . They are capable of creating a work that could serve as a model for many others, especially for those who do not permit this work . . . Thus, values are being wiped out, erased, which could benefit all of mankind. But what meaning does "mankind" have now? People's nerves are being destroyed, the meaning of life is lost, no philosophy is able to help here. Expelled, lost, ruined, before rescue can reach them. Every week several of them die, passing away slowly of hunger and mental anguish, and if the day of liberation should come, it would find them unable to find their way back into life, to work, and to creativity. Gone, gone . . . (university Hindu scholar Otto Stein, Prague; university professor Baerwald, mathematics, Prague; university professor Hugo Ditz, chemistry, Prague; Professor Fröhlich, mathematics, Prague; Professor Wilhelm Caspari, cancer researcher, Frankfurt; Leo Birkenfeld, piano, Vienna; Rudolf Bandler, singer, Vienna).

Face of the Ghetto, June 22. Suddenly summer is discovered, as the sun burns down and the sky, with blue and white clouds, spans the rooftops so the streets are long and wide enough to bear normal, city traffic. But the sidewalks are bumpy, dotted with holes and cut up by sewage gutters, running from the house gates uncovered to the outside so that one runs the risk at any moment of getting one's feet stuck in the running urine. The streets are, as mentioned, long and permit quite a deep view, a perspective that could stimulate any watercolor painter. Everywhere the stories of the houses have simple iron balconies. The shutters of the shops are closed, the nameplates erased, the store windows sealed. Here and there in a dirty, low window a sign is visible: JEWISH SHOEMAKER; DOLL CLINIC; STATIONERY; BARBER; MANICURE; GERMAN REFUGEE SEEKS WRITING ASSIGNMENTS; PLATE PAINTER; JEWELER—all in grotesque spelling or in Yiddish. One also frequently encounters pieces of paper posted on the wall: "Attention! *Ich geb arojs jiddische Bücher zum Leinen* [Yidd., I give out Yiddish books for reading] . . ." This is a private Jewish lending library with several dozen worn books, older Yiddish literature.[18] Nearby, the official food distribution center, that is, bread, vegetables, milk (for children), meat and sausage, coal (briquettes). In addition, signs for doctors and midwives . . .

People stumble and limp through the streets. Their gait is not the gait of normal people in the streets of other cities. Back bent, stomach sagging, legs unsteady . . . People, the masses, the groups—children, old people, and cripples—don't fit into the frame of pictures of cities . . . somehow they have been arbitrarily forced in. The morphologic observations arouse horror, sympathy, and—despair of humankind, knowing that this condition was arbitrarily created. The idea of creating such a city could only spring from the minds of Lombroso patients [Cesare Lombroso was, among other things, a psychiatrist who studied the criminal mind]. But it exists and lives and calls on the world in its hours of greatest loneliness: "Come here and look at this wonder. University professors, who held forth in the lecture hall, running around with a pot looking for soup, famous singers pushing coal carts, lawyers standing guard in a carnival uniform (armband and colorful cap), renowned chemists and actors waiting in front of decaying barracks for a call to be placed with some ressort (straw, junk . . .). Such an engagement means a daily supplement of 15 dkg bread (bran) and 5 dkg sausage (later, soup, fatless stuff). And for this supplement, people fight as if their lives depended on it. All these figures occupy the long alleys with the locked, once Jewish, but mostly Polish, stores, whose signs and inscriptions have disappeared, only here and there traces are visible to the schooled eye . . . If only a camera could memorialize this curiosity, this devil's spawn of a city, this Ghetto Litzmannstadt, which, like a ruler over the medieval ghettos, has the right and obligation to look down on it in its ghetto backwardness . . . And the most peculiar aspect: Hohensteiner Strasse, formerly Zgierzka . . . Both sides of the street lined the full length with wooden planks and barbed wire . . . the tracks of the streetcar running between them. Trucks driven by Poles and Germans move in between, the one-horse carriages with the funny little horses in Russian style, these are the Polish coachmen with their plate-shaped caps, the *izvostshili,* the Polish workers at the electric wiring, the German soldiers, at night still at M . . . [illegible] a little piece, singing and stomping. Early in the morning, the water sprayers come from Litzmannstadt, but the water wets only the small strip between the fence and the barbed wire, which extends along the sidewalk on both sides of the ghetto street. The best way to describe this "extraterritorial" path is as a *corridor.*

NOTEBOOK C

Remembrances, Private Diary 3

In every office of the ghetto a picture of the Eldest, like Melech [Hebr., king], *even a calendar.*[1]

May 12.[2] The cool weather is a welcome break. The evacuees are at least able to carry a lot on their body. Everywhere women are sitting and making little sacks for inside the clothing of the departing. Moving scenes. By contrast gruesome scenes at the railway station. Hands up, wedding bands and watches. Death threats, so the story goes. One kilogram of margarine 8 marks, ¼ kg of bread 60 marks. When they are psychologically totally destroyed, people will dream. Thousands are lying on their cots dreaming. One tells the story: When my father appears in my dream, it means something good is going to happen. Therefore, the danger of being deported now has passed. I can feel it, I know it . . . allocation of ressort shoes 30 marks, one pair of soles = 125 marks, one piece of candy = 1 mark.

May 13. Received 5 dkg of bread as a birthday present. Enduring hunger with dignity. One assists the other, especially now when hunger . . . [illegible] than before. Incredible excitement in the city, as if alarmed, households destroyed, since individuals are already gone. Hundreds into hiding. Police come again in the night, tearing people from their beds. Henuschi[3] will cry today—as usual—and be sad. Money no longer buys anything, only in exchange for clothing and shoes. Feeling that from now on a new time, perhaps even liberation. Carts with baggage. Blankets and cushions may still remain in the ghetto. Pfeffergasse. Hagglers with the meager belongings of the strangers. Now pulling the carts, women and young girls—ghetto has become almost all Polish, since the Germans are gone [O. R. means Jews in both cases]. Shops open only at three o'clock, since the owners work in the ressorts.—At night, emptying of beds, due to shortage of candidates for transports. Enormous excitement, expulsion ending today, supposed to continue. People are loaded, taken away, and they vanish into the unknown like air . . . terrible night—from the beds to the station and the train . . . Wednesday—concert (Mozart) filled with young workers. Three hundred people from the old-age home evacuated, from the home the seventy-nine-year-old Bech Engel.—Many over eighty, came from Germany and Austria. Professor Baerwald (University of Prague), the most renowned mathematician in Prague, and wife died at the end of April 1942, starved to death in the camp. Professor Otto Stein (Indologist), Buddhism, second transport from Prague.—

May 14. Clarinetist Leo Birkenfeld (Vienna), skin and bones, starving in the hospital, torn from the hospital bed at night, transported, deported. A goat was spotted in the field. Three live chickens. One egg = 20 marks, one suit = 30 dkg bread.—A Jew ploughing with a pair of oxen and three Polish Jews nearby look on. Bread? Terrible prices! Misery compounded by tribute. You are Jews? You will be repaid. Margarine = 1,000 marks.

May 15, 1942. Outsettlement of Germans [Jews] said to be over. New *geserah* [Hebr., decree, also anti-Jewish decree]. Thirty thousand Poles [Jews] are supposed to be outsettled. There's talk about new settlers coming in. Nobody knows anything specific. Dreary day, rain, cold. What is going on outside? Margarine 700 marks. Chaimki: 1 mark = 4:1.

May 16. Potato peels in the kitchen, 1 kg = 20 marks, in the ressort, with medical prescription, 1 kg free of charge = raw peels, washed, cooked, put through meat grinder, eaten as a delicacy with sugar. Jews in surrounding villages come to Marysin.

May 17. Evacuating! But what then? What happens afterward? What's on the mind of the arrangers? Without professional training, for years idle, aged, without clothing or underwear, without instruments, without pencil or pen, without the slightest possibility of making a living, with torn rucksacks and knapsacks, without linen and without blankets, street beggars without being hardened like this sort of people, humiliated and outcast . . . What then? Whereto with us? Who has been thinking about it! What will happen tomorrow? How will this end? And the other family members? Dispersed over the face of the earth . . . Without contact. Severed from any human company for the last six months. . . .

What do people do who are all without anything to do? Work at their living quarters: pumping water; doing laundry; cleaning; mending; rubbing; standing in line for rations; keeping clothes in order; polishing shoes. Women are knitting; embroidering; making sweaters and stockings; extending socks; sewing . . . Since the end of April, thousands are turning over the soil, plowing, planting, weeding, even ten-year-olds, weak, malnourished . . . And with all that, now in *May* the entire ghetto goes hungry.

Suddenly prices fell, since the deportations of those who were settled in have stopped. Now Jews from nearby villages are supposed to come in . . . New excitement, but at the same time worry since the ghetto will apparently be maintained. The official nature of the Litzmannstadt ghetto says it all, namely, the infamy of seeking to downgrade us, to cast us out, to humiliate us. Maximum prices for May 5 and 14: bread 400, margarine 1,000; now, bread 200, margarine 45. One hundred thousand human beings ask each other daily: Did you get your fill from the soup? Did you already eat the whole bread ration for the day? How will the next allocation be?—*Vegetables, potatoes, sauerkraut* are unavailable, even turnips are no longer to be had.

May 17. Jews from the surrounding area settled in the ghetto, that is, only parents—children remained there.—The children, whimpering, torn from their mothers' breasts . . . Anguish. Question being asked: Why? Nobody can give an answer.

May 18. Rumor: Evacuation of the local population is to begin soon. Today more details from newly settled Poles from the neighboring villages: lived there without ghetto, fairly well nourished (bread on the black market 8 marks). Male heads of families called up to the market square presumably for an assembly, were instead loaded on a train and brought here. The men are to go to the coal mines in Dabrova,[4] women remain here, instead of being registered they are immediately put on a train and dispatched to somewhere. Children are taken off the railway cars during the ride and separated from their parents. Today the ghetto is swarming with men and women from the surrounding countryside, good-looking faces. They are supposed to work. Thirty thousand in all are supposed to come. (Why then are thirty thousand of the local population taken away? Nobody knows.) Owners of Iron Cross First Class and badges for having been wounded are called up by the German authorities (Baluter Ring[5] = house of the Gestapo), are asked if they want work, and will probably get the job. Meaning privileged position.

May 18. Gathering, washing, cleaning, cooking dandelion stems, a three-hour process, *since nothing but sauerkraut,* chives as salad, in the pot = 50 marks.

May 19. Strange figures among the new arrivals, like teachers, young girls, some wear short lambskins with legs wrapped *opaaken* [Yidd., in rags], like a caftan, were lying over the roadside ditch without any kind of luggage . . . these people are expelled, not evacuated: the picture of the Wandering Jew, of the fugitive, expelled, hunted Jew. Bread sacks hanging around their necks, little knapsacks, children over ten, part of the luggage had been brought by train, waiting for lodging, back and forth . . . They still don't know where they will spend the night . . . *Don't forget: All this is the solution to the Jewish question.* Hold it fast in memories, think about it and fill it in with individual episodes . . . Gold, etc., surrender, that is, because of robbery of the German people. *Evacuating,* in order to separate parasites from others. *Ghetto* in order to mark Jews as a piece from the Middle Ages with a yellow star. Myths: to fulfill the legend of Ahasver . . . From this, there is no redemption.

May 20. Four thousand came from the villages. Yet now barely one hundred ten thousand. Twenty thousand died within the last twelve months, thirty-five thousand Polish Jews and twelve hundred "Germans" evacuated, that means there are sixty-seven thousand fewer people, plus four thousand; new births are almost zero.

Many horrors were forgotten.

Many horrors (atrocities)[6] went unwitnessed.

Many horrors were of a kind that those who described them were not believed. But they must remain alive in human memory.

A little glass of vodka = 3½ chaimki.

What is being sold in the shops? Broken mirrors, old toothbrushes, broken combs, torn nightgowns, eaten, worn shoes, hairnets, mud chalk, pulped paper by weight as toilet paper, ribbons, tooth powder, socks, gloves, hairpins . . . brushes and combs at premium prices, likewise powder, lipstick, and other cosmetics.

May 21. Some of the new arrivals were sent away for agricultural work; some were sent back to their original home.

Quarantine in Marysin and the city. Typhoid fever. [. . .]

May 22. The home is being dissolved. First day of Shavuot [Feast of Weeks, Jewish harvest festival]. Giving of the Law at Mount Sinai.

Everybody is too weakened to cover long distances, even standing in line for rations is tiring. Since the deportations, the general restlessness did not go away. Fear that the rations won't be distributed on time, causing hunger during the periods of cessation.

May 23. Brzeziny.[7] Question: What happened to the little children of Brzeziny? A mother, her child hidden in her clothes, was taken away. An officer at the railway station told a mother: Cover it with a blanket. Then he threw it into the car as a package so that the child was taken along. A *shegetz* [Yidd., non-Jewish boy, also a knave, a rascal] throws the child out of the window as if it was a doll. *Yeled* [Yidd., child, baby] a *mess* [Yidd., corpse].

Human fates in the ghetto:

1. An old woman, eighty-five years old, left alone in the old-age home—father, two sons, hunger, daughter dead (wire), formerly a professor of mathematics. Hunger.
2. Wife in America, daughter in Tel Aviv, son missing in Poland, another son uncertain in France; the man has cancer in the last stage, [taken] to Kolo.
3. A blind war veteran, former reserve officer, Iron Cross First Class and other honors, taken to this place by mistake, he wants to get back to the Ashkenes, but prohibited as Ivri—rammed by civilian Gestapo as he passes harmlessly on the sidewalk, seriously injured, broken arm, hospital.
4. *Longing:* everybody for something else; for children, for grandchil-

dren they never met, for food, for landscapes, for books, for something indiscernible, nebulous; and in the end just longing in and of itself. The object disappears, the senses cannot grasp the outlines of the object of longing in the fog of hunger. . . .

May 23, 1942. Everywhere in the kitchens peeling potatoes prohibited so that the peels won't be sold separately at usurious prices. The Eldest sets the official market price of cigarettes at 1 mark, since the black market demands already 2½ marks.—Declaration: The entire ghetto is a work ghetto, all those who don't or won't work will be outsettled.

Shabbat. Second day of Shavuot. The Eldest, temple *maftir* [Hebr., Torah honor for concluding verses]. Speech: The entire ghetto must work.—The ghetto collects everywhere leaves as spinach. [. . .]

May 24. Sunday. Noise in Marysin and screaming by those who now arrive from Brzeziny. No word so far about the thousand evacuated as "Germans." Days go by quickly (so yesterday my own lodgings, maybe Mendelssohn . . . or some other spot). Everything revolves around two questions:

1. Aren't we going to starve to death?
2. Will the *Geulah* [Hebr., redemption] come in time?

May 25. Declaration: Jews must salute Ashkenes officials in uniform. Standing in a closed room until he gives the sign to sit down, men lift their hats, women nod their heads, likewise greeting of guard at the ghetto gate, also when an official passes in a car, as well as civilian Ashkenes.

Already close to five thousand people from Brzeziny. Another thirty thousand Jews come from the surrounding villages; ghetto again work ghetto.

Renewed appearance of hunger; pain in the nails and toes without visible symptoms. Inflammation of the nostrils, pain in the limbs, pain in the shoulder blades.

Concerning soup! A scene: Five women are sitting in the street on a rock with their bowls, eating soup, red soup. Eating? No. They slurp, gurgle, drink, tilt the bowls to swallow the last bit of a drop. On a stone staircase nearby, again women, one of them in her time a renowned Viennese opera singer . . . Along the walls of the buildings young and old men with pots, drinking soup. On the ground in the grass, between weeds and wildflowers, children slurp soup . . . On the stairs to the workshops, people in tatters, with wooden shoes, of which nothing but the wood is left, in their eyes no longer craving of hunger but hopelessness, acquiescence in all that might still come, holding out their soup bowls toward the door behind which the soup is being dispensed. Always the same problem. "Is something in the soup? Is it thick or empty soup? Will my hunger be stilled for a few hours?" And despite the soup's being commonplace, and despite the complaints that follow the consumption of the soup, the stomach longs for this kind of nourishment, it demands it, the soup is the stomach's companion in all those many months while it lives, suffers, hungers, dreams in the ghetto, this diabolical construction. These verbs have no literary value, no literary origin. They are as real as all other realities of the ghetto. They form the frame for the picture "Soup." In the cemetery, at the edge of the stones, those who work there have *soup.* One can hear the *scratching* sound.

Schools are for the time being prohibited. Thousands of young people without mental occupation, contrary to the Jewish need for books and learning.

Im eyn Torah, eyn kemach! [Hebr., "Without Torah, no bread!" from *Sayings of the Fathers.*]

May 25. There is no mail inside the ghetto! "Mailbox for Jews' mail." No mail, no telegrams, no telephone, no messengers, all personal favors.

May 25. Leaves as spinach. People tearing weeds from cracks in the gutter, collecting leaves and dandelions in the meadows, stopped and forced to hand it over. All the green stuff is designated as animal fodder.

Because of typhoid fever among the new arrivals: Quarantine! Fifty people in one room, sleeping on the floor!

Of forty-seven hundred new arrivals, half (men, women, children) have been dispatched further on. The rest remain for the time being.

Again: About thirty thousand are coming from the surrounding villages.

Names: Zenon Cymbalista, shoemaker, B. Alphabet, midwife.

May 26. Must paint the zigzag of in- and outsettlings! (Don't forget Nuremberg, and so on.)

a. Into the ghetto.
b. Nuremberg, Cracow.
c. Germans in.
d. Poles out.
e. Germans out.
f. Neighboring Poles in.
g. Some of the same out.
h. Again, Poles out.

In the course of this confusion, thousands die.

May 28. *The home is dissolved!* God makes the Jews work like slaves, carrying burdens, sleeping in holes, and . . . wasting away . . . Cemetery: January 1 to May 9: Ninety-four hundred people dead. In the ghetto, one hundred twenty horses, fodder, mixed fodder: barley without kernels, straw, here and there an old piece of bread, perhaps potatoes, eat grass.

Bess-Oilom [Yidd., House of Eternity—cemetery]. Tree-lined paths destroyed, trees (beautiful acacias, dwarf palms, and umbel-bearing trees) uprooted, landscaping destroyed. The roots torn out by Jews for heating fuel. Holes filled in, character lost. Furthermore, the hall plundered of lamps, equipment, beautiful fine-wood pieces. There are many interments, workers, the office busy from morning to evening, a shul [Yidd., synagogue], where there is sometimes praying and learning, and sometimes taken away standing. Kitchen, one thousand soups. The beauty of the most beautiful cemetery in Europe (splendid variety of trees, but unfortunately too splendid, even ostentatious, headstones and family crypts) is there "put into the earth . . ." Many millions of dollars invested in gravestones. The wealth of the Jews of Łódź, who created the textile industry, is visible in the cemetery.

Caretaking of the ghetto: The declarations are addressed to "My brothers and sisters." Then comes the lash with the whip. [. . .]

May 30. *From the collective into private apartments.* Nobody knows where he will be housed. Suddenly he gets an assignment from the housing office, hurries to get there with his belongings—some hole without furniture, without a stove, without a bed frame, filth everywhere . . . Has to sleep on the bare floor . . . if permitted to take a small chair or table, it's immediately used up as heating fuel . . .

Blessing. Book of Numbers 6:24–26. This is what the priests are to say to the children of Israel as they are blessing them: The Lord bless thee, and keep thee [24]. The Lord make His face to shine upon thee, and be gracious unto thee [25]. The Lord lift up His countenance upon thee, and give thee peace [26].

Without clothing vouchers, without nourishment, desert, Deuteronomy 8:4. "Thy raiment waxed not old upon thee, neither did thy foot swell, these forty years."

Deuteronomy 28:37. If you don't obey . . . "And thou shall become an astonishment, a proverb, and a byword, among all the peoples whither the Lord shall lead thee away."

May 31. A sudden heat spell, stench in the ghetto. Living quarters crawling with cockroaches and vermin, sticking in clumps to the walls. Prices are falling daily. For the last ten days bread has dropped from 400 to 140, margarine from 700 to 150; radishes, chives, sugar, etc., available on the market . . . [. . .] The home is being moved out after seven months of a life fit for a human being[8] . . . Excitement. Where, how, what shall we cook? No bread at all for three days, that is, following a good time: fear of hunger . . .

June 1. Move from the home being ordered. Each person gets half a loaf of bread and 1 dkg of margarine.

***Face of the Ghetto.* May 1942.** Concerning novella: "He Searches for the Secret of the Ghetto."[9] Faces are shriveling, thin so bones are visible everywhere, death skull, a horrid sight. Collapsed temples, protruding ears, unshaven, stubble beards, like convicts released from prison. Add to all this the bundle on the back, and the picture of the *Wandering Jew* is complete.

Water and bread. When a beggar asks for something, the minimum is water and bread. In the ghetto these are rarities; *bread* is the most expensive item. In the old days, a Jewish beggar would get a piece of sugar instead of a coin, put it in his sack. June 1—bread 150, margarine 130. Prices are falling because many don't even have money anymore to buy the official rations.

How does the ghetto feed itself? Rations, food coupons, special food coupons,[10] kitchens . . . proceeds from work. Where does the foodstuff come from?

Misery, hunger. Whey, fresh leaves as salad, used to be thrown out as weeds. Hunger. A policeman holds a slice of bread in his hand; ponders whether he should allow himself to take another bite; debates with himself. "Can I afford it? Will I be able to get more bread tomorrow? Will the rations work?" Some resist, some don't. He prefers to light a cigarette (1 mark) to drive away the hunger rather than eat more of the bread. Such scenes are played out everywhere.

Lending library. Rare old books which are usually hard to find: Thackeray (*Vanity fair* [*sic*]), Seneca, Gorky, Dickens, Disraeli, Bellamy, *Salambo* (Flaubert), old Yiddish books, Polish and even Russian books.

Blessing. Genesis 22:16–17. "By myself have I sworn . . . that I will bless thee, and in multiplying I will multiply thy [Abraham's] seed as the stars in the heaven, and as the sand which is upon the seashore . . ."

Job 1:21. "Naked came I out of my mother's womb, and naked shall I return thither. The Lord gave and the Lord has taken away. Blessed be the name of the Lord!"

Proverbs 3:11. "My son, despise not the chastening of the Lord, neither spurn thou His correction."

June 3. [. . .] Winter campaign. The ressorts are producing winter caps and straw covers for shoes—winter campaign (!) prepared with foresight.

Genesis 50:24–25. Joseph 24. And Joseph said unto his brethren: "I die; but God will surely remember you, and bring you up out of this land unto the land which he swore to Abraham, to Isaac, and to Jacob."—25. And Joseph took an oath of the children of Israel, saying,

"God will surely remember you, and ye shall carry up my bones from hence."

(The bones remain here in the ghetto Marysin.)

Mood between the wires. At night, electric streetcar.—Bridge walkways built of wood. Poles, Germans, soldiers.—Most incredible effect to be for *the first time* completely cut off from the world . . .

June 4. Curfew in the ghetto, nine o'clock. In the ghetto advanced by a quarter hour so that the Jews are home on time—by contrast with Litzmannstadt. Hired for work in cultural archive (theater, music, folksong).[11]

June 5. Salad from radish peels. No objection from anywhere, in contrast to potato peels, which, according to some doctors, have no nutritional value, and others think they are harmful. "The world is so beautiful and we are cut off from it," says an old Jew who has never been outside. [. . .]

June 6. Boot shiners in front of the Catholic church: Grandfather with grandson, a seven-year-old, charming boy, gives exemplary shines; gives Block two shines for 25 pennies each, speaks German, Yiddish, Polish. In the church a storeroom and workshop, a wonderful structure from Czarist Russia. On the opposite side the Kripo [criminal police], passing by prohibited.—*Jewish policemen accompany two Ashkenes civilians with filming equipment, chasing passers-by off the sidewalk.*—Saying: You would long have been lying in Marysin [cemetery], if . . .

June 8. Every day, thefts. Last leftover food bits. A little piece of bread . . . Came back from the old-age home. Envy of those who get the soup "from the bottom where the vegetables and potatoes are resting." [. . .]

NOTEBOOK D

Remembrances

June 8. Thieves, thieves . . . The *big* events are penetrating the wire fence.

Face of the Ghetto. At the street corners, barefoot children saccharine original . . . Men as brown as the hamals in the Balkan, with ropes, as carriers of burdens. Jew not recognizable . . . Broken *windowpanes* . . . In a dark room in the back, despite bright daylight, lies a dying man in an old, broken-down bed (pillow and cover full of fly dirt and roach blood).

Picture.—Oy, veh is mir.—These can be seen by the dozen in the main streets like Hanseaten Strasse, Sulzfelder Strasse, Franz Strasse. At the same time, active trading in front of the houses, senseless busyness. Girls use *windowpanes as mirrors,* girls at the machines, ressort clothing—lingerie—applying lipstick . . . Mixing with the beggars—all are wrapped in tatters—fabulous girlish figures, blond in attractive clothes, coquettish, little hats, permed, manicured, pedicured (in modern summer sandals).

Suddenly wire. Through Hohensteinergasse—characteristic of ghetto layout—all *along wooden planks* with barbed wire. People move between rows of houses and the wire. Between wire and wire, electric streetcars and horse-drawn carts, bicyclists, cars, hauling carts (Polish coachmen). Two wooden bridges were built, 5.4 m in height, so that the Jews can pass the street and continue on their way.

June 9. At the edge of the ghetto behind the wire, from the old-age home, unaccustomed noises are heard: roosters crowing, hens cackling, gramophones, radio music, clock chiming . . . like a *dream in a dream.*

For the first time at the cultural center:[1] one-story building without any kind of façade, pleasant, looks like an early Greek temple. Nice cloakroom, foyer, theater hall. Orchestra plays on the stage. Conductor Ryder[2] of the old school, musician does heavy manual work partly in ressorts. Beethoven, Fifth Symphony, violin concerto . . . Greatest contrast to the ghetto, a miracle, therefore incomprehensible. But proof that the metaphysical needs of the Jews in the ghetto cannot be suppressed. What more could one say about this?

I am sure the Jewish people will be eternal, but not like Wandering Jew, nor a singularly appearance in the history of humanity. The atrocities according to the necessaries of Getto are not able to break the resistance of the Jewish forces and souls. We can truly say: The future belongs to us, if though we at present are tired and weary the hunger, cold and beats [original English unedited; italics added by the translator].

Dissolution of the collective, classification, and private lodgings: getting apartments. Finally people in the room. Luck: one upholstered chair, one washbasin, nails in the wall, cots put in order. Suddenly, in the dark room with only one, finally cleaned, window, a distraught-looking woman, torn dress, unkempt: haircut . . . lice-ridden. The closeness of old Russia: Dostoevski.

June 9. A resident at the old-age home (Genesener Strasse 26) was collecting signatures for permission to hold weekly Christian religious services. It became known. He was settled in with the rest.—By contrast: See earlier diary entries, a wagon full of baptized [Jews] were collectively outsettled. [. . .]

June 9. *Outsettlements.* Question: Smokers' coupons? Weekly supply of tobacco, twenty cigarettes, and a small package of tobacco with paper. Again, in the night, seven hundred men outsettled for work in Poznan. Women remain here. Anguish. To this day, unknown what happened to the people who were taken away to work (!) somewhere in the spring of 1940.

Revue III. At the cultural center, "Revue III" (the third revue in a series) was staged on June 6. The fourteen scenes offer proof, with few exceptions, the heritage of a good old style that is greeted with a friendly mien of recognition. It seems as if the time, the events of the last few years, has passed by the authors of the revue without leaving a trace. Individual scenes (Broderson, Jachimovics, Janowski, Gebürtig) run off, colorfully decked out, the themes of love, marriage, family, whereby the emphasis is on the poignant duets. The variety sometimes takes on grotesque forms, however, only on the surface. The texts are not very different from the duets of popular operettas, especially of the kind that are popular in America.

The writers avoid the possibility of capturing current themes—as they impress themselves on the observer in the Jewish streets of the ghetto—and presenting them to the people in the ghetto as the matchless, irretrievable events that they are. Even the sketch "*Getto Plotkes*" [Yidd., "Ghetto Rumors"] contents itself with superficial allusions. This would have been the forum to say something significant about the monstrosity Ghetto Litzmannstadt with wit and humor (gallows humor) and satire. The facts are so evident that one need not be a Sholem Aleichem to discover their humorous aspects. "Laughing is healthy—doctors prescribe laughing." To have followed this motto by Sholem Aleichem would have had, no doubt, the most charming results.

As far as the music is concerned, there are a few nice folksonglike themes in the so-called overture that are pleasant to the Jewish palate without rising above the flat level of popular music. Beigelmann[3] and Gebürtig demonstrate in a few numbers a feeling for strong rhythm. The great Russian Prokoviev is an asset for any revue; his music, close to the Jewish soul, can be an education. A big surprise is the *Fledermaus* waltz of the Viennese waltz king Johann Strauss. The audience feels this music as alien in a Jewish revue, even though it conquered the world. The piano accompaniment fails to find the verve which this music demands.

A particular hit was a dance quartet, that is, a number without text. The vitality of the four artists who performed the dance was especially effective, a brilliantly designed choreography whereby the male dancer was leading the three female artists. It was, no doubt, the high point of the evening, a peculiar vision. There was a twitching of shoulders, swaying of hips, stretching of legs, ending in a tap dance equal to the great international variety shows where the best tap dancers, that is, Negroes, can be seen. This must be especially noted. The audience, for the most part young people, even children, followed the acrobatics of the dance quartet totally enthralled, the tortuous concerns of the day overcome. No ghetto psychosis was felt here. Proof positive of the indestructibility of the Jewish spirit due to an inner faith that even manifests itself on an ordinary revue evening.

The decorations, created by the artist Schwarz,[4] showed a touch of an original flair for form and color, and demonstrated a certain skill and routine even where he borrowed from the expressionist sketches of the Blaue Vogel [Bluebird] and the Tairoff Theater in Moscow (Alexis Granofsky, Habimah, et al.). The painter Schwarz had the courage to realize his ideas of color even where text, music, and performance left him in the lurch.

In summary it can be said: An evening of entertainment for an audience that warmly received the tradition of the old, dated, Jewish theater as long as there is theater, a merry play to cheer up the senses. The ghetto has not yet taken up this tradition. This revue artistic presentation has not yet incorporated the ghetto.

One hundred five thousand people without a drop of alcohol, a *real* prohibition (even though vodka primitive is fabricated in three shops). In some shops in the courtyard, "lemonade" or soda water or "beer" of indeterminate origin.

June 9. Formulation "in good health and request money transfer" has been canceled.

June 9. Bris [Yidd., circumcision] attended by Ashkenes and filmed in beth cholim [Hebr., hospital].[5]

June 10. [. . .] *Latrine.* At the entrance, pools of urine, then gutter with dirty, murky water—one step, swimming with pieces of human excrement. Door to the seat cannot be locked—room dark, wooden plank messy, urine everywhere, stench, walls smeared with feces . . . Impossible to sit down, people are passing the door left ajar.

June 12. [. . .] Exodus 17:14–16; Amalek 14. And the Lord said unto Moshe: "Write this for a memorial in the book, and rehearse it in the ears of Joshua: for I will utterly blot out the remembrance of Amalek from heaven."[6]

June 12. [. . .] Police Jewish . . . see earlier. Police, a group of partisans of the Eldest, brutal, special class on the Ashkenes model, Gestapo. Numerous, since Chaim's bodyguard.

Hunger (outsettlement). People volunteer for German outsettlement since, driven by insane hunger, they are calculating that they will receive soup and a loaf of bread before the departure; hunger hallucination drives them there . . .

June 13. *Cooking* (for archive). Bread 80 marks, potatoes 12 marks, margarine 70 pennies to 1 mark.

Question: *Necessity teaches cooking* = a whole chapter, *cooking, heating, getting water,* tea, coffee, surrogates, whatever one has and what one doesn't have.

Daily death count sixty to seventy.

June 14. *Military gloves.* Work at home—one dozen = 40 pennies (sewing together). At six hours of work a day, one has to work three months to earn 80 marks = one loaf of bread!!! (Two hundred dozen gloves.)

Hunger. Potato peels, once so far in high demand, are hardly consumed anymore since lately after they were eaten there had been mass outbreaks of intestinal illnesses with diarrhea and fever. It turned out that since they were not cleaned thoroughly enough, fly excrement and other dirt stuck to the peels, which caused the intestinal and stomach ailments.

June 15. Dying: Frequently those who die on Monday and Thursday are registered a day later so that the bread rations due on those days can still be collected. These will benefit the surviving family members. Monday the fifteenth, fifty-nine deaths were registered; however, in reality, according to current research, sixty-seven—that is, 15 percent more.

Kripo—Fonye [Yidd., nickname for Russians; also, Russian soldiers]. The German: What do you have for me? Fonye: How can I be of service to you? Almost everybody in the ghetto had been ordered to report to the Kripo: Where do you have gold, diamonds, furs, valuables?—He has nothing. Gets a severe beating. Really doesn't have anything and so he can't report, he becomes a dead man.

Ressort gloves, aviator caps, overcoats, etc. They weave in the threefold curse.—

Concerning dying cemetery. At one time a *gypsy camp,* supposed typhoid fever, died en masse, *had to be buried in part of the Jewish cemetery.*[7]

A simple Jew reads Shakespeare's Coriolanus *in Hebrew.*

June 17.—Music, German classical composers in demand. Händel: *Largo;* Bach: *Air;* Haydn: Serenade, Concerto in D Major; Schubert: three songs; Beethoven: Fifth Symphony; Mozart: *Cosi fan tutte.*

Friday: Licht! Licht! [Yidd., Light!] (Well, buy candles!) [. . .]

Legal Position of the Praeses. Is the Praeses [Rumkowski] also the representative of the highest court? Is it possible to appeal to him?

Rabbis: fifteen local, four German. What are they doing now, these fifteen, plus four German, rabbis? The *rebunim* [Hebr., rabbis] are 100 percent Chassidim [followers of Chassidism].

June 20. In the church (Church Square), eiderdowns and upholsteries are being stored; after being cleaned, they go to Ashkenes and the bombed-out areas which had to be evacuated by their inhabitants. Church as storehouse.—Opposite the parsonage as Kripo.

June 21. Curiosity: Schools, instruction, prohibited. *Children grow up without any instruction!* Private lessons are also prohibited. Without any schooling, even without technical schooling. Wild primitive Jewish life useless.

Kabbalists and Chassidim. Are there any followers of the Kabbalah [Jewish mysticism] here? Are there direct followers of the Baal Shem Tov [founder of Chassidism]?

Polish private elementary school in Savishnitz 22 (Dworska) for children up to ten years of age; do they also learn to read, pray, and speak Hebrew?

June 23.—"He Searches for the Secret of the Ghetto." A man on his deathbed: "God laughs about the perfidy of the being he created. Among them are many who today are still in high places . . . If I only had a little of the optimism that is carried around here . . . Now I am lying here between life and death, a peculiar condition, but this 'in-between' belongs to a category that only a few people are able to enjoy . . . Therefore I feel, in spite of everything, as an exception, as a chosen one, whereas the children of Israel have been pushed back into Egypt . . ." Hallucinations. Dies.—

June 23. Thieves . . . stealing a pot of soup next to you . . . eyeglasses from the pocket . . . the matches from the box . . . a piece of paper which you prepared for something in the shop.—[. . .]

New hopes for nutrition: young red beets and white radishes. Through the town a cart with bad potatoes, which are supposed to be distributed quickly.—New hope for the end of the *milchome,* in which Fonyes work *shitovim mi maala* [Hebr., Russian units from the air] and make of the Ashkenes *irim a churban* [Hebr., German cities in ruins].

Prices are rising due to a day's delay in bread distribution. Garlic 3 marks = 1 dkg, onions 1,5 = dkg, bread again 120 to 140 marks per loaf, potato 35 marks, pot cheese 10 dkg = 6 marks. [. . .]

Plague: flies no deterrent, bugs, fleas, vermin, cockroaches, lice.

See *Hunger* or *Soup* or *Dying.*

Group pictures of indescribable suffering: father evacuated, mother dead, daughter wire, son dying of hunger, another brother for weeks at the Kripo, brother-in-law old-age home with swollen legs . . . Neighbor similar story . . . almost all the officials of the transport are in Marysin cemetery.

Hunger in every face . . . Again the question: What is all this for? The pain of creation is visible here, and with it concert romanticism: "This is where I want to go with you, o my *love* . . ."

June 25. *Face of the Ghetto.* Only wool caps are seen, no hats, no new dresses, now under the burning sun, people in short jackets lined with old dilapidated sheepskins.—[. . .]

June 26. To show: what Ashkenes has done: the limits of the ghetto and how Ivri then extended the limits—creative work, also *organization.*

Men who can handle a scythe and a sickle are to report for "work detail." Today *ishe beim drut d'rharget* [Yidd., a man was shot at the wire]. No more questions about how, why, who?

Face of the Ghetto. In every office a picture of the *Oldest* [original English], calendar, school report card, enjoys flowers. Everywhere at every latrine vegetables. Pictures [original English]: What pictures? [. . .]

June 27. The first little red beets, white radishes, dill, young onions, but almost only on black market; at gardeners or vegetable shops, in the *vegetable book.*

Four kinds: food card (groceries), bread card, vegetable book, cigarette card.

Winter 1941–42. Longing for spiritual-religious inspiration. Jewish religious service, Friday evening, second transport Prague, Dr. Lamm and Dr. Barth. Room filled to the brim; in the room next door, the baptized too have need; wife of Professor Biedl only [wants] to live among Jews . . . The Roman Catholic and Protestant Jews have set up their own religious services in Zidovska (restaurant), Sunday morning Catholic, afternoon Protestant.—The relationship between the baptized and the Jews is very bad . . . out of fifty in the camp, twelve are baptized. . . .—At the time of the outsettlement, the Kripo assigned the Roman Catholics and Protestants their own railway car.

Sealing of the ghetto. In contrast to the medieval ghettos, the present-day ghetto is "closed" through a misunderstanding of the term on the part of the Eldest and the Ashkenes. [. . .]

Street names. German names from the time between the conquest and before the establishment of the ghetto. Now street names: left of the bridge no signs but retained old condition with old Polish names; left signs with letters like A, B, C, and so on, and cross streets with numerals.

Which parts of the ghetto (details) should be pictured? Before every posting of kitchen rations, great excitement: What's going to happen? How much will the rations be this time? . . . One Jew says to another: *"Oy, beganvet er uns!"* [Yidd., Oh, how he robs us!] (when he gets a meager ration).

June 27. *Obligatory Saluting in the Ghetto.* It has been noted lately and repeatedly that the order that all German officials are to be saluted is not being followed. I draw your renewed attention to the fact that all German officials, in uniform or civilian clothing, are to be saluted by the ghetto inhabitants. This order to salute extends also to passing cars.—The salute is performed according to firefighters' service order by standing at attention and especially by removing any head cover. Women and persons without head cover salute by nodding their head. Failure to follow this order will entail the *most severe punishment.*

June 27, 1942. Proclamation: "Obligatory Saluting in the Ghetto"—difficult to carry out since it is impossible to take note in a moment's passing of speeding cars, aside from the fact that the passersby have enough problems not to fall into one of the open gutters on the miserable sidewalks, furthermore, terrible dust—then totally impossible even for keen observers to determine the origin of the car. *Civilian officials* are not recognizable since they are in the wave of the human mass without a star not clearly recognizable, especially in bright summer clothing; they are not recognizable by their physiognomy since there are thousands of blond, blue-eyed. . . . How should children understand this? Furthermore, it is also a difficult order to follow from a psychological standpoint, since the Jews shy away from making any kind of motion, and even the slightest sign of a connection causes discomfort. Order not feasible, threat of punishment therefore absurd.—[. . .]

Conclusion: picture of a moment; Ashkenes in civilian clothing stops at a cooperative, in the midst of a huge crowd an elegant Jewish woman and her husband, makes her stand on the sidewalk. "Just pose for me," took three shots with his camera. "Don't you have children? Why don't you have children?"—Frequently SS men without uniform grab passersby and hit them in the face. Obligatory salute, a soldier served a Jew with a barrage of kicks.—An officer salutes a lady and stands aside when the lady tries to give way to him on the sidewalk. [. . .]

Yiddish Folksong

Unter majn kinds wigela
Steht a waisses Zigala
Das Zigala is gefohrn handlen
Rozinkes un Mandlen is sehr siess
Mein Kind wert sajn gesund un frish.[8]

Today neither *rozinkes* [raisins] nor *mandlen* [almonds], the folksongs of a bygone day have lost their meaning, for a normal Jewish life no longer exists, no more *shadkhen* [marriage broker], *melamed* [teacher], *chusen-kalle* [groom and bride], *cheder* [room of study], no more independent handicraftsmen, and even no more flowers to pluck. [. . .]

June 30. Formulation "here and healthy" without the mention of "send money" is again permissible. Money is flowing in, in meager amounts since most of those sending money have likewise been outsettled from Vienna, Prague, etc. Earlier postcards used to come back with the note "Addressee evacuated," so their fate was known. Now, since the ban on mail for the last seven months, fate completely unknown. We hear that the Viennese were sent to Cracow and from there to an unknown destination.

June 30. Yiddish, Knut Hamsun's *Hunger* (German lending library, Hohensteiner Strasse 19) (Hanseaten Strasse 17), *Soifer* [Yidd., scribe, especially of Torah scrolls].

Saccharine: November 1941 = 20:10 pennies
May 1942 = 3:1 mark, 200:3 = 70 x more expensive
June 1942 = 6:1 mark
Bread: 500 marks "chaimki"
June 30 = 110 marks
Margarine: 600 marks
June 30 = 220 marks
Matches: 3.IV = 1,50 marks maximum price
Oil: from 7 marks to 700 marks in May
Cigarette: November 1941 = 4 pennies, beginning of May = 2,25 (black market)

Official title: *Department for the Insettled:* Fischgasse 8.

July 1. Funeral, cart is racing away. Life-threatening scenes, police beating people over salad.—*Phantom "Łódź"—Golem* . . . Borrowing a pencil at the post office = 5 pennies, reading a newspaper = 10 pennies.

NOTEBOOK 13

The Questions. Novellas. Special Notebook for Questions.

DR. OSKAR ROSENFELD

[. . .] Face of the Ghetto. *Melody of the Ghetto.*

"Sacharina originale sechs a marek" . . . to be sung (motto).

June 1942. Even though the design of the city plan had been left to the whim of each architect, it is still possible to recognize a system of main and side streets. A design motive was absent, of course. The growth of this part of town proceeded more in a vegetative than in a constructive manner. Nevertheless, the well-inclined observer manages to imagine a certain harmony in the chaos of houses and barracks, a harmony of a higher order, however, than the one that corresponds to the laws of mechanical systems. The streets lined with houses that once belonged to Polish inhabitants resemble the streets of middle-size European cities in the Balkans, for instance Belgrade or Bucharest or Sofia, not more than three stories high with narrow, primitive balconies on which laundry is hung out to dry. The doors and gates as well as the display windows are locked with an iron crossbeam. The walls still show some traces of Polish signs and inscriptions. The memory of the Slavic fellow citizens has almost been wiped out. Here and there a sign has been forgotten. Some entranceways are like caves, these are the hideouts of the criminal element, as in the Trödlergasse—or Pfeffergasse [alley]. (Its former name was Faiferufka.) In the garret of the rear building lived a Polish woman who not only provided the criminals (thieves, burglars, muggers, arsonists) with lodgings but also furnished the requisite equipment and tools. She had a rich store of varied accessories for her companions: masks, beards, wigs. She created the blind and the lame. She equipped her accomplices with false papers: in such-and-such a place a fire or a flood broke out requiring collection of money, etc. Her masked agents worked the Łódź underworld as much as the city itself. They also went beyond the city limits to inexperienced provincials whose hearts were more willing and on whose wallets the demands were not as great. They were successful, brought in booty. Poor Jews who heard that in some little town the shul burned down donated money or a Torah scroll or food for those who had been burned out, and the collectors had only one duty, to deliver a percentage to their mother, the Polish woman in the Faiferufka. Through these streets, once inhabited by underworld figures,[1] proletarians, and lower-middle-class Poles, now shuffle former citizens of Vienna, Prague, Berlin, Frankfurt, Hamburg, Danzig, Luxemburg, Munich . . . partly clad in fashionable wear like tourists who had been transported to an exotic place, between the locals, those deported from Łódź, that is, those driven into the Litzmannstadt ghetto, but the mixture doesn't seem to work. Some figures and groups belong in the ghetto from a morphological standpoint, since they have always lived in the ghetto that was Poland, and figures who—European in dress and attitude—won't permit themselves to be amalgamated. Such a process can succeed only slowly and gradually. The outsettlement of approximately eleven thousand Western Jews in May 1942 alleviated the problem. After this outsettlement, a deportation that had, no doubt, a lethal end, the "German elements" in the ghetto had disappeared. The small remainder was no longer able to change the character of the ghetto streets. Again men in caps and women in head scarves are predominant among the passersby . . . with the exception of a few singular coquettish figures. All this weaves and pushes and hobbles over the pavements of the filthy streets, the shrill noise of the street urchins pains the ear, dust whirls up, the clouds wander along dreary and dank, gusts of wind at every street corner, a cool, almost cold beginning of July. [. . .]

Concert at the cultural center. Through an outskirts-type area, past decaying barracks and open latrines, wanders a man who had by chance somewhere at the post office or a clinic or even the quick-fix kitchen gotten word about a concert on Wednesday, toward Marysin, the elegant quarter of the ghetto—some kind of cottage—where, next to homes for children, orphans, and old people, are charming little houses, which are inhabited during the summer months by employees of the ghetto in need of recreation, vacationers, so to say. This place can hardly be called a *datshe* [Pol., weekend home] or a health resort. But those lucky enough to spend a few weeks there in peace and quiet away from the ghost ghetto are the envy of everybody . . . Now back to the walk to the Wednesday concert, toward the cultural center.

The splendid term "cultural center" dies on one's lips at the sight of the actual house. The term dies, but the house does not disappoint. A one-story, extended structure with flat, unadorned walls and wide windows, flat roof, grayish-white and horizontal divisions like an early Greek temple at the time when the ascetic Doric style was still representative of Hellenic culture. The house *represents,* and we, therefore, want to praise those who made such a choice. Rather than being at the front, the entrance is at the side, directly next to the fence, an open gutter, clutter, and all around the dreariness of the ghetto in all its brutality.

Several groups in front of the house. Mostly younger people. Well-dressed locals, very young girls, and even children. At the entrance opposite the box office a handmade poster in Yiddish and German announces the program. People look at it, read, many write down the various musical numbers, for program notes are nonexistent. Seating (only seats) for 1 mark; 75, 50, 30 pennies does not cover the cost of a program. There is also an office and a cloakroom—not to speak of the roomy, well-aired foyer with tall windows opening toward a formal garden, giving the impression of a cosmopolitan occasion, especially during intermissions when cheerful, smoking concert goers of both sexes engage in serious conversation, in Yiddish, Polish, German, or even English, about the just-heard musical pieces.

The hall resembles a theater. The musicians are sitting on the stage; behind them, that is, in the background, sets that inadvertently remind of Saturday's revue performance due to the sidings and the dismantled prompt box. Below the ramp, a piano that frequently has to take on the role of contrapuntal accompaniment. Twenty-five rows with sixteen seats each, two dozen wall chairs fill the hall, holding four hundred people, and it is sold out every time.

The members of the orchestra appear onstage a few minutes after six o'clock, in dark street suits, serious, silent, as is fitting for this type. It must be said that most of them work during the day in some ressort—like making straw shoes or sorting stinking rags or gluing soles or serving some such magic. Most of them are string players, that is, violinists, cellists, violists. The flutist and trombonist even together with the pianist don't stand a chance against the bow-wielding majority, besides the fact that the conductor's gentle soul would not permit such a dispute.

It is not allowed to belittle the conductor despite his personal modesty and reticence. A man of advancing years, about sixty, with a lively face, bright sparkling eyes, and a gray goatee that bounces up and down coquettishly below his expressive mouth. His gestures are vivid, his arms have a wide reach, not like the so-called practical conductors who hold in their feelings and presume to take control of even a gigantic orchestra with short bobbing motions. With his back slightly bent, his legs spread apart, the agile, slender, little man bounces up and down as on a swing or—maybe more precisely—like someone who is himself a spectator who follows the rhythm of the music that is just being performed. He, Theodor Ryder, is the person said to be responsible for the program. His heart seems to belong to Beethoven and the Romantics (Mendelssohn, Schumann, Schubert), although Bach, Handel, Haydn, and Mozart are by no means neglected. If he had the music material available, he would no doubt also present Jewish music, pieces by Josef Achron, Gustav Mahler, Arnold Schoenberg, or even Eastern Jews who find their inspiration in the Jewish folk soul, like Weprik, Krein, Engel, Rosofsky . . . But it is useless to dream of such possibilities, to harbor such illusions. Just as there are no eggs or lemons in the ghetto, there are also no musical notes, no instrumentation, no scores. Ryder conducts from a little hand score in which not all instruments, and therefore not all entries, are marked, but the orchestra functions with such precision that the few "pointers" with the baton suffice.

Four hundred people each follow the playing on the stage. It doesn't bother them, they even take it as natural, as fate or the will of God, that before them in a dimly lit hall, directly adjacent to one of the cruelest realities, through the movements of a gesticulating man with a yellow star on his back, Beethoven becomes audible, and exactly that Beethoven about whom so much had been pondered and written, and exactly that work which is seen as the most profound revelation: the Fifth Symphony. It is not good for ghetto people to lose themselves in fantasies. Their nerves require tender care. When the concert is over, they must find their way back to the daily soup (or to desiccated potatoes). A singer still demands to be heard. Rudolf Bandler of Prague is one of the most popular. His deep baritone leaves room for the murky as well as the grotesque and the burlesque. He sings arias from Italian operas, he sings them in an enthralling Italian parlando, and when he sings a ballad by Loewe or a Schubert song, then even the souls born in the ghetto feel as if they were at home, remembering perhaps the poetry of Schiller and Heine, which, as is well known, had been some of the favorite verses among the Eastern Jews until their own, Yiddish literature pushed aside these German poets.

A short crescendo: some fantasy from "Mignon" or an overture by Mendelssohn or a little piece by Smetana if not Jacques Offenbach, who, unfortunately, is only represented with "La Belle Hélène." The orchestration of many pieces falls on participating pianists, as for example the young man from Prague, Kurt Behr, and thus a family stands together, entrusted with the task, to provide, once a week, four hundred downtrodden souls with two liberating hours. In this sense, the cultural center brings honor to its name and mission.

Mood *tliah* [Hebr., gallows]. Shabbat, February 20, 1942. Friday 3 Adar 5702. On February 20 in the forty-second year of the twentieth century the heavens opened toward evening for Shabbat. Shabbat, 4 Adar 5702, "and God showed me faces. There it happened that the word of the Lord came unto Ezekiel in the Litzmannstadt ghetto. And he looked and beheld . . ."

Friday, collective, six o'clock in the evening, impersonal declaration to all members of the collective. Suddenly people disappeared . . . [illegible], therefore beware of spies: meet at nine o'clock at the Fish Market—*basar* [Hebr., meat] market (at the time of outsettlement market for good bargains of German products bought and sold). Rumors: military parade; directives from the German military; the Eldest will speak.—Afterward some reported that they knew . . . The sick had express dispensation from attending the meeting. Shabbat from nine o'clock on a queue of men and women being led by the room commandant through the almost empty streets across the "little bridge" at the Old Market Place between the ghetto and the city, past Hamburger Strasse to the Fish Market. Along the way local passersby asked what was going on . . . Nobody had the answer. Frost. Clear. Biting wind. Terribly uncomfortable being in the open air. The closer to the square, the clearer that something terrible was about to happen. The streets usually teeming with people on Shabbat—empty . . .

The rumor of the *true* drama seems to have gained credence in the ghetto, none of the local inhabitants want to risk being forced to participate and therefore remained at home.

Goaded by the sharp commands of the Jewish police, took their places, men in the front, women in the back, similar queues were streaming toward the square from other directions. It didn't take long. Shortly before nine o'clock, Fish Square was filled with a human wall, was encircled, a horrifying silence, a few locals out of curiosity.

Finally the masses begin to understand. Sense of foreboding during the march that they were to attend an execution scene (or a witch burning); in the square, many for the first time, *gallows.* It had been *erected* early in the morning by the Jewish police. Several women fainted at the sight, others fell into convulsive sobbing; several of the men managed to send some of the women back home or took them (secretly!) to nearby apartments. Those who wanted to go later found the street blocked off; then order to seal off the surrounding area of Fish Square.

Tliah: quite low on three steps, small podium, to the left across from the post office for newly settled a rectangular trapdoor; above the trapdoor a vertical balcony, at the upper end a horizontal beam with a hemp cord.

A cold shudder went through the onlookers . . . No more illusions, no dream, raw reality, for everybody knew who was Ashkenes.

Several well-fed, field-gray SS officers. At the corner of the square, soldiers with mounted machine guns to keep the crowd in check. Nobody had the courage to flee. The transport leader warned of *most severe* consequence for anybody who tried to leave. *A few* managed to get to the collective. An Ashkenes car was parked not far from the square.

Word making the round: cause and candidate. Cause: Jewish star; another variant: a communist wanted for a long time, flight only a pretext. Left wife and child behind to take better care of them from Germany (name: Herz, Cologne). *The wife is said to be among the onlookers, unaware of what's happening.*

Men are quite numb. Some of the women somewhat worried. The

Ashkenes men are in a good mood, well fed, smoking, looking cheerfully at the crowd.

Almost an hour and a half. Cold is intensifying . . . rubbing to generate warmth, with hands on the knees. About eleven-thirty suddenly complete silence. From the direction of Zgierz, probably from the Baluter Ring (Gestapo headquarters, office of the Praeses—government square), appears a man without a hat, flanked right and left by field-gray soldiers, his gray hair in the wind, no collar, open neck, moving closer slowly, in a short winter jacket . . . directly to the gallows. His gaze falls on the gallows. Most onlookers, especially the women, avert their eyes, others turn their backs to the square; many look nevertheless sideways to the spot where the scene is to unfold. (Tragic irony . . . joke, perhaps to be released again!!!) Most of them after all witnessing for the first time such business and desire for sensationalism. Since none had ever attended a witch burning or torture or pillory, they didn't know how to behave, didn't find the right style; tugged embarrassed on their clothing, clenched the fists, and waited for a sign that was to tell them what it was they should do. Suddenly the silence was so horrifying that the healthy voices of the field-gray Ashkenes could clearly be heard in the square. A man of more than eighty suddenly remembered hearing from his room a strong voice by the wire around midnight, a song that began with la-la and ended with "and if the world were full of devils," and began to make, quite unexpectedly, his own observations about this. Yes, this old man even rolled up the torn gloves for a moment to make sure that his fingernails were clean. A woman her lipstick.—

Not a word was heard. Silence. The candidate shivered in the cold. The field-grays in furs. His overcoat was taken from him. He folded his hands. Saw the entire scene, the crowd. Implacable. Mounted the steps to the podium. There was met by two Jewish policemen and a third man who busied himself callously with the cord.

It was said that a Jewish policeman, a well-known communist, had been ordered to assist in this execution—as a deterrent. Completely dull expression of the crowd, who didn't like to see *Ben Israel* [son of Israel] under the gallows. Sensationalism won out over disgust, women there with handkerchiefs over their faces but peering nevertheless, men completely dispassionate. The symbolism—a people pilloried—

did not enter their consciousness. The bareheaded man shivered, folded his hands. Something was wrong with the cord. The Jewish policeman handled it very clumsily. The field gray standing next to him straightened it out, busied himself; the Jewish policemen in their excitement had made a wrong move, not well familiar with executioner's tool, more used to *tefillin* [phylacteries] (observation of an onlooker). The moment came when the crowd thought something was going to happen, a declaration or reading of the sentence or some other matter. But nothing. Continued silence. When the man saw that there was no escape, he again folded his hands and suddenly, with a lamenting voice: "Why don't you let me live . . ."

Many expected instead of this plea some kind of demonstration as a legacy from the crowd, some inspiring motto. But nothing of the sort. He was no hero in our sense. Now eyes averted from the gallows, dull thumping was heard of heavy material and wood, a few seconds later the convulsing body, dangling. The crowd was even able to look at it for quite some time—seconds (counting to thirteen). The corpse softly in the wind. Rigid features, rigid limbs.

The field grays gave a sign, Jewish police gave a sign, and the crowd quickly began to disperse, going home, the wife of the delinquent was present . . .

The body remained hanging the entire Shabbat. The Jews avoided the place.

Remedies. Talkie [original English]. The construction department received the order on Friday at five o'clock in the evening that a gallows had to be erected on Fish Square the next day, at seven o'clock in the morning; exact specifications: wooden beams, bent iron hook, long, thick, and strong . . . A man from Germany was entrusted with this job. Worked diligently and thoroughly. Finished the job. Taken to the square. This worker was—as it turned out—a close friend of the executed Herz from Cologne. Became mentally disturbed, died of a "broken heart."

Later, gallows, which was taken away, was borrowed by the Gestapo.

Later came an order for a gallows for twelve people, an exquisite construction, a true model. A single hand movement and all twelve are swinging at the same time . . . [. . .]

Face of the street. Everything is old, mummylike, as in an herbarium, people, houses, trees, memories. Even fresh vegetables, as soon as they are brought into the ghetto, shrivel, the leaves shrink, the little tails of radishes and turnips wilt . . . Everything looks as in a secondhand shop, smelling like old *tefillin* and prayer shawls [Yidd., *tallesiem*] . . . [. . .]

Christians, Poles: Talkie. Seventy-five-year-old housekeeper, in service from great-grandmother to great-grandchild, came along during the drive into the ghetto after sixty years of service. Wives of many doctors, judges, engineers, that is, intellectuals, in all more than one hundred "Aryan" Poles, even some with Ashkenes blood (!) with Jewish star.

Spoon. Spoon. Always just spoons, knives and forks unnecessary for taking meals since there is nothing to cut (knife) and nothing to spear (like pasta, baked goods, firm foods—fork). There are thousands of young people who have never handled a knife and fork.

Music. "Would like to hear music."—"Have forgotten what music sounds like." And I approach the telegraph wires and hear the rustling, I've often heard beautiful things, etc. [. . .]

Dying hospital. In the middle of dying a new neighbor reads Romain Rolland's *Jean-Christophe* in Yiddish. Carpenter ressort no. 4. Finger smashed for Ashkenes. Conversation. Gospel. At the same time, Tanach. Another from Brzesziny tells a story. Cleaning woman, English teacher in Łódź. Says: "I'll emigrate = America or Argentina or Palestine or Russia," tells she was driven from Łódź to Tomaszów, from there to Łódź concentration, then ghetto. Lost everything. For two years no news about husband, son, parents.—Two children with broken limbs taken under an apron by parents to the hospital. Quiet. It is Shabbat, July 25, 1942, after Tishah b'Av. *Nachamu* [Hebr., consolation]. Two Jews begin to pray. Children are crying. A nurse scrubs the floor. A dead man is taken away. One carries the dead man outside. Loss of any historical consciousness, no connection as in the old days in the *kehillah* [Hebr., community] and *chevra kaddishah* [Hebr., sacred brotherhood—burial society]. A seventy-year-old spent sixteen days at the Kripo, two in front, three behind, was bloodied with beatings, almost nothing but cold water, now stomach tolerates nothing anymore, slowly wastes away since he can't eat.

Nights in the ghetto. One goes to bed early. Except for various ressort workers (laundry service, cleaning service, dye works, for Ashkenes military), everybody is in bed by nine o'clock. Women already have done their cooking, washing, ironing, and mending . . . Family life is nonexistent, no movies, no lectures, no social entertainment, *nine o'clock curfew.* The workers who come back from the ressort at two o'clock work the afternoon shift. Those who come home in the evening, about six or nine, are working mainly in the morning. Everything is chaotic. The son doesn't see the father, the husband doesn't see the wife, because they usually work different shifts. Children lie around in the streets, courtyards, latrines, gutters, wallow in refuse, become street vendors. Chaotic. Wasn't better in the old days, either, lower middle class, barter, coffeehouse, tavern, door-to-door salesmen, shops open until eight or nine o'clock. Upper bourgeoisie, elegant lives, high society, only Jewish workers had mechanized their lives and therefore formalized. Of one hundred thousand people, eighty thousand are in their more or less meager places of rest, their overnight lodgings, by nine—for it is hardly possible to speak of apartments. They lie around and ponder. What will the next ration bring? A surprise like a moving-picture show.—

Chassid. Morning in the hospital. A man, strange to look at, thin, long, with decaying teeth, a grinning laughter, famished. He pulls the prayer shawl, big, filthy, and well worn, over his head so that his entire face is veiled in it, and says, veiled in this way, the blessing over the tallith [Hebr., prayer shawl]. Then he pulls back the tallith, his face becomes visible, piously enraptured, the head appears beautifully formed—Near East like the figures in illustrated Arabic and Persian fairy tales—places the phylacteries rather quickly on his left hand and arm, then the *shel-rosh* [Hebr., frontlet], a big rectangular box placed on the forehead, and begins to pray swaying back and forth. *Shachrith,* the morning prayer, with the beautiful parts (now trembling). All around him in the hospital, gestures, the things of morning after a heavy, feverish night, odors, noises . . . For a long time his face still radiates with the fervor of his devotion.

Golem ghetto. Never seeing Alphabet,[2] speaking with him, always finding new pages, don't understand him and don't understand that he is so little understood, can be interpreted like the ghetto, which he symbolizes.

Two Spoonfuls of Soup. (A jester who amuses everybody.) "*A human being sins for a bite of bread.*" Hospital room. Twenty beds. Twenty thousand flies. Summer. Two children, legs stiff from lying. Quiet. Old people.

Several devout people. Reading Tanach, Gemarrah [second part of the Talmud]. Somebody is brought back in after operation . . . Swollen legs. Most, thin skeletons . . . Suddenly a doctor comes up to an old man: Your name is Warshafsky, you are eating a child's soup? One soup, two spoonfuls, the child has . . . You old glutton, now even deny. I was being told. (Earlier he is seen looking around.) . . . He contradicts, doctor getting more and more agitated, the patients butt in, have seen. The poor child doesn't say a word, does not complain. The doctor to the nurse: "Starting tomorrow, smaller portions in favor of the child." Warshafsky whines, protests, defends himself, calls on God: "You'd better not call on God, he doesn't like this very much." Another: "Just for two spoonfuls of soup." A third: "Whether you eat roast pigeons—which are not meant for you—or hard stones, I don't give a damn about it." Warshafsky: "Me, a sick man." Suddenly, a new one, looking fantastic, Gospel reading: "We are all sick. The entire ghetto is sick. Stop this kind of talk. Better yourself. It is a disgrace to act like that. What will the foreigner from Vienna, the professor, think of you? You had no upbringing, you're uncouth fellows . . ." Another: "Uncouth fellows. *Mir senen* [Yidd., we are] all Jews, without exception, without protection. You'd better not butt in." Another: "You noble soul, fine gentleman, feels like an aristocrat among us." The young man, agitated: "Yes, it is necessary that I teach you some manners. As long as I am here in this room, there will be order. I will not permit you to smoke. Smoking is not proper for the sick. Bad air. I'll open a window . . ." Another: "Oh, my god! Opening the window, the fellow is crazy . . ." "Air is health, where have you been living up to now? In a farm shed!" Suddenly: "In a farm shed? He's insulting us, that fiend . . . God punish him for it." Warshafsky moaning: "Two spoonfuls of soup, the child offered it to me, no, leave it be, why should it be taken back to the kitchen . . . I? Taken away? I know you too, you bread *shnorrer* [Yidd., scrounger] . . . took the bread crust from another child, made him believe he couldn't chew it." Warshafsky: "God, oh, God." (Talk about rations, outsettlement Warsaw.)

(God shall give us bread for as long as we still have teeth to chew.)

A very old man, the jester: The Talmud says: "Man does not exist to complete his work. One starts eating the soup, another finishes it off." The phrase is lost in the turmoil, only a very young boy who understood laughs. "But the Talmud also says: *Rachmanes* [Hebr., mercy] requires a heart." Then a debate that the Messiah is really due now. The doctor returns from his rounds: "Listen, Warshafsky, tomorrow you'll go back home to your wife, we have no use here for gluttons and thieves like you. Taking the food away from a child . . ." Leaves furious while Warshafsky gets up, gesticulates wildly with his hands and wants to say something. "What, you are accusing me," somebody calls out, "I have denounced people, have informed . . ." "Aha, Warshafsky, what's that supposed to mean?" Warshafsky fends off, but the other keeps on crumbling. Old people interfere, but a young fanatic: "The horde of Korach [biblical figure, rebelled against Moses], rebelling . . . what a scandal . . . Judaism, Jewish history, gives you examples of how to conduct yourself, but you (he trembles), one should appear among you and preach to you every day . . . Gospel. The teaching . . . How is the Messiah supposed to come if you are so evil and low . . ." "What's this? Are you our rabbi?" somebody protests. "Give me knife, so I can stab . . ." Nobody knows if he is talking about himself or the young fanatic. The nurses gather around, there are no knives or forks, only spoons for soup . . .

All eyes are on the young fanatic. A preacher in the desert . . . a redeemer of the imprisoned . . . Necks are being craned. The pious one has slipped under his blanket. The second one calls: "*Shma Israel* . . ." [Hebr., "Hear, O Israel" (central Jewish prayer)]. The young man wants to speak. Words fail him. Suddenly, Warshafsky: "What does he want, this *meshumed* [Yidd., baptized Jew]?" The word creates *incredible* excitement (*Poshe* [Yidd., criminal] *Isruel*). Some really believe this. The young man remains silent, sits slowly down on his bed, his eyes are glowing. Whispering! *Meshumed!* But nobody knows if it is true or merely speaking ill of him . . . Meanwhile the down feathers are flying up wearily, disappearing. "Darkening, darkening . . ." "Two spoonfuls of soup . . ." Silence. In the dusk, gleaming cigarettes. Nine o'clock, the sick are moaning, groaning, burping, and the "o-woe-is-me" of the humiliated Warshafsky saws the time into ghastly, melancholy pieces, which the "o-woe-is-me" of the man who had surgery saws into immensely melancholy pieces.

Talkie. Working, toiling, being humiliated, robbed (at every step of the way, from home to last crumbs of bread, money, gold, jewelry, furs, shoes, eiderdowns of the outsettled and their leather straps), going hungry, freezing, shooting at the bridge, shooting at the wire, cemetery, *tliah* . . . Nearby the siblings from Cologne, Düsseldorf, Hamburg, the police, daughter in the rag ressort, wife embroiders emblems . . . daughter collapses; son, because was kind to children, beaten by a field gray; from the second son he gets a suit from Oranienburg . . . After that, decision that he could only take care of his wife by fleeing to Germany, and from there . . . Caught . . . Scenes . . . *Tliah.* . . . Before that had himself been looking for work in the rag ressort, but since he was shortsighted he was unable to tell the wares apart; furthermore, too old: sixty-four years old, most famous *chemist,* Professor Hart from Frankfurt.

Witnesses, how the whole family was wiped out . . . *Völkischer Beobachter* [a Nazi newspaper], croaking hole Litzmannstadt, calculating calories . . . The death rate of the insettled.

Beginning: how the ghetto arose!!

Chassid. *Rachmanes* and *Hamokem* [Yidd./Hebr., God] = the seat (of the world). *Ato bochartonu:* Chose us and placed obligations on us, not because we are smarter, better, etc., than the other nations (no, for Jethro was a goy who gave Moses advice on how to bring order into the camp), but because he promised to lead the children of Abraham, Yitzchak, and Yakov to Canaan, and we, therefore, have to bring the teaching with us from the desert. This isn't chauvinism or race prejudice. Everybody can be part of it if he lets himself be *mallet* [Yidd., circumcised] and takes on the laws and keeps them.

Learning. Why learning? So that one knows how to behave, getting to know everything? No, through learning of Torah, holiness comes into a person, it changes him and makes him ready after the process for good deeds, without which nothing positively Jewish exists. This transformation is very important, only found among Jews. [. . .]

Hunger. Talkie. Winter day. Nurse Chana, sentimental, sees a few sparrows, throws some bread crusts into the snow. Sparrows are flying down . . . [illegible], beaks partly in the snow. There and then, a young man (German) flings himself on the sparrows to chase them away, the oldest sparrow drops a bread crust from his beak, the German takes it, knocks a breadcrumb from the beak of the other one, and eagerly stuffs it in his mouth. [. . .]

Hunger. Not that this or that person is going hungry, for many go hungry, but that an entire city should exist in a permanent state of hunger as if this condition were a law of nature, by some cosmic plan, the will of God. It couldn't be otherwise. Just as fish, due to their constitution, according to the plan of creation, are swimming in the water, that's how human beings in the ghetto go hungry. It must be stated as simply as possible.

Hunger = a permanent condition, not limited by time as elsewhere but invented as *a torture,* hunger that leads to biting the dust, not as transition to a normal life later on.—Speakers go away: liver, one has to eat everything if one doesn't want to starve to death. The starving Chinese, for example, are not required to do anything, but here they demand labor, organ, and they say: "The ghetto too is in the war," mental and physical output of strength. Is it a dream? (He says goodbye, a figure à la Golem.) Or is word of Rumk[owski], "Only a remnant will remain," being fulfilled?

Here artificially pushed into a country where all around everything flourishes. Of . . . [illegible] made, carried out by wretches of the lowest mentality. There is only ration, nothing else (what is lacking: besides soap, fuel, hygiene, pharmaceutical medicines), people who put eight children to hard labor, collapse. And later: a society that has died out, humiliated, been kicked, robbed of concentration, abused, families crushed, still in the ghetto clothing, furs, shoes, the last wedding ring, outsettled, shot. All the while constant fear, all of this boundless, without limits, and the uncertainty, what then?

When will the good or bad end come? No lodging, no bath, no drinking water, no heating fuel, no clothing. Nothing exists. Closed off by brutal force. Foreign organizations would surely feed the entire ghetto, but they are not permitted. For one hundred thousand inhabitants, a dollar a day could easily be done; after all, the king costs billions. Even the rural inhabitants all around would deliver their products against other wares (from overseas). But this is politics, annihilation. With all this complete restriction, restriction of mail, of those who were "expelled," not a trace, and in all this constant threats. Eighty percent of the ghetto works for Ashkenes for starvation wages, not only for *voisko* [Pol., military] but also for civilians, have no scruples, emblems, dirndl dresses (costumes, etc.), see the gloves for the military beside the low-quality foodstuff, as, for example, potatoes. And looking at the death rate, percentage twenty times higher than outside.—

If Ivri is responsible for Ashkenes misfortune, then he would be responsible for Israel's fortune, how is this supposed to go together?—The *yeshuye* [Yidd./Hebr., redemption] must come *mehero beyamenu* [Yidd./Hebr., in our day], otherwise it is too late . . . (He passes by wherever he sees symptoms of hunger.) *No beggars, because there is nothing to beg for.* Driven to insanity, suicide, incurable disease. And the terrible fear not to live to see the end and having gone hungry for naught.

NOTEBOOK 22

Golem and Hunger

Just as the black hearse drove past us on its way to Cemetery Marysin, I met him. I had never seen him so calm and collected.[1] Every word he spoke to me seemed to me the result of a long thought process, and the words themselves were simple, understandable to anyone. We walked through the ghetto together. We passed the long queues at the vegetable center, the potato handout . . . the kitchens, the grocery shops, that is, the distribution centers, the bread handout . . . Unfortunately, I cannot repeat word for word what Eternity [in the original, first, "Alphabet," then crossed out and replaced] told me. I lack the gift of retelling. Neither am I able to reconstruct his theses in as logical a manner as he did. I lack the experience, the vision, maybe even the courage of the heart. Therefore I beg of the future reader, who has a claim to the original, to forgive me if he hears from me only a faint echo of Eternity's words; if I confuse them with a jumble of facts and thoughts. I am unable to remember the finer points of his guidance. For my memory has become weak. I am myself in the grip of the most widespread ghetto disease: dimming of the memory . . . not being able to remember things just heard, the names just read. There is a flicker in front of the eyes, a droning in the ears, one hits one's forehead, racks one's brain, attempts to conjure up the past. To no avail. Thus I struggle to jot down the few remarks which Abram Eternity—that was my mentor's name—made from time to time as we strolled through Ghetto Litzmannstadt, reserving my right to amend my notes occasionally and as needed. "You have no doubt," he told me while we halted our steps opposite the *kolejka,* that is, the gathering crowd, "read about hunger in India and China. Ghastly occurrences! The soil is desiccated, the grain dries up, sometimes even a plague of locusts, a pity! Thousands, even countless thousands, die within a few weeks because nature has failed them. Nature leaves human beings to die of starvation. Just as floods and volcanic eruptions spread over the landscape, destroying anything alive, man and beast, a drought over far-flung areas turns them to zones of famine, forcing living beings to wander elsewhere . . . They wander, run, flee, ride . . . seeking to save themselves. To . . . [illegible] escape nature. The municipality, society try to help. Assistance committees rush to the afflicted areas in overpopulated regions. Those with good legs and a store of provisions are able to save themselves. A walk of a few hundred kilometers and he is beyond the danger zone . . . It is also possible to protect oneself by avoiding the danger zones, by emigrating . . . The world over there in China, India . . . is open to anybody.

"Go from town to town as a beggar and you won't starve to death. The poorest of the poor can give you a handful of rice, a piece of bread or fruit . . . you don't need a passport, no visa, no exit—. . . [illegible] if you want to wander a thousand kilometers unimpeded. And you don't lose your pension if you do so.

"When Germany suffered from a shortage of food after the lost war, a generous plan of making provisions available was created. Fat and meat and other lifesaving products poured in from everywhere. Billions in credit were granted. Goodhearted neighboring countries took in children from impoverished homes. Holland, Norway, Switzerland, Denmark, were feeding German children. Those who had enough money could also live very well in Germany itself. Millions of the defeated were not lacking in anything. Foreign countries delivered anything against payment. Many countries that produced a surplus were happy to pass along their excess goods. If you had money or credit or well-to-do relatives and friends abroad you could emigrate, seek out the bountiful tables overseas. Nobody prevented you from living wherever your fancy directed you. And even at home, you sat at your own hearth, slept in your own bed, made music on your instrument, and when you felt like it, you took an airplane to somewhere—Paris or Venice. Happy, such a hungry man! Happy, such a nation that lost a great war and is nevertheless permitted to go on enjoying life and being productive and eating to its heart's content! Now the defeated nation was freer and less bound than after the lost war, than during the years of shortages and reparations. If you don't like it here, emigrate! The world is your oyster! But the dissatisfied citizen remained. Thousands of mansions were built, their rooms filled with works of art.—The people who lost the war and supposedly suffered privations bought French masters, established art academies, philosophized as ever. (Bauhaus in Dessau, Laban's modern dance, the School of Wisdom in Darmstadt [Keyserling!] . . .) The Germans followed their every whim, and, with the clouds, their dreams went north and south . . . and in the midst of their dreams they sometimes received delicacies from relatives and friends abroad . . . for a few pennies one could buy a glass of beer or wine and forget the woes of the world. The forests provided fresh air and color, the sea roared, and any enterprising soul could undertake an excursion through the beautiful world—even without a passport. Nobody went away hungry from my door. Unemployment was a great evil, but it did not corrupt the defeated Germans. There was no sign of a moral decline. On the contrary: Beautiful verses were being written, individuals displayed a certain pride, they longed not only for bread but for infinity as well. Immense is the world! And rich! And full of fruits. Any wayfarer is embraced. The world of seekers for work and bread permitted them to live after their own fashion, and, if they were skilled or lucky, they rose in the ranks—all the way to the stars. The defeated in war loved their fatherland, their truncated, beautiful fatherland, more than ever . . ." Eternity would have gone on raving for a long time if we hadn't been startled by the noise from the crowd in front of a vegetable shop. We heard screams, moaning, shouts . . . we saw Jewish policemen beating down on a cluster of children with the handles of their whips . . . and on old men and women who were waiting with their soup pots, knapsacks, and sacks, for fifty decagrams of turnips. "That's hunger," said Eternity sadly. "This is the kind of hunger that gets lodged in the guts and wallows there and spawns excesses. It's a miracle that nothing more horrid is happening than what we are seeing every day: the thrashing about of the human beast . . ." I didn't dare contradict him. "This hunger," Eternity continued, "is not something temporary that suddenly broke out. Nobody can claim that it was demon nature that brought this over us. It was given to us as a present, forced on us . . . A diabolical gift, shackles . . . we are shackled to hunger. To going hungry. We are constantly hungry, whereas all around us everything flourishes, the soil and the animals. And one thing more: Not a small segment of the population goes hungry, not five in one hundred, rather, the other way around—

five in one hundred get their fill every day. It is not the case that here and there somebody goes hungry, no, it is an entire city, an entire state, existing in a constant state of hunger as if this state were preordained by some cosmic force—that's what makes this condition so lamentable. As fishes, in accordance with their constitution, swim in the water, so the inhabitants of the ghetto go hungry . . ." A policeman in front of us was taking two women away. They had been plucking dandelion leaves from the edge of the road to cook and to eat, in violation of regulations. "You have to eat *everything,* if you don't want to bite the dust," they declared when they were arrested, but this objection did not help. They had violated a ghetto law. The women and the policeman had just disappeared around the corner when an excrement wagon pulled by seven people attracted our attention. "The man on the right, with the wooden shoes and the sheepskin vest," noted Eternity, "was lecturing only a short while ago at the University of Prague . . . That's hunger . . . For twenty-five decagrams of bread he volunteered to haul excrement. As he pulls the cart together with several companions in the ghetto, people used to the refuse of Balut, he thinks of India . . . of the dreams he once had . . . a strange fellow . . . pulls the cart and smokes a short English pipe, which he bought in Delhi. That's hunger . . ."

Eternity furrowed his brow. A cold wind blew at us from a shadowless nearby alley, making our teeth clatter. "And next to the excrement workers," he continued, "not far from the latrines, where the muck is being pumped, are heaps of potato peels, turnip leaves, refuse vegetables, foul radishes, and similar stuff, and this miserable, stinking stuff, in the process of decay, is being dug out of the holes by children and old people, happy to be gathering a handful. Hundreds fall ill from such nourishment. Dozens die of it. And even if the sick and dying are aware of the cause of their suffering, they still don't mend their ways. Hunger is stronger than fear of the danger . . . By the way, for whom should the thousands who have been transported here from the West save themselves? For whom suffer the pain when the nearest and the best have already succumbed? Marysin still has room left for more victims . . . And should they recover, get back on their feet, then hard labor is awaiting them again; labor that they detest and that will bring them down very quickly again. Hunger in the ghetto is not limited as it is, for instance, in China or India, where a few weeks of dearth and misery are followed by a period of normal life. Hunger there can make people croak, rouse them from a vegetative existence, and return them to Mother Earth. Our hunger has been contrived as a form of torture, initiated by an insidious scheme . . ."

How often such a thought has preoccupied me and thrown me into despair, without the courage to express it! Now I heard it from the mouth of my companion Eternity, without fully comprehending what was being said. Eternity didn't like pauses. "There, there," he pointed at a yard strewn with rocks and wooden slats, "they all carry their hunger openly in their faces. Each one has only one desire, all have only one desire: a thick soup! What a story the soup vessels could tell—the tin, ceramic, aluminum pots, the soup dishes carried with straps and belts around the body! When over there, in the Far East, the time of hunger comes to an end, people continue to follow their old, accustomed occupations, men, women, and children, so that the traditional rhythm returns to life, with a future and with hope . . . That's how those over there are doing . . . but here every day the situation gets worse. Here almost every starving creature is lost. He is too weak himself to take on the arbitrary guile of the ghetto. He is not allowed to sing, to dance, to learn, to teach, to pray. The nation of priests—'You shall be a holy nation' enslaved through lowly, degrading work. Buried forever, not like miners who when buried are usually rescued and receive the sympathy of the whole world . . . when they are rescued they once again see the light of day and God's beautiful world, they are permitted to laugh and to whistle and to enjoy the good things that are plentiful all over the earth. And if they cannot be rescued, they return to the earth . . ." Eternity took a deep breath. These last words had excited him. I could see that he still had much to say, but he stopped in view of the crowd waiting for soup. We came closer, looking into the wilted faces and extinguished eyes, hardly a spark of a will to live was to be discerned.

"Ten hours daily of unaccustomed work will destroy any hope . . . going hungry and working at the same time—such a condition will break the strongest soul. Even the certainty that only *work* will spare the ghetto of the worst cannot appease the minds. Three years of ghetto did not bring about a complete change in people. If in some remote areas of China or India a famine would break out for a few weeks, the world would know about it and would try to help to get these people back to a normal life. Here, the aliments are already allocated, rations parceled out. This means: A new form of existence has been created for us, which we are expected to recognize as legal, predestined, even just . . . even though every living breath resists this notion . . . Not only are our stomachs revolting, if longing for the life one once knew can be characterized as a revolt. But psychic depression is not even the worst, the daily despair, the hours of loneliness. No, this isn't the worst. Look around you: People hold out their tin cans, possessed by craving for grabbing the few pieces of potato that will thicken the soup . . . Every potato is a building block for tomorrow . . . 'But I am seized with fright only then when I have to realize that the craving is slowly fading away and hopelessness is taking its place,' a citizen of Łódź once confessed to me. I replied without much faith in the persuasiveness of my words that one can only live in the ghetto in calm if one recognizes it as stable, eternal, valid, until the end of days. However, one gives up the hope that life will someday again be worth living. One has to give up once and for all the thought that it could be otherwise. Each resident has to tell himself: I must live in the ghetto the way others live outside in their cities and spaces. If you have made up your mind that this is the way it is, then the ghetto no longer holds any terror for you. It seemed to me that there was much truth in this, but who among us is strong enough to accept such a thesis? We who have been deported here from the West, certainly not . . ."

Eternity remarked that all discussions of this kind are not able to still the hunger and that all desires and dreams are secondary to hunger. We had been passing a few grocery distribution centers and were approaching Brzezinska Street where several shops offered "illegal" food supplies for sale. We passed through a stinking anteroom, drenched with urine, and from there entered a room that served as part living quarter, part business and kitchen. Next to a dirty scale was a variety of foods like cheese, preserves, babka, also garlic, onions, spices, candy, sour pickles, piled on greasy paper. The dried fly shit didn't make these things any more appealing. "Do you want to buy bread?" a young woman with a frayed, flowery head scarf whispered to me. "Or maybe sugar . . . we don't need that much . . ."

Eternity gave me a nudge. "This is hunger . . . people are selling what they deny their own hungry stomachs in order to be able to buy the rations or medication. Bread . . . sugar . . . The question is how long these people can hold out . . . those who give up part of their bread and sugar have lost all human sense of measure. We, who receive soup twice daily, that is, therefore are not walking at the edge of death, would not be able to sell even a gram of our ration without endangering our health, even our life—but however this may be, we are unable to breach the wall that has tightened around us, and we are, therefore, also unable to avoid the senseless acts that are committed every day . . ." I looked in Eternity's bitter face that was drained of all blood. "Shall I once more compare our situation with the famine situation, which we have heard about in India and China and the famine-ridden areas of the world war! Our hunger defies any comparison because it entails other factors; these are factors that don't come into play there, specific ghetto factors, psychic symptoms . . . The end result of a process that began with expulsion from our homeland, degradation, deprivation of all rights. All is lost if hunger is joined to homesickness, fear, despair, or even weariness of life. An organism depleted by hunger cannot withstand such psychological assaults. This barren landscape," Eternity described a motion with his hand as if to encircle the horizon, "a dreary climate, filth, dust, flies, excrement in yard and street, all these plagues of ghetto life encroach on us day and night until we collapse. Enemies compass our body from all sides. We don't know which of the threatened parts we should protect first. We are constantly exposed to assaults on our heart, lungs, stomach, nerves. The muscles dwindle, the bone frame becomes brittle . . ."

Eternity's eyes followed an old man carrying rotten wooden slats on his shoulders and wiping the sweat from his brow from time to time . . . "This man has lung disease. He doesn't know it yet. In a few days, he'll lie down on a cot and won't rise again. Tuberculosis as a consequence of malnutrition. The latest ghetto disease. Following dysentery, flu, typhus, and typhoid fever, finally tuberculosis as mass disease. In the Middle Ages this was called—plague!" We had drifted into the area of Marysin. A wasteland was surrounding us. "The surroundings alone are enough to make us weary, to sadden the soul, to fatigue the feet." We halted our steps at a wooden plank. A woman brought "lunch" to her husband in a tin can—soup. What slurping, hissing, gnashing . . . grinding of teeth . . . Like a beast of prey that received a big animal bone . . . Ghastly to listen to . . . "That's hunger . . . — And again and again . . . One man goes insane . . . a woman commits suicide . . . And always a ceaseless, merciless race with death.—Only a remnant will remain . . . Within one year, the ghetto lost half its population (one hundred sixty-five thousand down to eighty-five thousand).

Study (Animals in the Ghetto)

I was on the way to friends who were working a *djalka* not far from the Dworska, in the direction of Marysin. A villalike little house flanked a part of the short side of the property. It was toward evening, before sunset, still warm, so one could sit outdoors. I recognized Mrs. Halpern, a dentist and emergency physician, in the window. She carried a table and chair outside . . . Under our feet sparse, thin grass . . . Bushes with leaves, first cherry blossoms . . . A yellow butterfly passed us . . . "What's going on in town?" Town—that is, the ghetto. There's no ghetto atmosphere here but a sort of country one . . . "I am exhausted, happy to be far from life in the ghetto. Happy to spend all day in the clinic . . . Tumors, abscesses on the back from poor nutrition, in the leg . . . even on the head under the hair . . ." "This is not the worst . . . the worst is when people collapse; happy as soon as I offer them a chair or even a couch . . . It's not possible to help. The ressort soup is not enough . . . and the ghetto doesn't have more to offer . . . How long will this still go on?" A stork is flying overhead . . .

"That this should be possible! That he is allowed to fly without asking them!? To be moving about freely in the air? Hard to believe . . . We have become accustomed to this prison to such a degree that any moment of freedom appears unbelievable to us . . . Who among us can believe today that he once lived in an apartment with several rooms, a hallway, bathroom, furniture, etc. . . ? That he could come and go and cook and eat like a human being? A dream, a long-forgotten dream . . . The stork comes from the south, perhaps too soon, he doesn't have to regret it, he will not be arrested and condemned to permanent imprisonment . . ." I continue: "A few days ago I saw three goats and six sheep in a meadow near Marysin, grazing, eating, and enjoying life. For a few moments, I was completely happy. What? Animals in the ghetto? Free, without shackles? Without fear of being 'outsettled'?

"What's new in the ghetto? Ration? Coupons? Outsettlement? Will they leave us alone here until the end of the war? Again and again driven out?" The woman's face becomes distorted, creases suddenly appear around the corners of her mouth, her gray eyes fall shut. It seems to me that her hair has taken on a deeper shade of gray. An airplane above us. Noise from a motor . . . It flies east . . . "Toward the East, wonder what is going on there . . ." After a pause: "Will we be redeemed? Is redemption still possible for us at all?" [. . .]

Zgierz: November 11, 1939. A rabbi had to pay 300 marks for the gasoline used to set the synagogue on fire and had to sign that he and ten Jews had set the fire. [. . .]

Concerning Outsettlement Winter 1942—January, February, March, 1942

STUDY (MY OWN PIECE)

Woman—comes to photographer Marinak, who had constant business at the central prison since he was taking photographs of those who had been arrested (dead people on cots, etc., ghastly scenes), and requests of him: "Intervene for me with Shulem Herzberg, the commandant of the central prison, the confidence man of the Praeses, to have my husband set free." "I'll do my best, will go there . . ."—"My five children sick. I myself almost famished, I implore you . . ."—Marinak goes with *teke* [Yidd., briefcase] under his arm. Winter, frost . . . Comes to the prison. The gatekeeper, believing that he has photos with him and has come to photograph, admits him. He asks for Herzberg. He is not available, has visitors . . . [illegible]. People come to Herzberg to discuss with him matters concerning the outsettlement. He offers them schnaps. Sausage. Wine. Buttered bread, etc. They start drinking. Gradually, merry atmosphere. Deriding those marked for outsettlement, making fun of them . . . Finally, Marinak enters. Sees scene. Begins to plea with Herzberg. He, half drunk, . . . [illegible] choler . . . "Nothing to be done . . ." Gets ever merrier. The others look on. Scene. Herzberg crooked Order Service. Cap. Gives guests jewelry, stolen. Finally. Herzberg signs the piece of paper. The woman outside two hours in the cold. Marinak brings the news. Happy, tears in her eyes. Thanks him. Saved.

Three days later. The Order Service reports to the groggy Herzberg. They are still four hundred fifty-seven short of the stipulated number of fifty-three thousand for outsettlement. Winter. Frost. The rescued man is torn from his bed at two in the morning. Resists. Says: "I have been freed by Herzberg." Shows the piece of paper. Useless. He is dragged along. Wife and children, half dressed, go to the train station. In the graying morning. Wife and five children freeze to death. In Herzberg's apartment, heat. He yawns. The Eldest telephones, asks if everything is all right, the necessary number reached. "Yes, everything in best order . . ." [. . .]

Terrible faces: people cross the street, wilted legs like wooden poles. They don't recognize each other—Subject: soup . . .

NOTEBOOK E

Notes as a Reminder. The Most Important Questions. Outsettlement of the Insettled.

Continuation—Diary

Wire. Concerning dying (Völkischer Beobachter: croaking hole of Europe . . .). Nobody is allowed to pass the bridge near the wire fence before seven o'clock in the morning. A young man wants to go to his father's workplace to let them know that he is sick. Passed the bridge in the early morning dawn, is shot to death by a *Stahlhelm* [Germ., steel helmet].

In the ghetto too the Eternal is among us.

Outsettlement of the Insettled

Before being transported to the train station, those marked for departure (expulsion), every day approximately one thousand men, women, children, were taken to the central prison where they had to stay for two days and two nights. The Jewish police herded them together like sheep. The police frequently appeared at the lodgings of the unfortunate lot and forced them to get going immediately. Many were taken unceremoniously from their beds to the station . . . At night . . . Always at night . . . It seems that this is a time befitting the terror of the deportation. And now, with the expulsion order in their pocket, they came. All around the central prison they were crowding together. Like a train of the damned, those selected for torment, destined to enter the inferno, appeared the throng of children, women, old people, and men with their sacks and knapsacks. The scene resembled a carnival or a gypsy camp. People waited and begged to be let into the prison. The first declaration concerning this transport stated that holders of the Iron Cross First Class or the Purple Heart (thus, only Germans) were exempt from the evacuation. But since the pertinent documents of most of the people thus honored had already been confiscated back home, even these "privileged" ones had to undertake the journey into the unknown.

On May 2, the central prison was filled for the first time with those who had been banished. The ghetto gave them soup and bread. On May 4, it was off to the railway station. Rainy, cool. There the German Kripo held sway. A wild scene ensued at this first transport. The Kripo took away people's rucksacks and bread sacks. Any kind of foodstuff they carried was taken away. Blankets, pillows, warm clothing. Despair. What to do? Hopeless. Along with it all, whippings for those who weren't able to go fast enough. *Threat of being shot!* Hands up! Nobody was allowed to carry anything by hand. Wedding bands surrendered. Complete beggars.

This made the rounds. What to do? People everywhere in the ghetto began selling their meager belongings. Vehement trading in the alleys and courtyards. Increase in grocery prices. Bread 700, margarine 1,000, two pieces of saccharine 1 mark, three thin strips of chives 1 mark. The Jewish police takes away anything superfluous already in the collection camp, partly into their own pocket. Wagons filled with luggage (blankets, pillows, etc.) are seen returning to the ghetto. People rise up. Some collapse along the way. They were putting on all the clothing they could fit. Four shirts, several dresses one over the other, sacks sewn into overcoats, so that no luggage is necessary . . . In the stairwells, hallways, yards, in the prison, they lie pressed together like herring. Good thing the weather is cool.

And in all this, there were hundreds of volunteers. It cannot be any worse "there" (presumably Kolo, 90 km away); perhaps even more bread and potatoes in case of farmwork. Here potatoes—1 kg = 35 to 60 marks, one cigarette = 3 marks. People from Vienna, Berlin, Cologne, are the first victims. The transports continue. Again and again the same complaints. Leather straps together with the rucksack cut off by Ashkenes at the railway station. It's considered to be a stroke of luck if someone is allowed to keep a small package. Purchase of reichsmark: chaimki = 10:1. (When criminals are discharged from prison, they are allowed to keep all the baggage they had brought along.) And the trading increases. Shoes, clothing in demand . . . A gigantic end sale. The wares disappear, of course; after all there are no normal buying sources. The soup, which used to cost 20 pennies in the shops, is now 6 marks, thick soup up to 15 marks. The rise in prices made the departure easy for many. Maybe the farmer out there will give us something for our work, bread crusts, potato peels, fat rinds, we'll gladly eat from the pig's trough, as long as we can get out of the ghetto . . . Since many sell their rations (flour, fat, vegetables), the distribution of the ration is being postponed by three days as a punishment—until the transport is completed. Therefore, terrible hunger. From May 10 to 14, the most severe famine in the ghetto. Not even potato peels. Dandelion leaves as salad are being collected in the open field, already *parnosse* [Yidd., a living] . . . paid for picking, prepared as salad.

On May 10, a wagon full of baptized, not Mosaic, Jews departs. Evacuations continue, sales continue, soup 28 marks, potato peels 14 marks, potatoes 90 marks. Allocation of ressort soup is being sold for 30 marks, one pair of soles 125 marks, one candy 1 mark. Women sit and sew pockets for the inside. Touching sympathy, a piece of heart goes with every one who is departing . . . excitement grows, since it is not certain whether more are to follow the preliminary ten thousand. Then suddenly another two thousand! As a result, raids in the streets to scrape them together, some collapse, nobody pays attention anymore . . .

From the old-age home too, three hundred fifty people are evacuated, more than eighty years old, and just as in the past, the blind, the lame, the dying, the tottering old men, are taken into the ghetto, thus it goes on from the ghetto . . . May 13 and 14 pass in terror. Excitement, the mailman appears. Is he carrying an expulsion order? May 15 last transport. And now it was to be the turn of the local population. This was to be the final chord of the outsettlement. The ghetto again supplied twelve thousand human beings, not counting those who have been put into the ground in the cemetery.

And suddenly from the surrounding villages come Jews . . . Polish Jews . . . and so it goes.

Depiction of the Mood (Provisional) {. . .}

The tragedy is tremendous. Those in the ghetto cannot comprehend it. For it does not bring out any greatness as in the Middle Ages. This tragedy is devoid of heroes. And why tragedy? Because the pain does not reach out to something human, to a strange heart, but is something incomprehensible, colliding with the cosmos, a natural phenomenon like the creation of the world. Creation would have to start anew, with *berajshit* [Hebr., "In the beginning," first word in the Hebrew Bible]. In the beginning God created the ghetto . . .

July 3. The trucks of the Ashkenes can been seen on top of the bridge, driving through Hohensteiner Strasse between the wooden fence and barbed wire—the inside of the open cars can clearly be seen: the most beautiful red and white radishes, salads, turnips, carrots, fruit . . .

They race by, enticing as in a fairy tale, while nearby the ghetto inhabitants, who are working for the Ashkenes, feed on rotten old black berries, 25 dkg a day, now and then regurgitated vegetables and from the new gardens for 5 marks, green stuff (*greens* [original English]) unfit to feed on. Chives disappeared, 1 dkg of garlic 4 marks.

July 4. A beggar—truly a rare sight—knocks on the door. Nobody goes begging, almost all are beggars—gets radish peels, holds them tight against his body, sneaks away, cane in hand, *sheepskin in July,* like Rembrandt. Passes a pregnant woman.

July 5. *Today a good day.* Even though one hundred five deaths, also several uncomplicated births. Here must be taken into consideration the fact that interruption of pregnancy (artificial abortion) is permitted—because of the difficulties of nourishing an infant.

July 4–5. Night. Fire in the ghetto. Since the ressorts are working for the Germans [original English], the fire brigade of Litzmannstadt also comes charging out at night . . . Terror in the Hohensteiner . . . *Noises from the other side:* whistling of the factories, smoking chimneys, singing *balmelchom* [Yidd., soldier], cars and nocturnal fire brigade sound sirens, banners on the streetcar, Hohensteiner Strasse. Months ago borrowed pencil from the post office for 5 pennies.

One hundred four thousand human beings—summer without drinking water. People borrow a pitcher of water from a neighbor for cooking. Renewed hunger. No vegetables. One kilogram water turnips 20 marks, margarine 250, bread 150, Quaker 60 marks, potato 25 to 30 marks.

Nobody says "please" or "thank you" when asked for something: in Polish, *prosze pana,* but German = *bitte,* doesn't exist in Yiddish.

Horrors of winter. Heating, hunger, frost, no warm clothing . . . crowding at the hospitals, hardest labor—pulling heavy loads in the streets, getting water, frozen water pipes, toilets, saving light, darkening, children all day in bed, enormous mortality . . .

Humor in the ghetto. Especially directed against the Eldest, comments about rations, much from the Talmud, etc.

The ghetto's melancholy received in the concert a religious character.

Wisdom in the ghetto. Talmudists, Chassidim, people in the street (vendors), etc.

Ghetto Litzmannstadt is the Golem among the cities of the world. Need to draw a figure that wanders through the ghetto and combines in himself all qualities = *symbol of the ghetto:* apparition, resembles the Eternal Jew, Christ, Golem, police, field grays, and so on.

Evacuation from Loewenstadt (Brzeziny)

NIGHT OF MAY 15 (SHABBAT)

Brzeziny 18 km from Łódź. Seventeen thousand inhabitants, of which 5,750 are Jews. Ghetto: Eldest of the Jews, Felix Ikka, for two years. Mainly tailors (even before the war) for military ressort, navy, air force, army. Food allocation ration one family: one room, one official: one room, one tailor: two rooms, better treatment. Wages by the piece. Official's weekly pay, ration per week: ¼ kg of sugar, 10 dkg artificial honey, 8 margarine, 3 butter, ½ kg flour, vegetables, soap, coals . . .

Outsettlement: Friday, May 15, in the afternoon. Jewish policeman led women and their children up to the age of ten to the community marketplace . . . These women and children taken into empty houses in the driving rain. Terrible wailing, sleeping on the bare ground. Three o'clock at night, Gestapo from Łódź beating with whips. The women remained, the children thrown onto trucks, "That's shit;"[1] also the sick with their children and old people unable to work. Eight o'clock in the morning, the women were taken back to the ghetto. Shrieking, wailing. The mother: "There's never been a night like this before." Automobiles with children taken to Galkuwek and there again thrown into the railway car, accompanied by Jewish police from Loewenstadt. When the Jewish police treated the children well, they were beaten by the Gestapo until the blood was flowing. Then the police cars of the Gestapo returned to Łódź.

After the action with the children, the Jewish police went from house to house on Saturday, May 17, demanding that all Jews report to the market square, in some alley, with rucksack and bread sack. At first there were fifteen hundred people—men, women, and children over ten—who appeared at the market square. At the market square women, children, and men were separated . . . The older men, older women, and children were loaded onto a wagon in individual groups, their baggage separate, twenty human beings per wagon, taken to Galkuwek. The healthy ones had to walk on foot to Galkuwek. Here in Galkuwek they were all, in the same groups, chased onto the train with their baggage, the cars were sealed, the windows closed, German police served as guards. The train remained in the station all night, six o'clock in the morning left for Łódź.

Arrival in Łódź. When they arrived in Łódź, they were taken over by the Jewish police. Housed in barracks, in part in the camps abandoned by the insettled.

The first fifteen hundred were followed by another three thousand, all in all forty-five hundred human beings, among them older men and women, disabled for work, and children over ten. (Of those, twelve hundred were immediately sent on; three hundred sixty men to somewhere for forced labor.) Of the Jewish population in Brzeziny of about five thousand seven hundred fifty, one thousand nine hundred fifty remained. Work camp in Brzeziny, three hundred as handicraftsmen and day laborers (illegal workers) for cleaning, etc. Most of the tailors were also sent away.—The rest were sick, invalids, etc. The evacuation was carried out in spite of the authorities' knowledge in Brzeziny (Loewenstadt) of the raging typhoid fever—within the time of the quarantine.

About Ghost "Ghetto"—Dreams: and Other Things

Embedding dreams in *hunger,* in the way to the cemetery, into walk to the ghetto courthouse, therefore, daydreams. The *Golemness* must repeatedly be emphasized.

a. Delicacies, the land of Cockaigne, bordering on the erotic, repeating itself, always oranges, blurring into lemons, breasts.—
b. Dreaming of father, then a pleasant surprise . . . Fact, got 10 chaimki from Prague.
c. A wealthy man distributes loaves of bread . . . , etc. Wrestling, beating, police . . .
d. Seven hundred million Jews are running over rural road between potato fields . . . Bombs from airplanes, then machine gun . . . Then gas . . . Then the clothing with bloodstained holes sent back to the ressorts. The dreamer has to clean them, recognizes his father's suit. . . .[2]
e. He is still Professor Clinic, in a white coat, is to be buried alive, since white coat like shroud . . . suddenly Jewish police push him into the wagon, outsettling him, putting a cap on him as doctor, is happy, awoken, spilled black coffee with his foot, which he had readied for brushing his teeth.
f. A beggar wanders through the city: a rare picture, Rembrandt . . . This beggar walks slowly (describe the itinerary . . .) to Polish-German library . . . asks for the remembrances of Socrates . . . then Faust (describe in great detail).
g. The entire ghetto works: *Y'ladim* [Hebr., children] and *s'kanim* [Hebr., old people] . . . People of weak characters participate, give orders, degrade their brothers and sisters to slaves for a coupon, for 5 dkg of butter, a can of sardines, or 4 dkg of sausage.

Someday the question will be asked: Did Chaim Mordche [Rumkowski] do right in face of the *sakune* [Yidd., danger]? Will he be held responsible by somebody? Was he the smart one? The true *shofet* [Yidd./Hebr., judge]?

Readings

Hamsun: *Hunger.* Kubin: *The Other Side.* Zola: *The Belly of Paris.* Carlyle: *The French Revolution.* Maurois: *Disraeli.* Dostoevski: *Crime and Punishment.*

The category *capital and work* is unknown in the ghetto. Neither the capitalist nor the worker is to be seen; neither anonymous capital nor individual private capital; neither the exploiter nor the proletarian.

We are living in a *commune*. Of the one hundred four thousand inhabitants of the ghetto as of July 1942, about one hundred thousand are of equal rank. The remaining four thousand are living under somewhat more favorable conditions due to more generous food rations and more hygienic surroundings. That is all. The ghetto as such, its highs and lows, can be experienced/enjoyed by all in equal measure. There is no channel through which victuals flow from different reserve. That's why the only trade is that of rations that people save from their own mouths; *earlier,* still gifts (delicacies) from abroad and contraband. Since May 1942, modest home production of vegetables—without assignment for the open market, furthermore, with secret traders who somehow got these goods. The strange thing about it is that:

1. Many of these articles (products) are not available at all, like tropical fruits, delicacies, white flour, canned goods, meat and fat, sausages (only with coupon), vegetables, fish, oils.
2. The raw material for preparing countless dishes didn't exist, couldn't be delivered.
3. Because everyday objects, such as shoe polish, toothpaste, soap, alcohol, medicinal articles (opium, iodine, ethyl alcohol), medications, bandages, shoestrings, rubber goods, electrical goods, were unavailable. There was no source from which—even for large sums of money—the lacking products could be obtained. (That's why the rusty nails, old toothbrushes, and shoe-shaving brushes . . . empty bottles, corks.)

Look, for instance, at the kitchen ration of July 8, 1942, for ten days. One and a half kilograms potatoes, 30 dkg flour, 10 dkg oatmeal, 10 dkg peas, 12 dkg sugar, 12 dkg margarine, 10 dkg substitute honey, 9 dkg coffee (ersatz), 25 dkg salt, 1 dkg nitrite, 1 dkg paprika, ½ dkg lemon extract, a little piece of soap, a package of laundry detergent, ⅒ liter vinegar, one flypaper = 4 marks.

Workers' extra allowance for ten days: 1 kg potatoes, 12 dkg peas, 20 dkg sugar, 5 dkg butter, 13 dkg coffee, one fruit soup, half a piece of soap, 10 dkg barley 2½ marks.

July 9. *Wood center.* In the courtyard, wood leftovers from the wood- and fashion-producing ressorts, specifically pieces from models, slats, shavings, wood rinds, are lying around in the burning sun. Overseers check to see whether some pieces still usable for production, should be sorted and packed away. Girls, women, children, former professors, doctors, writers crawl around on the dusty, filthy ground to hoard their 10 kg in bundles, rucksacks, or baskets.

July 11. *Carrots.*—Wildfire: *vegetables at the grocery store,* particularly red and yellow carrots . . . So what? Right around the street corner noise is heard. Right . . . a cart pulled by human slaves . . . Green stuff—leaves and tiny heads, red and yellow . . . crowding at the front door . . . Several children manage to push their way through the crowd: shopping nets, baskets, sacks, strings, even pots, cartons, and similar containers. Doorkeeper. Won't let them in. The crowd pushes with ever more rage. Suddenly as if everywhere, police caps. Sticks are seen being swung . . . The police flogs, lashes out. People absorb the beatings. The noise intensifies . . . Wild faces, swollen veins, enraged eyes . . . desperate faces. Finally . . . the door is broken down. They are inside the store. Police behind them . . . wild craving: 1 kg carrots, one bushel of turnips . . . The hunger.

The first *agricultural* lecture held in Polish. Formerly in Yiddish.

July 13. Again hunger. Prices rising. People remember that in January 1941 the decagram ration of vegetables with water turnips was 3 dkg per head. Back then (see!) fifteen hundred people died during that January, no coals . . . hunger and cold. Lying down in the evening, frozen to death by morning . . . An entire family, except for one boy whose legs had to be amputated. Why not us? We are guilty, all of us who are allowed to live while others pass away . . . All of us in the ghetto are guilty that it is this way . . . "I was teaching in the school in freezing, 7-degree temperatures and still this was a beautiful time . . . , "a former teacher relates. [. . .]

July 15. *Dying.* Near the big bridge, woman is lying prostrate on the ground. A policeman approaches. A woman doctor arrives, moves on. Policeman waves male doctor. He shrugs his shoulders after examining the woman, leaves . . . None of the people crossing the bridge pay any attention to this scene. Death, simple, over with. The Jewish problem is being solved in installments. [. . .]

When someone dies, people nearby and the military doctor remove gold teeth and valuable fillings from the dead person's mouth.

Photographs: The bridges. View from the bridge on the city.

Henuschi: My thoughts are with her!

Uniforms in the ghetto . . .

Cholent [Yidd., popular dish for Shabbat] *kitchen:* potatoes with barley, cooking overnight, horse meat, Friday, women with pots covered with paper, on this paper name and address. The numbers are called out on Shabbat, the cholent is passed to the women through the window in a cold, drafty yard. [. . .]

July 23. Today is Tishah b'Av. Nobody has a feeling for it. Several Chassidim at the hospital are reading the Kinne [Yidd., Book of Lamentations].

July 24. *Outsettlement of the insettled.* Story told at the hospital. Kripo at the railway station during outsettlement. [. . .] Little package of bread, 5 dkg margarine, 10 dkg sugar, little packet salt, paprika—stops him, outer garments, warm overcoat, taken off, rucksack cut off, train whistles. "Now, run!" And the Jew runs, field grays behind him, door to railway car slammed, he has been robbed of everything.

Conversation about the situation: Spain (Marranos [Spanish name for Jews forcibly baptized by the Inquisition who secretly observed Jewish practices]). What does Insel [Germ., island—Rosenfeld's code word for England] want? The power of Fonye.—Secret agreement between Insel and Horowitz [code word, probably for Hitler].—A *mabul* [Hebr., flood] will come. Destruction of the world. Another: Apocalypse (see there).

July 27. *Outsettlement Warsaw:* Rumor, all Jews are to be evacuated from Warsaw. At the same time rumor that potatoes will again be part of coming food rations.—Warsaw, indeed, violent evacuation of ten thousand Jews a day at gunpoint and under shootings. Not outsettlement but expulsion on a staggering scale as previously from Łódź into the Ghetto Litzmannstadt. The Eldest of the Jews in Warsaw—suicide.[3] All of this is not strategic but Jewish matter. [. . .]

July 28. *Twenty thousand flies.* Plague of flies. Hospital. A hallway with seventeen people, one hundred flypapers with two hundred flies in one week, that's twenty thousand flies. An interesting statistic.

Chassid: reassigned to the junk ressort next to dirty rags. *Loshen kodesh* [Hebr., holy language].

1. Contains no word for sexual organs. Reference always to "shame," "disgrace." From this derives the shying away by Eastern Jews, traditional-orthodox Jews, from anything sexual.
2. When somebody speaks in some room to someone in no matter what language, it is unclear whether the person addressed is male or female (*ten li; teni li*). That's why the speaker will out of shame avoid saying anything obscene or depraved within earshot of witnesses.
3. Behind every word is another word, a secret unto eternity. Let's take for instance the words "Abraham," "Isaac," "Jacob" . . . It is possible to glean many secrets from them and, through an ever-widening link of letters, create a line of words that likewise reaches into infinity. These beatitudes and secrets are already contained in the Torah itself, which countless kabbalistic and mystical writings, for example the *Zohar* [mystical commentary on the Torah, main work of the Kabbalah], try to elicit. Centuries upon centuries will pass to advance step by step from secret to secret, to discover beatitude after beatitude.

July 30. A flat region, all the way to the horizon. A barren land. No great ideas. This "staggering" of the commune, see Russia and China. Up on mountains, lofty feelings, deep thoughts: Horeb, Sinai, Nebo.

Look up poems Pharao, see Talmud Chassid. Love your neighbor as yourself, as you *love* God, and the *love of God* (not out of sense of duty or fear of punishment) is the reason for keeping the commandments (Torah).

August 3. More reports about expulsions, area of Warsaw. Jews captured together, women and children torn away, men shot dead. At the hospital, a victim with bullet-shattered shoulder (came here). Remembers Turek near Kalisz [two towns near Łódź]. Otherwise also unrest because of provisions. One loaf of bread for a week since the end of

July, that is, 3 dkg less daily. Five kilograms of potatoes for four weeks. Supposed transport difficulties according to Ashkenes because of *milchome,* therefore delays.

August 4. *Talkie.* Talkie takes on ever greater dimensions in the conception. Three parts: action, dialogue, music (sound). Music:

a. Sensing noise of the street.
b. Motive of the excrement cart, removal of the dead.
c. Town crier in the street.
d. *Nigun* [Hebr., melody] in the Chassidic school.
e. Singing in the ressorts.
f. Revue (Beigelmann).
g. Folksongs.
h. Ashkenes field-gray choir is heard from beyond.

Beginning of *tikvah* [Hebr., hope].

August 5. The sick at the hospital. In the ressorts almost all normal. Former textile manufacturers in Łódź. Now it becomes apparent what the Jews had achieved for the Polish economy: *production, ready-to-wear clothing, export.* Ashkenes despoiled all of this. Partly destroyed, partly taken over. *Talkie.* While children and old people scour the refuse for potato peels and the like, trucks pass between the wires along the Hohensteiner Strasse with the finest vegetables, beer, wine, oranges, meat; coachmen and chauffeurs, cheerful with cigarettes in their mouths. Clearly to be seen: Hunger is artificially created. For the *Polish peasant* is still producing. He too must be recorded.

August 6. Again rumors. Excitement in the ghetto. A Jewish delegation is said to have visited the namesake [presumably the German ghetto administration] because of the intervention. He promised *soff* [Hebr., end] in eighty days. Ghetto filled with hope and excitement as it hadn't been since the winter, as if the Messiah was near. "Really? October?" With all this again hunger . . .

Fear in the ghetto. Ditches everywhere since the time of preparations against air attacks. Guard at the ditch. What for? Nobody knows. Who knows for what purpose the graves are still being guarded! Perhaps to murder us and throw us into the ditch or even alive at the end of the day? Similar ditches with masses of dead soldiers piled up on top of each other . . . People look at each other terribly sad without saying a word.

Dying at work. People are weak and sick, they go to the ressorts for fear of losing their worker's ration. There they collapse in the midst of the heavy labor (bakery, joiners' workshop, metal, wood), don't make it back home. On some days up to five people. Outsettlement Warsaw is said to be continuing.

August 7. [. . .] *Talkie.* Professor Hart from camp to private apartment = path à la Golem to Brücken Strasse. Furthermore, photo entrance 10 Altmarkt. Lodging of Dr. Nathanson,[4] picture of departure from Frankfurt à la Baron Mayer; before, new suit, *pour le mérite* [French medal of merit], where later, Jew's star.

August 8. Hospital I is said to be designated for liquidation and to be turned into a ressort. German commission inspected it already; preparations are under way. Has central heating whereas the other sections do not. Acquaintance with Dr. Vogel, a physician from Prague; tells of death of his brother, who, during the train ride from Prague to the ghetto—due to mental disturbance—had conflict, made remarks against Ashkenes, taken to prison Litzmannstadt for a so-called court hearing, and was shot. Details of the circumstances not known. Fear to survive. "On our bones Palestine must be developed, the only hope . . ."

August 9. Remembrance of potatoes—February to May, completely rotten and still being eaten with skin, no peasant would have the heart to feed such potatoes to his pigs.

August 10. Dying. Appendix comes to the hospital. Is not operated because the doctors postpone . . . Dies early in the morning with the words "Don't let me suffer anymore." Lies around like a chicken.—Apathy, a second one. Delirium, dies twelve hours after being brought in. Nobody gives a damn about him. Both from Berlin.

Hunger. While one hundred thousand people go hungry, a few gluttons have strawberry preserves, condensed milk, wine, liqueur, fine cigarettes, and so on.

August 13. *Starvation-wages bread.* Price of bread, on the black market, from November 1941 to May 1942 = 8 marks to 700 marks. June–July–August = from 150 to 200. Young workers in the ressorts (tailors, joiners, et al.) earn 20 marks a month for seven hours of work daily. Have to work ten months for one loaf of bread. *Very good ressorts [pay] 60 marks a month;* selling part rations (honey, oatmeal, sausage) to buy rations.

August 14. Again several thousand Jews from the surrounding countryside tossed in here, men and women separated, children left behind, unknown. Expulsions from Warsaw continue.

Ghetto sickness. Memory loss, remembrance of people and things, especially names. The names of one's best friends, of towns, books, etc., are lost.

August 15. I weigh 47 kg. Lost 10 kg since Prague.

August 16. Field-gray Ashkenes were shooting near Hohe Brücke [Germ., High Bridge]. One of the wounded taken to the hospital. The story goes—big and supposedly healthy. Again hunger. No potatoes and few vegetables. Bread 200, margarine 250, vegetables 10 per kg, one pickle 1½, sugar, honey, etc., not obtainable. Dismay over bad rations. More soup instead of bread. Mortality increases, fear of winter.—One patient has been so completely crushed, morally and physically, by the blows from the criminal police that he doesn't want to eat and is slowly starving, getting *nifter* [Yidd., finds deliverance].—Renewed hunger. The Eldest prohibited the private gardeners from selling their produce, therefore nothing but secret trading, that is, black market. At the same time *bituchen auf soff* [Hebr., hoping for the end].—

August 18. Ghetto again in state of agitation because of events outside. *Milchomo* [war] in critical stage—the same time rumors: Horowitz-Hanoar [Hebr., "hanoar" = "youth"; Horowitz-Hanoar is O. R.'s code for Hitler Youth] to be brought from over there to us, pogrom, but ghetto administrator (Ashkenes) prevents it.—Sensation: 20 (!) dkg of sugar part of the next ration. Nurse comes to the bed of a patient: "Oh, life is hard and narrow." *Narrow is life!* Finally found a word: narrow.

August 20. *Hunger.* Hunger as at the beginning of May. People are collapsing in the street. Bad rations: no honey, no flour, 1½ kg potatoes for ten days.—*No vegetables.* Collapsing in the factories, especially terrible the straw ressort.—One pickle 2½, two radishes 2½, hardly any bread on the black market. Terrible. Fear of pogroms. Domestic potatoes are expected in four to six weeks.—At the same time, glowing optimism with regard to *soyne Israel* [Yidd., enemy of Israel; antisemite].

August 21. Again rumor that a few weeks ago Horowitz-Hanoar wanted to enter the ghetto but were prevented by the Ashkenes ghetto director (Biebow)[5] since he wants to have calm and order. A man with a sense of responsibility.—Alarm. It is said that Fonye bombarded west of us. No details known.

August 22. *At the night from 21 to 22 (Shabbat as usual) many Jews were been hunted from Warshavie and other villages (little towns) to Getto. A great deal dead during the voyage. I am told that this action was a sort of pogrom in order to make a trouble under the Jews round the Getto and into the Getto; but the truth is unknown. Luggage robbered, two* erschossen [Germ., shot dead]. [Original English.]

August 23. With regard to Warsaw, it's being told that machine guns have been set up in the city, Ivri shot at and hunted.—Again one thousand Jews arrived from the area of Ozorkow without anything, aggravating the food situation.

Ghetto diseases. Mental apathy. Loss of sense of time, loss of eyesight, weakening of memory, see note for August 14. Reread Zangwill's "Voice of Jerusalem." Demands religious tradition despite being politically Zionist.

August 24. Statues of Virgin Mary removed from in front of the Catholic church on Kirchplatz [Church Square]. Poles passing—through Zgierzka—are still lifting their hats. Incredible hunger since there is no fat at all in the workers' allocations.

August 26. *Ghetto diseases.* "Beware of stomach typhus"(!). No unboiled (!) water; no uncooked vegetables (!). Neither cooking facilities nor warm water easily come by. Cleaning *toilet,* where there are only open latrines. *Flies!* No flypaper. Mass deaths of dysentery!

August 27. Village 40 km from Łódź, Zduńska Wola: *yeladim* separated from old people and parents, *yeladim* ordered to lower *rosh* [Hebr., head]—then shot with revolver, adults too came to the ghetto. Of these, the older ones immediately again unknown whereto deported, only work people left here.

Rumors of differences between Fonye and Insel. Ashkenes foreign minister presumably with Fonye. Mood depressed. 1,130,000 kg of potatoes arrived. Hope for some nourishment.—Concerning Zduńska Wola, about 40 km, children said to have been shot to death; mothers forced to bury their own children, some of the parents shot too.—Corpses brought to the ghetto.—

August 28. *Letters home. For several months only preprinted cards with "healthy," but address and name written by the postal official so that the addressee doesn't even get to see the original handwriting.*

August 31. New stern proclamation: "Strictest Blackout," only 15-volt lamps, under punishment.—Hunger. Guided dying people in the street.

September 1. *Hospital evacuation.* Evacuation of the sick from ghetto hospitals under special circumstances. Without warning, the Jewish police surrounded the hospitals at five in the morning, streets blocked off, the sick taken out, put on truck, and taken away by Ashkenes, whereto? Despair of the sick, flight over the wall, with assistance from nurses. Great lament in the ghetto. Horrible tragedy for dear ones, doctors, the entire personnel, etc. What will happen next? Introduction to the fourth war year in the ghetto.

October 1. [. . .] Arrived from Zduńska Wola, twenty-seven dead, twenty-three men, four women, some of their names unknown. Families separated: two people in the ghetto, the others where?—Hospitals with infants, women who have just given birth, amputees, severely sick, cripples, removed in one day.—Seems beginning of a new outsettlement. Terrible atmosphere despite delivery of 1 million kg of potatoes.

September 2. In March 1940, psychiatric ward still in Łódź evacuated, eliminated. July 1941 in the ghetto psychiatric ward evacuated, eliminated.

August 31. Various ressorts impose ban on admission.

September 2. *Hospital evacuation. Fate of the residents unknown.* More and more new details come to the fore, flight in various disguises. Patient leaves the hospital in an aide's coat. A woman taken away one hour after giving birth. Surgery torn away during forceps delivery (already on the day before, wild car racing of Gestapo through Zgierzka). Some tore open their wrist arteries with fingernails—suicide.—Front entrance blocked, passage only on opposite side. Since about two hundred patients have fled, those who had been referred to the hospital, relatives of the sick and people from the old-age home, were arrested. All at night. Woman asked to report for presumably stealing her child from the hospital. Examination of the child shows that it is healthy and therefore has no need to be hospitalized.—As a control, the list of the sick is revised so that those who fled can be tracked down. Many of the relatives wandering aimlessly through the streets, wringing their hands, insane, collapsing. A sick man flees, lodging is searched for him. Encountering father-in-law with a long beard. Since beards are prohibited in the ghetto, he had not been out in the street since the injunction. Is taken away. Situation of hostages (?). Patients who had left the hospital two days ago are tracked down, loaded onto the wagon, away . . . Reportedly all shot (?). Answer to inquiries: "This is for our blood." Interpretation: Events at the front!

The ghetto speaks of nothing else. Terrible depression despite 1 million kg of potatoes. Fear: What else lies ahead? For the High Holy Days? The Eldest is circumvented. He only heard about the *Aktion* one and a half hours after it began.—Infectious diseases: (all hospitals have been evacuated) housed in private lodgings: typhoid fever, dysentery, tuberculosis. Infectious and surgical wards will, so it is said, be set up. The doctors from the hospitals are wandering through the streets in despair.—Hospitals I, II, III, and IV converted into a ressort for joiners' work.—When somebody says "Only a miracle can save us," others present will shake their heads negatingly and make a gesture that means: "Nothing! Long live the devil. We no longer believe in redemption. We don't believe in miracles . . ."—On September 1, at eight o'clock in the morning, the Eldest in his cart drawn by white horses races through the Lagewnicka, in direction of hospital, his collar pulled up, a cap pulled deep over his face, a picture of misery and yet somehow of dignity at the moment of greatest responsibility. Those who had fled are ordered [back]. The sick had to report on September 2. Resister was shot as entering the Ashkenes' car.—Ashkenes commission visited the Baluter Ring—details unknown.

September 3. Wide discussion of blackout order. Noncompliance no longer punished with arrest but with severe beating.

Baluter Market. Central nerve of ghetto life. The entire ghetto apparatus is housed there. From there emanate all decrees, proclamations, that regulate the ghetto community. A square of three rows of houses framed by a rectangle, on the fourth side the electric train, German guards, opposite the Jewish police headquarters (Order Service, chairman of the Order Service, Rosenblatt),[6] this is where people are taken. The house of the Praeses next to Ashkenes.

The Praeses has a staff of assistants. Enormous pace. Quick decisions necessary. Receives order from outside and organization from within.

Secretary Dora Fuchs[7] controls all strings. Miss R. Wolk. Praeses high-pitched voice. Mood from laughing face, humor, Jewish humor. Some matters already settled partly in the anteroom, partly in office. The most important discussions—with the German authorities. The central office is hard at work issuing directives, receiving information, typewriters. Ceaseless telephoning.

Ceaseless import of goods from Litzmannstadt for the ghetto administration. From there to the various distribution centers in the ghetto. A narrow-track electric train line was built so the products could be dispatched more quickly. The central office supervises all work ressorts, chairman Aron Jakubowicz[8] supplies the raw materials and delivers everything to the Germans. [. . .]

Friday [September] 4. (Nine years, three hundred sixty-five days.) Conference with Ashkenes. By order from Berlin, outsettlement of all children between the ages of one and ten. Old people from sixty-five on without exception, also from the workshops. Official Weygand received the order to be carried out immediately within the next few days. This concerns about eighteen thousand souls. Potatoes being sealed away to avoid black marketeering. Exempt are policemen, doctors, and supervisors, and their children. A piece of paper from the old-age home to the office: "Please save me, the house is surrounded. Rosa Steiner, writer, Vienna." By eight o'clock already great excitement at the office, lack of will to work.

Detail: Begging on knees, *"Just not the children,"* but fruitless. The outpowering [O. R.'s word: *Auspowerung*] of the ghetto: At the church again hundreds of eiderdowns and pillows, at Hohe Brücke. Haste of those destined for outsettlement moving like an abject seamless queue—*never seemed more senseless.*

[September] 4, Friday. *New outsettlement. Children and old people.* Terrible heat. Proclamation. In the morning 8 kg potatoes, from September 11 to 30. But brings no joy. Outsettlement of children and old people. Rumors: In the Volborska,[9] Polish workers under German direction, setting up trenches. What for? In small pubs, people affected by children and parents: "See Pharao Mizrayim!" A nice Rosh Hashanah gift! Finally at two o'clock, posters: At 3:30 P.M., the Praeses and a few other gentlemen will discuss the evacuation at the Fire Brigade Square (Hamburger Strasse *tliah*). New hope. Rumors: children saved. Rumors: postponement by three months. All without foundation. Tomorrow, Saturday, all ressorts and shops closed. What about the lunch-time soup? New concerns. Women, weeping and hand wringing, besiege Kierowniki (director) to intervene. Praeses comes racing in his car. Incredible traffic on Hohe Brücke. Everything is boiling, seething. Behind the church wall eiderdowns and pillows, goose down. Working women are lying on them, some are eating their soup in the burning sun. Children call out their saccharine original, all hell has broken loose. Crowds, all around policemen, trying to calm. But mood desperate. What is still ahead of us? What is the Praeses going to say? Will he have a calming effect? By what means is the deportation carried out? [. . .]

Breakfast: 5 dkg of bread, noon: ressort soup: a *feast*—5 dkg coffee mixture, 1 dkg sugar. Preview of Praeses' speech: I feel for you, mothers and fathers, powerless . . . did everything to save the fifteen hundred children . . . tears in his eyes . . . Thousands of people Hamburger Strasse 13 . . . the crowd trembling, desperate: "We are the victims of those who were permitted to remain behind, also the children of the supervisors, policemen, etc." Did nothing to calm the crowd. Heavy atmosphere persisted. It was said that the Jew Gertler,[10] the middleman between ghetto and German authorities, went to Berlin to plead for alleviation, a postponement on behalf of the children. (Many later annulled.) None of the doctors, policemen, firemen, collaborators, were spared. Praeses: "Those who don't work must make room for the workers . . ."[11] Bitter cries from the crowd, even men. Before the Praeses, David Warshawski,[12] ressort supervisor, addressed the crowd in Yiddish, and Judge Jakobson[13] in Polish.—

Night from Friday to Saturday, November 5. Sobbing—screams neighborhood. Children taken away by Jewish policemen. Alarm, bombs, antiaircraft fire?! A warm night. Nobody is able to sleep, as before the end of the world. In the Zgierzka, Ashkenes voices, speaking of four bombs . . .

Saturday, September 5. Quiet morning. No midday soup . . . Will the intervention be successful. Are there exceptions? Day breaks, again hot, waiting in vain for thunderstorm. The evidence division is working toward outsettlement.—In the Sulzfelder, wagon with Jewish police who are to take away the children. The chief of the county Lask cart no. 1 for work use. "The Eldest of the Jews horse-drawn cart no. 7." Scenes. Mother ran out of the house trying to prevent police from entering. Police are driving people away from the front of the row of buildings. Terrible heat. At three o'clock yellow postings; proclamation: "General curfew from five o'clock until further notice. Exception: doctors, police, firefighters, and people with special passes. Violators will be evacuated." Grocery shops empty, street vendors with food have disappeared.—Religious people contemplating suicide. The human brain cannot comprehend it . . . Anybody who is going to survive this will suddenly find it all disappearing, and won't believe it himself . . .

Hunger, catastrophic since ressorts locked, therefore no midday soup. Bread partially consumed, next distribution not before Tuesday, September 8, 1942.

Sunday, September 6. Four o'clock in the morning the children. Lamenting and screaming next door. No human sounds, only animal mothers, bawling and whistling. Children themselves quiet, just whimpering. Until morning. No sign of life in the city; only the authorized, food workers, refuse workers, fecalists, doctors, called-up officials, firefighters, police, [people] with special passes, are allowed in the street. Terrible hunger. Exchange between man and wife: "If we could at least go together."

Blind rabbi: "Who will take care of him?" A dog has a dog tag, but husband and wife will be separated . . . What then? Another exchange: Ghetto gives no answers! To the "Why?" (*"Madua?"*) and "How much longer?" (*"Ad matai?"*) are added *"Whereto? Where are they sending us?"* The Eldest mentioned the number: thirteen thousand old people, eight thousand children, all in all twenty-one thousand, that is, 20 percent of the ghetto, to save 80 percent.—Children of the cadres also have to go, as well as those of the doctors, and others. Only the *children of the police* are exempt.

Henuschi. My thoughts are constantly with her.

From Pabianice: six tailors are still working there, and a Jewish coachman, 3 marks daily, working from five in the morning to seven at night.

Report: None of the old people were let go, only the eighty-four-year-old Mrs. Poznanska[14] (Marysin!).

Ghetto in the ghetto. Closed off from the world: no mail, no newspaper, no radio, no telephone, no gramophone. Ghetto created from five o'clock on September 5 *curfew.* Absolute: ghetto in the ghetto. Tuesday, September 8, bread distribution (!). One million kilograms of potatoes are stored. What will done with them? Bakeries are not working! What will happen? Will the ghetto starve to death? Human beings without provisions. In the house a mother with three children among them an infant without bread, potatoes, fat, vegetables.—The terror continues. No directives for expulsion yet. Children, the sick, the old are going at any rate—in contrast to the norm up to now. Mental abnormality. Terrible heat. Digested vegetables, cabbage half eaten by grubs. Fear that *Aktion* will be taken over by German authorities if the Jewish police is not up to it.—Whimpering from the lodgings continues. Everything up in the air. Longing for rain. Zgierzka too very weak, this Sunday Ashkenes go on excursions. Freedom. Never felt it as on Sunday, September 6, 1942.

Jeremiah 31:15ff. "Thus saith the Lord: A still small voice is heard in Ramah, lamentation, and bitter weeping, Rachel weeping for her children; she refuseth to be comforted for her children, because they are not . . ."

Sunday/Monday, {September} 7. Night of thunderstorm. Cool at daybreak. Policemen surround Zgierzka and buildings elsewhere on the double, break in. Take away children. In front of the entrance gates one-horse carts (lattice carts). Suddenly from the entrance gates weeping women, young girls, old women, driven onto carts, children thrown like packages. In front a field gray with whip, next to him soldiers, rifle, revolver, *steel helmet,* windows have to be closed, threats against faces behind the window, people picked up randomly. All ordered to line up in the yard. Full of questions (?), off. Hospital is said to be collection camp. Fear and dread in the ghetto. Monday, six o'clock in the evening, all is quiet.

Tuesday, 8. Said to be normal bread and ration distribution. Still no decision. Curfew. All are going hungry. Nothing to eat since early morning. What will come? No news whatsoever, not even rumors. Bread bakeries are said to have been working during the night. So bread today after all? Suddenly at three in the afternoon. Building supervisor: vegetable book and 1 chaimki for bread. Each person gets a loaf of bread. Later, bread card! Down in the yard and in neighboring yards, the building supervisors with blue bread cards, all around excitement among residents, profound quiet, overcast and rainy after five weeks of heat. What day is it? Date? Nobody knows. Already three days of house arrest. It's all brilliantly staged. "They had already surrounded our house and then moved on to the Franziskaner [Strasse] because the block was too small. They are to finish up today, only seven thousand people short. When they reach that goal, our house will be saved . . ." Rumors, speculation. Tired faces of the Jewish police. Some of them eat bread crusts, are hungry. Rumor that people are picked up by whim, therefore excitement even among the "protected." Question "Whereto?" is no longer being asked. Where are the children? Have the transports left the ghetto yet? . . . Questions! Fear of the night. In the yard restless residents, pacing back and forth. Two hours have passed already, no bread! And what tomorrow? Nothing to eat in the house.—

September 8–9. At night. Screams during sleep.—Neighbor service at the cemetery. Because of the curfew, none of the dead can be registered. Police are alerted and have corpses picked up by cart, directly to the cemetery. For days decaying bodies, withered, yellow, blue, swollen, stinking. Only name and street. An official has to inspect every corpse: 40 dkg of bread and 10 dkg of sausage. Doctor in Marysin. Death certificate: weakness of the heart, famine edema, among others, neighboring building surrounded since Tuesday the eighth.

Now September 9. Call at six in the morning: Get dressed, get down here! Putting on double and triple layers, without overcoat and hat, sudden cold. Lining up in the yard. Two dozen people, field gray with whip. Where do you work?—Where is your wife? Your daughter.—Pause. How old are you?—Pause. Wants to take me. Jewish commandant whispers something in his ear—saved. "The real old ones are going." Blind Rabbi Krakauer (Komotau) and wife. Conducting themselves heroically. Went without *siderl* [Yidd., prayerbook; Hebr., siddur]. Fortunately they are carrying some food and many layers of clothing. Still hope that they will stay here.—In the morning the twelve-year-old Rosenblum boy in our yard was hiding in the ruins of the house—shot to death by field gray with rifle—part of daily routine. Afternoon quiet. Inhabitants from the yard congratulate each other, as they emerge again here and there, for having been saved. Older gray-haired women appear: "God be praised . . . Mrs. X . . ." Tears in their eyes. Old people who had been hiding suddenly return to the houses, weak, nothing to eat for days, supported by relatives so they wouldn't collapse.—The presumed number of twenty-one thousand was already exceeded so that for the time being no further outsettlements are in the offing. Hunger is borne more easily after overcoming danger. Curfew still in effect. Millions of kilograms of potatoes are waiting. Tomorrow? Today borrowed 70 dkg of potatoes for midday and evening soup, prepared with flour, 20 dkg of bread already eaten, that means watch out. Dreary, rain. Alone in the apartment since the rabbi and wife were taken away. Maybe they'll still come back? Would make me happy—a flash of light that would be able to reconcile me with much. Smoked three cigarettes out of nervousness.

Intermezzo. Interaction with Ashkenes. 2x the week an Ashkenes is traveling with the Eleck [electric streetcar] *cross the Zgierzka in order to see his wife from the far. He is disappearing like he is been coming and he send to her money with jewish workers who are engaged in the City. A gallant gentleman* [original English].

September 9 in the evening. Curfew still in effect. No rations, no potatoes. A woman approaches me in the yard: "What is left for me in life? My twelve-year-old boy was shot today (Rosenblum), my two six-year-olds and fourteen-year-old girl were taken away." She sobs. Her husband comes out, figures à la Chagall, silent. Suddenly woman: "Sister mine," embracing her, touching scene, a young fellow, nephew, weeping with them.

People in the house congratulate me: Bender, Dr. Rabinow, Ginsbergerova, the young Eibuschütz, Dr. Laborat, Dr. Gelbart, several women from the building: "Why not color your moustache?" somebody asks (for younger appearance). Dusk descends. Groups in the yard: In front of you a ruin, to the right, outline of Litzmannstadt, left, a church.—Despite deepest depression, hope for *nezuchon-bituchon* [Hebr., certainty in the final victory].

Henuschi lies awake. What is she doing now? Is she working, is she contemplating? How does she live? Does she have news from Wilma and Erich?[15]—

September 10, Thursday. Still fright at every knock on the door. Unable to sleep: It's being said that patrol will come back once more. Many jumped from the carts and were saved, police looked the other way. With potatoes, flour, sugar, margarine. What is there to cook today?—Alarm in the night.—Rifle shots in the Zgierzka at night. What is going on?

Yesterday, Wednesday, a patient who had fled the hospital on September 1 was caught. An "evacuee" from Prague, a cripple. Testifies that Dr. Gelbart had aided him in his flight. Dr. Gelbart is arrested and shot on the spot.—Nothing is known about the transport. Still no rations! What will be tomorrow? Since August 20, I have been cooking for myself: soups, coffee, potatoes. Since autumn of the year before ghetto has decreased from one hundred sixty thousand to ninety thousand, of those twenty thousand died, fifty thousand were evacuated (first thirty thousand locals, then ten thousand from the West, now a mixed group of ten thousand).

September 10. Suddenly sun. I am washing my shirts, night robe, before that handkerchiefs. Another night of lying alone for a long time, unable to sleep. Fate of the Krakauers hard to bear. Dreaming in waking state of this couple. Thinking of siderl and tallith—tefillin bag.

Interesting conversation: "Has the number of twenty-one thousand been reached yet?" Uncertain. But the demands are escalating. Last year they demanded ten thousand.—The ten thousand were surrendered (double meaning) to them. Then more and more. That is why nobody knows what the next day will bring . . . Praeses was reportedly close to suicide (!).

September 11, Friday. Patrol in Marysin. Ashkenes supposedly marching through streets shooting at groups of people. Second patrol is still awaited in our complex. Absolute terror. I too very agitated, cold shivers despite sun. I already scrubbed the toilet, cleaned the garbage bucket, took it down, cooked, washed, ironed. Stomach cramps, attacks of diarrhea, am smoking a lot. Potatoes 8 kg + 4 kg (work), but unable to cash in because of curfew. *A car like all prison cars* with little window visible, packed with people who had probably been taken from their lodgings and taken to the central prison for further transport. Fear and dread, because of Erev [Hebr., evening] Shabbat and Erev Rosh Hashanah. Been reading a lot in Tanach [Hebrew Bible], especially Devarim [Deuteronomy] (laws, blessings, and curses). Unfortunately, lost Rabbi Krakauer . . . Could the danger have been avoided? No, for the order came from Berlin. Voices are heard: "Tribute! Ransom money! The bank of the Eldest has enough jewelry and gold, rugs and furs, etc. . . ." Rumor: It's being negotiated. Rumor: Children will be released at the last moment. Today, Friday, sixth day of curfew. Not a trace of change. The streets are deserted. A few anxious people behind the windows, waxen faces, silent. Atmosphere as after a pogrom. All that happened is still incomprehensible. What happened some time ago with the gypsies? Will I see my friend, my father, my brothers and sisters, again tomorrow? Nobody knows anything of the others' fate. Field-gray police cars are racing through Zgierzka. Nothing eaten besides bread soup. It's four-thirty. Hanging washing out to dry. Wilma, Ernst, Erich, what is happening to them? Do they have any idea?

September 12. *Henuschi more and more deeply concerned.* Five o'clock in the morning. Get up! Revision. Got dressed at dawn, cooked coffee. Lining up in the yard, then to the Altmarkt Square. Staged flight beforehand. Commandant tells me: "Don't do that, you'll get shot." Giving up plan, back to the yard, street, groups. Ashkenes grouped together in neighboring buildings, pulled people out, onto the cart, pushed me aside, saved. This is how we are standing on Altmarkt Square for two hours. Back home! Going with father . . . [name illegible], gut Shabbes [Yidd., good Shabbat]—Yom Tov—going to bed, sleep hopeless. Cooking barley with flour.—Colored my moustache and hair brown with coffee.

Talkie. Police announces: Somebody is in the throes of death upstairs. Ashkenes: You'll guarantee on your head that the man will be dead by noon.—Second case: A seriously ill man in bed, Ashkenes pulls revolver, shoots him point-blank, parents pulled away, five-year-old child remains; three carts pulled up, filled with people, Goodbye!—May God help.

Sholem Aleichem: May God help, that God may help!—An actor disguised as excrement leader locks himself in the dung cart, unrecognizable, saved.—Shabbat, noon. Cooking barley. What lies in store? The end or another patrol? Rabbi Krakauer's fate?!—

The seven members of the rabbinate (rabbis of Łódź) arrested and sent away together with the ritual slaughterers and slaughter supervisors. Considered to be dispensable. Ghetto is to be called "work camp." Transformation, may even be alleviation. Five o'clock in the afternoon. Waiting for potatoes 8 + (5 kg). Waiting for 25 dkg of pot cheese according to work card.—Unknown woman crying, her mother and children had been taken away. Begs. Receives dry mix of coffee.—Everybody is waiting for six o'clock. First day of Rosh Hashanah. Tomorrow, Sunday, maybe the curfew will be lifted. Haven't left my room for a week.—Thirteen thousand had presumably already been transported by this morning.—

Ration for everybody, no special coupons for workers, bread for six days (!). At last some sugar and margarine, but when can we go pick them up?

Two proclamations: Six o'clock proclamation that the curfew is lifted.

Proclamation ghetto administration, signed by Biebow (first proclamation from this functionary in the ghetto). Starting with the fourteenth of this month, again normal work schedule since the outsettlement action is completed.

Biebow proclamation: *"The now recognized workforce,"* that is, those who work, "are protected and will be adequately fed." Calm since the hospital really turned into joiner ressort. Eldest proclamation of September 13: Improved provisions, prohibition of trading in foodstuff, protection of the lodgings of the outsettled from looting.

A nightmare receded. People are coming out into the streets. All full of life, timid, but nevertheless again movement. We learn that all evacuees were taken to Litzmannstadt by cart or truck, no further details. Some were set free. End of outsettlement?[16]

Eldest: Women who were standing hungry in front of the potato storage place on Hanseaten Strasse issued 1 kg free.—Night rest.

September 13, Sunday. Cool day. Thousands in front of the shops to pick up their rations after seven days of curfew and starvation. They exchange greetings, wishing a good new year, as after an earthquake or a shipwreck. All went well? Who was taken? From me brother. From me mother. From me parents. From me children.

Talkie. A field gray tears a child from a young woman. "Leave me my child or shoot me." The field gray pulls his revolver. "I'll ask *you* three times whether you want me to shoot." He asks three times, each time she answers "yes"—shoots the woman point-blank. A few people come up and take the corpse away.—Terrible tragedies are gradually becoming obvious. Ghetto has twenty thousand fewer inhabitants. Hoping "*work camps.*" Desperate and starved people are hoping for an end soon, their only interest is food. It's all like a dream. Dark week. Nothing like this ever before. Today Sunday. Field grays with families driving through Zgierzka on an excursion.—Ban on mail persists: book, newspaper, radio, mail, letter, instrument. Everybody one meets, a second life. A resurrected friend: Dr. Josef Lamm,[17] and his wife, unheard-of, incredible. Saved like newborns, like hidden coming out of hiding places, returned to the light. Tomorrow, Monday, again *soups* from the kitchens, new hope for life!

September 14, Monday. Workday. Our division, "evidence," remains temporary. Big rush on the rations.

Talkie episodes. Polish worker at the wire to Jewish policemen who have loaded the children: "Aren't you ashamed to sacrifice your brothers like that? It will come over you someday." Woman, early in the morning—forgetful—works in the potato field, shot to death. [. . .]

After the outsettlement no sign of emotion for lack of experience, no reflex for such an unfamiliar occurrence. Cosmic like an earthquake.

Eighteen executions on Bazarna Square[18] Monday the seventh at noon, allegedly fled from the work camp and smugglers. Tagonorka ordered the gallows from a field gray on Baluter Ring. Jewish police did its job. Nobody talks about it.

One opens eyes wide, awake. Are you here? Fear of knocking on neighbors' doors. Potatoes 10 marks, three pieces of saccharine 1 chaimki.

Hunger during the outsettlement! Seven days without receiving food. How people in the building help each other. Much cooperative spirit.

Fourteen thousand five hundred people evacuated, ghetto now eighty-nine thousand inhabitants.

Daily routine, in a dream, lost in thought. Everywhere the question: How is the ressort soup going to be today? And the eyes shine: 40 dkg potatoes in each soup, wonderful! The Eldest has given the order for better middays (soups) from now on! [. . .]

Ashkenes soldiers outside the ghetto permitted a few Jews who had fled from evacuation to run away.

The hospital was evacuated on September 1; until September 16 nobody will know who was carried off and who is still in the ghetto.

September 16. Rumors about outsettlement on October 1, from sixty-five on up, cannot be verified. Vegetables arrived. Cabbage, radishes, parsley, pickles.—Commandant Rosenblatt is staying with us because his brother-in-law, a fellow lodger, has dysentery. I sleep, cook, do washing, ironing, in the kitchen.—Rumors about the situation outside. Are we at the beginning of another winter campaign?

Outsettlement. Talkie. Jewish police robbed [victims] during outsettlement and at the same time made it possible for many to be saved.

September 17. *Talkie.* Rumors of new outsettlement. Six Gestapo men kept one hundred thousand Jews in check during the outsettlement.—Rumors that the outsettled were taken to Litzmannstadt. From there clothing brought back here as used material. Apparently all gassed as "unusable," that is, no longer alive.[19] Of course, unable to learn anything positive. Intervention at this point is useless.—The pillows, that is, bed-feather warmth, for warm vests for Ashkenes military winter campaign.—Sensation: Bones in the ressort soup! However, the bouillon goes to the kitchen personnel.

September 18. *Outsettlement.* During the outsettlement actions, sixty in the ghetto fell victim to shootings and hangings. Rumor: Seventeen executions in Bazarna, three shootings in the cemetery, the rest while standing in line for potatoes on Hanseaten Strasse (Lagewnicka).

September 19. Children presumed to be in the town of Wieluń (near Kalisz), under supervision of Jewish women. Other version has it that they are in Poznan for blood transfusions. Similar assumptions already made during winter evacuation. Nothing is heard about the older people. Sudden cold spell.

September 20. Erev Yom Kippur [Eve of Day of Atonement, highest Jewish holiday]. For several days air raid alarm. A final decision is presumed imminent. Everywhere discussions about the possibility of a winter campaign. Foreboding of frost to minus 35 degrees [Celsius].—Many mothers had been hiding their children and had gone in their place. Now deliberations what to do with these children.—Rumor that tomorrow, Monday, Yom Kippur, all rabbis will be taken to the *tliah.*

September 21, Yom Kippur.—Terrible. Diarrhea all day. All factories have been working.—Cholent instead of soup for the first time, but didn't eat it because of stomach. Cold nights, early frost, feeling miserable despite *very good news* [original English].—

Henuschi: What is she doing today?

NOTEBOOK F

September 16, 1942. *Draft of a "Cultural History of the Ghetto."*[1] During the world war, the Germans set about to discover Eastern European Jewish life, to preserve it, to capture the folklore in its immediacy, and to apply it to their cultural studies by leaving them their freedom.—But as they marched into Łódź, world war, they sang antisemitic songs. See "Vilnaer Troupe," Arnold Zweig, Dehmel, German Theater, "Dybbuk."

Now memorizing, using, effacing, destroying, giving a different morphological form, distorting, crippling, presenting to the world as the ugly parasite, and wanting to liberate. "Work camp," to make the Eastern Jew work, elevate him to the German work ideal.—(To show the way to a police state, autonomy under force of circumstances.)—The Jews want to break the encirclement (see private sale of foodstuff, street sale, sales cooperatives) . . . First determine the morphological structure of Jewish life in Łódź: important *rate of mortality, occupation levels,* also with regard to relation to Germans and Poles, outward form, social outlook, Manchesterism, *longing to go abroad.*

Now (insert): no industrialization, mechanization, socialization, coordination, since no desire to take over means of production. Occupational change took place, though, but without technical or mental retraining, *without schooling.* Amateurish and yet achieved much, due to adaptation of talent. Precisely because all regimentation is absent.

No factory work: Tradition is lacking, freedom of those who place the orders, freedom of those who carry them out, joyous pride in work, desire to continue it, personal taste, love of material.

Everything dominates us: fear of not finishing, desire for a workplace, craving to fill stomach.

Child labor: Missing is the home atmosphere. Barely leaving workplace, again ghetto misery. No models, no school. No pride in work.

Above all haven't seen, any *form,* learned. For these children the world does not have the face of reality.

All other workers: They don't see the purpose of their work, don't experience the effect of their hands' creation. The product is alien to them. No mental connection between creator and creation, no relation of master to his work as a shoemaker takes pride when he has finished a pair of shoes.

Competition: He doesn't strive. Cannot advance, build a career, just wants to keep his workplace. Concern: How will the soup be? [. . .]

September 21 and 22. Read *Sayings of the Fathers,* immensely rich, use as motto here and there. Clear contrast to Nazism, understandable enmity against Ivri. [. . .]

An important factor that determines the structure, the mood, in the ghetto, curiosity, melancholy: is *deafness of the soul,* ingratitude, alienation from the time, more refined Jews do not exist, not on the surface. Total morphological transformation.

September 23. Heard that all factories will have to work on Yom Kippur. In shirts, gloves—in the apron camp Franziskanska (Baniu), hundreds of Eastern Jews were shopping on YK, no Western Jew was to be seen. Hardening of the human spirit, deafness of the heart, alienation. Basest mentality doesn't matter. What kind of human beings are these? Terrible: downcast, melancholy, sobering. Say something about this: picture in the streets, thefts.

Today rain, thinking of Zurich four years ago, return to Prague. Henuschi was startled—there began the evil.

September 23. Got box of shoe polish in the office. Walking with doctor along the wire Zgierzka. Police come up to us, reminding us to walk very *quickly* because otherwise danger.—Ashkenes orders all prescriptions from the pharmacy, looking for acute illness or *suffering.* Danger of deportation for suffering—what craftiness.

September 23. Suddenly a lot of Polish workers have come to the ghetto. What for?

September 25. *Outsettlement. Talkie.* Children torn away. Horse-drawn cart drove off, mother remains sitting in the corner. Father takes tallith and *tefillin,* whereupon mother to kitchen work, before then packed and stored children's clothing and other things in a bundle. [. . .]

September 25. Shabbat. Eve and Sukkot [Feast of Booth, in remembrance of the exodus from Egypt]. Large quantities of potatoes arrived, 5 kg of vegetables (4 kg turnips and 1 kg radishes) per head especially. Received special rations, among them 10 dkg of butter, sago and baked goods, zwieback.—Terrible diarrhea, ghetto sickness for the second time.—

Talkie. The female conductors of the electric streetcar—in men's clothing and coquettish caps covering their long blond hair—look up into the ghetto windows when driving through Zgierzka. Excellent mood today since going to *Neila* [Hebr., closing; service ending Yom Kippur], according to feeling.—

Prices decreased: one loaf of bread 50 chaimki, 1 kg sugar 50 chaimki, trying to get rice and coffee against dysentery—at all cost. Tomorrow, Saturday, I'll give reading of novella "The Secret of the Ghetto," that is, Prague-Łódź. Looking forward to it. It's being said that the Kripo is inspecting houses for hygiene.—Planning to read today for the first time by electric light in the evening.—Thousands of cases of typhus.—Reports about the last group that was expelled: supposedly being fed in Poland, alive.—Dr. Natanssen visits quite often, is in a good mood.—Home in Marysin still functioning.—Praeses through the streets on foot, crowd gawking at the man in high-heeled boots, he chases them off with loud voice, painful scene.

September 26. Shabbat and Sukkot. Haftorah [Hebr., conclusion; reading from the Prophets], Zechariah 14. For October: 13 kg potatoes. Breathing sigh of relief. What comes after, what in between, unimportant. We'll hold out. No more fear, not even of the winter frost = 6 kg coals and 4 kg peat.

September 27, Sunday. Nighttime alarm.—Since the last outsettlement all proclamations and all work in the office in German language.—Fingers worn and rough—brutal from peeling potatoes.

September 28, Monday. Leaving house, Church Square, man and woman are sweeping fallen leaves, *autumn* mood: absolutely no seasons . . . what fallen leaves . . . what fallen leaves as little in the heart as blossoms . . . nothing touches me . . . thousands of people at the break of dawn, like beggars with soup cans. . . .

Zechariah 14:1: Behold a day of the Lord cometh, when thy spoil shall be divided in the midst of thee.[2]

September 29. The size of the ghetto is being reduced. The area of Franziskanska will be cut off in favor of Ashkenes. Renewed evacuation of thousands within twenty-four hours. New lodgings being assigned to them. A big tumult. The commission is working. In addition, establishment of new ressorts, for this as well, dislodgings.—Terrible Jewish police, a special category of human being, brutal, criminal. The spirit of the tormentor, fearing their own caste, moral censure—"Guardians of the City" . . . decide what is good and what is bad . . . collaborating with the official criminals . . . they are called by name. Somebody calls out, *"Wos stajt ihr du, ganoven, gajt awek, gajt ahejm"* [Yidd., "What are you standing around here for, you thugs, go away, go home"] at the men loitering in front of the potato- and coal-storage place.—

Face of the Ghetto. **September 1942.** In the morning when people rush over bridges and through streets to work, the observer does not have the feeling of being among Jews. Petit bourgeois types and proletarians from the East or the Balkans, just like the ghetto city itself: physiognomy, in clothing, in gait . . . The sweeping gestures are absent, the loud voices are absent, as, for instance, among Italians, the French, Spaniards, or even people from the Balkan area. The atmosphere is dampened, oppressive, only on occasion explosive. Goethe's saying "the language of the Jews is language with pathos" is not valid here because the *pathos* has disappeared completely from their lives and reemerges only sporadically.—The faces are dull.—Most ardent wish: "Not to have to eat any more soups" (called here the "middays"), no more liquid stuff—nothing can be read in them [the faces], not even suffering. Predominantly Slavic types. The "Eastern Jew" as in Yiddish literature and painting (Chagall et al.) no longer exists. Absent are side curls, beard, kaftan, velvet hat, peaked caps; even *tsitsit* [Hebr., prayer fringes] are nowhere visible. Since there's no piety, almost no studying of Thora and Talmud, a certain gleam is missing in their eyes too, reverence and absorption, dreamers of the ghetto—an obsolete romantic concept. The ponderous boy, the teaching elder—only somewhere in secret . . . A sukkah [booth] had been put up for a dozen Chassidim, otherwise no trace of *Yomim Neroyim* [Hebr., Days of Awe, High Holy Days], of Sukkot, in the ghetto.—What will happen on Simchat Torah?[5]—Today for the first time.

Thinking of Henuschi, made coffee, aroma, remembering Henuschi, her morning coffee, also still in Prague.—Ghetto in good spirits. Potatoes, cabbage, turnips, rolling without interruption. I myself feel as before an impending tragedy . . . suddenly . . . catastrophe Ashkenes . . . and what then?

Horror talkie. I'm starting to hoard for fear that in case of collapse there won't be any replenishing for a long time.—Prices have fallen, bread 50 to 60 marks, 1 dkg onions 1 chaimki, no fear of hunger and cold! Potatoes 3 chaimki, but garlic 2 marks per dkg.

September 30. *For "The Secret of the Ghetto." Ghetto finished.* A group of Jews across from the potato distribution on Hanseaten Strasse; a boy with rotten teeth, lying on the ground, a grin on his face; an old man, bald, traces of *payes* [Yidd., sidelocks] visible; women in head scarves, flour carriers, coal carriers, loitering figures, cart with horse—hearse pulls up. Coachman, the *grober* [Yidd., gravedigger]. The old man asks: "For whom have you come?" "Somebody will be found, don't worry. We've enough corpses in the ghetto!" "And who will come for you, coachman?" "Nobody needs to come for me. I'll have my mare take me to Marysin. She'll take me there without a coachman. She knows the way. And then, she is the best mourner. She'll certainly come. Whether relatives will come to the burial is uncertain. My mare will accompany me, I can count on her, hee-oh . . ."—A hot day, potatoes and vegetables with interruption.—Strict blackout, have to prepare water and sand.—

October 1. Getting up at five-thirty at the break of dawn—washing.—For the first time in the ghetto cholent at the bakery, excellent: peas, potatoes, meat, garlic, onions, oil, paprika, salt, eight hours in the oven. Cooked vegetables, potato goulash, etc., by myself for the first time.

Humor: When does an inhabitant of Łódź eat chicken? Either when *he* is sick or when the *chicken* is sick.

October 2. Daily question: "What's new in the ghetto?" In contrast to what is going on outside, about which only rumors!

In the decrees (proclamations) the phrase "ghetto inhabitant"! A particular race!—

Suicide, fifty-year-old local resident, from the fourth floor Lagewnicka out of desperation, couldn't bear life any longer . . . nervous breakdown, no positive motive.

October 3. Thirteen kilograms potatoes, for November and December, 13 kg potatoes each. Concern about storing them—the leaders are riding in their cars, personal and proud—the strange sect of human beings who are ruling in and over the ghetto.—Work hours from eight in the morning to eight at night.

Germanization of the ghetto = All reports in *German. Sonnabend* [Germ., Saturday]. Street name. However, now only in letters and numbers. For example, O, P, R, or, 6, 4. German is easy because it's the basis of Yiddish. Tragic situation that Jews are carrying with them the medieval German argot until 1942. During first occupation of Poland 1914, similar fate. If it were Polish or Hebrew, the situation would be different. Misfortune: German education, affinity for Ashkenes culture. *Goethe, Spinoza.* Caption under Spinoza's picture: "Signum reprobationis in vultu gerens"—"Carrying the sign of depravity in the face." Goethe to this: "This could, of course, not be denied when looking at the picture; for the copper etching was terribly bad and outright hideous, whereby I was reminded of adversaries who will distort first anybody who is the target of their ill-will and then oppose him as a monster" (*Dichtung und Wahrheit* 14 B).

October 3. Strike of the women who peel potatoes in the kitchens since their second soup had been withdrawn.

Spinoza. Secret. The masses venerate the books of the Bible more than the word of God itself. ("You," says Reb Yossel, "venerate the word of your leaders more than the word of God, and that's why you must perish, run afoul of your Jew hatred.")

October 3. Shabbat: For the first time officially working on Shabbat. New rule: from eight to eight, twelve hours.

October 4. A new expression for God: "*The one with washed hands,*" the being that I am not allowed to name because I haven't washed my hands yet.

October 5. *Talkie.* Yesterday Simchas Toire [Yidd., feast of Torah joy; Hebr., Simchat Torah] as a guest at Praszkier's.[3] Beautiful service with a *chasen* [Yidd., cantor], called up to the Tojre [Torah], with three Sefer Tojres around the table as back home, rolled together, *hagbe* [Yidd., lifting of the Torah; Hebr., *hagba*] and *aliye* [Yidd., going up to the Torah; Hebr., *aliyah*]. Then a meal: schnaps, cholent (barley, peas, potatoes, meat), aspic, chopped red cabbage, coffee with honey cakes, Yiddish and Polish songs; Zionist Caro[4] about Simchat Torah. Judaism and Jews won't vanish, in the end there is always immediately a beginning, thus eternity, no enemy can destroy us . . . Beautiful atmosphere, time spent wonderfully Jewish, thought much of Henuschi, even of her meatloaf . . .

October 6. *Talkie.* Ashkenes with a rifle and Ashkenes in civilian clothing with a briefcase beating passersby off the sidewalk.

October 7. The end is in the air. When? Uninterrupted potato supply. Rumor that Ashkenes want to keep them for themselves? . . . In case Łódź is bombarded and the ghetto isn't.—No more bread for the last two days. What would Henuschi say to this?

October 8. Cool after wonderful summer days, Polish autumn. Many suicides.—Typhoid fever in the building, three cases.—When will this end? Everybody says: "When the war is over . . ."—New vegetable allocation. Prices: bread 65, sugar 70, tomatoes 12, pot cheese 70, coffee 400, vegetable and potatoes are falling. Some ressorts (saddle makers because of lack of leather) curtailed, whereas straw shoes [ressort] was expanded. Still working for Ashkenes. In the tailoring (ladies') ressort perfect products of good material made by Jewish women for the department stores[5] of the Ashkenes.

October 9. Terrible news: It is said that six hundred thousand were deported from Warsaw. Ten human beings have already arrived here. No known details. Here, great excitement, since the same is feared despite balance in the ghetto between work and production apportionment.—We've been living in the shadow of death for three years . . . since September 1939 many Jews have been shot to death by Ashkenes . . . Gone through a lot . . . What meaning do little details have in face of death, who is always standing at the door? Petty things! Constantly under threat, any moment can bring death . . . chased away, shot, starved, beaten to death by the thousands . . . Every day new victims . . . The closer the end, the greater the danger . . .—

Evacuation Warsaw. Dreary, rainy, cool . . . Bitter disappointment about predictions of the end . . . Today 26 kg potatoes for November and December.—News from Warsaw. Of the remaining four hundred ninety thousand Jews all but about thirty thousand were lately evacuated, families totally atomized, deliberately, completely. Dissolution of this *Yishuv* [Yidd./Hebr., Jewish community]. Up to now relatively free life, of late establishment of ressorts, ressort participants living in closed circles, taken to work by leaders and brought back, workday from seven in the morning to six in the evening. However, freer life: business with Poles, trade with profit, entertainment, coffeehouses, restaurants, Yiddish theater, Polish theater in the Jewish quarter, bars, dancing, elegant women, etc. Since the situation has apparently become critical, fear for Ghetto Łódź. Six people from Warsaw arrived. Everybody here is upset. Proclamation Biebow of October 9: "Warning: Whether it's a matter of petty theft in the ressorts or food ressorts and so on, whether against war economy or food supply, I shall take strictest measures. Signed: Biebow."

(In the afternoon the housing commission appears! Fear that I must evacuate apartment! Terrible, shortly before winter. [. . .]

October 12. Must suddenly evacuate apartment; furniture gone, bed in the kitchen, sleeping there *today* for first time. Going to move to Hohe Brücke. Depression as never before because of rumors: Marysin census taking?! Building of barracks for potatoes or for concentration camp? The Eldest is said to be curtailed, the whole ghetto administration taken over by German authorities. Will it get better? Work ressorts expanded for war effort, on the other hand, decrease of officials?—I'll sell everything and eat! Cooked and ate potatoes three times today.

Face of the Ghetto. Cold autumn. No more sandals, no more bare feet. Loud clanking: wooden shoes . . . goat hide, but also summer coats . . . beggar figures who have nothing to wear. Soon dark . . . All stairwells dark, no light because of blackout. People walk through puddles, sewage, dirt . . . Horrified expressions because horrifying things are expected again . . . Gradually again faces, as last winter, pale, yellow, mummies in tatters, clanking of the wooden shoes, yellow skin, grayish black clothing, filthy whitish gray surroundings . . . [. . .]

October 15. Apartment in Zgierzka 24/4, for the time being fallen through. Have to see Praeses on the seventeenth. [. . .]

I am sleeping and living in the kitchen. Terrible existence . . .

Laws in the ghetto. Whatever isn't taken care of immediately won't be taken care of at all.

See: my apartment!—Everybody wants it. For small favors the ghetto dweller demands *revenge,* doesn't let go. First he offers his help, then he demands compensation, that is, a favor in return. Reading Schiller, prose, am captivated by this brilliant storyteller.

October 16. *Hunger. Death. Bridge.* When it was being built the Ashkenes didn't think how much effort would be put into surmounting it. Bridge weakens the human being, decimates, many perished in the achievement: bridge. But not meant as a perfidious design, otherwise they would have built the bridge even higher. Some have to pass the bridge six times daily, sometimes carrying heavy burdens.

October 17. Awaiting German commission for inspection of ressorts. Gray-haired people and children should not go out into the street in the next few days. For fear of *chappen* [Yidd., being caught] and being sent away. Dark mood. New allocation of potatoes for January, February, March = 39 kg on credit (11.9 chaimki).

October 18. Again desperate mood: In Marysin fencing in of Jews under Ashkenes' direction. Wooden, latticelike, with barbed wire, very tight, charged with electrical current, cut off from the other part of the ghetto. Nobody knows anything, and added to this is the fact that part of the cemetery wall has been breached and embedded in this construction. Fear of preparations for the great *nekume* [Yidd., revenge]!!!—I don't show my face in the street.—Cold, shivering, taking powder, constantly thinking of Henuschi, Wilma, Erich. When will the end come? We are all again in danger of losing our lives. Everybody is trembling, children and old people are being sent home for a few days from the ressorts.—Eldest still in the old position. Rumors about abdication apparently unfounded. Passed letter along to him because of the apartment, living in the kitchen is a torment—sleeping, cooking, eating, cleaning, studying, writing, storing potatoes, etc. Long term cannot be predicted. Air raid exercises under German supervision, many streets blocked off.—Hailstorm in the afternoon.—Prewinter.

October 19. Cold day. Summer suit. In Marysin 100 wagonloads of potatoes have been buried. Not distributed until April 1, 1943. Poles too drive through Zgierzka, very poorly dressed, serious faces, some cast a melancholy glance at the human beings behind the bars.—Stories are told about Warsaw: within one week five hundred thousand Jews were evacuated. Jewish police surrounded the block of buildings. People chased as they were found onto trucks holding three hundred people and taken away, whereto? Fearing for ghetto in winter. Eight thousand people are now working in the straw shoe ressort (straw wrappings for military shoes), Russian front winter campaign. Highest priority.—Air raid exercises under German supervision with Jewish police and firefighters, parts of the ghetto blocked off.

NOTEBOOK G

Notes for Remembering (remains manuscript)

October 26, 1942

October 20, 1942. More air raid exercises. In the very early morning parts of the ghetto blocked off. Soldiers near Hohe Brücke. Local traffic. Gigantic masses of people are making their way to work in the ressorts, soldier threatens with rifle when doesn't move along smoothly.—Cold.—Rushing to the office.—Evening in the dark kitchen. Having evening meal standing up or sitting on my bed in the dark. Light in the foyer, there I read Spinoza, "Theological-Political Tractate," bright and clear as nature, but for the last few days again horrified.—[. . .]

October 21. Frost on the rooftops. Winter. Still no place to live. Strictest blackout. Fear of bombings.—Reading Schiller. Prose. Freezing in the office. Cold, fever.

Eighty-nine thousand inhabitants, twenty-eight deaths, one birth. Stomach typhus continues to spread, three thousand official cases registered, more than two thousand kept secret, meaning more than 6 percent of the inhabitants have typhus. Despite cold, number of deaths has decreased since September from fifty to thirty; invalids, children, old people, evacuated. These fifteen thousand also must be regarded as dead. [. . .]

October 22. Mortality statistics January 1, 1942 . . . , 162,681 residents in the ghetto; 1,787 died between January and March 1942 . . . 142,079 reside in the ghetto; 2,244 died in March (1,411 men, 833 women), 72 human beings a day, 3 an hour. If compared to London with its 8 million inhabitants, this would be 3,800 a day, 1 million a year. On October 21, 1942, 89,000 in the ghetto. [. . .]

October 24. *Shabbat*—rain, bleak.—Dr. Kamenetzky[1] intervenes on my behalf with Eibuschütz[2] for coupon. Gigantic potato front, police real criminals who work over people with fists and clubs, yelling, trembling children carrying sacks on heads and backs as protection against rain, picture of wretchedness. [. . .]

See notebook "Studies." Eldest: two profiles. One: smooth, clean, calm, benevolent, religious, Jewish-traditional; the other: an enigma, sardonic smile, sly, crafty, deceitful = to be illuminated more closely as a character, after that, duplicitous actions, changing moods, sudden decisions, and, therefore, surprises. [. . .]

Bread Talkie. After the evacuation of September 1942, the closest relatives fell over the bread of the departed, in part without shedding a tear. Best friends feel no pain. Terrible coarsening of character and hardening of hearts. People don't answer questions.—[. . .]

Hunger. The mortality among men is three times that of women since the women have always been eating less than the men. We are living against the laws of medicine.—A miracle that with this kind of nutrition some of us are still alive, without albumen, carbohydrates, vitamins, etc. *Lack* of B-vitamins (since we are getting no albumen).

October 27, 1942. Couldn't sleep because of concern about a place to live. Have been told to move out of the kitchen. Warmed up potatoes in the early morning darkness and ate them for breakfast. Warmer day in the offing. Severe heart problems. Intervention. Housing department? What will be? How soon the end? Still have much to do on my work. Bleak mood despite good news from abroad, that is, rumors.

Soup. "Ressortka" is the name of the ardently desired. People in front of the entrance. "Do you have a midday to sell?" I don't answer, continue on my way. Costs 3 chaimki. From now on I'll be able to get good portions due to protection. Potatoes and vegetables are still rolling into the ghetto.—The Eldest is deeply concerned, downcast, unavailable. I am desperate over the lodging. For the time being, intervention not possible. In Marysin wagonloads of potatoes daily, furthermore, carrots, water turnips, radishes. Night work 40 dkg of bread and one soup; presumably distribution is already for April, May, June. [. . .]

October 28. Early in the morning at seven o'clock, several thousand wooden shoes clank across the bridge like prison inmates, nobody says a word, like corpses come alive, like ghosts clad in human clothing. The moon appears close as the sky gains color. Bridge flanked by hollering Jewish police, German field-gray guards at the white-red-black guard post are silent.

Henuschi thinks of *zlata Praha* [Czech, golden Prague].

October 29. Thirty deaths, five births, two stillbirths. Suicide rate is rising. Eighty-eight thousand eight hundred six inhabitants in the ghetto. *Potato front.* Masses, divided into groups and lead by police, move up to the gate near the scale. Scenes of beatings, mother with children, each one with a sack or rucksack or big basket, tired, weak, since six in the morning, many former lawyers, professors, musicians, etc. Some line up for days, even in the rain. Now warm night, wonderful sunny day.—Suicides with Luminal by Western Jews who carried poison with them. [. . .]

November 2. The whole ghetto in upheaval over potatoes from Marysin. Everywhere sacks being carried on backs, even children, on little carts, in baby carriages. Even on the excrement cart. The streetcar brings sacks of potatoes for a select few. Almost everybody has already consumed the November–December potatoes, I among them.—Ghetto administration (Biebow) gradually takes over the most important ressorts. "Signs—Eldest . . ." are disappearing. Yellow-black replaced by white-blue. Causes nervousness.—Plan to incorporate part of Brzezinska [Street] into the German part of Litzmannstadt was canceled, but Jewish residents are being evacuated from the buildings. Everywhere carts with furniture, people suddenly evicted from their apartments and placed somewhere.—Wonderful days, warm, sunny, soft leaves like back home.

Wintertime introduced, clock set back an hour.

Mood in the ghetto depressed for fear of winter and Ashkenes. Measures.—Balfour Declaration twenty-five years.[3] [. . .]

November 3. *Outsettlement.* Mrs. Caspari[4] gets paper of exemption from outsettlement. Everybody lines up outside in the yard. Jewish police take away the paper, hand it to another woman, who is freed for a bribe.

Attempt of husband to save his wife, to no avail. Police claims that Ashkenes tore up the paper. This is probably a lie. Professor asks me: "Do you think my wife is still alive?" I have no answer. [. . .]

Slogans of the Eldest according to Calendar Year 1942 (5702)

Don't walk along the wire. Don't sell the coupons for children and the sick.—To my last breath I shall look out for you.—Ghetto thieves will be pilloried.—In the ghetto, you cannot be working by the clock.—You are my only joy, my children!—We will share with you every bite (special coupon for members of the board!).—Newly arrived Jews are our brothers and sisters (hatred of Eastern Jews against *Yekke* [Yidd., jesting—derisive word for German Jews] and Daitsch [Yidd., Germans]).—Our work is our subsistence (wages, minimum, "chaimki" against reichsmark, inferior goods—ersatz). Nobody in the ghetto has [is allowed] to go hungry. (Speech of September 19, 1940.) Litzmannstadt Ghetto is a world (a work, a creation).—I want to be the orderly guardian of the ghetto (April 30, 1940).—I'll know how to deal with those who seek to damage the ghetto.—Young people must learn a trade. For the sake and for the benefit of the ghetto you all must walk in my path.—The problem of the ghetto dominates my whole being.—I shall not deviate one iota from my program.—

Other remarkable statements and episodes: Private property does not exist in the ghetto.—I cover my budget with work and requisitions!—The special commando does very good work of detecting hidden valuables.—Praeses tells about attempts on his life, also with knife . . . , but he would not let go! Children follow him with "bah, bah . . ." In 1940 until November 1941, more than 1 million chaimki in welfare money (from 8 to 16 chaimki per head upward of age categories).—

November 4. *One year in the ghetto. "Bituchen of an eck mehejro beyomejno"* [Hebr./Yidd., "Trust in an end yet in our day"]. There is no clock. The clock in the tower of St. Mary's Church shows permanently five o'clock! No noon bell ringing, no time.—Clocks and shoes in demand. No furs since they are prohibited.

Reading in the ghetto. Albrecht and Joachim Prinz: *History of the Jews;*

Spinoza: *Theological-Political Tractate;* Hess: Rome and Jerusalem; Pinsker: *Autoemancipation.* Haeckel: *World Enigma;* J. J. Rousseau: *Confessions;* five volumes of an art history; novellas by Turgenyev and Gorki; Pentateuch (in the original). (Haven't read but available: Sokolow: *History of Zionism;* Hamsun: *Hunger.*) Schiller: *Prose,* Heine: *Prose,* both bought in the street. A few pieces about Łódź. Sholem Aleichem: *Autobiography* (Yiddish); P. Hirschenbein: *Settlement in the Crimea* (Yiddish); Bergelson: *Story* (Yiddish); Kraepelin: *Psychiatry;* Blume: *Lectures on Freud.*

November 5. Everywhere pitch-dark stairwells. Everything is dark. Beginning at the break of dawn one walks over the dark stairs of the ghetto, bumps into others, only a small light at the window of the stairwell . . . Terrible collisions . . . but outside moon and full light, streetcar Łódź to Zgierz!—*Starting today, again concerts at the cultural center,* on demand of Biebow.

Of the newly settled the men's death rate is four times higher than that of women. Of those, 40 to 50 percent are former Eastern Jews.

Henuschi. Handing over a sort of will to Dr. Oskar Singer[5] and Dr. B. Heilig.[6] For all eventualities. Feeling weak in the heart, cold in the feet, shivers, and with all that enormous hunger. Ate 40 dkg of pot cheese, even meat patties with 70 dkg of potatoes and still hungry. Heart trouble. Pinching *à la angina pectoris. Again the first grayish black crows under a bleak sky, autumn and winter mixed together.*

November 7. [. . .] *Latrine.* Open latrines in the office: on one side sits a man, a woman sits opposite him, next to them men pissing, all without modesty . . . woman holds the door to the plank-toilet shut, next to her a man's hand with lit cigarette . . .

In the area of Łódź are "Jews' camps." At the post-office counter a woman employee who fills out preprinted form . . . "is in good health." Not even one's own handwriting is allowed. For eleven months *mail ban.* People are all blowing their noses in the street, pinching nose with fingers, tossing snot on the ground. Today cholent (without peas, only potatoes), selling price 7½ chaimki.

November 8, 1942. Cold, mood bad despite *good news from abroad* [original English]. New allocation of vegetables. Police (Special Division) themselves stealing potatoes, etc.—Special commando of women introduced: director is Dr. Bondy,[7] pretty, young women selected.

Hygiene. Everywhere on the stairs, even to medical doctors, spit, yellow sputum, not cleaned up; even the doctors ignore it. Disgusting.

The Eldest spoke at the cultural center: For the time being, no more potato allocations.—Female special police will take care of the children orphaned since the outsettlement in September, supplied with uniform and boots. Today got for the first time the second soup in the kitchen, waited like a beggar with pot and spoon.

Finance. "Chaimki" also called "Rumki."

November 9. Plan to get to Marysin takes on firm form. When there, well taken care of.—I'm freezing in the office. Have to concentrate on conversation with neighbor, Mrs. Plocky. Left without breakfast, since no bread. [. . .]

Kolejka [Pol., queue] at the vegetable place, police shouts and bludgeons. The Eldest officiates several times a week at weddings, of course reform, since the rabbinate is banned, orthodox ritual not possible. [. . .]

The Eldest still on top, inspects ressorts. Gertler ("Gertler Jugend," they call the Jewish police) performs weddings. Very lively, is constantly seen in the ghetto.

First snow. First snow at noon . . . Cold. I'm sitting in the unheated office with stiff fingers.—Again rumors about outsettlement of ten-year-olds and those over sixty.—We all feel in deadly danger, since recent warnings make us expect the worst. Again Messiah spirit, we're hoping for a miracle. Only a miracle can save us: otherwise we will either starve to death or freeze to death or be beaten to death. Potato supply getting low. I am thrifty with flour and flakes—who knows how long the misery will still go on.

November 11. First frost, frozen water puddles, fear of winter—no coals, wood a rarity, sold in the street at fantastic prices for 2½ chaimki per kg.

November 13. Continued cold. Lodging situation tragic! Sold potatoes, facing starvation!

Talkie. Curiosity. A twelve-year-old girl, Therese Saleszki, was taken from Litzmannstadt to the ghetto since she was presumed to be

Jewish. The girl's parents are missing (whereabouts unknown). Another correct version: During turmoil in Litzmannstadt, Therese was thrown over the fence and taken to the ghetto.—Thirty-two deaths, no births. [. . .][8]

November 15. *Henuschi.* Invitation to [stay at] the home in Marysin for one week. Looking forward to it, however, [will be] separated from the archive desk.—Still stomach typhus. Still no lodging.—*Psires* [Yidd., rumors, news, reports] bring good tidings. Apprehensive of November 28 because of Henuschi's excitement.—No more potato allocations.

Children abandoned by parents because of outsettlement, adopted into families for pay. More than six hundred orphans already placed. [. . .]

Hunger. A miracle that we are alive. Nutritive elements: albumen, fatty acids, carbohydrates, sodium, water, and spices.

"Strength and courage are the consequences of a balanced nutrition: constant lack causes timidity, cravenness, and weakness." *Meyers Konversationslexikon* [popular German encyclopedia], vol. 14, p. 394.

November 18. Mood in the early morning hours: kitchen gray, dark outside, light in the Zgierzka from street lamp . . . first Basa, then Escho . . . [illegible], then Mrs. Goldfarb, then Mr. Goldfarb . . . coffee, washing . . . toilet . . . gradually daylight . . . I rise from my cot . . . in slippers . . . unable to cook . . . They are eating raw grated radishes on bread everywhere for breakfast, even in the offices.—Yesterday, medical exam with old Dr. Loewy because of Marysin. Still no lodging, no hope of finding one. Reading novellas by Stendhal (Henri Beyle), (refreshing) in the cold foyer in the evening.—Yesterday bath in a tub in Volborska. Unconfirmed news about the children who were evacuated in September. Allegedly working in Pabianice, healthy . . . [illegible]. No trace of the others. [. . .]

November 20. *Marysin.* Reporting to home Marysin. Tub bath in the morning, then long wait in the open air at the police precinct, Catholic parish yard. Waiting for the streetcar. People give us curious looks. Finally cart with straw, a streetcar for cattle, we jump aboard, riding past straw sheds (for straw protection ressort), past hills (piles of straw), for potatoes. Everywhere people are digging. Bleak, wet, cold autumn, rain. I am freezing in the beautiful room. Very good reception. The Eldest appears[9] in the dining room of Home I. Says that the popular Mrs. Poznanska has died at the age of eighty-seven. I had visited her that morning. She had a messenger tell me with weak voice: *Utro!* [Pol.,Tomorrow!] Beautiful death. The Eldest had taken good care of her. [. . .]

November 21. Huge moon over cemetery Marysin. Unbelievable, fantastic. Above the mausoleum of the Poznanskis. Mrs. Poznanska, eighty-seven years old, died. Idea, go there to live and eat at the home. [. . .]

"The world is a book of which one has read only one page if one knows only one's native land." Eighteenth century.

November 22. First frost, terribly cold in Marysin. Evening November 21 gramophone; Caruso, synagogue songs, Liszt rhapsody . . . a little music and sentiment outside the ghetto. Asking if I can stay in Marysin. Prospect very minute. I am finally scared of winter cold. Feet stiff.

Work for Ashkenes continues in the twelve ressorts. Gigantic snowshoes. Wrapping of braided blades of straw as overshoes, impossible to walk or run. The only ones standing in snow and cold: guards . . . [. . .]

Curiosity. Biebow orders establishment of a movie house for workers' relaxation. At the same time continued terror on the part of the Kripo, preparation for new "outsettlements." This contradiction is part of the system. [. . .]

November 23. *Henuschi.* Today on top of everything, blizzard and freezing temperatures. Good mood because good *psires.* Perhaps rescue after all. Thinking of Henuschi, Vilma, Erich, Ernst. Perhaps yet good fortune of reunion. Concern about lodging and board. No potatoes, no more bread.

November 24. Winter, frost, and snow. Freezing terribly. Still no lodging. Choice: Marysin or city? *Psires* good and confirmed. Curiosity. A city of eighty-eight thousand (that is, one hundred thousand) inhabitants, without schools, teachers, instruction books, synagogue, movie theater, radio, gramophone, without woods or fields, without shops, without a home, without musical instruments, where everybody eats the same food, *without drinking water,* without newspapers, without a library, without coffeehouses, without restaurants, without hotels, without games or sports, without cars, bicycles, without pets (dogs, cats, hedgehogs, goats, rabbits) . . . coals, vegetables have to be gotten an hour and a half from Marysin . . . no carriage, no cigars . . . no wine, no beer, no schnaps, no alcohol. [. . .]

Ressort: Jewish work and ingenuity. [. . .] Rags are being sorted by experts: long threads, short threads, cotton, sheep wool, etc. Reworked into fabrics, fabrics turned into suits, dresses, etc. [. . .]

Technical skills. Sewing machines repaired, various things made of old iron, steel, tin. [. . .] The entire ghetto works. Big plus account. That which every worker gets (in foodstuff) per hour = *28 pennies.* And besides, food mostly of inferior quality. [. . .]

Order of one million straw shoes: was delivered on time. Frequently the establishment of a new ressort within twenty-four hours is ordered. That too is done. The German commission of experts (professionals, not politicians) rate the work as very good, they are amazed about the talents of the workers. The ghetto is secured through work. [. . .]

November 27. *Leaving Marysin*—I'm without living quarters. Don't know where I will sleep and eat tonight. A singular case in the ghetto that somebody has no bed to sleep in. I'm without bread, without potatoes. Never felt as forsaken.—And tomorrow is November 28.

Henuschi. What is she thinking? Does she know, the poor dear? Does she remember November 28, 1937? The chicken and the poppy-seed cake. My darling . . . Will I see her, will she see me, again? . . . How long will this go on? [. . .]

Curiosity. F. O. D. New characters in the streets: young women as police F. O. D. (Frauen-Ordnungs-Dienst [Germ., Women's Order Service]), barrettes with colorful fringes, sporty overcoats with belt, ski pants, sport shoes, grayish green loden with yellow star on the right-hand chest, in their hands a club. Coquettish, the cap tilted to the side, like girls in uniform in the operetta. The charm of novelty soon gone, hardly anybody pays attention to them.

Kripo patrols the streets. When they find two Jews talking to each or walking together, they come up to them and hit them over their heads, saying: "*Gite zeitung?!* [Yidd., "Good tidings?!"] Right?! *Gite zeitung.*" That is at a time of allegedly good news from outside. [. . .]

November 30. Terrible storm, like a thunderstorm from Siberia.—New rations without flakes, butter, matches. [. . .]

Inquiry with the Department for Insettlers whether there were twenty Jews from Amsterdam in the ghetto. Proof that Jews from abroad were also subject to being outsettled.

Rumor that Norwegian Jews will be taken to Warsaw—88,092 human beings in the ghetto. [. . .]

Face of the Ghetto. After a terrible blizzard, ghetto is white and dirty white.—Everywhere carts being pulled by bundled-up people with a little wood, coals, vegetables, excrement, etc., without horses. Here and there a German car, inscribed GETTOVERWALTUNG [Germ., Ghetto administration]. *Kolejka* in Lagewnicka in front of the fence of the vegetable center, children with sacks; mostly women, old and young, with rucksacks or baskets or bags made of dirty, old linen . . . They are waiting for 3 kg of vegetables. Five people are permitted at one time to enter the place where the vegetables are lying around in mud and snow and are being weighed . . . Pushing, fighting, hitting, cursing . . . The shivering crowd pushes forward. Woe to him who would try to cut ahead of the person in front of him! The policemen are yelling, hitting randomly, thrashing, pushing against the chest—they have learned the tone and behavior from the Ashkenes. More and more people joined the queue. It passes the "kitchen," a few of those waiting in line lost their patience and went into the "kitchen." "Do you have a piece of paper?" A piece of paper legitimizes receipt of a portion of soup. The piece of paper costs 3½ chaimki. At the time of cholent—up to 7½ chaimki. Renewed pushing and shoving near where the soup is being dispensed.

Outside, the tired, bundled-up figures pulling a cart with various loads. Again and again the excrement cart, people with mummy faces. In the daylight, the bright snow makes them even more ghastly, more ghostlike. [. . .]

December 4. Yesterday a pleasant Chanukah evening at Jakob Schipper's. Festive mood, lit menorah [Hebr., candleholder]. *Broche* [Yidd., blessing]: friend. Address by Caro; Praszk[ier]. Tabaksbl[at],[10] familiar, religious-national atmosphere far from all politics of the day. Neighbor Herschkowic invites me to his apartment. Dr. Feldmann touching because of lodging. Sang in Yiddish and Hebrew—as in the old Zionist days.

Henuschi. Memory of Herzl. (Tomorrow with Zionist Neumann.)[11] Wonderful winter evening, thought a lot of Henuschi.—Yesterday, December 3, three young girls (who ran away from work in Poznan), brought to the ghetto by Ashkenes SS according to sentence—sabotage, shot, in the central prison shot in the forehead, among them a seventeen-year-old girl.

New decree: Whoever doesn't report to the office loses soup and wages for the day.—Ghetto confirmed as work camp, therefore no question of outsettlement, no fear of food shortages.

There is no margarine, no food storage places, no cellars. Vegetables and potatoes are stored in the foyer on the frozen ground, under the bed, in the kitchen, frequently on the supports between the two bed frames . . . covered with dust and dirt, smell, rot . . . almost everywhere. [. . .]

Gypsies. Snow time. December 4. Gypsy camp. Near the end of the ghetto, Sulzfelder, toward the town. It was said they were altogether about five thousand human beings, also the remnant of former concentration camps in various countries. What's happening with them, a puzzle. [. . .]

December 15. Possibility for lodging. Kitchen is no longer bearable. Ten deaths. Eighty-seven thousand eight hundred forty-seven in the ghetto.—The Volksdeutsche woman Neumark left the ghetto after the death of her Jewish husband, Judge Neumark, is going to Berlin.

December 17. [. . .] Dense morning fog as in London where Henuschi is, temperatures dipping.—Good *psires* from abroad, but not confirmable.—Flour and eggs are supposed to come, incredible surprise since I haven't seen an egg for fourteen months. *Have been living in the kitchen for the last two months.*

December 20. *Dying. Hunger.* During outsettlement (winter locals), sixty people couldn't come along; were pulled off the wagon, remained in the cold, froze to death.

Deaf-mute after burial of mother and sister in Marysin, fell, couldn't make himself heard, froze to death.

Doctor takes food and bread ration cards from patient who is expected to die within twenty-four hours. Patient dies . . .

Talkie. Mother and daughter die. Neighbors, [who] neglected them, break into the room, steal bread, sugar, flakes, bedcover (the dead daughter is embracing her dead mother . . .) . . . throwing some rags over the two bodies, return and pull out even the oven exhaust pipe . . .

The Eldest speaks brusquely to the audience at the cultural center after a concert, after a revue—questions of the day. "Power" (that is, Ashkenes) over potatoes, cleanliness in the lodgings, bathing institutions, laundries. Gesera [Hebr., anti-Jewish decree] need not be feared. Typhoid fever. [. . .]

December 26. "*Work deployment*" (the term from over there).

Winter arrived. People are losing their patience. Answer to the saying "It's good": What's good? This is the fourth year . . . again and again: tomorrow, the day after tomorrow. I've lost my patience.

December 27. Celebration at the cultural center = two years' tailoring ressort and associated trades, mainly rugs.

Exhibit by the statistics department and rugs: say something about that. Praeses acts like president of a republic: speeches in Yiddish, a young girl speaks Ivrit [Hebr.], then Yiddish. Some voices: *loshen kodesh!* Then academy, Praeses is speaking. Lasting one and a half hours at night. Present: three fat sausages, 20 dkg of bread, candy, and cigarettes. The ghetto glorifies itself, celebrates its own enslavement (pattern: partly ornamental, partly figurative—motif ghetto).[12] Besides incredible vitality, proof of Jewish talent for trades and arts and crafts. Making everything out of rags, out of *shmattes* [Yidd., rags, tatters, clothing] for the Ashkenes power.

At the center: Praeses, Jakubowicz (director of all ressorts), David Warshafsky.

December 28. Not used to fatty stuff, stomach ailment in the morning.

December 31, 1942. From twenty-eighth to thirty-first severe food poisoning after the banquets. Winter has come. Question of lodging still not solved.

January 1, 1943. *Henuschi.* A winter day in November.—Renewed hope of seeing Henuschi again.

Fire in the clothing ressort Dworska 14. Women, Jewish, design clothing for Ashkenes. Incredible that Jewish taste and sense of form should make the *fashion* for Ashkenes; living isolated from the world and still fashion: *flared skirts.* [. . .]

Face of the Ghetto. Women: scarf over head. Long pants, à la ski, of strong, spotted, dirty linen, tied at the bottom to wooden shoes, the latter in tatters. Sometimes they wear men's caps, also men's jackets. Men: sheepskins without sleeves, shirtsleeves of dirty material, pants patched together, no shoes, old spats covering feet, which are wrapped in several pairs of socks, head lowered, face not visible because of earmuffs, which also cover the cheeks . . . The gray and matte brick red are visible under the dirty white snow holes and puddles.

Use word "puddle" in the stories.

New Year's Eve celebration in the ghetto: big party at Miss Fuchs' place. Also at other people's, women coifed and in elegant evening toilette, etc. Alcohol. [. . .]

January 5. *Work.* Ashkenes demands six hundred workers for Poznan. People from Czarnickiego and out of their beds at night. Again fear of outsettlement.—Winter, snowstorms.

January 7. Back in Marysin for recuperation.—Discussion with artist Leizerowicz[13] about the mood in the ghetto. Nietzsche's "The crows are shrieking, swirling townward in hasty flight. Soon snow will fall—blessed is he who now has a home! . . ." [Translation by B. G.] Our conversation reaches a certain depth. He wants to paint my portrait. Gradually one gains a new perspective of things, especially ghetto things.—Professor Caspari is also here, discussion about nutritional values, etc.—

Eighty people selected.—Leizerowicz tells about an Ashkenes whose eyes fill with tears when the fate of the Jews is being discussed. Exceptional case. The Ashkenes at the Baluter Ring are cheerful, singing. Who knows why?—

Talkie. On Marysin ground. Behind the wooden fence and the wire, fifty Polish children ages eight to ten. Children whose parents cannot be located (outsettled, *geharget* [Yidd., slain], fled, etc.). Farm labor under Ashkenes supervision. Daily 10 dkg bread and two portions of soup (thin with vegetables).[14]

January 8. [. . .] Ghetto is becoming dejudaized. Young people speak Polish. Yiddish is quoted like a foreign language. [. . .]

January 18. Illnesses. Lack of fat, anemia. Women without periods, erotic sense completely dead, especially among the Western Jews, therefore also no marriages. [. . .]

January 21. Fifty Jewish workers have come to the ghetto from Berlin. Telling stories of alleged terrible bombardments of Berlin.—Furthermore, forty alleged *tliahs* in Litzmannstadt for Ashkenes communists from Volhynia.—Suddenly big thaw. Have been informed that I will get an apartment at Dworska 1. Departing from the home.

January 22. Friday. *Outsettlement September.* All gone. I remain alone with Professor Caspari.—Jewish police throw infants through windows into the street onto a horse-drawn cart. Not a sound from the children.—Later an Ashkenes gives a child a nice apple.

January 23. Shabbat. Thaw. First inkling of spring. Heart in emotional upheaval. Prices are rising. Bread 160, sugar 1,30. Outsettlement 1942. *February.* Even the dead were taken along, thrown into the railway cars. [. . .]

January 27. Air raid alarm at night, what is going on? Fonye pushes forward, Ashkenes retreats—so they say.—Beautiful winter day. Told to stay at the home until further notice. [. . .]

Name: *Eternity.*

New ressort: *bookkeeping office work* for over there, since there is apparently a shortage of help due to call up.

Cemetery. The former walkways and tree-lined paths, as well as the cemetery gardening shop, used for graves.—Thaw. [. . .]

January 31. Beginning to think about other novellas. With which one shall I begin? Difficult since the material was directly used in the first book. [. . .]

February 5. Evening party of young people. Telling about experience. Great suspense and mood. I myself don't expect any changes in the next few weeks.—Day before, cheerful conversation with Praeses in Yiddish. Have good hope of being well taken care of until the end, if there is no outsettlement.

Hearse pulls up at the home. On the cart, a wooden plank with a black cloth. The outlines of the dead man, head and half-pulled-up legs visible under the cloth. Hearse is full.

Potatoes 20 chaimki, oil 3 to 5, butter 5 to 6.

Two hundred and seventy Jews who worked for two years in Germany now arrive in the ghetto in deplorable condition: wrung out, thrown on the dung heap, and housed in Czarnickiego.

February 6. Storm.—Inkling of spring. Again several experts housed in the city.—What about the Janissaries [Turk., core troops of the Turkish army]? Today Shabbat. Again fear of outsettlement.

February 7, 1943. A little peace and quiet.—From Czarnickiego, twenty-eight dead carried away in one night. Forty to the hospital. Most of the former workers from Germany brought here because of malnutrition. Dying slowly in the prison.

February 8. For several days a posting—proclamation: When *several* people, that is, a round, read newspaper—death sentence!

February 9. Renewed winter.—Girl in the home reads original *Magic Mountain;* Maurois, *Disraeli; All Quiet on the Western Front;* Penguin books, etc. [. . .]

February 12. Types: eighteen-year-old writer gives reading in the home kitchen, looks like a twelve-year-old.—Evening: song recital: Schubert, operas, Russian, popular Viennese operetta songs. Happy to be conducted. Tomorrow new repertoire, maybe a literary reading.

Terrible excitement in the ghetto: Jews from Lublin and Białystok, where outsettlement and pogrom, were brought to the central prison.[15] Perhaps in connection with the front (?). Here the local ghetto administration confiscates canned meat, which was once allocated. A shame that it wasn't distributed sooner. Who is responsible?—

February 13. [. . .] Home—afternoon. A redheaded child sings Polish folksongs, touching . . . reminiscent of the "Bluebird." Sings song about Marysin, what the Praeses has done for the children's home, that he was a mother substitute for the orphaned children . . . never will we, dear Praeses, forget this, dear Praeses! Tango! The audience nods, a smile, reflex to hearing refrain on the lips, some hum along.

What's happening over there? People under the *tliah?* Are these acts of revenge?

February 14. In Białystok, German posters with text. This is what will happen to you, if you are not victorious! Two Germans hitched to a cart, a Pole holds the reins, a Jew cracks the whip.—Supposedly.

Blizzard, terrible storm.—Completely without news from the outside world. *How are Henuschi, Vilma, Ernst, Erich?*

Many of the Jewish workers brought here from Germany, Poznan, the northern parts of Poland, etc., are dying in the prison. Partly malnourished, partly weakened by hard labor that drained them of all strength = *exhausted* [original English].—Praeses declares he cannot sleep in the city, therefore Marysin, where he takes a one-and-a-half-hour walk alone in the evening before going to bed.

February 15. Dejected mood. Storms. Rain. How much longer. Dreamed of Henuschi.

February 16. *Cemetery.* Walk through the cemetery in stormy weather. Next to luxurious graves, family crypts (Poznanski, Kohn, et al.), the small earth elevations of the recently departed, by date next to each other, not by name, hopeless in their loneliness. Terrible accusations. Grave ornaments torn down, even metal letters screwed off the stones. At the majestic entrance door to the *kitchen,* where the cemetery workers get their soup. Here many millions of pounds invested. Many German inscriptions. Here and there shriveled, but still green, cypress trees.

February 18. *Ashkenes.* Change of mood among Ashkenes apparently noticeable here. Several Ashkenes railroad workers speak in friendly tones, saying they had found among the Jews many good and decent human beings. Parting scene for one who is going to the front. Jew wishes him a happy return, covers his face with both hands, sobbing. Touching scene. Conclusion: *They* too want an end.

One hundred and eighty totally emaciated workers from Poznan arrived. Skin and bones: 10 dkg bread, two portions of soup and coffee. Three-hour walk to the workplace, ten hours of work, at five o'clock early on the way, back at seven o'clock. Many too tired to eat the left-over piece of bread in the evening.

Concerning Białystok: Approximately two thousand people loaded onto a railway car, taken away: father, mother, daughter, jumped off the train. Mother missing. Father, daughter (broken arm), in the hospital, father suicide, daughter adopted by Praeses.

Renewed fear of outsettlement (May!) if not radical change of the situation before then. [. . .]

February 20. Redheaded boy plays on his harmonica Mozart's *Eine kleine Nachtmusik,* Schubert, Russian songs.—Girl tells story: "Mother lost, brother murdered, sister deported," and goes dancing over in the Bawjarna until one o'clock at night.

Proclamation from Praeses: "Strict warning! *Blackout.*—Threat of punitive measures by cutting of electricity."

February 21, 1943. During alarm, a Jew accidentally near the wire at night. Guard shoots, seven times, man over thirty dead. Buried Monday, February 22, bloodstained clothing.

February 23. Rising prices and hunger. Bread 200, butter 8, potatoes 22, vegetables 11, one candy 2 chaimki, garlic and onions not available. Butter by contrast again in coupons. [. . .]

Hearse—door in the back opens during fast ride, coffin falls out. Upstairs large number of tallith, taken to the cemetery. Tallith and tefillin the most important symbols of the Jewish religion. How far hunger has gone, when Jews sell tallith and tefillin for a few chaimki to buy rations. . . . Bodies wrapped in linen cloth—stitched together from remnants.—Tallith over shoulder and head . . .

Eroticism: So-called dignitaries are now seen quite publicly with their lovers in the street, left trembling their wives and now strut with their cats . . . Done quite shamelessly and publicly, especially young policemen. In connection with that also corruption: allocations, positions in ressorts, coupons, vacation home, clothing (Fein and Bunin?), etc.

Show in the book the stages leading an orthodox Jew to sell his tallith and tefillin.

February 24, 1943. [. . .] *Soup.* Psychosis. Everybody eats, stuffs himself with soup, more soup—the craving for food overrides all considerations, liquid—fear of swelling in the legs, etc., drive people to absolutely wanting to eat—even soup. Psychosis!

Ashkenes *spy* [original English]. They go through the ghetto with "Magen David," lurk and denounce. Dangerous! But we have no interest in political discussions, etc., since the end is known and we have no way of changing anything about the current situation. Otherwise no sympathy for England, who has betrayed us terribly with regard to Palestine. [. . .] Sensation: letter through Red Cross from South Africa, Johannesburg, Dr. Ginsbergova.

February 25. First sign of life from her husband after three and a half years, directly to the ghetto: letter read, English parts translated, wanders from hand to hand, comments, sacred object, put back into envelope . . . Despair in the ghetto. German commission. Baluter Ring therefore blocked off to passageway. Restlessness. In addition, rumor that in a speech outside the slaughter of all Jews (allegedly) was announced. Impossible to verify. [. . .]

February 27. Behind the kitchen, Marysin women rummaged through the refuse of potatoes, peelers carry it away in scarves.—Pots away. Soup 8½ chaimki. Pallid sun. *Milchomo* has no end. Will there be another war winter?

White horse pulling the cart that brings soup containers to Marysin. Nearby the long straw shed. People, lying around on piles of bundled straw, are slurping the soup. Telling jokes or staring in front of them. The horse's mouth is as smart and expressive as a camel's. Sniffs. Opens the upper lip, the skin quivers, lets his tail, stuck between his hind legs, hang down. Turns the head toward the soup-eating figure, sad, melancholy, his eyes half covered by his lids, as if he wanted to say: "I know that I too live in the ghetto, that I am not an Aryan horse . . . etc., but be patient!"

The Poles. On the tracks between the wires, two young Poles pulling sled, show the Jews next to the wire their derrières: "Up yours . . ."

Others are shoveling snow and throw it over the wire onto the sidewalk of the ghetto.

When they pass by in the streetcar, they stick their tongues out at the Jews.

No understanding here that England and Poland are allied. Woe, when the underling becomes the overlord! On May 3, Polish national holiday, placards with "Death to the Jews!"

Depravity of the Polish police toward the Jews.—In the war against Bolsheviks, the intelligent Jewish soldiers were pulled back and put in concentration camps.

Polish compatriots pulled the boots off the feet of Jewish prisoners in the war in 1939, not the Germans.

March 1. Types. Solo dancer now has leading role in the central office for the work ressorts. Coffeehouse singer and jazz musician actively using his talents in various ressorts. [. . .]

March 2. Storms—northwest—not cold. Terrible pain in the hip muscles. Either lack of vitamins or neuralgia. For the time being no medication against it.

Henuschi. What is she doing? How is she living? Has she gone as gray as I? What about Hans? Vilma, Ernst, Erich? Greatly concerned about them all! Evi and Georg!

Hunger. Despite new ration (March 1–14), bread 200 chaimki.

March 3. Spring is in the air, some sun. In seven weeks Pesach. Will we have matzot? Important question as a gauge.—Hail—question for our table: Isn't it enough already? What does "he" gain if another one hundred thousand *Yehudim* [Hebr., Jews] perish?—

March 5, 1943. Today beginning of new life for me in the ghetto. Left the home and was taken by Ch. Praszkier to his house (apartment) and housed in a room. Got a meal—carrots. I'm surprised and touched by the kindness of the Praszkier family, especially the mother, a woman of gold, a *sadene Yiddene* [Yidd., real Jewess]. So I'm back in the ghetto where the struggle for animal life continues unabated.

Latrine. In Koscielny Square above the yard a toilet installation: open seating planks since the doors don't close, hindered by piles of human excrement. At the entrance and in the place itself piles of feces and urine puddles. A well-manicured female hand holds the door when one wants to open it inadvertently. It belongs to a beautiful young girl I had seen in the office. She too sits on the plank without shame in the daytime. However, the room that contains eight "seats" is quite dark.

Everything is encrusted with dirt, used toilet paper sticks to the shoes, we carry it into the yard as at every corner somebody—resident of the building or stranger—relieves himself in broad daylight.

Historical significance. If one wants to draw a leading person's attention to the historical significance of the ghetto, one makes a defensive gesture. He doesn't want to know, his gaze is fixed on the everyday. Any debates are therefore difficult, it's impossible to get closer despite the Jewish soul. The significance exists in the fact that for the first time in the history of mankind a community has achieved this and this under coercion. Spontaneous inventive spirit. Courage and confidence in oneself—a Robinsonade on the continent. The term "ghetto" has received a new meaning. The contradiction: on the one hand, as punishment isolated because harmful to "people's body" and parasitic—on the other hand, creative. Achievements demanded out of nothing, and reached. In this case, the German coercion had a favorable effect.

Female police—F. O. D.—dissolved.

March 17. Sunday. All ressorts closed. General situation improved. The ghetto works; therefore, hope that provisions are secure. At the moment, soup 8 chaimki, other prices accordingly.

Proclamation: What will be planted in March! Visual tables according to German pattern, excellent: salad greens, cabbage, strawberries, radishes, etc.—Proof that it is possible to sow and harvest in peace. The ghetto hopefully will be able to produce large quantities of vegetables itself.—Two women doctors were called to Pabianice to the Jewish work camp where apparently many Jews are still working (not as ghetto).

Vigantol against vitamin deficiency: The pharmacy received thirty little bottles, some of them sold immediately, others called in and handed over to the special commission.—I myself am in urgent need of Vigantol.[16]

I

The frost shed a whitish gleam
Over my head,
Making me believe I am an old man,
And that gave me great joy.

2

But soon it thawed and went away.
My hair is black again,
Making me fear my youth.
How much longer still to the bier?

3

From even dusk to morning light
Many a man turned old,
Who would believe and it wasn't mine
On this entire journey.—

NOTEBOOK 11

Ideas. Effect of K. Literature.

Studies: Narrative—"Resurrection"
Ideas—August 1942
Started in Mid-1942 (Remains Manuscript)
About the History of the Ghetto Litzmannstadt

DR. OSKAR ROSENFELD, MATROSENGASSE 1/42

Studies

Wedding. The realist: Some marry out of want, others out of plenty. In both cases it is the social situation of the ghetto that determines the motivation to get married . . . The young man is lonely, working from early morning to five in the afternoon at the ressort, comes home to an empty, desolate room, has to prepare a meal . . .

Longing for companionship, a desire to escape from being alone, makes him look for a companion, whoever she may be—she is supposed to be an assistant, a companion sharing the same fate. Two weak people can become strong together . . . The rations are the same, twice the amount of coal and wood expands the possibilities . . .

He is Director Kierownik. He has coupons, extra rations, special allocations. He lives—compared to other ghetto inhabitants—in abundance. He wants to make a young woman in the ghetto happy. And she! She feels fortunate, believes herself to be saved, to be able to make it. About the time of the ghetto condition. Hearts find each other in the atmosphere of a prison cell . . . They don't think of the future . . .

That's the *social* condition. But, say the philosophers, why shouldn't a man and a woman find each other? Why should the longing of the sexes for each other die out? *Marriage* in itself without social conditions? Without social reasons? It is to be considered that eroticism has died completely. That this category of human life was totally lost, that it must even be regarded as something extraordinary! Just as the more delicate aspects of life were lost to us, just as music, literature, spring, flowers, and the like, so also love . . .

Religious perspective: Demands establishing a family, marital life, children, the bearers of the *brith* [Hebr., covenant], children of Israel, descendants. . . .

Generally: It's a marriage of uncertainty. Wife and husband can be suddenly torn apart by expulsion: *courage to matrimony.*

Ceremonial: Praeses at the cultural center almost every week, thus the religious atmosphere is absent though Praeses tries to put emphasis on a nationalist character. How much of the religious aspect is being preserved? Inasmuch as the *chussen* [Yidd., groom] puts a ring on the *kalle*'s [Yidd., bride] finger and says the traditional blessing. The Eldest and another Jew are witnesses. The Eldest officiates. The marriage is as valid as a marriage with a rabbi and with the agreement of the current (German) civil authority. Mostly young people, about ten couples a week. Local people.

Earlier outsettlement. First outsettlement from the ghetto. From Łódź into the ghetto. Woman and child torn from their beds at night. December 1939. Two electric trains to Radegosts [Radegast]. With rucksack and sack, beaten by accompanying soldiers, people walked into the camp, about three thousand. Factory area. Soldiers: into the camp. Who has a cigarette lighter? Who a cigarette case? Both taken away and beaten. From one at night to nine o'clock in the morning in a big factory hall. Door locked. Door opened. "All out to shits!" says the soldier. All went into the yard. There a long wooden plank, a sort of bench. All together: old men with young girls, men with women, children with men, etc. While we were sitting there relieving ourselves we were being photographed, in part close-up, also from below. I can't get this scene out of my mind even though it was three years ago. Purpose: to show with the pictures that Jews have no shame as they are shitting, without regard for the sexes . . .

Back in the hall. Soldiers: "Hand over all money or you'll get shot." Some hand over their money. Later, again soldiers picking several men from the crowd, taking them outside, several shots. "If you don't hand over money, gold, jewelry, you'll get shot like they were shot . . ." Repeated several times. Beatings all day . . . Doctors forced to remove human excrement with bare hands, among them the Łódź doctor Eichner, later went to Warsaw. After two days in the cattle car, eighty people are dead at a temperature of 20 [Celsius] below zero. Direction Cracow. Terrible scenes in the cattle car . . . Children whimpering, people moving their bowels, some lick icicles to still their thirst . . . at several stops Jews brought us food. Masked cattle cars . . . Behind Częstochowa, again taken from the car: "Everybody out for shitting." Same scene, again photographed. Toward Cracow. A few fled back to the ghetto[1] . . . [. . .]

Religious life. Officially there have been no religious services since *Yomim Neroyim* 1941. Circumcision carried out unofficially. Sukkot huts not allowed. To be *metaher* [Hebr., purified], mikvah [Hebr., ritual bath] not allowed. Ceremonial *levaye* [Hebr., burial procession] not allowed. Matzot: still some for Pesach 1942. *Shilchelach* [Hebr., carrying out of religious obligation] in private apartments. Rabbinate does not exist. Weddings through the Eldest. Bar mitzvah not official. No Beth Midrash [Hebr., temple, synagogue]. Children up to age ten are put in children's homes supervised by women teachers; from ten, work in the ressorts. In tailor and joiner ressorts division for youngsters who want to learn these trades. Unofficial teacher instructs math in Yiddish.

Toire [Yidd., Torah] is not being taught, children grow up without traditional Jewish religious life. On occasion a father will look for Hebrew (Torah) instruction for his son, but no teacher since money has no value. Some Torah scholars demand coupons for themselves or their children as an honorarium.

Morality. Most personalities of "elevated social position" have official girlfriends, as they say here: love affairs. These girls and women have no shame and parade openly as the official mistresses of the respective candidates.

Study—Composition

SIMULTANEOUS ATTEMPT OF A CRITIQUE OF "I. W. N. N."

Camp life: People with soup bowl, etc., money comes in, a few marks, buying soup or dumplings at inns, even a bit of schnaps. Company gets together: highlight some characters, the soprano, painter Gutmann, the one-armed industrialist, etc. Haven't exchanged any memories yet about back home.

We are moving closer together. Singing in the evening. During the night to the latrine. Three-quarters of the conversation passes in concern over food. In all this, thoughtless hours, reading, smoking . . .

I haven't seen Professor Hart for several days . . .

"Haven't seen him? He died . . ."

Artist Gutmann paints silhouettes of the ghetto from the window of the school (camp collective). He is elated, delighted, raves about the beauty of the barren landscape, because he doesn't know yet what despair is. He still has provisions (white baked goods, preserves, goose fat), etc. Bring earlier characters to life.—Show how erstwhile illusions "we will persevere" are breaking down.

The first *slow* dying because impossible to get to the hospital. Running against the wall of "protection" for the first time. Transport leader Kagan, good-looking, gets soup from the thick bottom,[2] and still into the hospital. Someone is dying. Has a nice, big, aluminum soup bowl with strap ties. The neighbors eye it. Each one would like to inherit the bowl . . . envy, fear; the dying man could give it to an outsider . . . Despite misery and want they have become petty. Calculating that this pot holds more soup, for back then at the beginning everybody's pot was filled to the brim.

Unclear feelings. For the first time the question: What is the ghetto? For each person something different. Some have advanced to ghetto big shots. Getting the prime positions: doctors, department of insettlers, postal service, ressort (explain), even judges (Wilczek). Beginning to understand the ghetto (!), penetrating the inner clockwork of the ghetto.

A few months of this squalor and milieu have changed us more than the passage of years before. Not that hidden, evil instincts were unleashed, but we learned that to live merely in order to live, a few spoonfuls of thick soup were worth more than all the ideologies and human sentiments and prayers . . . We only knew one thing: *To spare our nerves* was as important as eating.

The transport leader shows his true face, ruthless.—Intrigues—a few join him, others remain in the opposition.—In the end the *nese* [Yidd., miracle] collapses.

Concerning toilet: one sit-down toilet only for the sick. Permission to use it needed from the guard at the door, who is dependent on the leader. This *toilet* is the downfall of the opposition (witnesses: crowding, no toilet paper, for the first time use of Tanach, Heine's poetry). Some are trying to push their way in. Impossible. Going into their pants. Stench. Washed. Fight over a scrap.—Threats of reporting don't work. Origin of the slogan: *I'm going to the wire.* Very little sense of belonging, camaraderie.

Conversation at the bedside of a dying man. Not much interest. Just go away. Quickly to the soup. He decays visibly . . . Symptoms of death—rattling. At the hospital this is a daily occurrence. But in the hospital one need not worry about the everyday.—Just got money, but 15 chaimki is not enough, a loaf of bread costs 18 to 20 chaimki.

Victor Deutsch has the *élan vital* that many are lacking. He already knows after a few days in the camp where to get the best and cheapest dumplings. Without money—sells something or other . . . loans out a hot water bottle for one night until morning, gets a few sugar cubes in return, Prague, and for this a few dumplings . . . and smokes . . . people who have never smoked in their lives are smoking. The Croatian cigarettes Bragava and Rama and Ibar . . . half a cigarette . . . saving and looking for butts . . . Chaimki 10:1, very crude. When somebody in Prague sends 500 crowns—a small fortune, and for 50 chaimki two loaves of bread.

We can see the hunger in the veteran ghetto inhabitants . . . begging children to tell where the soup is being distributed . . . a twelve-year-old girl follows me like a prostitute because I once gave her a crust of bread and the rest of my soup.

Victor: "Don't look at her, yell, chase her away, or you'll never get rid of her." Victor knows his way around, but I don't follow his advice.

The coffee often comes late and is, therefore, cold so that we don't use it for washing and prefer going into the yard directly, and I can wash up at the well. Conversation at the well. Young girls too join. Open blouses despite the cold. Very little timidity, hardening. Nearby the long wooden plank as latrine where we sit like swallows on telegraph wires, and not too far from there the garbage dump . . . Potato peels, vegetable leftover, stinking cube-shaped stuff, molded bread (everything rotten, some have to pay for their avarice, their parsimoniousness, with the loss of their bread leftovers).

Children are rummaging around it, crawling around in it, fishing something out, and putting it into an apron or pot. For the first time I also saw Professor Hart . . .

Toilet question is worsening more and more. A woman from Prague (see elsewhere) invents a house toilet against a fee . . . Nice evening. People are singing. *Volga Boatmen* . . . Johann Strauss . . . *Ave Maria* . . . Schubert fanatics. Garfinkel comes for a visit—characterize him. Possible sensation. Letter Red Cross, South Africa (see notice February 25, 1942, Notebook G). Then again soup. Describe the smell, the longing for something else to eat, revulsion against coffee.

For the first time wire. A real live wire. Now writing a poem about the wire with the concluding line: "The wire is good, keeps us away from life's follies." Irony . . .

I'm getting to the hospital. The man screams, "Oy, veh is mir . . . Mother, Father, give me a piece of bread . . . Crush our enemies . . . kill those who torment us, and give me a piece of bread." I'm annoyed because I can't sleep. I yell at him: "If you don't be quiet, I'll put you out into the yard . . ." The next morning he is dead, exhaled his soul. I'm deeply sad, I'm ashamed . . .

The first suicide—jumps from the window at the school.—Life goes on. Monotony. *Idleness.*

The first ghetto diseases: pain in the toes—nails . . . emaciation, inability to sit, lower back hurts . . . big scene because a woman had brought in a little piece of bread outside eating time and eats cheese. When the scene is over, to calm things down, conversation about family. Wife there, son there, daughter there . . . all torn apart: They don't know that we're here . . . Wonder what they are doing over there . . . what they are eating over there. In New York, five cents will buy a huge, big sandwich: sardines, sauerkraut, cheese on white bread, olives, etc.

The stomach juices are stirring. "Stop it already, such talk is dangerous." Professor Hart falls off his cot.

Outsettlement in the winter—meanwhile it's February. Bread 600, reichsmark = 1 chaimki . . . (Elsewhere!)

Walk through the ghetto, see elsewhere: *Face of the Ghetto.* Horror of the ghetto begins. We are going to the cemetery. Hearses . . . [illegible] snow, winter. We are burying one ourselves . . . [illegible] (See corpse to the cart at the home Dr. Loewenstein.) People are dying here and there. And everybody believes: *I'll* survive.

Mice in the *room* of the private apartment. (First must-tell: collective is dissolved. People are moving into private apartments.) Mice are freezing to death in the room. Key freezes in the keyhole. Somebody sees this. A slight fit of insanity. "I want to get out of this ghetto, go home, I want to drink coffee and eat buttered bread, nothing more than a piece of buttered bread . . ." They calm him down.

Hunger is intensifying. People turn against each other with enmity. The son would take the last bite from his father. Everybody has lost all sense of normal life.

A little sun, foreboding of spring. But cold in the evening, frost—minus 15 degrees Celsius. In the short breaks when eating is not foremost on the mind, memories come back, stirring up, finally calming, making one tired so that one falls easily asleep. Thinking again and again about one's youth and the mistakes one made and for which one is now being punished—ghetto.

"I cheated youngsters out of their money, could now be in America, Italy (?), Russia."—

Zionism: "If my Zionism had been genuine I would now be in *Erez.*"

"If my Bolshevism had been genuine, I would now be in Moscow," and so on . . .

Reproaching oneself is tormenting, leads to nothing, wears down the heart, the nerves.—

New diseases, new manifestations of hunger. We have become a different people. We no longer belong to the *world.* We are all dead for the world. The world has given up on us. We are lost, but we don't want to give up.

A devious way of starving us to death: a thin soup . . . Work is beginning: People are accepted at the ressorts.

Policemen, firefighters, night watchmen . . . Terrible revelation: One million kilograms potatoes frozen, therefore hunger continues.

A little flower—Mrs. Loewenstein weeps, says: "What a pity, my husband loved flowers so much."

The way people die—they don't know how to handle bread and soup; don't know what's best to buy for the chaimki that arrive in the mail. Bread, soup, coffee, dumplings, artificial honey, turnips—words that comprise our entire world. And filth. No personal washing for weeks. Clothes and underwear stink. Moldy smell. Dampness. Rot (see other mention) . . . Longing for two things: a thick soup and being able to eat undisturbed, in a chair, at a table . . . But the bones are hurting, emaciated. One contents oneself with it . . . It's all what one is used to. No mail delivery for four months. One no longer thinks about it. Everything has died out. Likewise also the longing? Have we forgotten the past? No!

But we don't want to think about it.

All talent has withered, is lying dormant. Memory lost. Somebody recalls: There was a concert at the cultural center. Gives a report about it. But others listen with only one ear. At the same time comes the news about the second camp.—Transport Germany (Berlin, Frankfurt, etc.), already more than one hundred dead. They are dead. Who knows what else is in store for us. And again, face of the ghetto.

Shabbat services. Lecture about famine in India. Minimizes the horror of the ghetto for us. For we are listening and talking to keep from going mad. Yes, even humor. Not only singing. Hours, days, are being passed this way. Stolen hours and days and weeks. Unable to stop them. Suddenly a *scream!* Nobody knows from where. But all are startled, and the room commandant, with a cigarette between the fingers, says: Time to go to sleep.

On the way to the post office, Koscielny Square, scraps of movie posters . . . German text. We are trying to reconstruct. Well-known names of actors, then completely hidden "Broadway 1939!"

We hear jazz singers, revues, girl dancers, etc. A dream, an absurd dream. Will we live to see this again? We talk about it, no lascivious word is heard. We sense: Eroticism has been lost.

The house (school) where we live is to be turned into a ressort. We are asked to evacuate. In front of the house, at the exit, gravestones used to line the side of the street. Not too far from there a few squat little houses. A young man, nephew of Professor Hart, voluntarily came to the ghetto from Prague because of a beautiful girl. They are going on walks together. Looks for an empty house. There the first kiss since arrival in the ghetto.

A man from Cologne wants to save his family, passes by the wire, behind the town. Train station. Ticket. Jews' star. Captured. Taken to Czarnickiego . . .

But it's already January. Add entry there. Then February 1942 *tliah.*

Gradually I am looking into the depth of the ghetto. Not only the face. There are hundreds here, even several thousand people, who regard their work in offices, bakeries, kitchens, storage yards as perfectly natural, even legitimate. They worry about their jobs, goals, aspirations. It is difficult to determine whether in their innermost heart there isn't something else that makes them forget. Or whether they have come to terms with their situation? They are laughing, making plans, scheduling for weeks in advance.

For the most part I am happy that my life is not that narrow, I am seeking to broaden the confines of life with my thoughts. I place myself into the universe, such a thought process heals me for a short time, lifts my despair. Sun, moon, stars, God, and I are one to me. Nothing can happen to me. I feel the millennium rushing past me—I am reading Spinoza in the ghetto, what good fortune, and I am discovering a beautiful *Zionist* matter, see elsewhere . . .

We are counting the days. Already one hundred twenty-seven days in the ghetto. Then we are calculating the days remaining to the end. Prognoses. No news, but rumors.

There's no news, no newspapers. On occasion somebody says he has seen a Litzmannstadt newspaper. Nobody believes him. Another tells that at the barbershop reading the newspaper is 10 pennies a head and more.

Rumors that the ban on mail will be lifted.

In every corner, people are working. Seeds. Plants. Vegetables, etc. A new scene. Proclamation: distribution of seeds. Is spring really here?

Hours of desperation, when will the sun's rays get stronger, days brighter? The wretchedness becomes more clearly visible: torn shoes, soiled clothing, hollow cheeks, heads grayer, legs thinner, it's not easy to cross the bridge.

A separate story: *Bridge!* For millennia. Mizrayim.

Dying is now accelerating. It's April. I'm visiting a mother and son. In November on the cot, Mrs. Brüll and Georg. We'll make it through. Both dead.

Where is X? Dead. Where is Y? Dead.—Dead. Buried. No longer any feelings. Robbers next to the dead begging: soup bowl, bread, shoes, pocket knife—especially when there are no surviving relatives.

No inheritance rights. Everything belongs to the ghetto. Still in autumn 1942: The nearest kin or a caring friend can claim a few small items.

Life is terribly gloomy. Human beings merciless. Alienated, with hardened hearts. Giving no answer.

Suddenly all Eastern Jews are strangers to me. Is it a real contrast between East and West? The opinion about it changes with the most recent experiences. Well inclined toward Boruch, Schipper, Neumann, Eibuschütz.

Long discussion about the ghetto. What it once was and what it is today.

Likewise: *hunger.* Hunger in the regions of China, India, hunger in the Ghetto Litzmannstadt.

And suddenly: I have to get out of the ghetto.

Contemplating how to arrange flight. I'm unstitching the Jews' star. I'm embittered.

Next to me a voice. Somebody calls out to me: "Sir, you don't have a star." It's a Jewish policeman. Warmth fills my heart. He takes it and stitches it on for me. "Watch out," he says: "If you're seen by an Ashkenes, that'll be the last of you."

I feel good. I suddenly belong to them all, the so-called Eastern Jews. We share the same fear of the Ashkenes, of our fate, of the hardships that are still in store for us. The few words "Sir—" saved me.

The next day we learn: Professor Hart or somebody else walks past the wire, moves on. Crawls under. Pushes against the beam, falls into the open sewer; tries to remember the outline of the street. Extraordinary precaution. Beautiful night, almost no wind. Almost full moon. He's afraid of the guard, he shoots (but at a rat).

He advances quite far, slips through, goes into town, train station . . . Is recognized by people who know him from Germany, welcomed, taken back, with food, even.

On his return unhappy nevertheless that he didn't stay over there.

Victor is supposed to get a good job: take over potatoes and vegetables for the kitchen. There he would have been able to eat. But too late. He's felled with swollen legs and face. Besides difficulties with a goiter (heart, see dictionary). Dies. Is buried in Marysin. After the burial back home. A smuggler brought bacon into the ghetto. We bought and ate. Diarrhea at night. Have to run. Our stomach and intestines can't tolerate fatty food. Terrible. The whole room, six people and a child are sitting on the latrine.

May evacuation. Ehrenhaft and wife, Ferler and wife, Engel and wife, Dr. Singer and wife, Ballenberger after a serious stomach operation . . . Taken to the station in Praeses' car during the night . . . bread taken away, straps cut off, unfortunately the weather is warm: All the clothes and undergarments too much to wear on top of each other.

We are still in bed. Saying: "Lucky ones . . . who knows when it will be our turn!"

One of us gets sick. Weak heart. Faints several times. Is lucky. Baron Hirsch is hospitalized where he dies before the great evacuation of September 1, 1942. Horrifying scene when the doctor says: "Screen."

How senseless all of a sudden is everything his forebears achieved, when *he* has to starve to death in the Jewish ghetto. "It's only the hospital and cemetery which really make clear what the ghetto is," says the chief physician, Dr. Levy, who had treated me. "No, no," he says, "retribution does not exist." And the man from a Chassidic home is atheist, nihilist. Has become a cynic.

Autumn is here. September 1. September outsettlement with all its horrors. A separate chapter. Needn't be specially noted here.

If something like this is possible, what else can there be?

Wherefore for still war?

Wherefore for still hunger?

Wherefore for still world?

Somebody concludes: When I left Lo . . . I had to leave behind my canary. He stayed in the cage in the abandoned apartment. Who knows how and if he's still alive.

There is little left to talk about: What comes after is only reverberation, echo, a trembling of the nerves. After this experience, our existence, always on the brink of death, has taken on a very simple form, restriction to the absolutely necessary. We are alive—some say—because we have reduced our lives to the most primitive level.

We are alive—say others—because we are still keeping alive the sentiments for what's great and just, and that which lies in the future.

We are alive—say some—because everything we do has to serve the preservation of life.

We are alive—say others—because we still have a sense of the metaphysical.—We have adjusted ourselves to the present situation, but our inner being is prepared for the future.

In store for us are: rifle, typhoid fever, gallows, death.

It's late autumn. It's winter. Two and a half years ghetto, one year "outsettlement."

Will we ever overcome Ghetto Litzmannstadt?

With this question we went on our way.

Dichtung und Wahrheit [*Poetry and Truth*]—Goethe.

Book 12. Concerning the Bible and Moses.[3]

NOTEBOOK H

Notes, Recollections (Remains Manuscript)

[. . .] **March 1943.** Celebration three years O. S. (Order Service of the police). Praeses thanks Commander Rosenblatt et al., hands out coupons, dinner. Rosenblatt and the three commanders, each receive a series of ghetto money autographed by Praeses. Eighty-six thousand five hundred thirty-four in the ghetto!

Curiosity. Three boys wrote a blackmail note to a woman demanding that she leave her jewelry at a certain place, otherwise they would report her to the Kripo. Boys of good families. The investigation division of the O. S. is investigating the case.

Legitimation. All workers in the ghetto newly legitimated in the name of Praeses. Purpose: induction of all inhabitants into work details. [. . .]

March 9. [. . .] *Health office, Dr. Miller,*[1] *Dr. Weinberg*[2] (illnesses, hunger, want). If the question of provisions is not examined from the standpoint of their pure nutritional value (calories) alone, a series of quite remarkable moments in the ghetto can be registered:

1. The emergence of hitherto little-known or disregarded illnesses leads to the conclusion that their causes have much to do with nutrition.
   a. A year ago scurvy and pellagra were being observed, in addition to more cases of famine edema and boils as well as abscesses.
      The cause of scurvy was lack of vitamin C, of pellagra vitamin B, of famine edema vitamin B and albumen, of boils and abscesses vitamins A and C.
   b. Nutrition didn't help much. During the summer, fresh vegetables, dairy products, etc., minimized the illnesses somewhat.

2. Scurvy and famine edema have receded somewhat at the moment. In their place are more violent occurrences of bronchitis and pleurisy, which are not always of tuberculin origin. Since vitamin C works against infections, all foods, such as sauerkraut, red beets, etc., that are rich in vitamin C can be regarded as beneficial.
3. Renewed frequent occurrence of what is called bone softening, that is, loss of calcium in the bones. The cause is definitely lack of vitamin D. Vitamin D occurs only in minute quantities in our food (butter). An alternative source of vitamin D is, of course, natural radiation like ultraviolet light (quartz lamp). Vigantol and cod liver oil are excellent sources of vitamin D. Since ultraviolet lamps as well as Vigantol and cod liver oil are hard to obtain for the masses in the ghetto, the above-mentioned illnesses cannot be fought with available means.
4. Illnesses that are due to lack of vitamins B and C could be minimized by supplementing the rations with addition of sauerkraut B and vitamin C. However, the general population should be instructed not to cook but I eat it raw since vitamins will be lost otherwise.

   Red beets likewise rich in vitamin C, red cabbage also rich in vitamin C, turnips too are rich in high-value vitamin C. Potatoes at this time of the year contain no vitamins, therefore supplements containing vitamins necessary. [. . .]

March 12. Rumor that Dr. Ley[3] is coming to the ghetto on an inspection tour. Certain preparations are being made.—Another rumor that nutrition would be improved. Supposedly the unit of 36 pennies per diem would be raised to 40 pennies (that is, the quota of the ration).

Ironies: Somebody informs the O. S. that a German commission is coming to the ghetto. Thereupon cleaning of the yards, streets, excrement removed, better hygiene. Information was wrong, but was successful.

Bride informs the police that somewhere a man had died. Police find the man, but rather than being dead, he is in agony. Turns out the bride produces a will in which the candidate had left everything to her—apartment, assets. Lonely death.—[. . .]

March 17. Rations taken for the first time to new apartment Dworska 1. Terrible pain in the ribs and hollow of knees despite Vigantol. Softening of the bones à la rickets due to lack of calcium (fat, butter, fresh vegetables, cod liver oil). How will all this end? A man named Stern secretly keeps a hen, she yields eggs for him (25 chaimki apiece), gets lost. Finds her near the door of Mrs. Schatten's chicken feathers—recognizes his hen by them. Animal stolen, suffocated in the transfer! Police complaint! How will the court decide?

Prohibition against wearing a beard, from the time the ghetto was established. Now gradually being forgotten. Here and there little beards are seen sprouting, also among young Chassidim, a hint of *payes,* a gleam in the eyes as if the *Shekhina* [Hebr., God's presence] resided in them.

March 18. Legs in great pain, terrible night, asthmatic cough, ribs hurting.

March 19. Pain, sleepless nights, should take calcium with Vigantol. Brightening in *Mizrach* [Hebr., East], perhaps *yeshiye* [Yidd./Hebr., redemption] sooner than expected.

March 21. Bright, cold Sunday. Consultation with doctor—rather than bone-softening neuralgia, nerve infection. More sleepless nights.

March 25. The Jewish police stops people in the street to find out why they are in the street in the daytime. Proof: legitimation. The streets are empty. German authority is expected (Ley or Greiser)[4] from the town. *Outsettlement? A hard day.* Thursday, March 25, is a hard day for the ghetto. Streets are deserted, a few people hurry along with a heavy heart. Atmosphere as during the week of September 1942. Nobody knows why he is being stopped and arrested. Deportation? *Houston Stewart Chamberlain* 1915. They are as swept away by a powerful storm: "Jews cannot be found since they are doing their duty as Germans at the front or at home" (world war).

March 28. Fear still in all bones. On the twenty-fifth I walked through the streets from my office. Policeman: "Are you going home?" I: "To get soup!" He: "Let me give you some advice. Don't stay in the street."

People are being captured, especially those who look sick and are poorly clothed, so-called *klapsidres* [Yidd., human ruins], dilapidated, broken-down, crippled figures! It's being said that about one thousand people (among them eight hundred fifty who had recently come from Poznan completely squeezed out) are waiting at the central prison to be transported to somewhere.

Outsettlement after all: A Jewish commission is said to go into the ressort in the near future and select older people who are unable to work for outsettlement; even into the houses. Because the ghetto is a "work camp." Interestingly: Eight hundred Poznan workers first squeezed out, now thrown on the dung heap as incapable of working. This is how a *tel* [Hebr., grave mound] for the Ivrim is made. All this is carried out by the Special Division of the O. S. About two hundred people were arrested in street raids and are being outsettled together with the workers from Poznan [. . .][5]

For Ashkenes. Orders for aviation troop: wrist warmers, knee warmers, head covers.

March 29. The one thousand are still at the central prison. For the time being no order. Today Praeses received order from Gestapo. Excitement in the ghetto since all further "actions" could *follow without limitations on age or job categories.*

Literature. J. F. Fries: "Concerning the Endangerment of the Well-Being and Character of the Germans through the Jews," Heidelberg, 1816.

March 30. *Outsettlement.* O. S. move into action during the night of the twenty-ninth and thirtieth. About one hundred sick people (lung tuberculosis) taken from their beds in Czarnickiego to the workers from Poznan. One thousand people are doomed. Terrible atmosphere in the ghetto, fear of outsettlement as in September. How many people will fall victim? How long will the outsettlement action last? Only the old and the sick? Terrible ghetto rumors. In the night foot stomping outside my window, wooden shoes, whispering, mumbling.

March 31. Twenty freight cars are actually made ready for the approximately one thousand people, many with lung ailments. Unknown whereto. Horrifying scene in Czarnickiego. A group of younger people loaded onto the wagon and taken to the collection camp, Kiddush HaShem[6] [Hebr., sanctification of the Holy Name], singing *Hatikvah* [Hebr., "Hope"; national anthem] . . . They were singing in greatest anguish a little piece of hope out of their soul. Auto-da-fé [burning at the stake by the Spanish Inquisition] was child's play compared to this ordeal.

March 31. Rain. Cold. Shower. Yesterday one thousand people taken away, only a few of them unable to work—mood of despair in the ghetto.[7]

April 1. Stormy rain, cold showers—outsettlement of yesterday forgotten in the ghetto.—

April 4. Oppressive mood, following the one thousand people—outsettlement is over. Aftershock only among those who lost family members.

Reading in the ghetto: Poetry and Truth [Goethe]; Heine; *Conversations with Eckermann* and *Tasso* [both Goethe]; Shakespeare.

People are singing. An old man, old material, sings Schubert's "Unvollendete" like a drinking song.

Diseases in the ghetto. Meyers Encyclopedia, vol. 10, p. 328 H, 1907 edition, sixth printing: "Greater ability to survive corresponds with a lower tendency toward illness . . . This is especially true of infectious diseases like tuberculosis, pneumonia, typhoid fever . . . all these diseases are less common among Jews or occur in milder forms. Particularly striking is the difference when it comes to tuberculosis though the majority of Jews are housed in filthy, unhygienic lodgings, that is, were at one time (ghettos) . . . The cause for the relatively low receptivity of certain diseases is attributed to the strict dietary laws, the inwardly directed and pure family life, and the moderation in eating and especially in drinking (alcoholic beverages), and on the other side by contrast, the cause for a heightened disposition for other afflictions can be seen in oppressive poverty, filth, and misery of the ghetto as well as the competitive struggle for existence. Even if all these factors for either greater immunity or disposition hold true, they are not sufficient to explain this strange phenomenon; it is, therefore, hard not to take into account the factor of race, that is, a biological race characteristic."

April 5. [. . .] *Ashkenes talkie.* Kripo comes to the house, visitation: one flight up to mother who is holding a child: "Where do you want me to aim, at the stomach or the forehead?" (Threatens with revolver.)

Names: Alphabet, Cincinnatus, Eternity, Stooljuice.

April 8. Cold, snow showers . . . Question whether there will be matzot for Pesach or rather additional rations. There's talk about potatoes!—Today burial of Cersky-Cukier[8] (tuberculosis).

April 9. Excitement in the ghetto, German authorities (twenty-nine people) inspected several ressorts, streets blocked off—talk of new orders, all this in stormy rain-hail weather.

Hunger continues. Question: What will today's ration bring? Supposedly neither potatoes nor anything sweet!

Religious tradition. Mrs. Elka Schapiro (ressort worker) received canned meat. Since it isn't kosher, she doesn't want to eat it even though she is weak and her feet are swollen. Doesn't want to sell it either since she couldn't sell *treife* [Yidd./Hebr., nonkosher] meat to Jews. The canned meat is still at the ressort. So still clinging to tradition. Thousands of people are sick therefore an equivalence should be set up since the sick are exempt and not bound by kashrut [dietary and hygiene laws of Judaism]. [. . .]

April 12. *Talkie.* During the night: Schupo [German police] talks with Jewish policemen. Two Jewish policemen are leading a man. "Whereto?" asks the Schupo. "To jail!" "So? You have a jail? What for? You are all here in a jail."

Extermination. A woman came from Zduńska Wola, had eight children. Now her mind on only one thing, to tell her story.

Humor. "One doesn't steal, one takes." Meaning due to corruption some people get from their protector and thus don't have to steal.

Religious life. Houses of prayer closed down in summer 1942, already in 1941 order to shave beards. All, or almost all, eat *treifene* soup. Kashrut does not exist. Pesach 1942, matzot for the first time made of rye flour.

Crematorium. Ozorkow near Łódź. Place where the thousand human beings are said to have been taken, see entries of March 29–30. Crematorium.

April 12. [. . .] *Struggle for power.* Stories about Dawid Gertler[9] and Marek Kliegier[10]—against Praeses. Revue of the "Special,"[11] *"Dawid is inser Vuter, Gibt uns Brojt"* [Yidd.,"David is our father, he gives us bread"]. Just as in ancient Rome when the plebeians selected some man and made him *popular,* that's the way it is here with Gertler and Kliegier. Praetorian guards surround both: "They were privileged among the troops through higher pay, shorter service, and special insignia. In (Special Division) the course of time they gained political influence, permitting them to enthrone and dethrone a series of emperors." Gertler and Kliegier like two consuls (*duumvirat*).

The Eldest. He wants to play the role of the one who created Noah's ark. Ghetto ark. He goes about his own way of preserving it, and if it should cost thousands of victims, he tears down everything that gets in the way, gets violent, lashes out . . . He has become *eved hagermanim* [Hebr., slave of the Germans]. He listens to nobody even if something good is proposed. When somebody has a plan concerning the children, he declares: "Don't play the big savior of the children, that's my role . . ." He wants to go down in history as the savior, *shomer* [Hebr., guardian], of Israel . . . This creates conflicts.

April 15. A few days before Pesach and still no decision about matzot or other allocations. (*Not yet decision concerning* [original English].) A bright sunshine, outright hunger.

April 16. Sun! Cold on the inside! Cooking without fat, without potatoes, without flakes . . . All are waiting for *deliverance:* 3 kg potatoes, 15 dkg preserves (turnips + saccharine), and 4 dkg margarine. [. . .]

April 17. Drafting *tnoyim* [Yidd./ Hebr., marriage contract] (engagement). E. Hirschberg, scientific department,[12] young Echezkiel Spiegel becomes engaged to Simrata Hirschberg. Set table. Shabbat. Havdalah [end of Shabbat ceremony]. Later signing of *tnoyim* as symbolic *mechuten* [Yidd., in-law], the father of the groom is not in the ghetto. Present are brother of the bride's father, son of Dr. Lemberg (he is Eldest of the Jews in Zduńska Wola, a town near Litzmannstadt), Lipschuetz (teacher at Hebrew high school in Łódź), and the artist H. Szylis.[13]—Brother reads *tnoyim,* makes speech, finally the father of the bride speaks, *mazel tov,* kisses, congratulations, evening meal with schnaps, meat, vegetables, babka [Pol., cake; in the ghetto made of potato peels and ersatz coffee), coffee. Going back home at midnight.

Loneliness. We live in house by house. Don't see each other as in a big city. Part of the daily routine. As one group leaves the house at seven o'clock and comes back at five, the other leaves at seven-thirty and comes back at five-thirty; their paths never cross but run parallel to each other. Thus it happens that one doesn't recognize a friend whom one has rarely seen for months, that one doesn't recognize the other. When somebody says, This one? Dead! This one? Died. This one? Outsettled . . . No news, of course. Mail ban for sixteen months.

Matzes [Yidd., unleavened bread]. In front of a grocery distribution center on Friday, April 16, people queue up to get matze instead of bread. All in all supposedly only 10,000 kg matzes for eighty-five thousand people. Praeses drives by. Jumps out. Chases people away. Hits. Thrashes. It was his wish that only Chassidim get matze. Immediately orders cessation of matze distribution. Matzes: a symbol of Pesach. Two kilograms bread = 1⅕ matzes. But people are yearning for a little piece of *yontiff* [Yidd., holiday]. A crumb of matze has the magic of evoking Pesach. Great is the longing for a bit of festiveness. For a little spark of hope. For preserving tradition. Matzes: in the *ghetto.* A little piece of freedom, a little piece of being a Jew! . . .

Today, Sunday, [April] 18, melancholy mood, dreary day. Everybody is going to get the extra ration and bread. Twenty decagrams brown sugar, 15 dkg preserves (turnips with saccharine), 15 dkg sago, 5 fruit teas, 50 cans red beets, one piece of soap, 5 dkg powder milk, 6 dkg cheese, 3 kg vegetables . . . But no potatoes. The ghetto is going hungry.

Talkie, 1940. Ashkenes at the wire. Is bored, shoots at passersby. Thump, thump. On some days up to ten people . . . Ashkenes looks into a yard from his post. A forty-five-year-old man is sitting on the ground reading. Ashkenes aims, shoots, hits him below the ear, the man screams, blood splatters.—Ashkenes picks up stones, tosses them against an opposite window to alert people. People are coming out, hear the man screaming, bring a stretcher to take him to the hospital, the man could be saved if the blood flow was stopped. "Bring the piece of dirt over here!" Ashkenes calls out. Then it happens. Ashkenes shoots his rifle from close range, twice; dead . . .

Nobody dares to go into the street. The seriously sick would like a doctor. The doctor doesn't dare to come. People dig holes into the wall of the yard so that they can get next door without having to pass near the wire.

Torn-down houses. One wooden house after another is collapsing.

Streets are changing. Back in 1940: "Whoever doesn't leave the Jewish district will be treated as a Jew." Still, many Poles remained. Ashkenes commission searched the houses. Many a Pole has tears in his eyes as he is leaving: "Take care of my house, my garden, etc." Leaving the place where they and their family had been living for decades like the Jews.

Talkie. A small town. Five hundred to six hundred Jews are coming from the provinces. Clothes taken off in a big building. SS says: "Nothing will happen to you. Just getting a bath. Cleansing. Delousing, etc." They leave. Tilted, slippery floor. Starting to slide into a sort of basin. Steam. Suffocating. *Terrible screams.* Dead.

Jews ask those who do these things: "We can't go on. Shoot us." Was no use. Have to. Or others are brought in and the resisters themselves are shot. And so it was done.—Clothes often sent to the ghetto for cleaning and the more inferior pieces left in the ghetto with permission of the ghetto administration.

April 19. *Toffi* children. Children are still calling out their candies, no longer 6 per marek but 2 per marek. They no longer sing *toffi* with the sharp double F but sing it strained, like "tovi," which is easier, less wearing on the speech muscles.

April 20. Yesterday Seder at Boruch Praszkier's with all the trimmings as usual, even eggs, which I have neither seen nor eaten in one and a half years. Brief, quiet evening from nine to ten o'clock. The night before something like festive mood in the ghetto. However without matzot, without wine. Dreary, rainy, without hope.

April 21. *Sky bright and fair. Pleasant sunshine. Little hope of better time. Around me dark faces. Meanwhile great suppers at the borders of the Getto, entertainments, performances in the culturhouse—and the people hungers. One kg turnip costs 20 "Chaimki" and I myself am not able to help.* [This and following paragraph in original English.]

April 22. *Passover-sensibility on the whole town. Private prayers to Lord. Nevertheless no one without care for the next day. A few sidurim* [Hebr., prayer books] *at the Zionist societies, first by the youth, the past chaluzim* [Hebr., pioneers] *on the hachscharah* [Hebr., training for immigration to Palestine] *Marysin.*[14]

Hebrew songs, among these "Techzakanah" ["Make Strong"], by Bialik.

Talkie and realities. After the company was gone, got undressed, in bed, light turned off. Knocking on the door. What's going on?

The black hand is storming the Jewish quarter of Varsovie [Fr., Warsaw], seeking to drive them out. They resist. Hands against weapons, rifles, and tanks—exchange of fire, siege. Will help arrive? All call out: Save our souls . . . The city is in flames!—How will it all end?[15] (Image of Czarist Russia.) People hide in cellars, attics, toilets, cemeteries, etc. From above, firebombs. Wild screaming and whimpering—*Shma Israel!* Does the world not want to hear? It doesn't hear. Shakespeare and Poe are silent.

April 23. One hundred twenty kilometers away anniversaries are being celebrated with revues and trite couplets, however, in *Erez* Israel with *tillem* [Yidd., psalms] and *tanes* [Yidd., prayer shawl] . . .

All waiting with dread: When will it be our turn? Does it make sense to be concerned about everyday things? The question "Where get the instruments of the hoplites [Spartan foot soldiers], weapons?" preoccupies the young and the bold, *all must be prepared for the moment of the danger and the enemy's attacs against us. Therefore it is necessary to cal the public opinion and not allow that the people further visite amusment and performances, on the contrary: that the whole population of the Ghetto may be prepared for the defense of life and honor* [original English].

April 25. Surprise: 5 kg potatoes, ration for two weeks. Worst kind of hunger overcome for short period. Black-market prices didn't go down.

Another surprise: huge queue at the potato distribution, but goods did not arrive.

April 26. Today, the potatoes are to be distributed, and in the kitchen "thick" soups.

Amnesty. Praeses pardoned light crimes and offenses on the occasion of Pesach!

April 27. *Hunger.* A beautiful religious service at Luzer Najman's—minyan men in the midst of a thunderstorm. See entry "Remembrances . . ."[16] Thousands of people are standing in line for hours for potatoes—desperate . . . Hunger on the last day of Pesach! Despair, nervous breakdowns, general weakness . . . No vegetables in the ghetto.

Marysin. On the way a yellow butterfly—stork—in the meadow three goats and six sheep . . . grazing . . . Otherwise no animals in the ghetto—no dogs, no cats, no rabbits . . . , etc.

April 28. *Work for Ashkenes.* A cool day, lucky is he who garnered his potato ration. Half a million straw shoes ready for the Russian winter campaign. One million kg straw prepared for further work.

April 29. *Face of the Ghetto.* Again, as in the year before, all around barracks, wooden houses, latrines, people at the roadside, even children, with spades and shovels [*djalka*] working the ground, nearby already a bit of greenery, even cherry-tree blossoms and almond bushes directly behind the fence . . . some in shirtsleeves, some wrapped in goatskins, some in loafers or wooden shoes [*trepki*] . . . The Jews are planting, their own vegetables expected by mid-May. Nearby wooden houses and even solid buildings are being torn down on order of Ashkenes . . . Mortar is flying, the thin-leafed trees rustle, mostly birch trees . . . The Jews are lugging heavy beams and planks on their shoulders like beasts of burden . . . Small carts with their meager possessions. Discolored bedding, broken chairs, broken dishes, a soup pot tied around the waist. Where are they moving to? Maybe back to where all is being leveled or separated from the ghetto? The sun is breaking through, bright blue between gray and white. [. . .]

April 30. *Henuschi.* Magnificent, cool morning after a terrible night, trouble breathing, thinking of Henuschi. I'm deeply concerned since I am without news, not through Red Cross either. What is she doing, the poor darling?

The leader of the Ghetto promises us that we will have enough of nourishment, victuals, and greens. The landmen here are working in all parts of the Ghetto. One sees women and girls and children with fieldtools—the best manner of defeating the bad time and the hunger. No one can live without the hope *for a good future* [original English].

Murder in the ghetto. The murdered thirteen-year-old girl *Ella Sznal.* The murderer, the twenty-five-year-old Chaim Israel *Brysz.* He confesses. Sold the foodstuff in three private shops.

May 1. Visiting Marysin, over meadows, sandpits. After two years, saw cows again; belonged to the Eldest. Milk cows.—Ghetto has been sealed three years ago.

May 2. Trial of Rathner and wife—card division because of food card fraud. Praeses demands the death penalty. The court sentences Rathner to three years' imprisonment. Fasting every two weeks, fifty lashes every month—corporal punishment. Court: strange sentence à la ghetto, under influence of Ashkenes, since in Polish law corporal punishment does not exist. The ghetto was established (sealed) on May 2, 1940.

Tidbit. The defense lawyer in court in favor of a defendant who embezzled food cards: "In the ghetto there are four kinds of human beings:

1. Those who have everything in excess, the best of the best.
2. Those who have connections with the first and who benefit as well.
3. Those who don't want to bite the dust and are looking around for rations, and who, if there's no other way, will organize them for themselves.
4. The vast majority who die of hunger.

"My client belongs to the third class, he wants to live . . ."

Tidbit. Spring 1941. Ashkenes demand that the Jewish court in the ghetto impose and carry out the death penalty for certain crimes (murder, listening to radio, smuggling). Ten judges resigned thereupon, four of them remained firm even though the Eldest had granted special protection to the judges.—Since then murder is a matter for Kripo and the German court, see entry April 30, Brysz.

May 3. Praeses demanded the death penalty for Rathner (see entry May 2) but didn't insist on it in order to avoid creating precedents. Ashkenes would insist on death penalty in similar cases in the future.

Praeses spoke on May 2 in Villa Marysin about postwar problems. He shouldn't rack his brain too much, the Zionist group is already planning for that time.—Afterward reception with bean coffee (!).

May 5. *Henuschi.* Again troubled nights—coughing, asthma, thinking of Henuschi's care in Vienna when she went to the pharmacy at night to get medicine. *Where she night hurried to the Svog-store and brought means against caugh* [original English].

May 6. *Wilma's birthday. Ghetto at once confidently: because of 8 kg Potatoes . . . Weather wet and cold like an autumn-day. When comes the happy end?* [Original English.] [. . .]

The Eldest. While he was living in Hospital I. Lagewnicka 34/36, orgies: looked out the window, called girls inside. At one time, the wife of a doctor. She refused. Whereupon her name was found out and the Jewish police were sent to her apartment and demolished the furnishings, floor planks ripped up, made a mess. The old man was also beaten . . . heckled by children who ran after the car . . . Ashkenes (Kripo) too gave him a few punches.

He himself has raised informers, declares: It is the sacred duty to inform the police of those who own jewelry, since the valuables pass into our hands and we will exchange them for food. Meanwhile it happened mostly that informing continued—up to Ashkenes, who then was using force and shedding blood. That didn't bother him: He has thousands of starving people and all of Marysin on his conscience. He says to himself: "We earn our income from our work and the requisitions, that is, confiscation of jewelry, furs, rugs, postage stamps, etc., shoes, featherbeds, iron, electric cooking appliances . . ."

May 12. Big gathering in my apartment. Mood: excited faces, but full of hope.

The Eldest wants to play a historical role for the future. Talks about leading the people out of the ghetto and marching in front of them. Has already intention of creating some kind of organization that will carry out the necessary preparations.

The Eldest. A primitive underling suddenly come into power, has only one wish: to keep himself in power. If he possessed any understanding of politics and had known the kind of partner he was up against, had he possessed the slightest diplomatic talent, had he negotiated, threatened, extorted, flattered, resisted—much would not have happened.

The others too, Dawid and Marek [Gertler and Kliegier], are totally deficient in this respect. Only in the exercise of power, without any foresight, without the slightest sense of dimensions, positions, possibilities, appraisal of the power relationships. [. . .]

May 21. *Talkie.* A train of inmates from Czarnickiego taken by the Jewish police to the Kripo, an abject sight as in novels by Dostoevski after Siberia . . . Professor Hart (with a pack on his back—laundry), "I buried my daughter yesterday . . ." How is it going? Better in the sun? Anything else new? Anything hope-inspiring?

Talkie.

1. A Polish Christian woman climbs over the wire into the ghetto. Schupo sees her. Doesn't shoot . . . the girl disappears.—
2. On the same day, three Polish smugglers with butter, eggs, etc., at the wire. Schupo lets them be.
3. On the same day Gestapo from the town: On the basis of denunciation, the commandant goes to Bess-Oilom, grave is opened, jewelry found with the dead.

Talkie. The ghetto has gone insane: The war will last another forty days! It's interesting to note how a rumor makes its way through the ghetto. Doubts, despair, belief, faith, unconditional trust: People start using their good soap and shoe polish, start eating potatoes.

Tidbit. Vegetable center. A woman lugs a sack with 2 x 15 kg potatoes. The director asks her: "Why in such a hurry? Don't you have potatoes left at home?"

She looks at him: "Because I ate the previous potatoes, I have the strength to carry *these.*" General laughter. [. . .]

May 23. During the celebration of the third anniversary, a toothless Jew in *trepki* [Pol., wooden shoes] says: "What can he do? Even if he slaughters us all, us here, somewhere will be Jews who will live to see his *mapule* [Yidd., downfall] . . . if not we, than in the United States . . . He won't destroy the Jewish people completely . . . What nobody has accomplished, he too won't succeed at, we shall live on . . . somewhere . . . we'll know what to do . . ."

Again *moire* [Yidd., fear] in the ghetto. A commission from over there is said to be coming. Warmer Sunday. [. . .]

May 25. Wearing summer suit for the first time so that winter is behind me. It would be terrible having to read up May 1942 . . . that is, outsettlement from the home in Marysin: Dr. Ferler and wife, Ehrenhaft and wife, Singer and wife, Engel and wife, and to let the figures pass before me: Mmes Stein, Biedl, Rosenberg, Adler, Markus . . . Farkas, Baer, Barihiuch, Arent, Bellak, et al. [. . .]

May 26. A cool day without any special character. Supposed to ask in Czarnickiego about the execution of Brysz . . . Don't feel like it . . . strange indifference . . . Otherwise sensation, in the ghetto concern about food always pushes all else aside.

People are adopting children since they get rations for them, which they withhold from them. For example, five rations for a five-member family, bread, two for the couple, in addition heating material per head, this means a fivefold ration for one stove. Part of the surplus (!) is sold under the table: bread and wood coal.

May 27. [. . .] *Ashkenes.* Execution Brysz in Czarnickiego. *Tliah* set up so nobody in the neighborhood could see it. Three Jewish policemen as executioners (henchman, two assistants), then examination of body by doctor. Discretion striking in comparison to earlier (see Herz—Cologne, February 1942). Is this a change in atmosphere? Isn't the food distribution a pure miracle? [. . .]

May 28. Didn't sleep all night and trouble breathing! Slept in the early morning with open window.

Henuschi. Again despair. Dreams of Henuschi, Vilma, Erich . . . How much longer?

Reviewing in my mind: Besides Henuschi, Vilma, Erich, Ernst: Linda, Emil Gerta, Otto, Hans, Feli, Franz, Gallia, Heini, Hans Bondy, Hans Klein, Evi, Georg, Wikinger and wife and daughter, Aunt Fanny, all the Jellineks, people in Bratislava, friends in Palestine . . . Lizzi Pisk, sculptor Weiss, Herta Ehrlich, Fritz Gross, Fritz Manyi Eri, Fanny Rust . . . Viennese friends from Astoria Beeth, de France . . . Prague friends: Rafael et al., people around the Hrad, Otto Schön, Herta Havr . . . Isi Kohn and wife, the Woihch family, Rand, Richter from Hotel Fischer, Lukanec, Dr. Frankl and Noemi, Gustav Boehm, Uncle Moritz, the Stadlers, Gruenfeld-Braun, Dr. Spiegler, the Geller family, Stricker, Friedmann, Ella, Kolb . . . Dr. Wiesen, people associated with advertisement (Goldf. et al.), Café Klein, Harry Prager, Grubner, film director Halery, Agadati, Bukspan, Uri Zwi Haller, Schlonski, Kanner, Bondy, Gelber.

Talkie. Have you ever seen a human being shortly before dying of hunger? His legs hardly support him, stomach caved in, sunken temples right and left, yellowish white coloring. Dizziness: collapses on the stairs despite cane. He's quickly administered some ressort soup. Another ten hours! Too late. Dies, slowly fading away . . . with a sigh on his lips. Every day a dozen. To be seen in the street, through open windows. They are completely wrapped in clothing because they are freezing cold.

May 30. Cold day. Potatoes are still rolling. Excitement in the ghetto: Waiting again for half a can of canned meat.—*From abroad fair records. What will be? No one knows any sure . . .* [Original English.]

For the story "The Secret of the Ghetto." Not in the basement but in the yard, wooden hut. Human queue into the yard . . . A small foyer: door, leading into Beth Midrash, half open: three long, narrow tables along the long side, flanked by benches, on the short side opposite the window high up a shelf with leather *sforim* [Hebr., Torah scrolls] . . . Candles . . . Terrible haze . . . sticky . . . moldy smell from old, rotten garments . . . And in all that, ecstasy. [. . .]

June 7. Zionist circle (Meilach Schipper) stimulates me to write memoirs. Maybe I'll start with a sketch in the next few days.

Humor. A black-and-white-spotted cow through Dworska to Baluter Ring. Everybody laughs; why? A young fellow says: "It's the first cow who made it to the Baluter Ring without protection."

June 8. [. . .] Something is in the air, says the ghetto . . . Cool day. We're waiting again.—

Humor. The Eldest as well as Gertler agree on everything except the agrarian question. The Eldest wants Gertler to lie in the ground, and Gertler wants the Eldest to lie in the ground . . .

June 9. [. . .] Ritual: A groups of Jews illegally obtained food with cards from people who were deported. Didn't go out for months and had a female relative get everything for them. Meanwhile their beards began to grow—Chassidic Jews. When they were caught and taken to Czarnickiego, their beards had to be removed according to regulation. Beards in the ghetto are prohibited by German authorities for hygienic reasons.—"Shoot me, hang me, but leave me my beard." . . . When he saw that his plea had no effect, since the Jewish police was dragging him to the barber standing at the ready, he begged him to leave him at least a little bit of hair on both sides so that a trace of his Chassidic soul remains in his countenance. [. . .]

June 12. Sabbath: You shall hallow the Sabbath day. Three *tliahs* at the central prison. Execution ten o'clock in the morning carried out by the Jewish police. Two candidates went from a work camp to a village, begging Polish peasants for bread. Caught. The third one tried to escape from the ghetto. Scenes. The delinquents were screaming. No use. Order from the Gestapo. The hearse was waiting in front of the prison for Marysin. All police chiefs including Commandant Rosenblatt as well as Gertler had to be present . . . Pathetic Shabbbath after Shavuot . . . Work and laughter in the vegetable patches. And then in the evening to the cultural center. Revue of O. S. with jesting and coarse humor . . . (*Tliahs* ordered on Friday evening! . . .) The executed are: Abraham Tondowski, thirty-one years old, Zduńska Wola; Herz Faygeles, twenty-three years old, Tomaszów; Mordka Standarowicz, twenty-nine years old. [. . .]

June 16 and 17. *Henuschi.* Terrible days—heavy cough, sweating at night, heart pain, have to take nitroglycerin, premonition of death for the first time. At the same time, rainy weather for days, which is actually beneficial for my asthma.—I have no hope for a good ending.

June 20. Feeling that the world will soon cave in on all sides. Will I ever see Henuschi again, she me? Daily and nightly questions. [. . .]

June 22. *Henuschi.* Ever more frequent dreams—Henuschi. Nerves tight to the utmost. When will the storm break loose? Humid day, gasping for air. Wheezing and pain near the heart.

June 23. Military commission from Berlin in the ghetto. Strict readiness. Streets empty. Everybody is in the factories. Quiet. Nervousness.

Ressorts being inspected.—Will probably be over today. My colleague A. S. Kamenetzky buried. [. . .]

June 24. No longer have any illusions. Counting on *milchama* [Hebr., war] 1944. Autumn!—Emanuel Hirschberg's scientific department has been dissolved. Equipment for the time being still in the ghetto. [. . .]

June 30. Learned last night that Dr. Heilig has died . . . forty years old, hidden T.B. A good friend is gone, a courageous colleague, excellent worker. Pain hard to overcome . . . After Dr. Lamm, who was deported, now my second comrade. Dreary day, it's raining, like autumn. The soul is just as dreary. Heilig's death hard to overcome, hadn't been prepared for such a sudden, tragic end. So far three victims in the archive: Cukier-Cersky, Kamienecki, Dr. Heilig . . . Who will be next?

Dr. Singer deeply affected, is charged with making the arrangements. [. . .]

July 2. It's being said that at the moment little work in the ghetto, except for wood and metal. Fear that people could be evacuated due to lack of orders. From the outside not a sound. For one and a half years, ban on mail. What is going on out there?

Henuschi. I'm dreaming of her every morning. How is Hans doing? Why has he never written?—Why not Henuschi through Red Cross?

Eighty-four thousand five hundred twenty-five inhabitants in the ghetto. Mortality fifteen to twenty-five daily.

July 4. *Outsettlement.* Mother with children, three already on the wagon; the third is torn from her chest by a Jewish policeman and tossed on to the wagon. [. . .]

Outsettlement May 1942. Is it true that Ashkenes demands outsettlement and the Eldest sacrifices the newly settled? This has to be investigated. [. . .]

Division of power. The Eldest put in power by Ashkenes: authoritarian, real commune . . . later real work camp. Food on the basis of *clearing* [original English] for work performed.—[. . .]

July 8–9. *Terror. Ashkenes.* Car drives through the streets. A frightened six-year-old girl hides behind me: "Oy, veh, they'll take me, Mamyshka will have no more children, two sisters already taken away . . ." (meaning September 1942 outsettlement).

Women's business. Prostitution. It's being said in the ghetto: They are carrying on too much. Every Kierownik has a girlfriend—officially. The young girls are being protected. For example, one sees many pretty girls in the kitchens (now strengthening kitchens, Mlynarska and Ceglana), appetizing, well groomed, round, and meaty. A man whose wife was deported gets married without waiting to hear of wife's fate. Praeses sent such a candidate to Czarnickiego, but that didn't solve the problem. Pretty girls are generally well dressed, good stockings and shoes, next to them thousands of wretched beggars.

Children. It's amazing: ten-year-olds in the factories. Busy at the machines in the tailor's workshops. Getting their rations, carrying wood and coal, heavy packs of vegetables on their backs; selling saccharine and toffi, working in the plants, helping with the cooking, etc. And with all that . . . [illegible] weakness, malnutrition, spindly legs, good humor, playing, smart, roughhousing . . . and in all horrifying to look at.

Talkie. At first good figures, finally death (dying, hunger, disease, gallows, terror, suicide, shot for amusement, hunted to death, of grief: loss of will to live—see Dr. Rosenberg after the death of his mother).

Curiosity. Mrs. Alma Eisenberger (Prague) was ordered to appear at Gestapo Litzmannstadt, where she was told that she had received citizenship for Paraguay. Probably left the ghetto (!!).

Diseases—month of June. Tuberculosis 265 + 26 = 291; total of 934, 60 percent TB in the month of June. [. . .]

July 11. *Henuschi.* Dreary, rainy Sunday. Idea: new ending, idea for novella "The Secret of the Ghetto."

Dreaming more often of Henuschi, trembling for her and about her. Strong impression of the book *Sex and Character* mainly because of the "I-experiences" and the loneliness. From there the idea for a new ending of "The Secret of the Ghetto."

Finally again desire to work. I'll be starting soon one of my projected stories. Wrestling with a concise style, structure. Perhaps the material requires a totally new form. Thinking of I. Babel in Malik-Verlag.

Today again B. I.,[17] new rations, among them 10 dkg fat and 1 kg potatoes. Elation to see again and again carts with cabbage rolling into the ghetto.

July 12. Yesterday I ate cherries for the first time in two years (from farmers) on the *djalka* [Pol., plot of land] in the company of friends . . .

Outsettlement September 1942. Somebody recounts embittered: Whatever Chaim may have accomplished while holding office, one thing cannot be forgiven. Address on Friday afternoon (together with David Warszawski and Judge Jacobson) before the Saturday curfew: "Give up your children, sacrifice your children, so others can be saved." On the following day, he appeared accompanied by Jewish policemen in Marysin, children's homes and orphanages were surrounded and many hundreds of children were dragged away. The nurses and supervisors wanted to hide the children, but by order of the Praeses, each directrice was responsible for the number of children.

Jewish policemen took gold and jewelry, and "saved" private children.

July 13. *A day of rumors.* Dawid Gertler was taken into town, overnight, didn't come back at night.[18] As a result, fear that this may have unfavorable repercussions for the ghetto. Since there is almost no food left in the ghetto, therefore hunger, that the ghetto is doomed.—In the end, a new chief mayor Litzmann, of whom, it was told, that he had no interest in preserving the ghetto.[19]

July 14. *The Case of Dawid Gertler.* Soon after Łódź was taken, Gertler made himself available to the Gestapo. His coworkers, figures from the underworld. Primarily good at detecting hidden jewelry and valuables. Followed frequently by severe punishment, even shooting. Later, after the establishment of the ghetto, he continued to work here, surrounded by his cronies. It was his job—as director of the "Special" and confidant of the Gestapo—to keep on coming up with new goods. In the spring of 1942 came the Herzberg affair, who was district chief in Marysin and director of the central prison. In this capacity he participated in the winter outsettlement, in the course of which he pillaged foodstuff of all sorts for many months. Also, jewelry, etc., was found in his possession. Herzberg disappeared, taken into town. His fate is, of course, unknown. *His fate is naturally unknown* [original English]. After Herzberg's fall, the time had come for Gertler's rise.

However, preceded by another episode: Gertler was arrested by the Kripo and accused of having worked with the Gestapo in securing gold, etc., in favor of Gestapo. Gertler's ribs were broken, imprisoned for eight months, didn't betray the Gestapo, finally freed through intervention of the Eldest.—Then quick rise. Gradually second to the Eldest in the ghetto. Foodstuff, meat, *djalka,* at his disposal. His people continued to sniff out valuables. It was he who, presumably, against payment of 1,000 to 2,000 marks, officially took Jews from the ghetto in big trucks to Warsaw and made money that way.—When he drove through the ghetto, people stared at him, admired him, envied him, à la Khan, mob-rule setup, fawning for his favor, presents for his people, coupons, etc., to push the Eldest into the background. Next to him the director of the work ressorts, Aron Jakubowicz, that makes three overlords in the ghetto. Frequent conflicts, which were resolved again, *sholem* [Yidd., peace]—but again and again power struggle, both parties trying to top each other in handing out gifts to their supporters. I saw confidants of the Gestapo à la Liliom and Ficzur; again and again valuables have to be tracked down. In mid-June 1943, gold dollars and gold jewelry, paper dollars, etc.

Now Gertler has fallen. Called to the Baluter Ring, put in a car, taken away. Search of his lodgings. He is said to have shared gold valuables with the Gestapo. At any rate, didn't return by the fifteenth, after three days. Will he have a successor? [. . .]

July 19. *Talkie.* Saw a group of people, among them women and young girls, taken by Jewish policemen out of Czarnickiego: shoes [*trepki*] clunking, deplorable faces. Dante's "Lasciate ogni speranzy roi ilicutrate" . . . All silent . . . no facial expressions, no horror, no hope . . . something like this unthinkable in our former earthly life.

July 20. New potato ration of 5 kg expected; prices: bread 220, potatoes 25 marks.

Curiosity. Who in future times will believe that human beings fought each other over a potato, had tears in their eyes, permitted themselves to be swept up in passionate excitement, were envious, revolted, sought protection?

July 21. I'm invited, Friday, July 23, on 20 Tammuz, to speak about Herzl (on the anniversary of his death) in the apartment of Boruch

Praszkier before Zionist friends. I'm curious myself to see whether I still have enough élan, enough dynamic, and enough stored "wisdom" to get and hold an audience's attention, to show that the old fighting spirit is still alive in me after almost six years of emigration, two years of them in the ghetto.—Today in front of revisionist friends for the second time.

Face of the Ghetto. Describe the absurdity which is more clearly visible on a bright day than in winter. People are carrying leaves of red beets (*botwinki*). They are stored in carts. Where is Gertler? Everywhere fruit trees: apples and Vistula [sour cherry] . . .

July 24. *Zion.* Spoke twice in a decayed building before revisionist youth. Splendid. Great time. On 20 Tammuz, anniversary of Herzl's death, in Boruch's apartment, conference on 21 Tammuz on the anniversary of Bialik's death, Herzl remembrances by Schipper.

Talkie. Children guiding, pushing, vegetable carts through the streets, charming, blond creatures—without any instruction, without a book, without a song. They have to make up everything themselves; card games: the cover of a cigarette carton, singing made-up songs.

July 26. Monday—beautiful, sunny morning—Dante delights me. Ghetto in uproar . . . *Vita nuova!* [. . .]

August 3. *Henuschi.* Still burning-hot summer weather—staying at home all day . . . Feeling fatally ill, dreaming of Henuschi. What's the poor soul doing? Is she crying her eyes out, *looking forward?* . . . [Original English.]

Starving. For two weeks: 20 dkg black flour, 25 flakes, 45 brown sugar, 25 preserves, 4 kg potatoes, 3½ kg bread . . .

Cut off from the world. Greeting cards "am healthy" have been stopped. Money too can only be acknowledged upward of 20 marks. Why? Because people are sending to their dear ones in the ghetto a few marks to find out whether they are alive . . .

Eighty-four thousand three hundred one inhabitants in the ghetto.

Viewpoints in the ghetto. Some say we must work, strive, produce, advance, to do all that's possible . . . playing the role. Kierownik coupon, etc.

Others say to feign senseless effort, since the ghetto is unnatural and cannot offer any satisfaction. It's a sin to *robot* [Czech, work] for Ashkenes, etc.

Ashkenes. Am druut! [Yidd., At the wire!] "Just hold out! You've held out this long, you must make it through the last lap. It will all be well."—These words were spoken during the hot days before Dante's end. The ghetto knew about it, everybody was feverish. Crazy rumors, some of it occurs later on. [. . .]

August 13. Terrible atmosphere, even despair—no new deliveries at the centers, neither potatoes nor vegetables. Fantastic prices.

Hunger. Botwinki leaves five times . . . fear of outsettlement . . . In the Marysin cemetery, trenches for air raids, therefore the rumor that Jews are being gassed, etc. Rug and straw-shoe ressorts have been liquidated, therefore rumor that the ghetto was to be dissolved. . . , etc. I'm still good for a potato allocation. Don't know what to cook in the next days. The ghetto is again going hungry . . . 84,187 inhabitants in the ghetto.

The cultural center has been closed . . . Ressort! One hundred fifty people from the ghetto brought in to work! It's being said that today 15 dkg of bread instead of soup and that neither potatoes nor cabbage is coming in . . .

August 15. At night. Again two hundred people dislodged during the night of Saturday to Sunday (August 14–15), presumably for work outside the ghetto. Again at night!

Unrest even though the worst rumors have already ceased. [. . .]

August 18. Indescribable hunger! No potato distribution in a week, no vegetables. Supposed to make do with 209 dkg flour for two weeks?! [. . .]

August 20. *Hunger in the extreme.* People are going to the *djalkas* to beg (against payment) for a few leaves of *botwinki* or something like that. One kilogram of leaves = 8 chaimki. At long last, potatoes! A 3-kg ration is distributed—relief. Most people fall over the 3 kg and devour it in one meal. For several days two hundred fifty men designated for work outside the ghetto, ready at the central prison, did not leave.

Young boys were suddenly dismissed from the central prison, perhaps there was a danger that they too would be sent out to work.

August 22. From the twenty-fourth on, 3 kg potatoes. The ghetto is breathing freely. Terrible heat—45 degrees! All are languishing. No way of cooling off—no bath—no tea—no fruit—no garden or forest—no water—no river! Indescribable suffering. People like draft animals hitched to carts, hauling excrement. Deliveries for the kitchens, children carrying wood, etc. At the same time, hunger . . .

August 26. *Curiosity.* Ashkenes trucks appear at the Bess-Oilom with *messim.* They blocked off Bess-Oilom for two hours and tossed the *messim* into freshly dug *kwurim* [Yidd., ditches]. All *be'sot* [Hebr., in secret]. The whole done supposedly systematically also in other areas to cover all traces of the *hargenen* [Yidd., the slain].

August 29. Turmoil in the ghetto because of *abroad!* [Original English.]

August 31–September 1. Again turmoil with Ashkenes: One hundred people taken from Czarnickiego, in addition twelve tuberculosis sufferers from the hospital. It can be assumed that they are lost in accordance with the familiar method. Reminiscent of Brzeziny. "Give me ten human beings," said Ashkenes to the Eldest of Brzeziny, a physician (!?). He takes inferior people with a criminal record (although only theft out of desperation), hands them over, among them the Jewish village idiot. All of them are somehow eliminated, report states because of sabotage. Ashkenes shows his skill, how he works, ten Jews destroyed and Berlin is satisfied.

The same here, now even at the last moment. They will claim that the elimination of tuberculosis sufferers will strengthen the workforce of the ghetto, that is, averted the danger, stabilized.

September 2. [. . .] *The question of Czarnickiego.* At the time of Polish rule, central prison of Czarnickiego. Since it was a prison, it had to be filled. Crime as elsewhere in the ghetto does not exist. Cheating, usury, forgery, manslaughter, serious physical harm, rebellion, political crimes, are absent. The only transgression is theft, and that of food.

Motive: hunger. Theft of public goods in cooperatives, vegetable centers, wood, coal, potatoes from passing carts, or corruption in the kitchens, larceny: two soups instead of one, exceeding weight limit, fake cards—from the deported, etc. Who passes the sentence: court—the "Special"—Praeses.

Punishments: Excrement[20] or several weeks = months at Czarnickiego. Now the following: Kripo or Gestapo keeping in reserve at Czarnickiego. For example, when exhausted workers come in from outside and want to recuperate a bit, they are put at the disposal of Czarnickiego. So it happens that they are placed on an equal footing with the inmates. Furthermore—and *this is the most important thing*—there is a constant number of inmates who are kept at the ready as commodity for the Gestapo in case a sudden demand is issued for delivery of human beings as workers or for some other dark purpose.

Outsettlement, if not direct work, means death. Therefore: Incarceration in Czarnickiego for petty theft of potatoes is as much as a death sentence, since during outsettlement he will be sacrificed and thrown into the insatiable jaws of the Ashkenes.

The "Special" too passes sentences administratively: for the most minute dereliction excrement, but from Czarnickiego.

Praeses too: holds to his disposition in Czarnickiego. A preposterous situation. Arbitrariness. Despotism without compare. Reverse: "The hungry do not understand those with full bellies." Unique in the history of mankind that human beings emaciated from heavy labor are put in prison afterward to be kept ready as *kapore* [Yidd., offering].

Jews are sentencing ghetto Jews to death.

Jews are putting Jews in prison whereby the impression is created: Jewish criminals. Something should be done about this so that one day not a single inmate remains in Czarnickiego, that Czarnickiego is empty! That would be the best refutation of the Ashkenes thesis.

Night scene: In Czarnickiego during outsettlement: some are frozen with terror, others weep, lament, and still others don't want to believe it, and still others resist. Singing of *Hatikvah* [Hebr., hope; Jewish national anthem] is heard . . . Family members held hostage and taken along if somebody stays in hiding!

September 2. All of a sudden sick people are being taken to the hospital by their relatives, in horse-drawn carts, etc., for fear of a surprise outsettlement. Ashkenes' cynicism, base hatred, such evil hard to comprehend, unprecedented.

September 3. Early morning fog, autumn in the air, and always the same question: Are the potatoes coming? For two weeks no vegetables; what shall we cook? Praeses discontinued meat allocation to the privileged. [. . .]

September 6. Terrible corruption among three groups who are feuding with each other: Praeses, group Gertler, group Jakubowicz. Each one has his praetorian guard, etc. . . .

September 8. *Tidbit.* Inferior soup at the ressort! One worker refuses to eat, pure water. Others don't take it either, out of solidarity. Kierownik intercedes. First workers' conflict. Kierownik tries hitting, the other one hits back. All solidarity, strike. Praeses intervenes, no good. Punishment: extension of work time by an hour, after the "Special" had arrested three and had to let them go again.

Dante perditus! Incredible atmosphere in the ghetto: rations appeared two days early, in addition, 3 kg potatoes = happened because hunger was too great.

Tidbit. Ashkenes Selner throws an apple into a Jewish apartment from his guard post. An Ashkenes control organ takes note, approaches the Schupo, takes away his rifle, takes him into town.—Polish coachman nods to the Jewish cart driver at the wire as if to say: "What does the Schupo still want with his rifle here? . . ."

September 10. Today blackout and alarm!

Saturday, September 11. *Tliah.* A man named Beckermann: Kripo makes house search! Discovered leather straps, supposedly from the leather ressort where he was working. Arrested, sentenced to death—gallows—from Berlin. Saturday (of course) the public hanging is to take place. It's been said that Praeses pushed through that he'll be executed at Czarnickiego. [. . .]

September 22. *Ashkenes.* When potatoes fall off the cart between the wires, he pushes them with his foot toward the sidewalk so that Jews can reach them. Some put them into their pockets and hand them eventually to a passing Jew. Ashkenes distributes apples and pears to Jewish children. Being admonished by another, Ashkenes gives present to Jewish policeman and says: "But if I should need you later, remember you owe me." [. . .]

September 25. *Ashkenes.* Ashkenes pulls up early in the morning in civilian automobile and a truck. Bess-Oilom is blocked off for hours, nobody is allowed to enter. Shots are heard . . . Nobody dares go near. Graves are dug up and filled in again . . . The Jews in the villages who helped with the affair as gravediggers, etc., are likewise *geharget* [Yidd., killed] so that no witnesses of the misdeed remain.

September 27. *Talkie, perhaps Ashkenes.* At the railway station wagonloads of passing Germans being evacuated from White Russia on their way to the Reich. Terribly sobering since only a short while ago German institutions were being established in Russia. Mood, of course, bad . . .

High Holy Days. Autumn winds, shortly before *Yomim Neroyim.* Both days at Boruch minyan . . . with *shofar* [Hebr., ram's horn], etc. Wonderful time, cold snack with *bronfen* [Yidd., liquor], much heart in it.—As it turns out, minyanim [prayer groups] were set up in many departments, also private *modlitwy* [Pol., prayers] . . . Singing was heard from the houses on the way to Marysin . . . On the first day of Rosh Hashanah at Luzer Najman's for supper . . .

October 3. Potatoes are rolling in masses. Today 3-kg ration. Hope that again before Yom Kippur. The eyes of the hungry are gleaming. Heating material: 1 kg coals and 3 kg wood for a month!!

Wonderful autumn days—midday sun. [. . .] Business with Praeses. People look up influential persons, giving them *psires*—getting goods in return. For example, at the "Special" or Jakubowicz or Provisioning.—Outrageous! If somebody wants to tell another person *psires* to give him courage, to keep his spirit up, then it's a moral deed, but not against payoff.

Talkie or novel. Chaver [Hebr., friend] listens to radio. Kripo comes. He hides the radio in his bed. Says to Kripo, What you are looking for is in the room next door. They go in, take furs, electric hotplate, iron, etc.—He is spared.

October 8. Erev Yom Kippur! Festive mood since Praeses succeeded in having the next day, a Saturday, declared a holiday. Pumpkins are rolling in—beautiful colors! Midsummer sun. This afternoon at five-thirty, *yontiff* evening meal at Boruch's, at Luzer's for *davenen* [Yidd., praying].

Attention! Splendid Kol Nidre minyan at Luzer's. The Eldest is present . . . speaks! Tells us that the ghetto had been in danger in August, which was averted only by assurances of the Wehrmacht [German army]. Later, Praeses guaranteed with his head peace and work in the ghetto.

Yom Kippur. Shabbat = Yom Kippur! Off from work. One hundred forty minyanim registered, besides many private, complete services. Sefer Torahs are openly being carried across the street to the house where the service is to take place. (In return all have to work 110 percent on Sunday, October 10.) Holiday atmosphere in the streets. Potato deliveries—pumpkins are rolling. Eyes are gleaming, father—mother—child—in the streets.

October 11. *Autumn winds from the Russian steppe.* First cold temperatures, foreboding of winter . . . without wood or coal. Today coupon but again no fat.

October 12. *Dying. Hunger.* A man of forty-two died because he didn't want to live anymore.—"I don't want to be a burden to my wife and daughter as a cripple."—

October 13. First big potato ration: 10 kg a head for three weeks! A sign that the ghetto administration doesn't want us to starve to death! Pumpkin is driving through town. Autumnal sunshine—warm, at the same time, a cold east wind. [. . .]

October 17. *Sunday.* Most beautiful sun, warm, springlike—with all that unrest, since the Eldest and Jakubowicz were in the town yesterday and officials of the ghetto administration were in the office of the "Special." People are queuing up for potatoes, tomatoes, pumpkins.

October 18. *Henuschi. Vilma.* Repeated dreams of Henuschi—Vilma, London—New York. Impossible to take notes every day . . . At the same time, premonitions of winter. Reading Henri Barbusse, *Hell.* Terrible, dreadful, grim book, *The Hell.* Wandering daily to Marysin for last four months, 200 x 3 km = 600 km, halfway to Henuschi. Autumn winds, portent of winter—without wood or coal. How will it all end?

Ashkenes. Manages to throw out a few potatoes with bayonet from the passing cart and kicks them with his foot behind the fence where a Jewish policeman picks them up for himself.

We're sick of the whole shit up to our necks. You're doing well. But our people won't come back from the Fonye front, they remain there as workers. [. . .]

October 20. Sun—sun—most beautiful May day. Suddenly hope of a good end very soon . . . Maybe this year, 1943, it will be all over . . . "There's hardly a human being who doesn't have a wounded spot somewhere after four to two years in the ghetto . . ."

October 24. More beautiful days . . . [met] today with the Jewish state advocates.

Cooking tomatoes as compote, peeling potatoes.

October 25. Sunday—spoke with Jewish state advocates—dark stairwell, through damp kitchen to a room full of beds: about the idea of a Jewish state and the world war.

October 27. Tuesday [met] with the revisionists about the situation in Turkey, the Middle East, and Palestine.

Gray, dreary, foreboding of winter, no potatoes, no pumpkins, no vegetables . . . [. . .]

November 4. *Hunger.* Cold, dreary, snow in the air . . . proclamation that shakes the ghetto.

"*Two Years Ghetto Starting November 4, 1943* (No. 401): As a result of the shrinking potato supply (ghetto administration has cut in half), I am forced to stop temporarily the distribution of extra soup portions." [. . .]

November 5. First winter cold . . . No wood, no coal, nothing to eat . . . not even a potato or ration or anything else cookable.

Ten lighters = 1 mark. [. . .] Eighty-three thousand four hundred sixty-nine inhabitants in the ghetto!

NOTEBOOK 15

Remembrances (As Manuscript for Author Only)

[. . .] The ghetto is something extraordinarily new inasmuch as the foundations for the moral education of the Jewish people have completely been lost, *religious*—or *national*—education. Children are growing up without these foundations, no substitute exists. Only one question: *Ration!* What will become of this youth? Wouldn't it be possible to introduce these children at least once a week to a piece of Jewish history?

Forms and colors of caps in the ghetto . . . describe in *Face of the Ghetto.*

Scene. Terribly emaciated! Rolling eyes! Allocation of four potatoes and four vegetables stolen! "I can't bear it any longer. I have to do something to myself! Nothing to eat . . . My sister is dying . . . husband and son lost . . . What is left for me in this world?" Tears streaming, nervous breakdown. Pulls herself up. Sits down in a chair. Gradually the agitation passes. Hums Solveig's song by Grieg without realizing what she is singing . . .

The Eldest. I saw him late at night . . . wildly staring eyes, hat with rim . . . boots shiny . . . he crossed the Baluter Ring, behind him several policemen as guards . . . he looked like a Roman emperor with his cohort . . .

He gave the impression of either a madman or a megalomaniac. Another time: He drives through the city: throws candy into the crowd.—A third time: Sees himself in *historical* perspective. A *Navi* [Hebr., prophet] . . . Hundreds of people work for him, write about him . . . He sees himself as a kind of Shabbatai Zvi,[1] but a genuine one who will hold out to the end without fail. Sees himself as becoming a hero in Jewish history.

During a scene between the Eldest and one of his opponents, the old man says: "*What are you telling me about Jewish history? I am myself a piece of Jewish history.*"

In his ill temper, yes, his wildness, he often loses all sense of responsibility. Often destructive, thousands have died because of his recklessness. Victims are par for the course, he says.

Psychological state of the ghetto. The ghetto nourishes itself also from—"rumors." Bad news is exaggerated as much as good news. It is important to determine what the psychological state of the ghetto is. Has all of it been reduced to an animal level? To a vegetable existence? Animal-like, or still hope? Some say that one must live one's life as if the ghetto were a permanent matter. Others say: The prevailing condition should not be recognized as permanent. Otherwise we will lose the strength, the courage, the desire, to live. Only inner resistance against the ghetto will preserve us. Both of these theses side by side.

Atmosphere à la Outsettlement

March 25 (1943). The streets dreary and drizzly and almost devoid of people. At the corners policemen on the lookout. Whispering: The young and old better stay off the street. They'll be captured and dragged to Czarnickiego. Ashkenes has demanded one thousand, short by several hundred. People are being captured like *dogs by the dogcatcher.* I get a piece of paper from Vera Heilig at the office: "I've been arrested. Please help me get out."

Desperate atmosphere in the ghetto. Renewed outsettlement? Which categories? Nobody knows—as usual—what is going on. This is how it continues into the evening. Meanwhile, fifteen of the eight hundred fifty workers from Poznan have died, the others are in pitiable condition. Unable to work anymore. About one thousand are sitting in the central prison waiting for what may come. Certain doom, Shabbat of March 27 still echoes. But in the ressorts they are celebrating anniversaries with eating and drinking. They call this "balls." The pariahs, the doomed, *klapsidres,* behind lock and seal, unable to embarrass the cheerful ones . . . Shame on the police who have adopted Ashkenes behavior. They believe they are able to protect themselves by acting in a brutal manner. Terrible embitterment—"We'll get even with you after the *milchome* . . ." So say some of the principled and courageous young men in the ghetto.

F. Schiller, from "The Mission of Moses" (from vol. 10 of *Thalia*):

> Two religions, encompassing the majority of the inhabitants of the earth, Christianity and Islam, are both derived from the religion of the Hebrews; without it there would be neither Christianity nor a Koran. From it (the Mosaic religion) came a precious truth . . . the teaching of the one God was temporarily disseminated among the people as an article of blind faith and was preserved until, finally, a few brighter minds were able to develop it into a rational idea. In this manner, a large part of mankind was spared all those sad errors to which idolatry ultimately had to lead, and the Hebraic version received exclusive preference so that the religion of the intellectuals did not stand in direct contrast to the religion of the people, as was the case among enlightened heathens.
>
> Seen from this viewpoint, the Hebrew nation must appear to us as an important universal-historical people, and all the evil that is customarily attributed to this people, all efforts of witty minds to belittle them, will not prevent us from doing justice to them. The disgrace and depravity of the nations cannot erase the eminent achievement of their lawgiver, let alone destroy the influence that is this nation's rightful claim in world history. [Translation by present translator.]

Idea. If that which happened here is possible—if the world has looked on the occurrences of the last ten years, then all that has been achieved up to now deserves to be destroyed. It was seen that the artists, poets, etc., did not have the strength to suppress the pernicious elements. They permitted themselves to be blinded by power, swords, medals, parades.

We know that the names of great men had greater value than those of propagandists and generals, but they remained silent and joined in. Woe to them! Something new must rise from the new flood in which not even Noah's ark would have a chance to save itself . . . [. . .]

Rescue. April 4, 1943. The question often comes up: How can the remnant that is still alive be saved? By ordering the powers that are seeking our destruction to halt in time? Is it possible to cooperate with them? Would they listen to us? Are they able to deviate from their goals? Or is all for naught? The doctor says: Rescue? What is there to rescue? Seventy-five percent are lost. Like a tuberculosis epidemic. In all of that, neither air nor nutrition. The ghetto is liquidating itself on its own—and for that one is supposed to sacrifice one's soul, conscience, heart, honor? Difficult question. We have to think of another way. [. . .]

Outsettlement autumn 1942. SS officer. People on horse-drawn cart, ready for the transport. Ashkenes pulls out revolver, shoots at a boy. The others, frightened, lean back to protect themselves, so to speak. "Don't be afraid, I won't do anything to you!" The boy in the cart collapses, backward. But he is not dead yet. Whereupon Ashkenes fires two more bullets into the temples. "Let's go!" And the cart starts moving. The husband dies, daughter, son, brother, evacuated, woman cleans room and furniture, cooks. As if nothing had happened. Earlier the pain was overwhelming and mourning lasted a long time. Now, only one thought: Spare your nerves in order to survive, in order to have at least this one consolation of *nekume* [Yidd., expiation].

Tidbit. Mark of Cain. "A man, a relative, who had seen the whole world—he also spent many years in Ashkenes [Germany]—said a few months after the beginning of the war, at the time when we didn't know the Ashkenes very well: "What he did cannot be avenged . . . , but we have to do one thing, so that the memory will not fade, so that the world will always remember its own disgrace: Every Ashkenes, big or small, must have a swastika burnt onto his forehead, into his forehead, and the Lord set a mark for him so that he could be recognized . . . see Cain."

The boy who told me this said: "I would finally like to live too. Don't want to live in Poland anymore when the war is over. Away. Somewhere. Getting married, enjoying life, experiencing something, '*Laiten glaich* . . .'" [Yidd., Like people . . .] Tears came into his eyes.

Psires = service. In my *cheder* [Yidd./Hebr., room] by and by—curiosity, excitement, noises, then rumors, Loew—news—looking at the window—some unexpected—finally—smiling, calm, secure, reproducing, most keep silent, only Fischer has something to say, talmudizes, etc. . . . Gradually quiet again—knocking on the door late at night, slightly startled—going to bed, reading, dozing . . . renewed hope . . .

NOTEBOOK 17

[. . .] *Face of the Ghetto,* May 1943, after Five o'Clock

After One Thousand One Hundred Ghetto Days

Water bellies, color elegance, impression: factory town—proletariat—Slavic types. In all that wearing makeup, in part out of vanity, in part to please Kierownik.—

The sun lies over the bumpy cobblestones. It illuminates the puddles, dries them so that a few hours after the rain dust flies up again. At five o'clock in the afternoon when the ressorts are done with their work and are spitting out their workers, children and the old next to men and women of middle age. The gates of the workshops open and herds of starved people in threadbare clothing enter the streets. Almost all carry baskets or pots . . . They chat, laugh, hurry . . . home in order to prepare the evening meal after ten hours of dull labor . . . But among the wretched also appear here and there well-dressed figures, mostly pretty girls, combed, curled, manicured, with round shoulders and round bosoms, well built, only that even they, these privileged children of the ghetto, show round, protruding bellies that detract from their otherwise undeniable charm. The round, protruding belly is no doubt the result of the nutrition, of the water in the potatoes, turnips, and salads, so that even twelve-year-olds look like pregnant women. One rarely encounters any Jewish physiognomies. The Slavic type predominates among both sexes, and especially among the children it is not apparent that they are the offspring of Jewish parents . . . But all, the girls in makeup who want to please the "playboys" of the ghetto, as well as the others in whom the desire for life's bare necessities has extinguished all that's good and beautiful, are enwrapped in the womb of worry . . .

(Different, of course, in Marysin!) Saccharine originals five for 1 marek. . . .[1]

Outsettlement September 1942. In September 1942, among those being outsettled was also a mother of two children. In an attempt to at least save her children, she was hiding them in the cellar whereupon she mounted, as one mounts a scaffold, the cart that took her first to the collection center and from there to somewhere. In her pain and the hurry with which everything was taking place, the woman forgot about her children. The children stayed behind in the locked cellar . . . A few weeks after the outsettlement, the janitor opened the cellar door to get some barrel or some other scrap, etc., and found the bodies—two children's bodies starved to death. The horrors . . . of outsettlement. In Prague they told us: You'll be going to a Jewish circle where you'll live in peace and work in your profession, so finally peace. Tens of thousands in the Łódź ghetto have found peace—in the cemetery of Marysin.

Talkie. Wife of a scholar. Daughter stayed behind in Germany. Son doing labor in Poznan. She herself has sold all her clothes piece by piece. Husband starved to death. She wears her husband's coat as well as his sporting pants, unabashed, uncomplaining—a hearty, courageous type! [. . .]

The victims a priori. Schmelz, *klapsidres,* Broch, Kalikes—these are the Jews who are lost with every outsettlement, these are the victims a priori.

Night Work in the Ghetto—Lecture for the Archive

Instead of "died": gone to his peace; gone to sleep; closed his eyes; stretched his feet; threw away the spoon; went baking bagels; went to meet his great-grandfather; packed his little bag; went his way; [Yiddish]: *verleigt mit'n Kop gemacht domino* [played dominos with his head]; shot out; *gegangen in die bagodim arein* [he went around in shrouds]; *gegangen in die Samtbäder arein* [he went into the velvet baths]; *gegangen sich auskleiden die Beiner* [he went to take off the legs]; *gegangen in loch arein* [he went into a hole]; *gegangen sich sehn mit die kvurim* [he went to see the graves]; *sich oisgeglitcht* [he slipped out]; *obgeplankt* [he blanked out].

For "buried": *areinrucken in oifen arein* [went into an oven]; *areinziehen sich in der dire arein* [went into the door]; *unter 7 schlesser* [under seven locks].

For "dead man": an enlightened one; *liegt in der Erd und pashed ferd* [he lies in the earth and tends horses].

Instead of Bes Hakvurah [Yidd., cemetery]: good place; pure field; eternal rest; free field.

Klobes [Yidd., curses]: *solst gehn verkehrt lederne shich* [may you go wrong in leather shoes]; *far dajn tir soll dir wachsen gras* [may grass grow in front of your door]; *bald sich soll man noch dir shiveh sitzen* [may they soon sit shiva—mourn—for you]; *wachsen soll auf dir schwammen* [mushrooms shall grow on you]; *a hohn soll nach dir krän* [a rooster shall crow after you]; *sollst verkapt weren* [may you lose your mind]; *die hint soln von dir haben a kolazie* [the dogs shall have a meal of you]; *man soll dich aheim bringen in a leilech* [may they bring you home in a bedsheet]; *dein leber soll hängen in a treifener yatke un a hint sol sie bapischen* [may your liver hang in a *treife* slaughterhouse and may a dog piss on it]; *sollst zegein wie salz im wasser* [may you dissolve like salt in water]; *der toches soll dir geschwollen weren von shiveh sitzen* [may your behind get swollen from sitting *shiva*].

Der malach-hamoves hot oif ihm an oig geworfen [The angel of death has cast an eye on him].

The soul of an informer wanders in a goat.

If you go to bed hungry, your soul dances in your sleep with the beggars. When a crow (Łódźer crow) knocks on the window, it's the sign that the angel of death has entered the room.

Agony: Signs of agony: when the sick person turns toward the wall; when the sick person asks to wash hands.

NOTEBOOK 16

August 4, 1943

"My Two Neighbors"

I

At that time I lived close to the wire, there, where the ghetto ends and the town begins. The room I had been assigned was on the fourth floor of one of the many wooden houses that everywhere dotted the streets like ornate barracks. They are grayish brown, dirty, crumbling. They bear carved gables. They look out through smashed-in windows. The front part has no lodgers. Ill-smelling sewage gutters clutter the path as one stumbles up the dilapidated wooden stairs. On the door, a Star of David cut of yellow cloth, held by a thumbtack. The names of the inhabitants are unfamiliar. On the landing, hole-ridden, greasy buckets containing sand, trash, scrap.

On the second floor, decomposing weeds, potato peels, stinking, broken dishes. Above that, just below the attic floor, dirty laundry on the line, hung out to dry. And everywhere, at the entrance to the house, on the stairs, in the corners, opposite the apartment doors, piles of human excrement of yesterday and today . . .

The house was uninhabited. Nobody lived there anymore. Shortly before I moved in, the inhabitants had been "outsettled," that is, loaded onto a horse-drawn cart and taken away—except for my neighbor. I hear sounds next door; the man himself, I have never met. When I leave my room, he is asleep. When I come back, he is at work. Lying in bed, I hear him come in. My dear, good neighbor. He doesn't disturb me as I am dozing. I am happy.

II

Summer announces its arrival with dust and heat. Not a strip of shade on the sidewalks. On the bumpy cobblestones thirsting leaves of turnips, radishes, and *botwinki,* fallen off the horse-drawn carts. These things are rotting, molding, in the streets. In the evenings, between six and eight o'clock, I pass the *corso* on my way home. People talk of potatoes, vegetables . . . of wood, of cooking . . . These are the daily concerns in the ghetto. I too hurry home. But I don't care much about the daily concerns of the ghetto. My stomach has become accustomed to the distasteful nourishment. I devour anything. *Yarmush, lebedar,* potato peels, dandelion stems, any kind of grass that grows between the cobblestones. Hunger can no longer do anything to me. The diseases of the ghetto, typhoid fever, dysentery, stomach upset, jaundice, tuberculosis, are seeking me out in vain. Nothing can be ruined anymore on skin and bones.

When I saw my face mirrored in a glass window yesterday, I wasn't startled. Only the fact that my temples, between eyebrows and ears, showed deep indentations and that my skull bones had become visible made me stop and think a bit. My hair is getting thin and gray, in some places even silvery.

Even when I was a child I had wished for silver-gray hair. Now it's making its appearance. I am tired and I fall quickly and easily asleep. The arm under my cheek, rushing in my ears—I am happy.

III

I hear my neighbor's name by chance. "Is this the apartment of Mister Cymbalist?" an old man asks me, wiggling his head. The head wiggling above the shoulders seems to be a nervous disease. The old man makes such noise with his wooden shoes that I have to strain my ears to understand him.

"Cymbalist," he repeats. "Doctor Cymbalist?" I nod in agreement. My neighbor, I think to myself, is Dr. Cymbalist. He couldn't be anybody else. That I hadn't known this all along! None other than Dr. Cymbalist . . .

The old man, satisfied with my answer, knocks on my neighbor's door. Not a word or sound from inside. The old man knocks again without getting impatient. Then he smiles, chuckles, turns around, and prepares to walk down the stairs.

"No Cymbalist . . . absolutely no Cymbalist . . . a mistake. Cymbalist doesn't live in the ghetto at all . . . Ran away to Warsaw at the beginning of the war . . . ," says the old man, and he stumbles down the stairs. Once arrived at the bottom, he gives off another chuckle. Thank God, my neighbor is not Dr. Cymbalist. I am happy.

IV

On the way home, in front of a bread distribution center, I learn that three hundred seventeen of our people died last month. Ninety-nine women and two hundred eighteen men. Wrapping the loaf of bread in an old, stained towel, I hurry home. The bread smells good.

I start preparing my evening meal. Here it's called *kolazia* [Pol., meal]. Cleaning the oven, splitting wood, breaking the coals, a few strips of tar paper as foundation, all this is essential for the preparations. The daily potato soup too—it alternates several times a month with cabbage and turnip soup—needs this.

We have learned a lot here. All men in the ghetto without a woman know how to make soup. This skill will come in handy someday later in life. We learned: to make soup and to be patient. Two wonderful virtues. I know that I will be grateful to the ghetto for them. After all, the ghetto didn't promise me anything. One must be just . . .

In the midst of my preparations I hear my neighbor's door. Cymbalist? No. But I want to call him that. Finally I've found a name for him. I don't have to rack my brain at night. He is Cymbalist. Not a word more to lose. I am happy.

V

At a surprising hour, my neighbor's voice becomes audible. It is soft, flattering, likeable. At first Cymbalist's speech is unclear. The words dissipate in the damp air. All I know is that the person he is speaking to is female. To a woman or to a girl.

"You're surprised that I'm home at noon? What? Why don't you say something? Strange creature! Or do you take me to be a fool, like most around here? In the ressort they say: 'Our boss'—they really say 'our boss'—'seems to have a lover at home. At work's end he gets nervous and makes sure he's first out the door. However, only for the last few days . . .' That's what they say in the ressort. What do you say to that, darling? Funny, isn't it. The people don't even know how right they are. Ha, ha, ha . . ."

After a pause, which is apparently filled with caresses for the roommate, Cymbalist paces several times back and forth. Suddenly he halts his step. I hear him cutting pieces of wood, breaking coals. Crackling in the stove, clanking of pots penetrate the wall to my ears. Silence. Flies are humming all around me. Dozens are sitting on the table, climbing over the windowpane, sticking to the pot containing the breakfast coffee. Some even try to crawl inside my shirtsleeves. The heat lures them on the boldest excursions.

What happened to Cymbalist? Finished with preparing the midday soup, he is pouring—I can hear the swishing—water into the pots. He puts one of them back on the stove. Suddenly he starts again. "A fine little soup . . . soup with parsley . . . What do you say, my child? I would've liked to get onions, but none were to be had in the street . . . But do we know what tomorrow will bring? Now all we can do is wait. Maybe we'll get potatoes again tomorrow. Stay quiet, stay calm, my dear!

"We've both lost our freedom, we're sitting locked in. You, you at least can hum, sing, you're God's favorite child and not dependent on rations . . . But we poor devils, we, we . . . Just wait, my little one, I'll be done right away. The water is boiling, it's steaming under the lid . . ."

Here Cymbalist broke off, took—so it seemed to me—a few steps to the window facing the yard, where I guessed the dish to be, and busied himself; a few seconds later I heard slurping and gurgling, all noises that accompany a hungry man's way of eating. Cymbalist filled his stomach and I was happy.

VI

On the same day, a few hours later, returning from work, Cymbalist entered his room with unusual alacrity. He had barely put down his *menashka* [Yidd., container] when he, apparently agitated and hasty, began pacing back and forth, stopping every second and dropping a few words. "Why aren't you saying hello, my darling? Are you angry? Was I not attentive enough to you? Tell me, please, say a word to me." The woman so addressed remained silent.

"This time we have light sugar. You'll enjoy it. My child . . . Light sugar, not the brown juicy one that bleeds through the paper bag. Do you hear? You must agree, I'm pampering you!"

After a longish pause, he continued: "Instead of answering, she nods with her eyebrows and taps with her legs. Nice behavior, that! I'd better not tell anybody what a bad roommate I have . . ."

I moved closer to the wall so I wouldn't miss a single word, lose a single breath. I had already become so used to Cymbalist's presence next door that his chatting and the silence of his roommate seemed quite natural to me. And still, my curiosity did not diminish. For a while I presumed that Cymbalist's companion was ill, very ill, and perhaps had to guard the bed, and that's why she was silent. His tender care spoke of a good heart, it touched me. I was even determined to offer him my help.

"We," he began again, "make the most beautiful clothing . . . charming blouses, night robes, aprons. Luckily you don't need any of that. Your dress was designed by the greatest of all artists. Noble in cut, elegant in color . . . ash gray I love best, especially a black dice-patterned waistline and back . . . Not to forget the yellowish brown of the skirt . . . Really a harmonious combination . . . Topped off with little black ankle boots, shoes to show off, or, what one now calls—pumps . . ."

He chuckled so softly that I had to strain my ears. Then followed a scratching sound with the legs, clapping of hands, and—to my greatest surprise—running about the room, knocking against the wall. A sense of foreboding seized me when Cymbalist suddenly changed his voice and started to get furious. "I took down the curtain to give you a lot of sun. I know you love sun . . . And now you bury yourself in the pillows as if you were cold! Shame on you . . ."

Then came a few more short exclamations. All this Cymbalist uttered tortuously. It seemed to me that his soul was suddenly embittered and his face, which was unknown to me, had darkened . . .

I was seized by a desire to knock on the wall and call out to Cymbalist that he should cease his lamenting and reproaching. But I did nothing of the sort. On the contrary. I tensed my nerves so that nothing that was going on would escape me.

A few seconds passed in indescribable anticipation. Not a sound from the other side—only a soft scratching with the feet, a rustling of the upholstery, a choking scream.

I walked to the side of the door. Next door, heavy breathing, almost rattling. "Now you have enough, beast, contemptible, faithless . . . why aren't you screaming when I strangle you, when I squash your legs . . . despicable tramp . . . Go to the devil!"

These were Cymbalist's last words before he left the room, slammed the door, and went down the stairs. I asked myself if I was happy but got no answer.

VII

I was overcome with weakness, which I had lately noticed more and more. It started with a flickering, bright-colored rings dancing before my eyes and a languid feeling in the cavity of my heart. My feet were cold; only with great effort was I able to clench my hands into fists. I stood by the window facing the yard. All sorts of people crossed the yard with hasty steps and disappeared behind rotten doors.

It was a little after five. The ressorts were spitting their workers out into the streets. Children carried pots wrapped in pieces of cloth, old people carried heavy burdens on their skeletal backs. "What is all this about? Why the haste? You'll get to your *kolazia* on time! Nice and slow! Patience, my dears . . ." I thought to myself.

I groped for the window frame to keep from falling. The weakness that had come over me forced me to cancel my plans for the day. Sentiments of longing and foreboding quarreled together in my head. Inadvertently I reached for my temples with both hands. All around, darkness descended. A rushing in my ears. My tongue searched for a wet spot on the palate. Suddenly I felt as if I had bitten into a lemon.

But in the midst of this condition, I was seized by the desire to find out what had been going on in Cymbalist's room. I didn't hesitate long. A few steps and I was in front of Cymbalist's door. I rattled it. It was not locked. Cymbalist had forgotten . . . I was happy.

VIII

There I was in Cymbalist's room, from which I had been separated for months by a thin plaster wall. I was standing in the room and looked around. On the window, which, like mine, faced the backyard, were big and small bottles in various colors, dried turnip leaves, and an almost new *menashka.* A red shred of fabric covered half the window. Below the sill, as far as it belonged to the interior of the room, were rucksacks, sacks, bowls, pots, and remains of coal and wood, all stored in chaotic order.

In a corner was a cute little iron stove. The floor, whose clay part showed rifts and cracks, was strewn with broken buckets and glasses, a dozen potatoes and radishes in the process of rotting. A cord extended from the window to the door, hung with damp pieces of laundry. The laundry pieces were dripping water into several pots and washbowls that had been placed there for this purpose.

Where did Cymbalist sleep? Did he have a bed at all? There, where the potatoes and radishes were lying around, behind the little stove, which was almost leaning against the broadside of the room, wallowed brown, dirty covers, which were perhaps new once, a long time ago; at the narrower end of the covers was something like a headrest: a grayish green linen sack filled with straw. I felt it. It was as hard as the straw sacks in prisons.

I was slowly retreating to the door when I heard steps. Somebody from below was approaching the attic floor. The steps were heavy and measured, ceasing from time to time as if the visitor was resting periodically. Did Cymbalist have friends or relatives who would visit him? What if somebody came in now and found me in the room? Was I a thief who sneaked in to rob Cymbalist of his meager possessions? Or did I even have an eye on the female on whom Cymbalist had bestowed in the last hours flattery and threats? However this may have been—the steps were approaching Cymbalist's room, where I was an intruder.

To leave the room and return to my own lodging seemed inappropriate. Counting the time that had passed since the stranger had begun his ascent, I figured he must have reached the attic floor already. I heard heavy breathing, rattling in the chest of a strong man, snorting from mouth and nostrils. Escape was impossible.

I, therefore, decided to risk an encounter with the intruder and even to defend myself . . .

As I thus deliberated, it occurred to me that a witness could betray me and prevent me from defending myself—my neighbor's female companion. Or I might find a friend in her. She was no doubt somewhere in the room, as Cymbalist had gone out alone. With a quick pull I lifted the cover from what I thought was Cymbalist's bed . . . nothing . . . no human being, only a mattress that was oozing musty straw, and on the mattress a torn towel singed at the edges, which Cymbalist apparently used to dry the stove.

After that—without any regard for the looming danger from outside—I poked through every corner and what was heaped up there: shreds, scarves, sacks, tar paper, coal pieces, and sundry unidentifiable stuff. I did this without thinking, without a plan, so I had afterward no idea why I did it.

Meanwhile, the stranger had arrived at Cymbalist's door. I heard the noise of heavy shoes. I felt his breath. I smelled his sweat. Since it was clear to me that he would try to gain entry, I pushed against the door to prevent him from intruding. My left knee pressed hard against the wood, the left hand held on to the door lever.

Suddenly I heard the jingling of keys. The stranger was setting about to unlock the door to Cymbalist's room. What was going on? Could a stranger have Cymbalist's keys? I placed my eye against the keyhole. As much as I could see, the man on the other side of the door was of medium height and indeterminate age. The little bit of gray hair that peeked out from under the white linen cap didn't indicate much.

Cigarette smoke penetrated the empty keyhole. Surprisingly, the stranger put the keys back into his pocket. "Why should I take the rucksack along," the stranger said to himself, "there won't be anything anyway . . . the bundle of papers I can carry in my hand . . . ," and he began to hum, to chirp, as if he had made a precious discovery. This was Cymbalist. Cymbalist in person. I recognized his soft, soothing, pleasant voice. It was Cymbalist and none other. My knees began to give way and my hand let go of the door lever. Cymbalist turned around, went back down the wooden stairs, cheerfully humming and chirping. He was in a good mood . . .

Cymbalist had hardly left the house—I saw him cross the yard—when I set out to look around some more. I pushed bucket, broom, rucksack, aside with my foot, without uncovering anything suspicious. Every object stood in a natural relationship to Cymbalist. Even the smell of ripened fruit and cognac seemed to me fitting.

I was about to leave Cymbalist's room when I noticed on the windowsill, a bit over to the side, a small, flat plate with a flower pattern, the edges of which were covered with white flour and sugar. A sight that didn't surprise me despite its rarity . . .

However, as I was examining the plate more closely, something caught my eye, something that was swimming in the middle of the plate. I was seized by sweet excitement. The swimming thing revealed itself as a kind of fly that does not usually occur in our region—larger than a common fly, not as shiny as the colorful flies of tropical countries. The fly was dead. Murdered, strangled. Waistline and back in a black dice pattern, belly and legs yellowish brown, the balls of the toes black . . .

Cymbalist, so much was clear, had given it to the fly and was now alone again. He doesn't need a female companion. The death of the fly does not bother him. He was humming, singing, and chirping. He had been venerating the beauty that rules the world outside. Happy Cymbalist!

IX

I, however, couldn't suppress a whistle of horror. The strangled fly stirred in me all kinds of thoughts. I repeated as far as possible the words Cymbalist had dispensed to his roommate a few hours earlier.

My throat was dry, my stomach was growling. Without much thought, I smashed the egg on the windowsill and slurped up the yolk with noisy delight. A few drops fell on my wooden sandals. Then I tore open the cabinet, took out a bottle, and drank: light, brown, aromatic cognac!

Done with the bottle, I bit into an apple that had somehow gotten into my hands. But when I was about to activate Cymbalist's radio, my hands froze, and Cymbalist was standing before me in the middle of the room. Neither on his chest in front nor on his back did he wear a Jews' star. There, where the Jews' star was supposed to be affixed, was a blood-red stain. Cymbalist looked at me with sad, pathetic eyes. His lips were contorted, he was incapable of uttering a sound. A feeling of being swept up by a blast of wind came over me. I felt as if some invisible being was pulling a silken cover over my ears. A profound sense of bliss permeated my whole being down to the tip of my toes.

I wanted to go and meet Cymbalist but I slipped, without hurting myself. Slowly, ever so slowly, the flavor of the apple and the cognac faded from me. My tongue was bitter and dry . . .

I groped for my pillow. Nothing had changed in my room. The water was steaming. The potatoes were done, the evening meal was ready. For a second, my hunger made me savor the most beautiful things. Didn't I have reason to be happy?

NOTEBOOK J

Notes, Remembrances (Remains Manuscript)

O. R., MATROSENGASSE 1/42, A6

[. . .] **November 11.** *Hunger.* Cold fog. Foreboding of winter. In the fields, hundreds of people harvesting the last stems of cabbage (without heads).

November 12. *Hunger and cold.* Snow—rain. Illegal prices: bread 360, sugar 3, oil 7, potatoes 50.

Potato peels much in demand. But the kitchens have to pass them on to the dairy department where they are transformed into vegetable salads.—Only a few can afford to peel the potatoes. Everybody scrapes them.

November 15. *Hunger.* Mrs. Brumlik (Prague, millionaire) begs in the *kolazia* kitchen for potato peels. A few hours later, she collapses of hunger, dies.

Contrasts: A carriage with dignitary going out to Marysin, from the opposite direction a hearse. The coachman a seven-year-old boy, laughing, cracking the whip. Loves to play coachman since there are no games. *No sports,* no exercise . . . for *eighty thousand* people. [. . .]

In the afternoon hours a posted proclamation appeared, signed "*Ghetto Administration, signed Biebow.*" Excitement in the ghetto! People line up in front of the walls. Text of the proclamation:

"Concerning: *Provisions for the workers.*"

With the proclamation from the Eldest of the Jews of November 3, 1943, No. 401, the working population of the ghetto was informed that smaller deliveries of foodstuff made necessary a cut in rations, *especially the rations for the workshop kitchens were thereby lowered.* [. . .]

This was the second proclamation signed by the Biebow administration. The first was after the September 1942 outsettlement.

November 18. *Hunger and provisioning.* The entire ghetto is preoccupied with the question of what will happen now: M. Kliegier (Special Division), Dr. Miller (health department) and S. Reingold (provisions) have taken over the provisioning on order of Biebow. Tomorrow, Friday, the first ration ordered by this triumvirate. Potatoes arrived on the last day, 240,000 kg. Will the coupons remain? A question of life and death for many.—Great excitement among all those affected.—Finally got two shirts from Bolek; the first in five years.

Henuschi. The poor soul spends the nights worrying and crying, I'm sure. I'm rugged, firm, despite terrible attacks of asthma, sleepless nights; keep going for Henuschi's sake. Why no letter through the Red Cross? What is happening with Vilma, Ernst, Erich? Will I ever see them again? Scant hope and yet hope! *A little hope and nevertheless hope!* [Original English.]

Knee in the ghetto. Praeses eliminated from provisioning, much of his power thereby taken from him. Yet, he continues to work, makes an appearance here and there, cares for the young women he had some time ago placed in the *kolazia* kitchens by assigning them to the leather- and saddle-making ressort—his own department. Admirable his attitude and endurance. Indestructible. Will triumph eventually over the lesser.

November 19. For the first time, rations not from the Eldest but apportioned from the ghetto administration. Autonomy of the ghetto—an illusion. Biebow can't stand the personality Ch. R.

Talkie. Nikodem Fischer. At the beginning of the ghetto, Nikodem Fischer was a courageous seventeen-year-old, a pretty, strapping boy. He crawls under the wire. Signals approaching streetcar to stop. It stops. He gets on. Rides into town. Since he speaks perfect German and Polish, he can get around there. After many adventures, goes to Germany where he finds work among Germans and is well treated. He apparently leaves this position of his own will, wanders around, and is caught. "Flight from the ghetto . . ." One day, the mother gets message from Germany, her son has been executed. [. . .]

Talkie:

1. Czech Jew is taken to Litzmannstadt Kripo, gets fifteen shots from a revolver.
2. A madman is taken off the railway car on the way from Prague to Litzmannstadt, they play a game of chase with him, he tells them the truth about the Nazis, he's *geharget* [Yidd., beaten to death].
3. Three young men, hospital-autumn outsettlement, are caught, taken to Ozorkow. There, forced first to dig a ditch, kicked in with the foot from behind . . . "Come here . . . open your mouth." Shoots into it.

Hunger. Late autumn. People—men, women, children, with sacks on the abandoned *djalkas,* looking for something edible left . . . cabbage leaves, leftover leek leaves, maybe radishes, potatoes. They dig through the ground without results. Only here and there a few leaves, they pick them up as if they were crumbs from the table of the wealthy. [. . .]

What will happen? No more coupons? Dependent on rations? Two and a half kilograms of potatoes a week? Without vegetables? Grave concerns. But the main concern: What effect will what's happening at the front have on us? Will we remain here? And for how long? Will we become at some point a war zone?

Nobody thinks about this most important question. Only private concerns and intrigues and ambitions! What a tragedy!

Hunger, theft, punishment. Six cases: People take a few potatoes from a full potato sack, putting them in their pocket, creating a deficit during reweighing (before leaving the place). Taken to the "Special":

1. Man over fifty, sick and weak, woman with four children, outsettled.
2. Woman, malnourished, fever, lung disease.
3. Supervisor declares he had turned the trick: forty-eight hours' detention.
4. Mrs. Rotlauf, torn about her hungry child. She and her child have not had a warm meal today except for ressort soup.
5. A young boy, without parents, a record for stealing cabbage, confesses likewise: twenty-four hours' detention.
6. Old man, severely ill, doddering. Terrible characters. Scenes. These are cases for the police. The court would be much worse. [. . .]

November 21. *Henuschi.* Dreary, foggy. London weather. Going to the Medinah-Ivrit [Hebr., Jewish State] people, giving a talk there for an hour. Back through the fog, coughing all night, thinking of Henuschi getting the medication from the pharmacy in March 1937. [. . .]

November 24. "Exhausted, exhausted.—The daily struggle, every hour anew . . . Who knows how long the suffering will drag on? . . ." So they say here among the people.

November 25. *Atmosphere.* Thursday. Spoke to the General Zionists. Returned with Chaim. Fell into open sewer filled with latrine dirt and urine. Injured my leg. Went home. Cold, freezing. Suddenly darkness on top of everything, something wrong with the electricity. No evening meal. The blue flame of the gas stove provides a dim light. A few friends in the room. Everybody deadly sad. We part. Going to bed without supper, only a few spoonfuls of the midday ressort soup. Getting undressed in the dark. Terrible night. Coughing, gasping for air. Early morning, severe leg pain, full of bloody crusts . . . And another day has gone by.

Thinking of Sunday, November 28, 1937, and November 28, 1943! What joy, what torment . . . [. . .]

November 28. *Wedding anniversary.* Poor Henuschi, I'm sure she's crying, sick with longing, thinks of November 28, 1937, when we went from Café Singerhof through the side streets! Vilma with white lilacs! Henuschi went home, I to Café Astoria . . . Gone! Gone . . .

When will we see each other again, embrace? A dream? An illusion? Despite five years, not a trace of distancing. I feel her breath, her hands, her love and care, as if she departed yesterday. But—but why doesn't she write through the Red Cross? I hear packages with good stuff are being delivered (from Lisbon) . . . Why nothing from you, my dear heart? You are alive and well, aren't you?

November 29. *Children.* They are not permitted to get any schooling . . . They are not allowed to sing, do gymnastics, march in line . . . No reading, writing, arithmetic . . . They are growing up like gypsies! Has there ever been the likes of it in the history of mankind? Are they all aware of this?

Dreary, rain, despair! Dark by five-thirty, hopeless, lights out. Sitting in my room in the dusk, a little gas flame, frying potatoes as once long ago at home in Koryčany . . . And again and again: my dear heart. On December 21, it will be five years, incomprehensible, a mystery . . .

Encyclopedia of the Ghetto

A group of people living together under extreme coercive conditions without the conscious intent of forming a community of common fate created forms that were only possible on the basis of the ghetto. Everyday life required certain norms of work and existence. It created its own structure, its own language, its own terminology. Nowhere in the world was there a human community comparable to that of the ghetto.

The change of all social, intellectual, and economic functions brought with it a change in the most commonplace conceptions. Concepts that until then were understood unambiguously everywhere among Europeans underwent a complete transformation. They had to adjust to the conditions that came into force with the ghetto. As soon as freedom of movement, the freedom to act, was gone, words, adages, sentences, too, could no longer be used in the conventional sense. The transformation of forms of living forced the transformation of forms of concepts.

Furthermore: Words and the word order were no longer adequate for the demands of the ghetto world. New words had to be created, old ones had to be endowed with new meaning. The three-language base—Yiddish, Polish, German—broadened the foundation of this process. This created the possibility for enrichment of the ghetto language as well as further refinement and the introduction of greater nuances.

Words, which until now had only an innate meaning, were endowed with secondary meaning. These might be ironic but also strictly factual. There was an especial opportunity to expand the meaning of Yiddish words. To the religion-bound, traditional word structure a more current meaning was added. In this connection, some individuals found an outlet for their talent of creating plays on words. Thereby, concepts arose in the way proverbs, or "words from the mouth of the people," used to be created. The source of these linguistic creations is the people, the masses themselves. Nobody can say when or where he heard this or that word, or this or that phrase, for the first time. The *phonetic* origin of these newly created concepts can be documented in countless cases. Since there is no newspaper nor any other printed word or written word that could be disseminated in black and white, the new formulation can only circulate from mouth to mouth.

A new formulation makes its way through the ghetto with the speed of a rumor. With ceaseless passion, hungry for anything worth hearing—even if it is something abstract—the ghetto man absorbs every word variant. For him it is news, that is, a living factor in the monotony of his existence.

Words for things of daily use have suddenly assumed prominence in the use of language. Since the concern for the meager products for a meal pushes to the side all other functions of animal existence, the objects connected with this concern gain the utmost significance—whether they be expressed in Yiddish, Polish, or German words.

Intellectual needs are pressed together in a narrow frame. They require only a few words, concepts, or word associations. The ghetto must renounce all technical assistance from civilization. Political and metaphysical aspirations are excluded. Religious functions are restricted to a narrow circle. What is left is only the area of nutrition and of ressort work, a paltry ground to nourish the unfurling of linguistic life.

And yet, within this limited sphere of intellectual activity, the imagination and humor of the people were able to unfold. A long line of poignant characterizations have earned credibility in the ghetto. Concepts with serious meaning have received an ironic connotation, everyday expressions have been elevated to a higher level. In addition, there are many words previously in little use that now have become very popular among all classes of ghetto dwellers. Polish words in particular have come into general use.

Overall, it is to be noted that the vocabulary has broadened within the confines of the ghetto. Everywhere we encounter expressions that were unknown before the creation of the ghetto or outside the confines of the ghetto. The atmosphere into which the ghetto is strapped determines to some degree the extent of the linguistic forms and vocabulary at the ghetto dweller's disposal.

A collection of these linguistic and word treasures forms part of the cultural history of the ghetto. In a future period, when the ghetto will be researched, such a collection, such an encyclopedia, will add to an understanding, where a mere description of the condition is inadequate. The word, the language, is the history of mankind. This thesis has long been proven by scholars; the language is a more reliable witness and source of truth than other, material artifacts.

The present encyclopedia makes no claim to be a complete and unambiguous explanation of the definitions of words. But it believes itself to be close to its set goal.

In order to achieve this goal, several ghetto personalities have been consulted who, on the basis of their position or their above-average talent (individuality), can lay claim to being inscribed in the dictionary of the cultural history of Ghetto Litzmannstadt. The names themselves must stand the test of objective evaluation. Some personalities listed may not have played an active role in the ghetto but can nevertheless be regarded as "prominent Jews."

A dictionary of ghetto language and ghetto personalities will, no doubt, have historical value beyond the immediate occasion.

Finally must be mentioned that the editors of the encyclopedia have attempted to do justice to the material without any preconceptions and to present thereby a building block for the cultural history of the ghetto.

O. R., DECEMBER 1, 1943

Little Ghetto Mirror, December 1, 1943

THROUGH THE CRACKS OF THE LAW

If the ghetto had a newspaper, and a newspaper with a court column, this column would be filled with the catchword "theft trial." But since the ghetto has to make do without such a literary pastime, as without many other things, the daily chronicler must rely on oral transmission, and occasionally the reports of the O. S. and the incomplete protocols of the ghetto court.

It's not facts that elicit our sympathies. Not even the persons involved, who are the wretched heroes on trial. That which goes on beyond the commonplace notion of theft in some cases are the circumstances under which the theft has been committed. Generally, criminal activity is keeping pace with the technical ability of the authorities charged with determining the facts of the crime, documenting them, and presenting them to prove the case. Evidentiary proofs without corpus delicti lose much of their persuasive force. In the big cities of the world, the tools of the criminal police are usually behind those of the criminals by several percentage points.

In the ghetto the criminal element does not have these general characteristics. Here, under the force of circumstances, a system has emerged that does not use violent force but gimmicks, tricks, cunning. In ninety out of one hundred cases, it's a matter of theft of food, petty theft. In some cases these robberies are carried out in such a primitive manner that one can only wonder about how little respect the thief must have for the investigative ability of the police. Then again, a theft will occur—snatching of potatoes or radishes or other kinds of vegetables—so openly in broad daylight that it presents no more than a public nuisance.

The scenes of the "crime" are primarily vegetable and potato centers—not to mention grocery shops where this or that employee misuses his position by swiping small quantities of edibles like sugar, preserves, and such. In these cases no skill is required, only a certain lack of restraint.

Different matter at the centers. The person entitled to the goods appears with a rucksack at the center. His social, familial, or professional connections assure him privileged treatment. A few more *buraki* or kohlrabi, a few dozen more potatoes, and he goes away happy after having deprived the center, that is, the ghetto, of this surplus by securing a bigger ration for himself. Even the most stringent controls do not work. For the eye of the law is itself the transgressor. The guardian is the accomplice.

More difficult are cases in which the candidate resorts to forgeries, that is, to manipulations, which must be registered as fraud. An example: The counterfeit money is confiscated by the police, and after the culprit has been punished, it is destroyed. What happens when the controlling power does not devalue the counterfeit money or leaves it up to the culprit due to the pressure of business? Then he can reuse it, everything takes its normal course, no fraud is apparent . . . These and similar occurrences have led to stricter controls in every way. In order to make it impossible for any one person to make off with more than the regular weight and to finally put an end to fraud and protection, every sack is weighed again before leaving the center.

But here, too, the hungry ghetto dweller's craftiness finds a way around. On the way to the scale at the exit, he simply takes out—depending on the ration—a few potatoes or some fruit and puts it in his pocket. The control weighs, notes low weight, that is, inaccurate scale. The "injured" party is compensated. The missing quantity is replaced. Until this trick too is exposed.

Again and again, the arm of the law collides with the plight of the citizens. A petty theft, a petty fraud, a petty burglary—signs of nameless misery and an imagination searching for a way out! But since even the world of the ghetto rests on the foundation of the Thora—right and justice—the poor culprit must be declared guilty. He consoles himself—until next time.

On a single day, the Special Division of the O. S. handled six cases of potato theft. Six cases, but basically one motive: hunger! The Special Division settles these cases without trial. A quicker and therefore harmless procedure. The six defendants had enriched themselves with a few potatoes through tricks, through manual or mental adeptness.

A man of about sixty, sick and weak, a woman and four children who had fallen victim to the September outsettlement . . . An elderly woman, malnourished, feverish, with lung disease.—A widow with visible erysipelas, in a torn dress, caring for a starving child . . . On the day of her arrest, she and the child had nothing warm in their stomachs except for the ressort soup . . . An old man, frail, trembling, a picture of wretchedness. These four accused were released. In addition, there were two young boys, orphans, with a record of cabbage theft. They got forty-eight hours of detention.

This is what goes on at the "Special." The court is stricter, sticking closer to the letter of the law. But life in the ghetto respects neither police nor court. It creates its own laws even if it results in detention or assignment to excrement removal.

O. R.

❁

December 1. [. . .] *Children.* A child misbehaves at a ressort. The soup is withheld from him, whereupon other children begin to strike in solidarity—all refusing to take the soup . . .

December 3. *Work for Ashkenes. Talkie.* On and on it goes . . . one day like the next . . . can this hopelessness be endured? How much longer? In Radegast, building of little houses and a roadway. Poor, weary, weak women from the laundry held back again, ten-thirty in the morning they are getting their soup, then dispatched to Radegast. Carrying stones, pulling little carts until eight at night without soup, without a piece of bread or anything warm. Terrible slavery! The next day many refuse to work again . . . A misery, noticed by few . . .

December 4. *Hunger. Hunger.* Sounds heard: A boy yells in the street, *"A razie is du!"* [Yidd., "A ration has arrived!"]. Immediately people stream from their houses; despite the cold temperatures they don't put on their overcoats and scarves until they reach the street, running to the grocery shops . . . Hunger! Hunger! The ration is for two weeks: 2 kg potatoes, 2½ kg rutabaga, 70 dkg of flour, 50 dkg of sugar, 50 preserves, 10 oil, 10 peas, 12 some kind of food. Fear of winter.

December 7. *Ashkenes.* Historical day. Today Director Biebow is addressing the Jews in public for the first time. Six o'clock at the cultural center. Here of late feather-and-down ressort is Dr. Glaser, Biebow's favorite. Everything was emptied out, lectern set up. Invited guest, Kierowniki, department chief and workers' representative.

Today, besides 10 kg rutabaga an additional 20 kg, furthermore, 5 kg of potatoes and 7 kg potatoes for seven weeks. Hunger.

But: The ghetto is supposedly an enterprise essential for the war effort, therefore nourishment, provisioning, among other things, for the winter. In addition, protected from outsettlement, that is, transfer of the entire ghetto. It seems that Biebow wants to maintain the ghetto until the very end. Difficult situation, since many factories in Germany have been destroyed by Allied bombings so that orders from there are sparse, if there are any at all.

Biebow himself is concerned about his future. Has pangs of conscience about earlier misdeeds (Zduńska Wola!) and would like to make restitution. This circumstance may be favorable to him and to us. For:

I foresee incredible battles and explosions before the collapse. All means, arson, gas, blamed on Bolshevism. All of Germany a heap of corpses and blood and horror. "Such is the agony of the Nibelungen."

Novel about a mother before outsettlement. Ella Goldberg Liebling tells this story: The mother was seized with unrest. "Let's go outside, somewhere, to hide in a yard . . ." We hesitated, were lying on our cots, though we felt the danger, but not decisive enough. At four o'clock in the morning she rose, went downstairs: "Going somewhere . . . why not hide." She went into the street. The Jewish police prevented her from hiding somewhere behind a wall, latrine, etc. She came back. Again: "Come, let's go to the attic . . ." We were too lazy to go along. Finally line up in the yard. Mother stays upstairs with a few people. Jewish police chases them down. Ashkenes sees her coming. "Get on the cart . . ." Without overcoat, without hat, without shoes, without a bite to eat.

Novel. Pain. She visits me. "How much longer . . ." Who knows. "I can't take it any longer. Everything is choking me. I don't care about food. My youth is gone. And yet: I would like to see Mother and Brother again. You know my brother, don't you? He goes to rich Jews in Prague. Has a portrait done of child, dog . . . I want to feed myself and sister and mother." But they say: "Now in a crisis?" "What crisis? If *you* are speaking of crisis, what about me who doesn't have 10 crowns in the pocket . . . For God's sake . . . They are responsible for the death of many thousands . . . Why not give a little something of their millions . . . these dumb, bad fools. Clung to the money and finally had to give it all to Ashkenes. I don't want to see them again. When it is all over I don't want to see anybody . . . Going somewhere[1] into the woods, among animals, birds, plants . . . don't want to have anything to do with human beings . . ." She jumps at me, holds on to me tight, bursts into tears, sobs, her body trembles: "Doctor, tell me, I must know, will we live to see it? I must live to see it, to see my loved ones again, tell me, you must tell me, give me hope, otherwise I'll waste away . . . Listen, you must tell me, give me hope . . ." Suddenly the sobbing stops, the eyes smile even below the tears. The face is waxen yellow.

"You mustn't let yourself go. Remain calm. Wait and be patient, short time. We'll see our loved ones again . . . We'll see our loved ones again . . . Trust . . ." She strokes my hand. Her wooden shoes make noise. She goes.

December 9, 1943. "We'll see our loved ones again . . ." Henuschi, Vilma, Erich, Ernst . . . and all the others whom I love so much and for whom I long.

Biebow said: "You, who have lived four years behind barbed wire . . ." What a perception. Promised work and provisions. Good luck in the ghetto: 2½ kg rutabaga a week . . . That's how far we've come already! . . . [. . .]

Ashkenes speech on December 7. "Workers, instructors, factory supervisors, and officials of the interior administration . . .

"You have been living now for four years behind barbed wire . . . The ghetto itself is a police matter . . .

"Politicizing (in the factories) does no good, for you are living behind barbed wire without the means to change your situation . . . The Eldest of the Jews is responsible that all orders given him by the authorities are carried out exactly.

"Special Division: We used to work very well with Gertler. Unfortunately, Gertler had to depart the ghetto a while ago. His successor, with all rights and authorities, is Kliegier. He is in constant contact with us and the Secret Police. It is the office that informs us about everything that goes on in the ghetto . . . When the Special Division does a house search, it is authorized, and it is in the interest of the ghetto, to confiscate all hidden goods of production . . .

"Also, I have never seen—as is customary among us—that passersby lend a hand when a cart gets stuck. Some time ago I stopped at a cart and gave a hand because I felt sorry for the people . . ." [. . .]

Tuesday, December 14. *Greatest tension.* Difficult day. At about eleven o'clock, the Eldest taken to town by three Gestapo agents. Fearful hours. Wild rumors. People remember July 12, Gertler. Will he return? What is going on? It is evening. Cart with white horse standing on Baluter Ring, waiting. It was night. Finally: toward one-thirty, knocking on the doors next door—Praeses is back. People give off a sigh of relief.

Then they try to find out the reason. Presumably control of provisioning. More quotas have come in than people in the ghetto. Card issuance office only seventy-nine thousand while the statistics department has more than eighty-three thousand listed.

However this may be, the Praeses is back, among the living. The blow has been overcome. The Praeses is working again—early at eight o'clock at the Baluter Ring.

A difficult night lay ahead. Fright struck the bones. Despite everything, the Eldest is the central figure in the ghetto. [. . .]

Henuschi. Still in bed with nerve information in the leg. Snow, dirt. It's all getting to me. Animated discussion. Continuing to study English. Thinking of Henuschi, dreadful foreboding!

Before Chanukah, memory of Prague—Aschermann 1939 . . . 5704.

December 21, 1943. Henuschi left five years ago. Five years! Longing and pain. Nothing but remembering . . . Eternally hers . . . Nothing else need be said! Nothing but hugs, kisses . . . , which I still owe her . . . To hold her in my arms . . . How she must be suffering . . .

Woman from Hamburg, husband died . . . Today Chanukah . . . bought one candle . . . 50 pennies, can't afford more . . . I am told that the shammes is not necessary. Burning the one little candle daily. Have set the table, turn on light, celebrate by myself . . . Room with three walls . . . instead of window, glass paper . . . but I celebrate anyway. In Hamburg, Mizrachi [religious Zionist movement]; would like to find a Zionist circle here . . .

She made a gingerbread for Mrs. X's birthday—of potatoes, flour, flakes, a little piece, about 2 dkg, as a present. Devoted, good soul . . . Touching . . . Tattered, torn, but suffering heroically. What can the enemies do to us?

Beautiful winter's day, frost and sun. Stinking turnip soup. I made a little tart with *danjak* for Boruch's child. Flour, flakes, milk powder, sugar, oil, salt, baking soda, flavoring.

Question being asked: How much longer? I think close to another year! [. . .]

Heating. Wooden slats, planks, window frames, beams, tar paper . . . All from demolished houses . . . Deserted streets . . . The houses disappear into the stoves.

Henuschi, Henuschi, how right the poor, unhappy darling was five years ago.

Chanukah—deep in the consciousness of the ghetto dwellers . . .

December 24. [. . .] *Suffering.* More than one hundred sick people were suddenly thrown out of the ghetto's infectious-disease hospital—in nightgowns and barefoot, housed in a few ramshackle buildings. In their place one hundred young Poles from the quarantine camp in Marysin[2] for young Poles with typhoid fever were quartered there. Jewish doctors had to care for Poles with infectious diseases. The Eldest wants to turn the former old-age home Geneserner Strasse into a new infectious-disease hospital.

December 25. Eve. This evening at Luzer Najman's together with a few friends. Chanukah Shabbat. I'm supposed to speak on this occasion. About the legend and about us, the living. No big words. We can light the menorah, each one is his own servant of the light.

Suddenly I remember Bessier v. Babothy—light!

Words spoken: "A servant of the light." Good effect. Unable to sleep the following night, plagued by cough and muscle pain . . .

Despite the winter, redemption is in the offing.

Painting in the Ghetto, December 25, 1943

For the painter, the ghetto can now take the place of a hidden corner in the Middle East, a piece of reality outside the realm of civilization, an inexhaustible source of themes. Painters who live in the ghetto are no doubt aware of these possibilities. It would be a sad comment on the artistic eye searching for topics were it to fail in the midst of such wealth. Painters who live in the ghetto don't need such a hint. What they might need is ideological guidance in matters of painting, that is, the representation of ghetto motifs. Here they wander hand in hand with the literary figures of the ghetto landscape.

The searching eye perceives:

a. The crooked streets with gabled houses, which don't fit into a busy world but belong to gardens in which human beings are seeking repose, especially the repose of the ether. The houses with wooden gables exhibit the style of bourgeois stability—even though we know that the people who lived in the area of the present Jewish living district before the ghetto was established were anything but bourgeois, but rather belonged to the proletariat and underworld.

b. Groups of people, pulling loaded carts, pushing, dragging, a task that is normally carried out by beasts of burden, horses or dogs or oxen.

c. Fecalists, young boys and girls, women and men of varying ages. Their dress displays a mixture of ordinary everyday clothing and heretofore unseen wrappings. Most women wear men's clothes, a kind of overall made of old scraps, scarves, and often colorful shreds of flowery damask taken from the bedding of the outsettled. The excrement container that they are guiding [through the streets] is usually in the shape of a concave cylinder, draped with a piece of cloth; on the outside, household containers and pots for the midday soup are often hung. Typical for this group is the posture of those pulling the cart, with extended, lowered head and knees turned outward, giving the impression of beasts of burden. Otherwise they also bring to mind the passage in the Bible that recounts the enslavement of the Jews in Mitzraim [Egypt].

d. Groups from the ressort kitchen. People of any age and sex carrying their soup vessels across the street. Many eat the soup right then and there, leaning against a wall or squatting somewhere. Striking here are the manifold containers: *menashkas,* bowls, pots, plates, even little buckets. The craving, the last means of expressing the constant hunger, can nowhere be mistaken.

e. The *kolejkas* in front of the grocery and vegetable shops. A variety of human types of the ghetto with rucksacks, sacks, baskets, bags, bundles. Especially striking here are the children. Next to them, the representatives of the Order Service, in face, dress, and posture, shining boots and armed with a *nagajka* [Russ., club], a visible contrast to the masses of people they are charged to discipline. The orange-colored stripes of their caps stand out unmistakably among the caps, scarves, hats, etc., of the crowd forming the *kolejka.*

f. Horse-drawn carts and trucks, loaded with potatoes or vegetables, behind them children waiting to catch something that might fall off, under threats from representatives of the Order Service.

g. Poverty-stricken lodgings of starving families, open beds, piles of refuse; food staples stored somewhere behind the table, underneath the bed, on top of cabinets, on windowsills.

h. Death: hearses driving to Marysin, the dying at home, the soup on the family table . . .
i. Hunger . . . Abstract and concrete hunger . . . Work in the ressorts . . . The bridge . . . The gate . . .

These motifs impress themselves inadvertently. Inasmuch as can be determined, it seems that the artists in the ghetto have so far shown little inclination to represent the face of the ghetto. However, it must be said that the circumstances do not permit them to go out into the street and to work outside (*on the open air* [original English]). Such confinement restricts the creative spirit. The ghetto can be represented either in its *crass reality*—this requires direct empathy, intimate knowledge of details, adamant fanaticism—or as a vision in the form of symbols. This depends on the specific character of the artist, that is, on his recognition, which can present to the viewer either the reality or the symbolism of the ghetto. The artists in the ghetto so far have seized upon neither one of these principles of style.

M. Brauner paints, with a broad brush, a few of the motifs mentioned, especially the above-mentioned motif of Jews in the role of beasts of burden.

I. Kowner works primarily with designs in carpet production and is therefore obligated to make do with the limited technique of this ghetto industry in form and color.

J. Leizerowicz belongs to several thinking artists; he is an artist of bold sketches, whereby he is seeking a style that could be called "tamed naturalism."

H. Szylis portrays small slices of the ghetto in a realistic manner.

D. Friedmann—the only one from the West—has a clear and sharp manner of drawing. He is attracted to what is illustrative in humans and landscapes.

Recurrent among all these artists in the ghetto is the demonic motif "The Bridge." All other themes are grouped around it. So far none of the five artists mentioned has produced a visual representation of the ballad of the ghetto. But this is still to come, no doubt.

(For details of painting in the ghetto and the artists mentioned, see "Encyclopedia of the Ghetto.")

O. R.

❁

December 26. A young man, stubble beard, spotted and tattered, enters. "I'm a Yiddish writer . . . would like to get to know you better . . . you are a literary expert, aren't you . . ."

"Yes, yes, sometime, next week sometime. Very busy myself . . . Later sometime." And yet important, to keep contact with such people . . .

Again and again concern . . . Fear . . . Will I be chased away from here after all?

December 27. *Children.* Heavy snow, 1 degree (*one degree above zero* [original English]). Two women from the laundry: early morning, about six-thirty. Dawn. One tells the other about politics . . . mentions names of countries and politicians. Looks around for anybody suspicious (*a suspicious listener* [original English]). A boy . . . As she looks at him, he says: "Hot nisht ka moire. Dos wos ihr weist, wis ich shin long . . ." [Yidd., "Don't be afraid. What you know, I've known for long . . ."]

Chanukah in the Ghetto, 1943

DECEMBER 28, 1943

"The living faith disappeared . . . what is left then is only the poetry."

This is how a superficial observer of ghetto life might summarize the way in which the holidays are celebrated here. The fervor of prayer—so it seems—has given way to ritual technique that feigns sanctity, traces of which are left only in the old and the pious. But—and every unbiased Jew has to acknowledge this—neither hunger nor cold can take away anything from the symbols of the festivals that are embedded unscathed in the tradition.

The difficulty of surrendering oneself completely to the magic of religious observance is primarily due to the lack of a suitable space. The Beth Midrashim have been closed down. There are only a few minyanim, which hold religious services in some hidden shul.

However, Chanukah doesn't require such houses of worship. Chanukah in the ghetto, as it was before in the entire East, is a family festival. It requires no official staging. The Jew who cares about remembering the Maccabees in a traditional way stages the festival at home.

In the streets, next to broken doors and on dirty doorsteps, sits some mummified creature. Through scarves and rags, the face is barely visible. This creature offers candles for sale. *"Lecht! Lecht!"* The call is heard. *Lecht*—that's usually Shabbat candles that are being sold every week on the eve of Shabbat. This time it's about something different: the candles for the menorah!

Not everybody can afford to give his menorah a full gleam. Eight menorah branches means, if every day a candle is added, thirty-six candles, with the shammes, thirty-seven candles, or, expressed in monetary terms, at least 18 marks, if a candle is calculated at 50 pennies. However, some families are able to afford candles for 1 mark apiece so that the "lighting alone" costs 37 marks.

And yet, despite space and financial difficulties, Chanukah is being celebrated this year in the ghetto with great dignity.

Many families have been lighting candles. Just as he had brought the *sforim, makhsorim* [Hebr., prayer books for High Holidays] and siddurim, tallith, and tefillin from the town, the master of the house brought with him, rescued, smuggled in, the menorah. On display are simple brass or wrought-iron menorahs, but also copper- and silver-plated ones, old pieces, new pieces, mass-produced and handcrafted, standup or wall menorahs.

Friends and acquaintances are invited. Over dark stairs, through damp yards and corridors, people are making their way to the apartments, which mostly consist of one room that doubles as living room and party room.

Many are festively dressed, all are in a festive mood. Some favored person, usually the daughter of the house, chants the introductory blessing as she lights the candles. It happens frequently that Jews from the countryside and German Jews from the West are suddenly brought together in one room and are participating in the festival. The lights are gleaming. Remembrances of Chanukahs past flash through the minds. Remembrances of youth, remembrances of student days, of happy years spent in freedom, of images that somehow had a connection with the Maccabees.

People are meeting "privately." Without the official ritual. As long as the menorah lights are burning . . . Children too celebrate Chanukah. People meet in the more spacious lodgings. Everybody brings a suitable present: some toy, a piece of babka, a hair ribbon, a few empty colorful cigarette boxes, a flowery plate, a pair of stockings, a warm bonnet . . . All this is auctioned off. Coincidence decides. The lighting of the candles is followed by gift giving. Ghetto gifts aren't valuable but are received with fervent gratitude.

In the end, songs are sung, Yiddish, Hebrew, also Polish songs. At any rate, songs that contribute to heightening of the festive mood. A few hours of celebration, a few hours of forgetting, a few hours of being immersed . . .

Chanukah 1943 was to be the last war—the last ghetto—Chanukah. So everybody is hoping. The participants exchange good wishes as they part—without words, mute, with pressing of the hands. The menorah lights go out. It's dark again. The people go out into the street. Ghetto life begins anew.

O. R.

January 1, 1944.—Beautiful winter day—bar mitzvah foster son (orphan) at the Praeses. Thirty-two guests. Called as the first to the Thora. Boy says Haftorah with Sephardic pronunciation and *nigun* [Hebr., melody]. Sounds splendid—until now completely assimilated. Praeses has achieved something very interesting here. Almost all guests (Kan, Schipper, Reingold, Jakubowicz, Bender, Stenchliwi, Najman, Schipper, Praszkier, Commander Rosenblatt, Blaugrund, et al.) called to the Thora. Afterward a little snack: fruit wine, some biscuits, nuts, but neither cholent nor sausage sandwich—Caro address to the bar mitzvah boy. Haftorah from Ezekiel about "Jewish state." Congenial morning . . . Praeses a few words: I hope it will all be well . . . Met Dora Fuchs and Aron Jakubowicz, with them all leaders of the ghetto.

January 2, 1944. Excitement in the ghetto—because of declaration *of the German leader against the jews in Europe. In the same time, a small number of people, hope for the soon end and for a better approvisation, but that is a sheer nonsense, because it is beyond the means of the Oldest. The potatoes are growing bad and frozen. The hunger is growing high from day to day and illness can not be defeated. An awful time! Signes of death without any interruption!*

The beginning of the new year is hopeless and wretched! What can you do? Nothing! We are prisoners. And I am looking forward to my brave and extraordinary wife abroad! She is weeping every day — I know it [original English].

January 4. *Praeses.* Yesterday evening, at five-thirty, January 3, again picked up by Gestapo and taken to town, presumably for a confrontation. Since the memory of the case of D. Gertler is true, incredible excitement in the ghetto, that is, fear. Fear as in the days of the autumn outsettlement. Didn't return during the night. Morning of January 4 comes. The entire ghetto is affected by what is happening. Everybody feels: Without the Eldest the ghetto will fall. No clues whatsoever.

Set free! At last, at four in the afternoon. I learn through a neighbor: "The Eldest is back at the Baluter Ring! Boruch went to see him!" The guardian of Israel does not sleep and slumber yet!

January 6. As a result of nameless suffering, the ghetto lives on carefree. *Fonye is approaching, but we don't feel a peril in contrary: a great number of people think that the liberation will come for us soon as the front is nearer to us. One don't hope, one is sure: The day of liberty is staying before the doors of the Ghetto. But I—I am sorry! . . . Each of the citizens thinks only: What will I eat tomorrow? Will become potatoes? Or other nourishment? Am I able to live in eating the minimum?* [. . .] [Original English.]

Little Ghetto Mirror

Cat privilege. One of the oddities of the Litzmannstadt ghetto: the absence of all domestic animals. The horses one sees in the streets do not promote the idea that only humans and animals together form a social unit in the sense of a normal community. Even man's most loyal companion is absent. Only starlings and crows give the ghetto dweller the illusion of the existence of fauna.

And yet in this area, too, the ghetto has its specialty: There is a handful of avid human beings who are allowed to keep a cat. These are the operators of grocery shops, these are food distribution centers.

The cats have the task assigned to them by nature to kill mice. Mice—the chronicler forgot to mention—exist in large numbers, especially in the halls where foodstuff is stored. Mice gnaw through the sackcloth containing flour, flakes, peas; mice penetrate the containers of preserves, sugar, bread.

To avert this danger and to kill the mice is the ressort of the cats. They too have to make *produkzie* [Pol., products; production] like all inhabitants of the ghetto. In return they receive a ration: 1 kg meat a week, good, fresh, digestible meat. The employees in the shops rightfully envy the privileged cats.

For the last week, that is, since the beginning of January, no meat has come into the ghetto, so even these privileged cats have no meat.

They walk around with heads hanging, sadly pulling their tails after them. A pitiful sight. The ghetto inhabitants' meals, like rutabaga, radishes, soup, they refuse. A real shame. Even they, the privileged class in the ghetto, finally have to learn, in January 1944, the serious side of life. They are now forced to share the fate of ghetto dwellers and go hungry. Man and animal. Getting one's fill is not the norm but the exception. Remember that, cat in the grocery shop!

O. R.

[. . .] **January 16.** Fear—*Wysiedlenie* [an outsettlement]. Commission in the ghetto demands statistical documentation of productivity in the various factories: hours, workers, highest performance, etc. At the same time, inventory of all machinery in the ghetto. Perhaps evacuation of the ghetto in Sustne and the surrounding area because of happenings at the front?! Nobody knows anything positive, only one thing: We are once again facing an acute danger!

January 17. *Henuschi.* First meeting with Henuschi in Café Astoria! *London News!* Proclamation from the Eldest: "On order of the authorities all *musical instruments* owned by ghetto inhabitants are to be surrendered [registered]."

Ashkenes theft. Calming in the ghetto concerning the commission, it is said that new orders [for goods] are to come in. Therefore, perhaps the ghetto will remain secure for the next few months.

Gold, silver, jewelry, furs, eiderdowns, sport shoes, typewriters, radios, postage stamps, old clothes. Any metal, bicycles, etc., musical instruments. [. . .]

January 21. *Hunger.* "Bitter, bitter! If we don't get some vegetables soon, people will fall in the streets like flies!

"Who knows how long this game will go on! Bitter! We're on the brink!"

Prices: bread 550, potatoes 80, rutabaga 25, radishes 35, oil 12, butter 10.—

January 22. *Goethe. Jews.* "The Germans will never perish, just as little as the Jews, because they are all individuals.

"The Israelites have never been any good as their leaders, judges, superiors, and prophets have accused them a thousand times; they have few virtues—mostly the failings of other nations: but in terms of individuality, persistence, courage, they have no equal. It is the most hardheaded people on earth; it is, it was, and it will be, so as to glorify the name of Jehova through all times."

Heavy, oppressive atmosphere . . . because of hunger and because of *abroad* [original English]. We will be evacuated, driven out . . .

Professor Caspari died, starved to death, broken down . . . since his wife had been torn from him. September 1942 outsettlement. [. . .]

Ashkenes 1940. An old man passes a Schupo near Massarska. The latter takes scissors from his pockets and cuts off the left half of the man's beard and kicks him with his foot in the behind . . . Jew goes to the barber . . . there Szylis . . . the old man can't pay, Szylis takes him as a model—the old man collapses at home of hunger . . .

January 28. *Hunger.* In the cold room with broken windowpanes, coughing blood . . . No bread, no rutabaga, no potatoes . . . therefore hunger, disease, cold. People succumb daily to these three evils.

Ashkenes. An old woman is ordered to report to the Kripo. What should she do? She owns nothing, not even a wedding band. The neighbor, a tailor in a ressort, calls to her: "Surrender immediately everything you have, gold, diamonds, jewelry, watch . . ." She has nothing.

"Then buy some reichsmarks and give them to the Kripo so they won't beat you."

Woman buys reichsmarks, goes to Kripo. "Let's have it, don't you have anything?" The woman gives the reichsmark to them. "Where did it come from?"—"Bought it. My neighbor told me to do it so I wouldn't get beaten."

The Kripo man says, among other things: "Sutter doesn't give you anything to laugh about and Rumkowski doesn't give you anything to eat . . ."

January 30. *Hunger. Tragedy.* Every day somebody from Prague dies of hunger. Nothing to heat the rooms with, nothing to cook, no medication. Doctors prescribe injections that are not available at the pharmacies, only on the black market; that is: Healthy people get prescriptions and buy up the medications, collect them, to sell them later for inflated prices. The sick, the weak—relinquish nutritive goods to be able to buy the medications that have become very expensive meanwhile. This is how these people go to the dogs. They give up nutritive goods in exchange for worthless injections and pills . . .

One kilogram potatoes 80 to 100 marks, 1 kg rutabaga 30 marks, one loaf of bread 600 marks, 1 dkg sugar 7½, one box of matches 12, 1 kg wood 6, one firestone with lighter 10, one paper bag 2, saccharine 1.

A worker has to work for six months before he can afford to buy a loaf of bread on the black market . . .

Hunger tremendous. Nothing to cook. Ration for two weeks: 60 flour, 20 grits, 50 sugar, 10 oil, 35 preserves, 5 margarine, 3 fat, 15 salad leaves, 1 kg radishes, ½ kg carrots.

With all that, heavy work in the ressorts: wood, metal, tailoring, shoemaking, straw, scrap material, white guard. . . .[3]

Slaves in the streets, pulling wagons and carts, yellow, cloaked faces.

Today, the anniversary of the "seizure of power." Of course, it's our fault.

February 7. Emigrants. Banished. "Isn't what we are losing a minor matter? Wherever we may turn, we carry two wonderful things with us: Nature is everywhere, and virtue that is our own." Seneca.

Hunger: "Soup is being spilled on the steps (stairs to the credit center). An old man pulls out a spoon he always carries with him, scrapes the soup together, swallows . . . That's hunger . . ." Story told by Meilach Schipper.

February 8. *Excitement in the ghetto.* Outsettlement atmosphere. The ghetto administration demands fifteen hundred human beings between the ages of eighteen and forty, healthy and suited for some trade . . . Discussion at the Eldest's. Lists are being compiled. For work? Whereto? Is it good? Or is something behind it? Reason states that on the outside, in some German factory, it would be better than here because there would be a firm, well-thought-out system and order concerning work and nourishment. Or is this the beginning of a mass evacuation?

"It's hard to say what is good! Should one be young, old? Sick or healthy? . . . In the end all is bad. We are prisoners. Banished, proscribed . . ." Everybody is anguished. Each one who goes away leaves behind family and friends, etc. When will this suffering end?

Getting together with *chaverim,* who decided, if necessary . . . to march into the field like soldiers . . .

Mrs. Maryam *Eternity.* Suicide by hanging.

Daily thefts of food of private people.

Sixty marks = 1 kg potato peels . . . Fantastic bread price! [. . .]

February 9. *Hunger and terror.* Unprecedented excitement in the ghetto! Hunger appalling. One box of matches 15 marks, bread, rutabaga, potatoes, also available at astronomical prices! Fortunately no frost, flu harmless.

Fifteen hundred are to be taken away. Whereto? The images of the fate of others of whom nothing is being heard rush through the mind. Fathers leave their children, husbands leave their wives behind . . . They should stay, don't want to go to the West. They love the Polish earth, the barren horizons and hopeless plains, the dark yards and damp stairs. Though the Pole mistreats, insults, tortures, humiliates them, a certain Polish patriotism is alive in them! Therefore fear. Only hesitantly do they line up at the commission. What will happen? Will the obstinate be taken from their beds?

Posting: Prohibition under most severe punishment to shelter those who want to hide.

It's five o'clock. The masses stream out of the ressorts and sections. They look at each other: Tomorrow you'll go, day after, I'll go.

People crowd around influential persons, begging them to intervene. For the son, the brother, the friend, the *chaver* . . . He shrugs his shoulders: "I can't do anything, have no means . . ." "Be well," says he to the one who received no consolation, "be well and go . . ."

Atmosphere as before a *shechita* . . . [Hebr., slaughter, ritual slaughter.]

Is this the beginning of the liquidation of the ghetto?

There's no clue. It is impossible to discern the pathology of this trade.

Onward! Excitement is rising, since nobody believes that it is only for work. During the night to Czarnickiego, those who didn't follow the invitation pulled from their beds. Despair, since many have already lost most of their family members and the rest wanted to stay together or go down together. Attempt to effect the freedom of several *chaverim* with the Eldest. Little hope, since the reserve is too small and fifteen hundred have to be scraped together.

Everybody trembles. Proclamation from the Eldest of severest punishment for those who permit friends and relatives to stay with them overnight, those who refuse to report and are trying to hide. [. . .]

Onward. Husband and wife with child leave their lodging to go into hiding. Police comes at night to pick them up. Beating in locked door. Nobody . . . Posting a note on the door: "Nobody allowed to enter apartment." Early in the morning, lamenting, weeping, sobbing. No longer terror but despair. They go to Boruch: "I can't do anything, can't help you." Mothers are screaming like wounded animals, roaring . . . We are helpless in the face of such tears. "Now," people say, "after we've suffered for four years, now that the end is in sight, we are to offer our heads? No, it's better to croak in the ghetto."

For when one of those designated for outsettlement does not appear at the collection point, the food ration cards for him and his family are invalidated. He himself *hefker* [Yidd., scot-free], Cain . . . a fugitive and a wanderer.

Gotten that far! Forced from his home and into the ghetto, name, house, assets, money, jewelry, furs, shoes, postage stamps, musical instruments, electrical appliances, typewriter, bicycle, everything taken away, put on starvation ration, to slave labor . . . finally, he is himself proscribed . . . Humiliated, tattered, in *trepki,* face unrecognizable, family lost, dead, poisoned, outsettled. Devouring raw potatoes, forced to steal, typhoid fever, lung tuberculosis, and at the same time terror of outsettlement: Who can keep his nerve after all that? Nobody will believe this. No human being can descend to such depths of terror.

Dostoevski figures always retain a glow of religious rapture. Here, this too has died.

A few pray early in the morning. On Shabbat, too, a few. All others are captivated by the thought: Will I get a good ressort soup tomorrow?

The sun falls on snow, it's thawing, warmth, a few laughing children's faces.

Bread 800, 1 kg carrots 80, potato peels unavailable, only through special protection (order of the kitchen department) . . . Ration today, Friday the eleventh, hasn't appeared yet. What is happening? Hunger to go on until Monday? . . .

NOTEBOOK K

February 12, 1944, to June 7, 1944

February 12. Extreme despair. No food (neither potatoes nor rutabagas). No rations, thus hunger—cold—fear of outsettlement. Some people brought to Czarnickiego during the night. All this forms the picture of the ghetto. In addition, no hope for a good ending . . . One has to be a great writer to describe this. Unique in the history of the novel. Dostoevski recounts conditions. Here the dynamic is generated by different circumstances. Absent is the freedom to make decisions, which therefore defies presentation through the means of the epic in the conventional way. We are compelled to find a new form: whether movielike or à la Dickens or Walter Scott or Cervantes or the Russian epic writers, only the future will tell. At any rate, it requires a long breath.

Again the hunt at night. People hiding in caves from the police who want to take them to Czarnickiego.

Heavy snow, first day of "Russian" winter! . . .

It's being said: "Oh, life is difficult! But if the mothers gave up their children in autumn 1942, then we too would be able to make it through! Now, the time for salvation has passed.

Sighs. Have you ever in your life heard a sigh of despair? Sighing "from the depth of the soul"? Here you could hear it.

Two proclamations on top of the misery of February 12:

Dispatch of Fifteen Hundred Workers to Outside the Ghetto

All persons who registered with the commission on Hamburger Strasse 40 are ordered to report immediately, on Sunday the thirteenth, at eight o'clock in the morning, to the central prison.

Those who are found ineligible for work outside the ghetto will be immediately dismissed.

Those persons who, for various reasons, have not reported to the medical commission will have to report by February thirteenth between eight and twelve o'clock at the latest.

All those who do not follow my orders are subject to the following:

1. Cessation of bread and food ration cards for the entire family.
2. Cessation of middays [soups] at the workplaces.
3. Punitive measures that do not depend on us. I am warning again against sheltering relatives or strangers and letting them stay overnight (whether during the day or night).

The ghetto population is herewith ordered to surrender rings of all sorts that they possess as well as other jewelry of silver or gold.

At the Special Division Hohensteiner Strasse against compensation.

February 12, 1944

Ch. R.

February 14. *Hunt of human beings. Outsettlement.* Outsettlement of fifteen hundred (sixteen hundred) workers from the ghetto is running into difficulties, it even proves at first sight impossible. Half the "candidates" are going into hiding. These hapless people remember that those who had been outsettled in the past, that is, people of the same category, either came back crippled, ruined, broken, mentally and physically debilitated, or else their whereabouts are unknown to this day. Terrible agony. They are spending days and nights in some dark hole, practically without food and without tobacco! Frequently together with their families since they fear that they might be taken to Czarnickiego as hostages. The Order Service seals, locks the empty lodgings. In some of these lodgings they made tabula rasa, furniture put outside, taken away, and made available to other parties.

What a hunt for human beings. Stopped in the street. Town like a ghost town since nobody without permit is allowed in the street between seven and five o'clock. This measure in connection with the appearance of the new administrative overlords Gestapo who will assume control over ressorts, etc.

In addition to all this hunger, cold . . . Nothing to cook. Cooperatives don't open before five, everywhere—especially at the coal distribution center—long lines into the night. Last ration shows—1 kg potatoes! What a surprise!

February 16. The terror still paralyzes every limb. Candidates are taken in groups to Czarnickiego for disinfecting. Food, bread rations, for families of those who had been in hiding are being blocked, barred from their lodgings.

Frost! Winter has begun. We're happy when the soup contains more than four half pieces of potatoes!

Bread 1,200, sugar 10, margarine 12, potatoes 130, potato peels 70, one cigarette 2 . . .

I am sitting at home, working on the statistics of the month, reading Heine prose: "The German resembles the slave who obeys his overlord without fetters, without a whip, through the mere word, even through a glance. Servitude is a part of him, it's in his soul, worse than material slavery is the one that is spiritualized! The Germans have to be liberated from within, it's no use from outside."

February 18. *Outsettlement.* Sudden winter! Snowstorm—from north, the Russian steppe.

A group of "workers" from Czarnickiego passes by my window every day, escorted by the Order Service in front and rear, like convicts. No expression in their faces, colorless from grief, hunger, and despair. Some smile or laugh: "It matters none how one goes to the dogs . . ." And people passing by, even though with sympathy, but without a thought, even for a moment, to how they might help.

H u n g e r !

Bread 1,200, sugar 10, potato peels 60, potatoes 220, oil 18 . . . All fantasy prices! Cigarettes 3 marks, 1 dkg tea 100 marks.

Compulsory saluting. Proclamation:

Compulsory Saluting of All People in Uniform as well as German Officials (Civilians)

On order of the authorities, I am drawing your attention, for the last time, to the fact that the decree of compulsory saluting of all people in uniform and of German officials (civilians) is in force.

Compulsory saluting is carried out by members of the Order Service and the fire brigade by standing at attention, and by all others by lifting the head covering, likewise at attention. Special care must be taken that during saluting the hands are taken out of the pockets and cigarettes out of the mouth.

Women salute by lowering their heads.

Disregard of this decree entails the most severe punishments.

Ch. R.

February 19, 1944. General curfew.

Proclamation {in German and Yiddish} No. 411

Absolute Curfew on Sunday, February 20, 1944

In connection with the action of dispatching fifteen hundred workers for work outside the ghetto, a general curfew has been ordered for Sunday, February 20, 1944.

Only Hospitals I and II will be open on that day. The pharmacy Kirchplatz, in Moth-Frischgasse, as well as rescue squads, will be open. All other divisions as well as factories and workshops will remain closed that day.—Workers without papers (legitimation card and kitchen service card) will be immediately arrested. All floors and cellars in the houses are to be opened on order . . .

Lodgings that were sealed by the Order Service are permitted to be opened by the owners so that they can pass the time in the apartments. I am pointing out one more time that on Sunday, February 20, 1944, every ghetto inhabitant has to stay at home.

February 20, 1944, Sunday. Severe asthma attack during the night of Saturday to Sunday, caused by excitement over events. People who are picked up for *work,* as slaves, treated like criminals, torn from their beds, torn from their families. In the early morning hours, two Order Service men appear at my door. Look briefly into the room and move on. Didn't take anything. About midday, I am in bed—a "Special" pays me a visit and tells me that the raid had a moderate result; sixteen hundred were supposed to be put to work outside the ghetto, but because of the general distrust, hundreds went into hiding. Terrible situation: food for the family blocked; some apartments sealed after the furnishings had been removed. How come back. Are we going to track down the ill-fated?

Finally, Sunday the twenty-ninth, they say that several hundred had been caught like rabid, mangy dogs. And what about the others?

How are they to find their way back into a regular life?

Now it's five o'clock in the afternoon. I am freezing in my room, all tricks at getting heat going failed. Another bad night ahead.

Results of the raid on the day of the curfew very minimal. Altogether twelve hundred forty "workers" in Czarnickiego. Effort to scrape together the exact number can lead to a catastrophe for the entire ghetto. What is the Praeses going to do? Will he draw the material from the pool in the ressorts and divisions? Within what time span? In all this, winter weather, wind from the steppe, and snowstorm . . .

February 22. "Compulsory saluting" posted again. Also announced, 5 marks—tin!

Raid. Outsettlement. Selling of coffee mixture on the free market by cooperatives (grocery shops) suddenly prohibited. Those in hiding are eating in their need the raw coffee mixture to protect themselves from starvation. It can be said without exaggeration: The Order is cutting the life thread of these ill-fated individuals. Twelve days have passed since the action. How much misery, tears, death? And all because of this infernal persecution.

February 24. *Hunger.* Sauerkraut, 1 kg = 130 marks. During the night, women too were picked up, about three hundred, the first "transport" is to leave in the near future.

Packages. Packages are arriving from Vienna, Prague, Lisbon, Rumania, Holland, Switzerland = bread, oil, preserves.

February 26, 1944. Lottery—mail packages—coffee mixture—raids.

Mail packages.

For the last several weeks, the ghetto has had a dozen "happy" inhabitants. Not in the sense that they have escaped from all the evils of ghetto life or that they have come to recognize that they have made it through what is mutable in life. No. Their happiness is of a simple kind: They received food packages from outside, from somewhere in the world. This fact can be described, without exaggeration, as a miracle. For, since December 1941, that is, more than two years, all exchange of mail between the ghetto and the outside world had ceased. Only when one of the insettled from the West gets a few marks is he able to acknowledge receipt with a preprinted form note. That's all. That is the bond between man and object outside the ghetto.

And now, suddenly, "gifts of love." There is no other way to describe these packages. They are coming, so it is told, from Vienna and Prague, from Holland, Rumania, even Portugal. The German Reichs postal service passes them on to the Jewish postal service, which in turn passes them to the sixth police precinct, from where the way leads to the Special Division of the Jewish Order Service. The Order Service informs the recipient, who reports to the offices of the Order Service, where the package is handed over. The content? Something edible, of course. Mostly bread, also oil, preserves, sugar, and similar rare and desirable things.—"Who is the sender?" the lucky recipient asks himself. But there is no answer to that question. The name of the sender is withheld from the package recipient. In the end, he contents himself with the fact that somebody outside thinks of him.

Ten to twenty packages like these have come into the ghetto on some days. And everybody who has been asked to report to the Special Division in order to pick up the package—usually weighing 2 kg—tells a tale of his shipment, he dreams of the past and is obsessed with hope to soon become a "happy" man again.

O. R.

Little Ghetto Mirror

Coffee mixture. The story of the coffee mixture has to be told as simply as possible:

During the days when—as the chronicle reports—sixteen hundred people had to be rounded up for work outside of the ghetto, many hundreds of the candidates left their lodgings in order to escape the posse, that is, the men from the O. S., and were hiding somewhere in the ghetto. To coax them out of their hiding places, they were cut off, as under a siege, from all access to food supply. Their food and bread cards were blocked and, to prevent any "illegal" nourishment from reaching them, so were those of their family. The refugees were able to live for a few days on their old stock of provisions. But when that began to dwindle and money, due to the fantastic rise in prices, was no longer sufficient, the persecuted reached for something that was as simple as it was natural: They asked their relatives and friends for coffee mixture, which on the free market in the grocery shop was available for 3 marks per kg. So they lived on ersatz coffee. But this source too was being plugged up. A proclamation to all shops prohibited the free trade of coffee mixture. This was the death sentence by starvation for the workers in hiding. Most of them—so the story is being told in the ghetto—came out of their hiding places. Deprivation of the last means of information, the coffee mixture, forced them to capitulate.

O. R.

Trading in Human Flesh, March 8, 1944

Not without inner consternation—even more, not without compassion—will the chronicler report about the anguish connected with the "dispatch of 1,710 workers to a place outside the ghetto." The day of this outsettlement resembled in many ways the September 1942 days of ill-fated memory. Anybody who has a bit of a memory and fantasy will recognize the symbolic character of these days with regard to the essence of Ghetto Litzmannstadt: *Terror and hunger as alternating interaction.*

The hunt for human beings brought out all desires, the good and the bad. Previous workers' transports had not yet faded from memory, so that all those designated for the February transport tried to save themselves at all costs. They escaped the nocturnal raids through flight, through cunning, through giving their last. All this didn't help much. The authority responsible for the transport warned the candidates in prominently posted proclamations not to try to shy away from their obligation to make themselves available. The warning was bolstered by withdrawal of the food allowance for the entire family. Nevertheless, the flights continued. Those who were hunted day and night were hidden in abandoned barracks, in holes, in attics, in backrooms at the ressorts, in areas unsuitable as sleeping places even for animals. The ghetto inhabitants designated for departure to someplace outside the ghetto (workers!) were being hunted like wild animals in the woods . . . This lasted three weeks, three long, agonizing weeks.

But even amidst the greatest adversity, some of the damned found a way out: They found a replacement. Despite the fact that these journeys "abroad" were regarded in the ghetto as life threatening, the fugitives found people who were willing to undertake the excursion in their place. The cost, the honorarium, was: two loaves of bread and 1 kg sugar. Or foodstuff equivalent to these products. For two loaves of bread and 1 kg sugar a Jew, in February 1944, would go out and risk enslavement, uncertainty, perhaps his undoing. So great was the hunger, so great the craving to still it. "It couldn't be any worse outside," was the thinking of the replacement candidates, "and for the time being I can have my fill for a few days with bread . . ." Two loaves of bread and 1 kg sugar are tipping the scale of a human life when terror and hunger and misery have transcended all bounds. The psychology of the ghetto inhabitants confronts science with heretofore unknown problems.

O. R.

February 27. Midday sun. Snow cover—and in Czarnickiego about fifteen hundred people who are waiting for a journey into the unknown! Twenty-four in one room full of lice, roaches, fleas! An ordeal even before the journey into the "Reich."

March 3. *Talkie.* The first transport is to leave tonight. Single people have already been given a number. Others in *reserve!* Waiting! Who knows what this night will bring . . .

Sixteen hundred people in a space made for four hundred!

Some are happy, for they received new wooden shoes before the departure, one loaf of bread, margarine, sausage . . .

Hunger—misery. A fourteen-year-old boy lets his dead mother lie in the room for eleven days so that he can get her food rations during this time . . . This would be a piece of world for Dostoevski . . .

March 4. *Talkie.* The suffering in Czarnickiego . . . appalling nights . . . At the same time orgies of young people on Baluter Ring with young women. Drinking alcohol, drunk in the street, left lying in the snow, bleeding abdomen (uterus), and taken to the hospital. Two perpetrators arrested by Kripo.

Hunger. A doctor begs for potato peels with tears in his eyes! An order by the kitchen department to the kitchens! But who knows whether this order will be honored since the transport division (for horses) takes priority! . . .

Sunday, March 5. *Henuschi.* Sunshine. Twelve o'clock in the sun. What is it like where Henuschi is? Already green and bright? Has the winter passed yet? [. . .]

March 10. Both workers' transports (1,710 people) departed for Częstochowa.[1] . . . Terror has passed. Supposedly favorable conditions there. Now new concern: Director Biebow is looking for about two thousand people to work in winter construction of houses in Marysin-Radegast (damaged by air raids).[2] With this, beginning of a new era. Difficulty since the prerequisites are absent outside . . . For the time being, evidence division left untouched. I am unable to work outdoors, physically unfit. [. . .]

Sunday, March 12. Six years ago today to Bratislava at Henuschi's urging! That was the beginning of the misery.

Dreary, miserable cough, distressing. Winter. Snow and excrement in the streets. People getting their ration and 20 kg coals. Within four months at the coal distribution center, barracks for ressort, within six months transfer of people from over there to us. Who knows what will still happen until then.—

It is said that the Eldest is not allowed to dispose of anything anymore; therefore, from now on no more bread and no more sausage. The doctors too are going empty-handed.

Musical instruments. The musical instruments handed in by the ghetto were evaluated by German experts and paid for. That is, the Eldest made about 2,400 marks in first-class violins, cellos, brass-, wood-, and jazz instruments. (Municipal orchestra, music school H. J. [Hitler Youth]—Reich music department mayor.)

Two cellos = 120, trombone, nickel silver = 20, accordion = 20, forty-four violins = 1 mark apiece, fifteen master violins together = 100 marks, a master saxophone = 40 marks, guitars, zithers, flutes, clarinets, saxophones, drums, trumpets, etc. = 2 to 3 marks apiece.

Produkzie. Whatever may be happening, no matter what the conditions under which the ghetto may be existing—it has one purpose: to produce! Thus reads the law Ashkenes. *Produkzie!* But Ashkenes is never satisfied. Only in the Bess-Oilom does he show satisfaction. All this works very well, every day there is plenty of *produkzie!*

Talkie. Outsettlement. September 1942. A horse-drawn cart in front of the house that houses orphans. Their parents had either died or perished on the transports from Lask, Zduńska Wola, Brzeznic, Pabianice.

Ashkenes in uniform with hippopotamus whip under his arm, cigarette in his mouth, next to the cart.

Early morning. The children are coming out of the gate to the house into the street; walking over the sidewalk they make a respectful curtsy, lower their heads slightly. They climb into the cart or they are thrown on to it by the Jewish police.

Then off they go. They go; that is, they are riding toward their end. Not a sound, no scream, no tear.

"Morituri te salutant . . ."

Life Writes Fiction, March 13, 1944

M. Klecztenski is a citizen of Ghetto Litzmannstadt. It is his duty to share with his fellow Jews the sufferings and joys of the ghetto. He has no desire to remember his former life, the years he spent abroad in Argentina and in Germany . . . On Wednesday, March 8, he is ordered to report to Baluter Ring. He appears. He is told to get himself furnished with "shining new" articles at the clothing and underwear department. Kl. follows the order, and, when he appears in this new outfit at Baluter Ring, he is taken to the police precinct where he is, so to say, placed in custody of the Gestapo. "You are Klecztenski?"—"Yes," he replies, without knowing what they are getting at. "You will go to Poznan with me." The official in civilian clothing turns to him, leads him to a taxi, and soon the two, the ghetto Jew and the German official, sitting next to each other in the taxi, drive off, between wires and beams, to the train station of the city of Łódź. Along the way, the civilian official treats the ghetto inhabitant with a certain civility, which he accepts with great satisfaction. All through the night they ride on the train to Poznan. When they arrive in Poznan early next morning, the two passengers wait for the train from Berlin, filled with military, to arrive. Kl. is standing with his companion on the platform when the train arrives, and out of the open window a voice suddenly calls out: "Papa, Papa!" Kl. is quite astounded when he sees his daughter and, behind her, his wife, getting off the train and greeting him. Now the companion takes the three people to a room in the station, where he leaves them alone. Years ago Kl. had been living in Argentina and had married a local woman. Later he moved to Berlin with wife and daughter. By accident he had been swept into the ghetto. His daughter, who was living with her mother in Berlin, had already a year and a half before tried to visit him in Litzmannstadt but had made it only as far as the city. She did not gain permission to enter the ghetto. She drove several times then in a taxi, back and forth between the wire and beams along Hohensteiner Strasse, trying to spot her father or something familiar . . . Without success. Since then she kept trying to somehow meet with her father. Through the offices of the Argentinian consulate—mother and daughter were regarded as quasi-Argentinian citizens—she at long last succeeded in arranging the meeting in Poznan. Finally father, mother, and daughter were sitting together at the station in Poznan. For six hours. Outside, two German officials were waiting: one to take the women back to Berlin, the other to take the father back to Litzmannstadt. The women are living in the Jewish quarter in Berlin, close to the edge of the city, a ghetto without wires or beams. The man returns again to the real ghetto. They talk about what they had gone through during the years of being apart. The furrows on the forehead and wrinkles on the forehead and in the face testify to the truth of their experiences. A novel ends. A new novel begins.

O. R.

March 17. *Tidbit.* Director Biebow accompanied by two German gentlemen at the Eldest's. Demands series "chaimki" with signature of the Eldest. Collectors' value.

Hunger. Babka, *plazki* [Yidd., potato pancakes], *klejselach* [Yidd., dumplings], made with *shulechz* [Yidd., potato peels], a difficult procedure, often several hours of preparation!

Humor. It is customary to drink the *soup,* eat the *coffee,* smoke the *tea,* sleep at the *ressort,* and work at *home* . . .

March 20, 1944. *Shulechz.* Rifke is happy. Due to a higher—let's say—intervention, she managed to get a written order for *shulechz* from a kitchen . . . every other day 2 kg of *shulechz.* Nothing to sneeze at. A kilogram of potatoes costs 200 marks, 1 kg of *shulechz* 60 marks. This means that 2 kg is a small fortune . . . Rifke, as I said, is happy.

She goes equipped with a sack in hand to the kitchen. Today nothing, maybe tomorrow, better day after tomorrow, about eleven o'clock before the rush of the soup distribution.

Rifke appears. Since she doesn't have written permission to be in the street outside of ressort hours, she is very nervous. The person charged with giving out *shulechz* to those who are authorized to receive it says, "Impossible! A commission! Won't make it today. Maybe tomorrow . . . day after tomorrow."

Finally God helped out and Rifke got her 2 kg of *shulechz.* It comes so easily over the lips: *shulechz!* But not all *shulechz* is alike! The *shulechz* that, in blessed prewar times, was being fed to the livestock consisted of nice, thick, golden potato peels for all Jewish children. But today, thin peels, dirty and dusty, partly dried out, partly just skin and bones, that is, without a trace of potato. But be that as it may! Main thing is that one can take home 2 kg of *shulechz* and prepare something tasty for the children, according to the housewife's talents.

Yes, the children! As soon as the mother enters the room, they fall over the sack with the booty of the day, that is, 2 kg of *shulechz.* Now it means working, lending a hand.

The *shulechz* is thrown into a bucket, taken to the pump in the snow-cold yard . . . It is washed, cleaned, separated from dirt and dust . . . Once more pumping, once more cleaning, after the presumably edible pieces are gleaned from the pile. Meanwhile it is late evening. The children are tired, almost falling asleep as they work. But there is no stopping, no break. After the cleaning, water is put up on the stove. The warm water is meant to wash away the remaining dirt and dust.

It's midnight. The housewife herself is tired. The 2 kg of *shulechz* yields about ½ kg when steamed.

Now it goes in the grinder as if it were meat.

The next day the *shulechz* is used in grated form. A child wants babka, another would like *plazki,* another prefers *klejselach.* The mother decides to make *klejselach* for the soup. The ressort soup, enhanced with *klejselach,* makes a full meal. The children say the soup doesn't smell good; that's because of the *klejselach.* But what do such objections matter? *Klejselach* from *shulechz*—so say the doctors and knowledgeable laypeople, stomach experts of the ghetto—has nutritional value even if you have to put forth a lot of effort to get some results. Maybe God grants us 2 kg of *shulechz* every other day . . . Half of life . . .

O. R.

March 22, 1944. There are two Kaufmanns, so the saying goes in the ghetto.

One for fire (Commandant Kaufmann of the fire-fighting squad) and one for water (Kaufmann, director of the kitchen department).

Luxusowski: These are 10-mark receipts made of metal.

March 23. *Despair.* Despair because of *psires abroad* [original English] . . . How much longer? All signs point to a long duration, no sign of letup, everywhere resistance, and in the country itself discipline is apparently unbroken . . .

No foodstuff from outside to be seen. I still own eleven little potatoes for the next two weeks.

Hunger. Talkie. "Is it strange that one is hungry despite the fact that one has a kilogram of bread in the cupboard? . . . One doesn't dare touch it when the daily portion has been consumed . . . And yet, what grotesqueness. Where in life has it ever happened that a person is starving, literally starving, when he owns a piece of bread that could still his hunger!"—"Good God, will we ever again see the light of the world? . . ."

"And the children . . . I'm coming home. I see my child going hungry and have nothing to give him. Not even a bread crust. For in the morning this bread crust would be missing . . ." [. . .]

Sunday, March 25. *Plan.* Without any external cause, I am preoccupied with the thought: What will happen when Fonye approaches? Must have a plan to prevent us from being chased away like rabbits. Make preparations now, but most of all the resolve not to give way without putting up a fight, not to proffer the neck to the henchman.

Monday, March 27. *Suffering* . . . At night snowstorm from the Russian steppe. Midday sun, doesn't help much. At night coughing, shortness of breath, angina pectoris, fear . . . muscle rheumatism, neuralgic pain, weakness in the limbs. I'm making plans in case of outsettlement. . . . Alone. The others don't want to hear anything about it. Maybe when it is too late? They're making plans for the long term.

March 29. There is no crime that hasn't been concocted by the brain of the Neanderthals [Germans] and that hasn't been carried out by the arm of the Neanderthal.

Situation. For four years—since March 9, 1940—we have been living without: books, newspapers, magazines, music, radio, gramophone, song, singing, sport, correspondence, countryside, air, woods, lake, swimming, bathing, gymnastics, walking, coffeehouse, restaurant, social gatherings . . . With: fear, terror, nightmare, hunger, misery, heartache, cold, frost, shadow of death, mass dying . . .

All is lost: honor, dignity, the past . . . Each one wants to save himself at the expense of the other, pushes his fist in your mouth to keep you from screaming . . . Thousands stagger through water and excrement and melting ice, carrying a *menashka* . . . eighty thousand human beings are eating ressort soup every day, a collective food that cannot be compared to Chinese rice food, for in that country there are a few dozen ways of preparing it . . . [. . .]

April 1. *Gleam of hope.* Sun, intimation of spring . . . 17 degrees [Celsius] in the sun. It is being told in the ghetto: Reports from Częstochowa of the Jewish workers who were recently taken there that they are doing well: two good soups, even some meat, working in a metal factory, etc. A few people were also met there who had been part of the outsettlement years ago. Thus there are still Jews alive outside the ghetto in the Warthegau [German name for area in Poland around the Warta river]. This gives rise to some hope . . .

Terrible nights . . . Cough, shortness of breath, cold sweat, sticky air despite open window. (*I am sleeping with open window!* [Original English].) The heart is aching, the stomach and rib muscles are aching . . . In the morning, almost collapsed. This is how it goes night after night for weeks. But we can't give up now, have to clench the teeth together and preserve our confidence, to be a part of the end, to live it, experience . . . Henuschi, to take Henuschi in my arms, to pay her back, make good for six years of suffering!

Can it still be grasped? . . .

April 2. *Sunday.* The ghetto bursts into cheers; it arrived: 1 kg potatoes, ½ kg red beets, ½ kg red preserved beets, 30 dkg of sauerkraut, ½ kg mixture of coffee! In addition to this a bit of sun and people are happy.

April 14. *Sick.* Been in bed for twelve days. Terrible throat pain à la angina pectoris. The doctors (Drs. Miller, Mautner, Natanssen) deny it, but the unsteadiness in the hands and the other symptoms are positive signs. Taking Iminol, Ephedrin, Strophanthin, nitroglycerine, etc. . . . Terrible nights, seeing the end outright in Marysin. Only the hope for Henuschi sustains me.

At the same time Pesach. Seder at Boruch's: nice table with matzot, *morer* [Yidd., bitter herbs; Hebr., *maror*], *chrojses* [Yidd. for Hebrew *charoset*], etc., even eggs . . . Then back to bed. Yom Tov mood in the ghetto, clean clothes, matzot. Praeses distributed thirteen thousand coupons for: ½ kg matzot, sugar, margarine, flour, preserves. For me especially through Boruch's intercession: 1 kg wheat flour, 1 kg meat, 1 kg sugar. As gift from Leizerowicz 1 kg matzot . . . Hand trembles. Should have a cardiogram . . .

On April 14 for the first time again at my desk at home. But still unable to produce. Hand trembles. Tightness in the heart area making itself felt again. Back to bed . . . *I am eating, reading, and sleeping with wide open window* [original English].

Don Quixote of La Mancha . . . amuses me again, hadn't read it for thirty-seven years, only Heine's commentary about it. Also Weininger's *Sex and Character,* with the insane Jew's capital and the excellent beautiful chapter on genius, memory, sex, piety, belief in immortality . . . Now, two o'clock in the afternoon. Luzer, almost in tears, welcomes me at the desk—Mother Praszkier is fixing me a daily meal of meatballs. Touching concern.

April 16. Still spring sun! Today again outside of bed. Great pain in the ribs, heart muscle . . . in addition to self-recriminations because of Henuschi . . .

Medications: Ephedrin, Iminol, Strophantin, natrium bromide, aspirin, Zanedo forte . . . Body is, so to say, poisoned, and yet I keep reaching for it.

About the Study "Hunger"!

One more thing in addition: the desire to survive as a moral obligation, as something that has been placed on the people of Israel because of Amalek [Biblical enemy of Israel, prototype of the persecutor; Israel is enjoined by God to destroy Amalek and remember his evil deeds]. Therefore hurry and fear; fear of not fulfilling this injunction. Surviving becomes a religious duty. . . .[3]

Atonement: Can this remain unatoned? It's ironic to see Ashkenes riding by in his automobile, commanding with his eyes, all around the slaves of the ghetto; he laughs, he believes himself ruler of the world . . . but atonement must come—as redress, so to say, for the suffering they caused: *That is the meaning of history.*

April 20, 1944. Cool day. For a short while out of bed. Surprise in the ghetto: special provision ½ can of canned meat, 5 dkg fat, 10 dkg vegetable salad. However, unable to suppress the hunger. Everybody is waiting for a potato or vegetable ration.

Deaths: The number has risen from nine to fifteen or seventeen a day, that's four hundred fifty a month, that is (on average), with seventy-eight thousand ghetto inhabitants, five thousand a year, or 6 percent, in contrast to the normal rate of 0.8 percent, or eight times as high. Transferred to London with eight million inhabitants, that would be sixteen hundred dead daily, forty-eight thousand a month, five hundred thousand a year! London is in part responsible for the death from starvation of one hundred thousand Jews. For it could have transported the entire Jewish population of Poland to Canada. Let's not always bandy about the term "war criminal." In London and New York and Moscow are the peace criminals. [. . .]

April 27, 1944. "Happy is the eye that sees redemption."

We are all waiting for redemption, liberation . . . No more patience to wait. Lost is all sense of the spiritual; only one concern: soup, bread, coupon. [. . .]

Saturday, April 29, 6 Iyar 1944. Increasingly urgent desire to say a few words of thanks to him who ties us to the world by bringing us consolation in the darkest hours . . . Idea to gather in a room for quiet assembly. A minyan.

6 Iyar . . . as last Shabbat before our faraway friends are coming closer to redeem us. The thought was met with agreement and so we met next door—in a spacious room around an oval table: Moshe Caro, Jakob Tyller, Shlomo Fischer, Shlomo Überbaum, Luzer Najman, Oskar Singer, Boruch Praszkier, Oskar Rosenfeld, Shaiye Wechsler,[4] Jakob Schipper. . . .

Nice, quiet atmosphere over good coffee, *lejkach* [Yidd., gingerbread] . . . O. R. said a few words on behalf of Shayek, who again and again was giving us the voice of the caller in the oasis (not the desert), bringing consolation and misery, and sowing hope. Then Moshe Caro along the same lines; finally Shayek about the idea that had carried him along through four years in the ghetto to this day . . . Everybody had the sense of historical hours, of a historical place.

Then in my room with Shayek and Tyller a half-hour of dedication to eternity, listening to the song of the ether, remembering the martyrdom of millions of European companions sharing our fate (photograph Grossman) . . .[5]

On the horizon a soft rosy band . . . this is how it appears to my friends, and faith in a speedy *yeshiye, mehero beyomenu* . . . [Yidd./Hebr., redemption, yet in our day.]

April 30. Then a peaceful, inspiring Sunday at the *chug* [Hebr., circle, assembly; study group] with lecture from the General Zionists, followed by an equally quiet and hope-inspired Monday, the *first day of May.* Still guarding the bed for several hours a day, outside, a cool, dreary day.—Coupon B I reinstated: 70 dkg bread, 10 dkg sugar, 10 grits, 10 preserves, 10 fat, 10 peas . . . every week!

We are keeping a lookout for the delivery of vegetables the way peasants await rain for their parched fields. Finally, spinach, 2 kg per person. In spite of it all—the suffering and hunger—no gloomy faces, on the contrary, hope, faith. Laughing, playing children, and people in the yards and at the fences who are working their few square meters—their *djalkas.* Potatoes? Uncertainty whether we will still be harvesting them here. . . .

In general, conviction that the end was imminent. Only a few singular skeptics, but without any concrete reason, more a matter of innate mentality.

Nobody speaks much *about hunger* despite the fact that it has never been as biting, as threatening. Mortality rate increasing, tuberculosis making the rounds among young people. In the streets *klapsidres*—these are decrepit figures, walking skeletons. Unimaginable for all of you far away.

May 3. The question gains ever greater urgency: Are we going to be here during the hour of the final showdown? Still be alive?—Outside, carts carrying raw material for the war, especially uniforms and cloth, partly also leather . . .

From over there, in the far distance—*from widest far* [original English]—singing that sounds like liberation and yet has so far always been deceiving . . .

Such bad soups—water with 2 dkg of potatoes—that most ressorts refuse to accept them, that is, they are striking. Even the children have been refusing the soup during shift change, casting the entire ghetto into great turmoil. In every ressort (and division), groups organized by communists that follow a slogan creating the above-mentioned atmosphere. An un-Jewish factor.

Reminiscence. Humor. Immediately following the establishment of the ghetto, the Jews began to work the soil, that is, to exploit *djalkas.* Since no fertilizer was available, some other means had to make do, and that's how they got the idea of using human *feces.* One load—this was taken care of by the local excrement workers outside their normal working hours—costing 2 marks. One day a fecalist was bringing in a load.

"This one is 3 marks . . ."

"Why? . . ."

"Because the *tinef* [Yidd., garbage] is from an assistant counselor. A noble *tinef.* It's worth the money . . ."

And the *djalka* owner paid.

Coupons of the Praeses. A young woman, swollen from hunger, as so many of her sex in the ghetto. The stomach, the consequence of too much watery soup, gives her figure its character.

The Praeses appears unannounced. Talking to the woman in brusque tone: "What do you want? What's your business here?"

The woman, bewildered, lowers her head.

"Sick?" asks the Praeses.

"Yes, sick . . ." the woman replies, trembling.

The Praeses looks her over from top to bottom. His eyes are arrested on her water stomach. He has someone note the woman's name and address, gives her a coupon, a sick coupon.

He thought the woman was *pregnant.* The water stomach had brought her luck.

Reminiscence. Square at Hamburger Strasse (Lutomierska)! Two Jewish workers escaped from Work Camp Poznan. They didn't want to die there from the abuses at the hands of Ashkenes but preferred to starve to death among their dear ones in the ghetto. That's why they took off. Were caught: one nineteen, the other forty years old.—

With hands tied behind the back, they are taken to the square, where two gallows are waiting. They get out of the Gestapo car. Only now does it become clear to them what is going on. All around the square, masses of people who had been driven together in the streets. Shortly before the arrival of the car, uniformed Ashkenes in the square, laughing, making noise, smoking cigarettes, talking loudly among themselves. The voices of those overlords are recognizable . . . One of them walks up to the gallows, shakes the beam. As if to make sure that it is solidly implanted in the ground . . . The two are dragged to the gallows. The boy cries, laments . . . Quickly carried out. The bodies twitch. It's over.

The Ashkenes salute each other. Laughter. Chatting. Cheerful . . . cheerful . . . Take off. *The brief "fun" is over.*

May 6. Vilma's birthday. One week before mine. [. . .]

May 8, 1944. Today, German commission in the ghetto, more than forty gentlemen. Excitement, since [they are] in the ghetto early at 7:30 A.M. Visiting a few ressorts. Air filled with rumors—*6 dkg parsley at 50 pennies.*—Sensation amidst the hunger. [. . .]

Remembrance of May to June 1942, when people had been picking dandelion leaves and were stopped by the police, since even these leaves were considered to be foodstuff and picking them was therefore prohibited . . . Now vegetation is so meager that nothing edible is to be gleaned from nature . . .

Words in the ghetto: Why is it so bad if it is so good?

May 9. *Hunger.* The gravediggers in Marysin are as hungry as the rest of the population.—Their arms and legs have become so weak that they no longer have the strength to bury the dead. On May 8, 1944—the number of dead rises during these hunger months—the burial of several corpses had to be postponed to the next day. Boruch takes a ride out to the good place to demand that his people get a third portion of soup . . . Otherwise the living won't be able to bury the dead.

Sensation of May 9, 1944. Since the end of December 1941, that is, for two and a half years, mail ban. Now finally traffic in stamps is supposed to be allowed again . . . starting Wednesday, May 10 . . . Open letter cards to the German and occupied areas. A ray of hope for those who have relatives or friends on the outside with whom they might renew contact and from whom on occasion they can expect a little package.

May 10. First day of spring with sun. Toward noon again warm. Out of bed. Studying photographs, writing dedication on two for photographer Grossman. [. . .]

May 13, 1944. A dreary, damp, warm day on which I am back at the archive for the first time in a long time. At night *a long train of recollection is going a cross my brain . . . in connection with Henuschi . . . The friends of mine are in the point to gratulate . . . A queer situation: my sixty birthday. I remember to the sister and Eric . . . What a awfully hour . . . And how long yet! . . . I am aspecting the next minutes! What they will bring to me?*

Alice de Bunom[6] *has brought a poem, Mos. Rosenkranz some flowers, Mr. Singer shakehands . . .* [Original English.]

1884–1944. Surprise! Shabbat! Boruch tells me to stay home at five in the afternoon. My friends are coming. Among them Shayek with a Sefer Torah cabinet, which he made himself.[7]—Then at Boruch's place decked-out table for the entire minyan. Natan appears, heard of the get-together by chance. [. . .] Singer, Fischer, Schipper, Überbaum, Boruch, Shayek, Tiller, Luzer, I, Caro, two photographers; suspense.—Boruch presents me with a beautiful album, in a beautiful, warm speech, with dedication from the *chaverim*. Then Caro speaks on the occasion. Celebrates me as a former writer and current teacher and leader who has enriched the ghetto Zionists, etc. Very good speaker.

Following, my words of thanks to all the *chaverim*. Finally

Dr. Singer, very skilled, adds to praise of Boruch and his family, I as the representative of the West. Through me all Westerners are celebrated. Schnaps, tea, little open sandwich rolls, *lejkach.* Excellent ambience. The photographer takes several pictures, among them Boruch's *b'chor* [Hebr., oldest son], also Yulek Grünberg, who hands me a bouquet of flowers.—Finally listened to Sefer Torah. Sacred words for the soul. (Album unique, a museum piece. Also a watch from Boruch as a replacement for the stolen Cyma [brand name of a watch].) We decide to get together every Shabbat at the place of one of the *chaverim.*

Ashkenes. Talkie. Kripo goes into the basement apartment. Dark. In the bed a very sick, tuberculous boy reading by a dim electric light. Sutter tears the book from his hand, hits him in the face with it, drawing blood. The boy faints, Kripo leaves. (Turning on light in the daytime is prohibited even in a basement!)

May 17, 1944. Workers moved out.

Twelve men, accompanied by five policemen, walk through the Dworska toward Baluter Ring. In their hands, sacks, rucksacks, bundles. On their backs, tied-together blankets, bedding, broken figures. Crowds gather on the sidewalk—it is three o'clock—even though the ressorts have not let out yet.

Screaming, surprise, gesticulating. Many children. A little sun. "What is going on?"—"People from Czarnickiego [going] to work outside the ghetto . . ." That's not so bad, I think.

Later Boruch and one from the "Special" tell me: "Fifty people are needed. People are plucked from the streets, taken from the coal distribution center, the quota has to be filled, so demands the ghetto administration. A woman next to me says: "Terrible! Again outsettlement!"—"You can't call that outsettlement, it's a matter of work outside the ghetto." While we continue to talk at my place—meanwhile it's five o'clock—the streets fill with people streaming from the ressorts, the noise level rises, the haste escalates, everybody wants to find out what the terrible thing was that had befallen the ghetto. For any expectation for something good has long died in the ghetto. Not even the belief in the delivery of potatoes takes hold.

A woman cries, sobs, laments. Another woman supports her, tries to console her. Probably, so we assume, one of her dear ones was caught and pushed onto the transport. The group that is forming around the woman falls suddenly silent. A man who joined them and looked trustworthy because of the wide, yellow band on his sleeve says something about a loaf of bread, which those who had been sent away had "now just now" received.

"A loaf of bread?" The people were shaking their heads.

"So I should . . . if this is true!"

The words "a loaf of bread" apparently had a soothing effect.

The passersby who had halted their steps went on their way brooding over a loaf of bread, which gilds the path of severest suffering.

Several of those who had been caught in the street are bolting, fleeing. Of the twenty who had been caught, fifteen made their getaway, they are being hunted . . . Impossible to catch them. But since fifty men have to be supplied immediately, the hunt continues. Finally. Evening. The chapter is closed.

Eyewitnesses report: A car with several Jewish policemen, of high rank, pulls up at the woodworking ressort. A few seconds later—the uniformed men jump off [the car]—the manager of the ressort appears, orders several workers to line up. The Jewish commission looks them over to separate those deemed fit for the purpose from the rest. Two to the right, five to the left. Three to the right, seven to the left. Five men daily. The workers don't know what this is all about. The rumor had been circulating in the ressort that workers were needed for unloading potatoes in Marysin, that is, something that would serve the ghetto. As soon as the inspection is over, the victims are taken by the Jewish police to the Baluter Ring.

A similar occurrence took place at the demolition center along the Brzezinska. Whoever has eyes to see will notice that the selection of the workers did not follow the principle of age or ability to work. Even the sick, the weak, and the elderly were being drafted.

The ghetto was as paralyzed.—Now, after five years of war, shortly before the end, Jews were "deported" from the ghetto to work outside. Deported? In work clothes, filthy, tired, with an empty stomach, they were being dragged to somewhere. They were not even allowed to say goodbye to their family, their wife and child and parents. That's not how one treats people of whom one demands and expects regular work performance.

"They are only going for ten days . . . not far from the town . . . to work in the fields . . ." This rumor alleviated the pain, the bitterness, and the melancholy of those staying behind. And in the late afternoon hours, one hears everywhere: "Tomorrow, in the soup, 1 dkg of flour, 2 dkg peas, 1 dkg flakes, and 10 dkg potatoes!"

"Yes, but 10 dkg potatoes gross . . ."

"Oh, how they will rob us . . ."

"They"—that's the kitchen workers who are entrusted with distributing the soup.

O. R.

Yankel the Folksinger. That same day, as night was falling, Yankel Herszkowic entered my abode. Broad, stocky, with sparkling eyes, shiny cheeks, fiery look, teeth like a beast of prey, in all that, a soft, humble look and expression. He is the singer in the ghetto. Shortly after the ghetto was established, when bread and meat could still be purchased in the open market but most people didn't have a penny in their pocket, back then the majority of the ghetto dwellers were starving in front of well-stocked shops—back then, Yankel became the troubadour of the ghetto. Troubadour and critic of human manners. He castigates the people and their behavior . . . singing his own songs in the style of balladeers, texts in a folksy Yiddish, which often sounds mellower and always more natural than the Yiddish of the literati.

He sings in the street, surrounded by the crowd. Mostly the very poor, the people. Themselves hungry and miserable, they have beggared a few pennies, which they give to their songster. Yankel is proud of his following. He says: "I want to survive the war, the ghetto. That's why I have to see to it that I get the necessary nourishment. There isn't enough for *all. Not all* can survive the war. That's why *the one* who endures will be the one who takes from *the others.* Those who stay alive do so at the expense of others. And I want to stay alive. I want to tell the outside world later on. That's why, I believe, it is necessary for me to survive the evil . . ." He smiles, laughs, his eyes and teeth are gleaming.

Pulling from his pocket a little piece of paper, a manuscript, he reads, sings, gives recitations . . . About the big shots and their little girlfriends, all of whom are mutually living well—photographer Grossman shows a photo. Seen from the roof, Yankel ringed by his audience. [. . .]

May 21, 1944. Six years ago, Henuschi was being hunted in Marienbad. First mobilization in Czechoslovakia. I am coming back to the

Andermann, she doesn't recognize me. Poor Henuschi, your suffering in Marienbad was for naught, her eagerness and love for me were not rewarded . . .

Talkie. Jewish State Party [original English]. A few words about the anniversary of Sokolow's[8] death and the situation in the *Jewish State Party.* Small living room. Two girls from the kitchen Lagewnicka 1/3. A minute of silence for Nahum Sokolow. Then *tikvah* before parting. Meilach takes me to the General [Zionists] . . .

We are traversing the bleak yard of a rear building; crumbling wooden steps lead to the first floor, directly under the roof. It's eight o'clock. The room is dark. A thin crack in the roof admits a little light so that the danger of people running into each other is decreased. We are passing the wall that supports the roof. Since there is no door, an opening has been made, about half the height of a man, through which the garret is reached. A few roof tiles assist in the climb, helpful hands are pulling the guests up.

The garret has been furnished as an assembly room. Long benches and tables, even clothes hooks. Right at the entrance young women are affixing blue badges on those entering. Dim lighting. The tables are covered. Rain is leaking through the roof, the last tremors of a May thunderstorm.

A sort of presidium. Also Boruch, the young Jakobson . . .

A young man, Gerson, has the floor. He is a streetcar conductor.

Commemoration of Sokolow as a genius in exaggerated manner, sweating. Then Moshe Caro! Of course, it is impressive how he delineates correctly, and in a clever way the personality, Sokolow, comes alive. A singer is called up. A young, masculine baritone sings the much demanded and much acclaimed *"Kol kore bamidbar"* [Hebr., "A Voice in the Wilderness"]. Then splendid ocarina players, virtuosi, mature musicality. Simple, modest, splendid human beings. About two hundred. At the end, softly, almost conspiratorially, the *"Techesaknah"* [Yidd., "make strong"].—We leave the room. Quietly. As inconspicuously as we came. Nine o'clock nightfall. Over the Baluter Ring. I wrap myself in my raglan. Going home alone.

Behind the barricade, the Ashkenasic *selner* [Yidd., soldier] whistles to himself. The stars are coming out, only a few people are still in the streets after a nerve-racking Sunday. Home into my room. Zanedo-Iminol, my friends accompany me to bed. Ghetto night.—Air raid alarm.—[. . .]

May 27, 1944. *Children.* Children sneak into the archive to steal *kolazia* cards to sell as playing cards. Big scene when they're caught. Crying. Threats of deportation after a terrible impression. Children offer paper roses as bribes. Where to find them? They'll scrounge money and buy paper roses with it . . . Terrible moral misery . . . ghetto is at fault.

Night. Again outsettlement. People torn from their beds because not enough volunteers reported for work outside . . .

Thirty men already taken in the night; were given bread, sugar, margarine, etc., to take along.

Twenty-eighth to twenty-ninth. Prevailing outsettlement atmosphere. A letter card from Częstochowa. From brother to brother: "Come if you can; it's better here than elsewhere. No easier place to survive the war." But fear is so deeply etched in, nobody wants to believe it.

Shavuot. Second day. Pentecost Sunday. Streets crowded as on a holiday in freedom. Nobody outside the ghetto can imagine the atmosphere of such a day. They are getting rations, coupons, *twarog* [Pol., curds], sausage, and all kinds of goods not yet received. Thousands of people in the *djalkas,* the sun is burning, a few tanned faces can even be seen . . .

But it is precisely the bright light and the sated green that throws the soul into even greater despair.

Now it's eight o'clock in the evening. I am waiting for Shayek and the others. Will we get word today announcing our imminent redemption?

Henuschi. I was dreaming of Henuschi. Arm in arm with her, she was guiding me, protecting me, keeping me warm. I regained my strength; then I was dreaming of Father and Mother as so often lately. [. . .]

Of the seventy-eight thousand Jews in the ghetto, seventy thousand are sick. Everybody has incurred some kind of ailment.—Suicide attempts in masses; insanity; stupefaction among younger people; manias. "Pants off, pants on, and the soup, that's what our life consists of," remarks a clearheaded one.—A separate chapter: the children (see notebook "Studies"). *Always the same story: lung tuberculosis.*

June 3, Shabbat, 1944. Shayek came with a golden heart and sang something for me. At first they were just words, beautiful words, resounding, touching the heart. I felt the deep meaning of the ether; that we are not alone on this earth, *that there, abroad, a world exists with human sense and spirit, and read to help us. But soonly I have felt. These touches are more than a simple reaction of the long loneliness and the heavy privations. An undescribably rapture moved me. I heard . . . heard tones . . . music . . . a slowfox. But now. I have perceived the real situation of the Getto-habitants but now I know what we have lost . . . There are moments where you can answer only by tears* [original English].

June 5. *Talkie.* The young Silverman, unknown to me, Zavišit, died—lung tuberculosis. The burial is scheduled for one o'clock in the afternoon. At eleven, Kripo comes to the apartment. Opens. The body is laid out in the middle of the room, the severely ill mother lying next to him. Kripo takes off, goes to Dworska 1, fourth floor.

The young man is to be buried, it is two in the afternoon. At that moment Gestapo appears equipped with truck and other gear, chasing everybody out of the cemetery. The bodies between two planks have not been buried yet, hardly covered with a few handfuls of earth . . . Interrupted right in the midst.

June 6. Tuesday. No sleep at night, against . . . [illegible] on my feet again, for the first time in the ghetto, had breakfast at seven in the morning. Shayek appears at eight-thirty, something has happened. . . .[9]

June 7. *Dying.* July 1942: Highest mortality rate in the ghetto, 1.99 per ten thousand.

76,701 inhabitants on June 1, 1944.

Mortality rate in May 1944, daily average 19.

Tuberculosis. Early 1944: January 1944 . . . 1.6 per thousand.

May 1944. Seventy percent of all deaths due to tuberculosis, which means in concrete terms: In May 1944 of about every 77,000, 13 human beings die each day of tuberculosis (lung tuberculosis)!

Continuation little notebook "Notes," starts June 1, 1944.

NOTEBOOK 20

Studies

June 27, 1944, Outsettlement, Last Stage

In the yard of the house at Kostelny 4, people are crowding with bedding, dishes, household items, underwear, clothing, etc. These are those designated for emigration. They are taking their last possessions to sell them at the central shopping center . . . [illegible] and RM. The latter [going] first to the central prison, that is, the collection center. Now nothing left. Everything they had scraped up in the course of four years in the ghetto, like household items and the bare necessities for their bodies, they are now giving up. They don't need it anymore. Journey into the Reich—last stage. Either quickly finished off there or seeing liberation.[1] For both eventualities household items are unnecessary. Mute. Without complaint. Fatalism. More like gallows humor. The good cheer of human beings who have not yet lost their faith in the ultimate triumph of justice. [. . .]

Outsettlement. June 1944. Twenty-five transports with one thousand each.

Hope remains alive that through some kind of intervention the transports will be halted or scaled back. Berlin—Vienna—Karlsbad—Prague—ghetto—Kutno (. . . Hamburg)? Whereto? Lost everything along those ways, only a piece of pocket mirror remains in which he, Professor Hart, sees his face: the countenance of a German physician (title page!).

Spirit. Talkie. They don't know (feel) how much suffering they have caused . . . The furrows of mental activity have been erased from the brow; and from their eyes the gleam of imagination, of longing, and of the mirror of the soul—everything that is spiritual has been eradicated, murdered, fettered, banished. Reverting to an animal state so that not a glimmer of hope, not the slightest atavistic thought, would cross the mind to bring even a trace of joy.

Little Ghetto Mirror, July 8, 1944, "Off to Czarnickiego"

The word going around is: "Off to Czarnickiego!" Each transport is to be comprised of seven hundred souls. And since it is very difficult to scrape together that number in a natural way, a firm hand has to help it along. If they hang your breadbasket higher, you will get an outright craving for the soup of Czarnickiego. And if you should resist even that craving, then a firm hand will get you out of bed at night and drag you to the collection camp. One should draw a lasting picture of the figures that, in the days of the twenty-five transports, were to be seen in the streets of the ghetto on their way to the central prison: with bundles on their bent backs, suitcases and handbags on weak shoulders, sweating children and old people walking alongside. Figures as those described by Dostoevski and other Russian writers. But among all these people, lagging behind them since she cannot keep step, a woman: loose gray strands of hair draping her shoulders, part of it hidden under a colorful head scarf; in place of a dress, a torn fur vest to which is attached a short girl's skirt of coarse linen; her legs are swollen and they hardly fit into the flat loafers; in her hands smaller and larger bundles, on the left shoulder a rucksack patched together from various materials; in front, dangling over her thighs, a soup bowl and a *menashka.* The old woman's back is bent to such a degree that now and then, when she leans against the side of a building, her weathered face and toothless mouth become visible. She staggers more than she walks. The ghetto pavement does not permit rhythmically regular strides. She too is a candidate for "work outside the ghetto." She too will participate somewhere out there in the work of reconstruction. She too must go. For she is—alone. Single people are favored for emigration. She lost her husband, children, and close relatives, and was left all alone. The lonely woman hobbles toward Czarnickiego. It is a beautiful, warm Sunday. The misfortune of being alone is being rewarded with the good fortune of being allowed to work outside the ghetto.

O. R.

Little Ghetto Mirror, July 26, 1944

"Cabbage, cabbage!" "For weeks no vegetables had come in, not to speak of potatoes."—Thus it is making the rounds of the entire ghetto. Nobody can ignore such observations . . . until they suddenly begin to whisper: "Cabbage has arrived. White cabbage," they say officially, "in large quantities. We'll get food. We'll have something again to put into the pot, to fill the stomach . . ."

And so it was. The cabbage was delivered. From Baluter Ring carts and trucks loaded with cabbage rolled through the streets: to the vegetable centers and from there to the cooperatives. Cabbage came from the city in a ceaseless stream. The light-green heads gleamed in the summer sun. Whenever one took a walk through the ghetto, one could see carts driving through the streets, in the front a coachman with an expressionless face, in the rear the Order Service man as the guardian, on whose shoulder rested the responsibility for the goods. "Cabbage keeps on coming . . ."

"I'm counting the tenth cart . . ."

"At least two hundred thousand kilograms are already here . . ."

"A nice ration!"

"At first for the kitchens. Next week the kitchens will have cabbage soup."

"Thank God for the variety." The cabbage soup came. It came daily. Some people ate cabbage soup three times a day, and cabbage soup became the main staple of sixty thousand people. In addition there were cabbage rations: 1 kg, 5 kg, 5 kg . . . cabbage, cabbage, cabbage! At home, too, cabbage soup was being fabricated. The ghetto wallowed in cabbage. The ghetto smelled of cabbage. Gradually cabbage weariness began to set in. The price of soup fell from 25 to 5 marks. People longed for the colonial soup, the so-called *klej* soup, prepared with flour and groats. An unfulfillable longing! And the cabbage kept on rolling into the ghetto. The water bellies became more distended. The stomachs revolted. The intestines didn't fare any better. Diarrhea became widespread. Nausea became a common occurrence. Every other ghetto dweller was suffering somehow from the consequences of overly intensive consumption of cabbage. During the day they drank cabbage soup, at night they passed it again in intervals. Thus a good night's rest was not very well to be had. The word went around that potatoes were coming soon, large amounts of potatoes, enough to supply the kitchens, when suddenly again—more cabbage rolled into the ghetto. Of course, everybody is so sick of cabbage, even the "little people" are beginning to sell their cabbage rations, when, completely but unexpectedly, a mood arises in the ghetto that cannot be put into words because the origin of this mood cannot be traced to any tangible factor. But, however this may be—the last week of July 1944 proves that psychic moments can overcome any physical privation, the last July week of the ghetto year 1944 is under a sign of hope that the Eternal, blessed be he, would deliver the ghetto from cabbage soup, *mehero beyomenu* . . .

O. R.

Little Ghetto Mirror, July 28, 1944

APOCALYPSE OR REDEMPTION

"Something can be felt in the air. Every night, alarm, blackout. The humming and rolling of trains with military through Zgierzka and near Marysin. *As can be seen, tired, war-weary soldiers in poor mental condition . . . Are they finally having enough? Five years of war . . . high time that it ends.* [Text in italics crossed out in original.] Today I saw carts loaded with cabbage and no convoy guards. Cabbage too is *hefker* [Yidd., ownerless], anybody's game. We've really come a long way. The centers are full, additional space for cabbage has to be found. The small pantries in the kitchens are not big enough, the cabbage begins to rot after three days, giving off a terrible stench in the areas surrounding the kitchens. This on top of everything . . . A price dive as even the London Stock Exchange has never seen. Money is gaining in value so shortly before the end. Soup 2½ marks, additives only valid until August 1. What a crazy world. Rumki are coming into their own again before they are being buried. The Praeses hands out coupons, the Kierowniki are polite, smiling at us, greeting us from high in their carriages. The word gets around that we'll be getting a two-week "iron ration" just in case that . . . If we only knew how and when! Today a *shishke* [Yidd., big shot], tomorrow a nobody. *Gevalt,* what am I saying! Tomorrow a new world. After five years of war we can finally breathe free! The word is getting around that we'll soon be redeemed . . . God shall provide . . . But while we are thinking about it, that is the moment when we will be permitted to see our children, relatives, and friends again. The lords of the ghetto plunder the ressorts for items that are out of reach for the ordinary ghetto dweller: shoes, clothing, leather bags, underwear, and also a lot of foodstuff. One pushes it off on the other. We are facing either apocalypse or redemption. The chest dares breathe more freely already. People look at each other as if to say: "We understand each other, right!" The Eldest knows that such looks are dangerous and he issues an order not to let the feelings of joy bubble over but to retain the same posture as before. It is still too soon. The eye of the sentry is still awake. A laugh can betray us, a cheerful face can endanger the ghetto. Therefore, quiet. Conceal it all . . . There are plenty of skeptics, nigglers, who don't want to believe it and still have doubts about that for which they have been longing and waiting for years. They are being told: "It has to come sometime, and now that the time is here, you don't want to believe it." Then they look with a vacuous gaze into empty space and bask in their pessimism. After so much suffering and terror, after so many disappointments, it is hardly surprising that they are not willing to give themselves over to anticipatory rejoicing. The heart is marred with scars, the brain encrusted with dashed hopes. And if, at long last, the day of the "redemption" should be at the doorstep, it is better to let oneself be surprised than to experience yet another disappointment. That's human nature, this is the human mentality of Ghetto Litzmannstadt at the end of July 1944.[2]

O. R.

❁

Editor's Notes

Notebook A

1. Mordechai Chaim Rumkowski, the Eldest of the Jews in the ghetto of Łódź, was born in Vilna in 1877 as the son of a worker. About mid-October 1939, he was appointed Eldest of the Jews of the city of Łódź by the German occupation forces and charged with setting up a Jewish self-administration as well as with providing Jewish forced labor. Rumkowski, who had been an insurance salesman and director of a Jewish orphanage, had also been a member of the Jewish community council of the city of Łódź.

   In Oskar Rosenfeld's diary, he is mostly called "the Eldest" or "Praeses." On occasion he is referred to by the abbreviation "Ch. R."
2. Jewish self-administration in Prague under control of the Gestapo.
3. In February and March 1941, about five thousand Jews from Vienna were deported to various Polish small towns like Opole and Kielce. Compare Hans Safrian, *Die Eichmann-Männer.* Vienna and Zurich: Europa Verlag, 1993, 97.

Notebook B

1. On April 11, 1940, "on order of the Führer," the city of Łódź was renamed Litzmannstadt. It was to commemorate General Litzmann, who had commanded a battle near Łódź in the First World War and who later represented the National Socialist Workers' Party (NSDAP) in the Reichstag.
2. Between November 5, 1939, and February 28, 1940, several thou-

sand people were transported, on order of Heinrich Himmler, from Łódź to the Generalgouvernement, that is, the part of Poland that had not been annexed outright to the German Reich. The original plan was to deport the entire Jewish population and a not-yet-fixed number of Poles from the newly created German province (Reichsgau) "Wartheland." Hundreds of people froze to death during these transports. The deportations were halted in February due to the intervention of the General Governor Hans Frank, who insisted that the Generalgouvernement should have priority in being made *judenrein* (cleared of Jews). See also Notebook 11.

3. Before the war, Marysin was a sparsely developed suburb of Łódź where the great Jewish cemetery was located. During the time of the ghetto, the Jewish Council turned several of the former summer homes in Marysin into nursing homes. Marysin was also the site of the ghetto's cesspools and several newly planted vegetable gardens.
4. A detailed description of this execution is in Notebook 13.
5. On December 6, 1941, the German ghetto administration demanded that Rumkowski make ready twenty thousand people for "labor deployment outside the ghetto." Rumkowski negotiated the number down to ten thousand. It was up to him to select who was to be "outsettled." After consultations with the Jewish Council, rabbis, and leaders of political groups in the ghetto, Rumkowski decided to follow the order. All of these deportations, lasting until January 29, 1942 (10,103 Jews), ended about 55 km from Łódź at the extermination camp of Kulmhof (Chełmno), which had been operating since December 7, 1941, and where the deportees were murdered in mobile gas trucks.
6. Between February 22 and April 2, 1942, an additional 34,073 human beings were deported from Łódź and murdered in the gas trucks.
7. The central prison on Czarnickiego Street served repeatedly as a source for deportations as well as a collection camp for those designated for deportation.
8. "Order Service" was the name for the Jewish police in the ghetto.
9. Rosenfeld himself refers at this point to Notebook E. Detailed descriptions of the deportations are also found in Notebook C. The so-called "outsettlement of the newly settled," that is, in October/

November 1941, from the German Reich as well as Prague, lasted from May 4, 1942, to May 15, 1945. A total number of 10,161 human beings were deported to Chełmno during this time span, where they were murdered.

10. The blind rabbi Dr. Krakauer and his wife shared living quarters in the ghetto with Oskar Rosenfeld for a while. Both were deported to Chełmno on September 9, 1942, and gassed. See also Notebook E.
11. Dr. Josef Wilczek, born 1877, a lawyer and for many years president of the Jewish community of Krefeld, was deported to Łódź in the fall of 1941.

    Notebook A contains the following entry with regard to the Seder night described here:

    > **Chapter Seder.** I'm citing in this connection Ezekiel 37. "The hand of the Lord was upon me, and the Lord carried me out in a spirit . . . And he said unto me: 'Son of man, can these bones live?' And I answered: 'O Lord God, thou knowest.' Then he said unto me: 'Prophesy over these bones. . . . Behold I will cause breath to enter into you, and ye shall live . . . and ye shall know that I am the Lord' . . . and the bones came together, bone to its bone . . . there were sinews upon them, and flesh came up . . . skin . . . 'I will open your graves, and cause you to come up out of your graves, O my people; and I will bring you to the land of Israel . . . I will put my spirit in you, and ye shall live, and I will place you in your own land . . .'" (Speech Krakauer, Zion speech Wilczek, at the Seder.)

12. Ghetto money was issued by Rumkowski and was called "Rumki" or "Chaimki."
13. Rosenfeld spells the words "Kripo" and "Gestapo" in Greek letters. The Kripo precinct on Koscielny Square was the center of constant violent assaults. Chief of the criminal police in Łódź was Dr. Alexander Zirpins, who had already made his mark in 1933 during the criminal investigation into the Reichstag fire when he exonerated the Nazis. After the war, he continued his career with the state criminal police in Niedersachsen. Concerning the activities of the Kripo in the ghetto, Zirpins wrote in 1941: "A type of work that is always carried out under the most unfavorable, most difficult, and filthiest conditions, but on the other hand presents a challenge and is as variegated as it is interesting and especially,

professionally gratifying, that is, it is satisfying" ("Das Getto in Litzmannstadt, kriminalpolizeilich gesehen" ["The Ghetto of Litzmannstadt from the Viewpoint of the Criminal Police"], *Kriminalistik,* no. 10, 1941, 112).

14. Even before the war, Marysin was the home of the largest Jewish cemetery in Europe. One hundred eighty-five thousand people are buried there.
15. The entries of May 7–10, 1942, are mostly in shorthand.
16. Allusion to Leviticus 26:14–41, and Deuteronomy 28:15–45, enumerating curses that will come over the people of Israel if they do not keep God's commandments.
17. By special order of April 11, 1941, the Protection Police announced that "any Jew who tries to crawl under or scale the ghetto fence, or tries to leave the ghetto in some unauthorized way [. . .], will be shot without warning." Original in the Polish State Archive of Łódź.
18. The ghetto had numerous lending libraries. The largest was the library of J. W. Sonnenberg, which had, in early 1944, seventy-five hundred volumes, eight hundred of which were in German, and a registered readership of four thousand. Sonnenberg had acquired his stock of books in the ghetto from people who had been settled there, starting his business in the ghetto with nineteen books in Polish. (The German authorities had closed all libraries temporarily in 1939.) Sonnenberg carried literature in many languages, fiction, school texts, encyclopedias, and scientific handbooks.

    Besides the private lending libraries, the ghetto had various smaller libraries belonging to political organizations.

    Rosenfeld wrote several articles for the *Daily Chronicle* of the statistics department concerning the lending libraries in the ghetto. On July 7, 1943, Rosenfeld makes reference to an article by Józef Zelkowicz, which was not printed in the chronicle but is preserved in the files of the archive.

> The decree of February 8, 1940, about the "systematic resettlement" from the city into the ghetto, regulates, among other things, the question of what is allowed to be taken to the ghetto and what is not. Thanks to this decree, the Jew was informed that his few pieces of fur-

niture and all of his possessions, for which he had been working hard his entire life, were now the "property of the state," and he was not allowed to either sell them or take with him. The decree states that the Jew is allowed to take with him into exile only bedding and family pictures and photographs. Bedding and family pictures—as different as they may be outwardly in their use—which belong, so to speak, to the most personal possessions, which Jewish families safeguard with particular reverence and piety. [. . .]

Bedding and family pictures—objects of particular piety—were officially accorded the Jew for his modern-day ghetto of the twentieth century. But not all classes of the Jewish population have family mementos such as pictures and photographs. The ancient "people of the Book," whose every phase of life had been regulated by the commandment of Scripture, tolerate [. . .] photography but see no more in it than a paper image, reminiscent of the appearance of a relative but expressing nothing of his character. [. . .]

Among the people of the Book, the memory of those near and dear lives in a different way in view of the heavy-linen- or leather-bound Vilna edition of the Torah, or the miniature but expensive Bible inscribed with the dedication of the forebears, written in ink for all times. Each heirloom becomes a memorial, a carrier of memories, a "memento mori." [. . .] The lawgiver presumably knew nothing about this type of remembrance. At any rate, the above-mentioned decree contains nothing about the taking along of books. [. . .]

This is the way the ancient people of the Book have always gone into exile, be it from Spain, from Portugal [. . .], from Germany, or from Łódź, naked and without anything more than a pack of sacred books on their shoulders. [. . .]

Family bedding and sacred books came to the ghetto with the Jews where prayers for the dead became commonplace and piety no longer had a place. [. . .] In the old days, if a book was accidentally dropped, it was picked up with awe and kissed as if in apology. In the ghetto, the books are lying around, dusty and moldy on the plain, damp ground, or heedless in some corner. In the interior, where the memory of the dead was immortalized in ink, are now nesting spiders and roaches. [. . .] While the beds served as fuel during the severe winter of 1941 in order to heat at least some water for the problem child, for

> the youngest and the weakest, the books continued to gather dust and mold. The people of the Book do not burn their books unless they are being burned and destroyed together with them. Even the desecrated Holy Book is not allowed to be burned but must be buried in accordance with the religion and law. [This translation from the German follows a translation from the Yiddish originally printed in the magazine *Laurentius,* no. 2, 1989.]

After the deportations of 1942, thousands of books remained behind in the ghetto. They were picked up not only by private lending libraries but also by the judicial office of the Eldest of the Jews, whose director, the lawyer Henryk Neftalin, was also the director of the archive, the population registry, and the statistics department in the ghetto. The closed library that was thus created contained already in the summer of 1943 more than thirty thousand volumes.

Józef Zelkowicz, born in 1897 in Konstantynów near Łódź, was an ordained rabbi who before the war was a leading ethnologist and writer in the Yiddish language. He was a contributor to many journals in Poland and the United States and also worked for the YIVO Institute in Vilna. In the ghetto he was one of the leading coworkers in the archives and contributors to the *Daily Chronicle.* Zelkowicz carried a large part of his writings with him when he was deported to Auschwitz in August 1944 and murdered.

Notebook C

1. Rumkowski had wall and table calendars printed with his picture and memorable sayings.
2. Entries of May 12 and 13 are largely in shorthand.
3. Term of endearment for Rosenfeld's wife Henriette. She emigrated to Great Britain in 1939 and lived in Australia after the war. Her daughter Eva, from a previous marriage, may still be living in Australia.
4. Town near Łódź.
5. Baluter Ring (Balucky Rynek) was a square where the offices of the

Eldest of the Jews and the goods depot, as well as the Gestapo headquarters, were located in the ghetto.

6. The word meaning "evil deeds" is in shorthand.
7. Notebook C contains a description of the deportations from Brzeziny and Babinice to Łódź in May 1942. In Notebook E is a detailed account of these events.
8. Up to this point, Rosenfeld had been housed in one of the homes of the Eldest in Marysin where his barest needs had been taken care of.
9. The novella for which Rosenfeld collected material and from which, as indicated in his diary, he gave readings in a small circle in the ghetto has not been found.
10. There was a certain number of people in the ghetto who held special coupons and thus had a right to larger food rations. Among them were especially functionaries of the administration of the Eldest of the Jews, factory managers, doctors, members of the Order Service, firefighters, and those doing the heaviest labor.
11. Within the "statistics department" of the Eldest of the Jews, which, together with the "evidence division," that is, the central population registry of the ghetto, which was headed by the lawyer Henryk Neftalin, the so-called archive was set up on November 17, 1940. Its purpose was to collect all documents of the Jewish Council and its departments. Especially, of course, it was to document Rumkowski's activities. At the same time, the archive collected information about life and events, and cultural and other activities in the ghetto. Its main task, beginning January 12, 1941, was writing entries for the *Daily Chronicle,* keeping a running account of population statistical data, information about the supply situation, production, measures taken by the Eldest of the Jews, suicides and executions, the activities of the Kripo and Gestapo, "insettlements" and deportations, as well as other occurrences. Later, portrayals of the atmosphere in the ghetto and short articles about the most varied subjects were added. Until September 1, 1942, the chronicle was written in Polish, then for two months bilingually, and after that in German.

    Starting in September 1942, Oskar Rosenfeld was a regular contributor to the chronicle. The last preserved edition of the chronicle is dated July 30, 1944.

Notebook D

1. Between January 1, 1941, and September 1942, concerts and lectures as well as revues and other cultural events took place at the "cultural center," a former inn for political meetings with a stage on Krawiecka Street. After the deportations of 1942 and the transformation of the ghetto into a purely "work" ghetto, the house was only sporadically used for cultural performances.

   Rosenfeld gives detailed descriptions of the programs and participating artists in Notebook 12 of his diary, of which excerpts appear in the notes.
2. Theodor Ryder, born 1881 in Piotrków, was a pianist, conductor, and music educator. Following his training and numerous concerts in Germany, France, and Switzerland, he returned to Poland in 1916. There he worked first at the opera in Warsaw, then in Łódź as conductor of the symphony orchestra and the opera as well as the radio symphony orchestra. In the ghetto he was one of the founders and the conductor of the cultural center.
3. Dawid Bajgelmann, a composer and conductor, was born in 1887 into a musical family in Ostrowiec, near Kielce. He played a great number of instruments, but especially the violin and clarinet. He became the director of the Yiddish Yitskhok Zandberg Theater Group in 1912. In the twenties, he was closely connected with two Yiddish theaters in Poland, Azazel and Ararat. A large number of his works were performed in the ghetto. In August 1944 he was deported to Auschwitz and murdered.
4. Pinchas Schwarz, an actor and painter, was born in Łódź in 1923. As a fifteen-year-old in 1938, he was admitted into the group around the Polish painter Wladysław Strzeminski, who belonged to the leaders of the European avant-garde. Strzeminski, together with friends, founded in 1931 the first European museum for modern art. Schwarz designed many stage sets in the ghetto. He also left his mark through constructivist sketches and photo collages for the scrapbooks of the statistics department, in which various activities of the Jewish self-administration were being documented.

   Pinchas Schwarz survived the Holocaust and has been working

since the war as an artist in Munich, Paris, and Israel. He now lives in New York.

5. The here-mentioned films have so far not been found.
6. In the diary, additional entries of biblical quotations from Exodus 17: Verse 15 follow: "And Moshe built an altar, and called the name of it 'Adonainissi.'" Verse 16. "And he said: 'The hand upon the throne of the Lord: the Lord will have war with Amalek from generation to generation.'"

   Deuteronomy 25:19. Amalek 19. "Therefore it shall be, when the Lord thy God hath given thee rest from all thine enemies roundabout, in the land which the Lord thy God giveth thee for an inheritance to possess it, that thou shalt blot out the remembrance of Amalek from under heaven; thou shalt not forget."

   Ecclesiastes 3:20. "All go unto one place; all are of the dust, and all return to dust."

   Isaiah 14. *Prophecy against Ashkenes!* [Rosenfeld's words.] Isaiah 25:8: "And the Lord God will wipe away tears from all faces; And the reproach of his people will he take away from all the earth; For the Lord hath spoken it." Isaiah 26:13: "O Lord our God, other lords besides thee have had dominion over us; But by thee only do we make mention of thy name."
7. From November 5 to November 9, 1941, 5,007 Roma from Burgenland in Austria were deported to Łódź; among them, 2,689 children. Eleven of them did not survive the transport in the unheated freight car. The Roma were cramped together in a few houses, the so-called gypsy camp, in Sulzfelder Strasse, without bedding or other furnishings.

   Again and again the German police engaged in cruel excesses, for example, forcing inmates of the camp to hang their own people. Due to the catastrophic, unsanitary conditions, dysentery and typhoid fever broke out shortly. Six hundred human beings died of hunger and typhus within a few weeks, or they were murdered. In early January 1942, the surviving Roma were taken by truck to Chełmno and gassed. See also Notebook G.
8. A well-known Yiddish lullaby: "Under my child's cradle / is a little white goat. / The goat went away doing business. / How sweet are the raisins and almonds! / My child will be bright and healthy."

In the ghetto arose a parody of the lullaby: "Nit kain Rozinkes, un nit kain Mandlen" ("No Raisins and No Almonds").

Notebook 13

1. With regard to the Baluty neighborhood of Łódź, see also the chapter "Der blinde Maks" in the book of the same name by Arnold Mostowicz, Berlin, 1992.
2. From this point follow, among other notes about Jewish philosophy and theology, comparisons between Spinoza, Maimonides, and Kabbalah, in search of the meaning of suffering:

> The slave condition in which Israel now appears (see "God") does not contradict its exalted destiny. For Israel was dispersed among the nations so that the heart of mankind would be permeated by its spirit. *Due to its calling, Israel cannot perish.* It resembles a seed kernel, lying in the ground and being trampled on from above, but it germinates and speaks and bears fruit. [. . .]
>
> *Suffering.* Conversation: What is suffering (see "Job")? Suffering is to reveal to a person those sins which are hidden even from him. The "just" *tzaddik* is to be led to self-examination and self-purification. God reveals to the "man" Job his omnipotence, wisdom, and mercy in the works of his creations and thus makes Job be silent. Job subjects himself to the secret of his suffering because he feels that he cannot grasp the secrets of the divine creation and, therefore, the cause of his suffering . . .

Notebook 22

Chapter title: The entries in this notebook contained an especially large number of abbreviations that have been spelled out here for legibility's sake.

1. A later entry at the end of the notebook:

> Concerning the Study "Hunger" (see earlier)
> Added to this is the desire to survive all this as a moral duty, as something with which the people of Israel were enjoined for the sake of Amalek. Therefore the haste and fear, fear of violating this commandment (develop more fully!). Survival becomes a religious command-

ment, like, "You will multiply like the stars in the heavens and the sand by the sea." Added to this is the expectation, likewise a duty toward God, of vengeance. "Retribution must come; we must be witness to this retribution . . . as compensation for the suffering we endured . . . That is the meaning of this last epoch."

Notebook E

1. The sentence is in quotation marks, and a little further on several passages are in shorthand.
2. Constantly, new transports with clothing arrived in the ghetto either for alterations at the workshop or for use in the ghetto itself. The origin of the clothing was registered with great interest.

   Thus the *Daily Chronicle* noted on May 30, 1942, the arrival of noticeably huge transports of clothing and other objects for use in the ghetto. "People are," says the chronicle, "considerably disturbed in view of passports, *tefillin,* and other personal objects that are found in the clothing." It seemed quite obvious that "the bundles had not been packed by their owners." Various documents also point toward bloodstains. This was even the case with clothing that was being sent to Germany from the extermination camp Kulmhof through Winterhilfe, the National Socialist welfare agency.
3. Between July 22 and September 9, 1942, about three hundred thirty thousand Jews were deported from the Warsaw ghetto, mostly to the extermination camp Treblinka, where they were murdered without exception. On July 23, 1942, Adam Czerniaków, the chairman of the Warsaw Jewish Council, took his own life when the SS commanded him to gather a children's transport. Czerniaków left in his diary the following note for the Jewish Council:

   > Worthoff and his colleagues [from the resettlement staff] came to me and demanded that I prepare a children's transport by tomorrow. With this my bitter cup is filled to the brim, for I cannot deliver helpless children to their deaths. I have decided to resign. Don't regard this as an act of cowardice or of flight. I am powerless, my heart is

> breaking with anguish and compassion, I can no longer bear this. My act will make everybody recognize the truth and maybe lead them on the right path of action. I am aware that I am bequeathing you a heavy burden. [Raul Hilberg et al., eds., *The Warsaw Diary of Adam Czerniaków: Prelude to Doom.* New York: Stein and Day, 1979.]

The deportations from the Warsaw ghetto continued unabated until merely sixty-five thousand people remained in the ghetto. In September 1942, the deportations were interrupted and did not resume until January 1943.

4. Presumably Dr. Hugo Nathanson of Hamburg, deported to Łódź from Prague in the fall of 1941; deported to Chełmno on July 7, 1944.
5. The wholesaler Hans Biebow, born 1902 in Bremen, had been appointed to direct the German ghetto administration in May 1941. Before the war he had built up a large coffee business in Bremen. In Łódź, he devoted himself primarily to the exploitation of the labor force in the ghetto and was also involved in setting up the extermination camp in Chełmno. Biebow tried in the course of time, through his close connection with Heydrich, to take over the directorship of Theresienstadt and other ghettos. In one telephone conversation, gotten through a wiretap by the Gestapo, there was talk of his aim to become the recognized "Jews' expert in Germany" (Telegraph of Investigation Bureau A Litzmannstadt of March 3, 1942). Wiretapping reports are in the archive of Yad Vashem. See note 12, Notebook H. Biebow was executed in Poland in 1946.
6. Leon Rosenblatt, born 1894, head of the Jewish Order Service in the ghetto. Before the war he was a bank director and reserve officer. In August 1944 he was deported to Auschwitz and murdered. Friedrich Hielscher records in his memoirs, *Fünfzig Jahre unter Deutschen* [*Fifty Years among Germans*] (Hamburg: Rowohlt Verlag, 1954, 362), a conversation he had with Rosenblatt in the ghetto about the participation of the Jewish police in the deportations. To get himself shot would be for him, Rosenblatt, the "simplest solution":

> But what will happen then? The SS has said that much already: then they will do the selecting. That means, those who have not been broken, women who are with child, rabbis, scholars, professors, poets,

will go first into the ovens. If I continue, I can round up the volunteers. They frequently push themselves on me. And sometimes I have as many as I am asked to report. Sometimes there are fewer. Then I can take the dying, pointed out to me by Jewish doctors, and if those aren't enough, then the terminally ill. But if these aren't enough, what then? Then I can take the criminals, but God forbid, who doesn't become a criminal in this place? [. . .] Who am I to judge? And yet: what if I can't fill the quota by other means? Frequently I can do without the criminals. But not always. And at times, even they aren't sufficient. Then I can take the very old. But what kind of standard is this? Mr. Hielscher, I am a poor Jew from Lemberg and I have learned my business and was an able commander of my battery [Rosenblatt was commander of an Austrian motorized mortar battery in the First World War]. But what I am asked to do here, I didn't learn. I asked the community leaders, the rabbis, the scholars. They all told me: what you are doing is right, stay and select us the way you have figured it out. And yet, Mr. Hielscher, I find no joy in life. I beseech you, in the name of the God in whom you believe: if you know of a better way than the one I have found, then let me know about it and I will bless you day and night. And if you don't know a better one, then tell me: should I stay or should I get myself shot?

7. Dora Fuchs was the director of the central secretariat of the Eldest of the Jews. She had been taken to Poland from the German Reich in October 1938 during the forced "expulsion" of fifteen thousand Jews with Polish citizenship. She survived the liquidation of the ghetto and the deportation to a concentration camp, presumably Ravensbrück. After the war, she emigrated to the United States.
8. Aron Jakubowitsch (?–1981), Rumkowski's deputy and overseer of the work ressorts in the ghetto.
9. Street at the southern edge of the ghetto.
10. Dawid Gertler, director of the "Special Department" of the Jewish Order Service. At first created as a bodyguard for the Eldest of the Jews and charged with "discovery" of smuggling and hiding places in the ghetto, the Special Division gradually took on important positions of power in the ghetto, for example, control of food distribution. By the end of 1942, it engaged increasingly in competition with Rumkowski.

For a while, Dawid Gertler gained some popularity in the ghetto. Thus the unknown author of *Notes from the Ghetto of Łódź*, written in letter form, which were found in 1961 in Auschwitz-Birkenau in a tin can that had been buried by a member of the inmate special squad:

> If a survey were conducted in the ghetto at this point concerning which department is the most popular at the moment, the answer would definitely be: the Special Division. And why? Because this department has made it its business to fight against theft and to improve the living conditions of the broad masses of workers. [. . .] The "Special" was a notion that aroused terror among the populace. However, since the young director of this department has officially assumed the position of overseer of order in the ghetto from the ghetto administration, it is no longer feared. On the contrary, the Special Division gives the workers hope, people know that they are no longer left to sink or swim. They are receiving their food rations under supervision of the "Special." [. . .]
>
> The rumor mill tells more details about the director of the Special Division. It seems he gains his strength from a cheerful nature. He likes to have fun with young people, college students, boys and girls, who would like to join the "Special." They want to help, do something for the ghetto. [*Briefe aus Litzmannstadt,* Janusz Gumkowski, Adam Rutkowski, and Arnfried Astel, eds. Cologne: Verlag Middelhauve, 1967, 57f.]

Dawid Gertler also worked as an agent of the Gestapo. His double role came to an end on July 12, 1943, when he was arrested by the Gestapo because he had been repeatedly successful in bribing members of the German ghetto administration and the police. Gertler was taken to Auschwitz, where he survived.

11. The text of Rumkowski's speech has been preserved. The original manuscript is in the Polish State Archive in Łódź. It reads:

> I must carry out these difficult and bloody operations, I have to amputate limbs to save the body! I must take children, otherwise—God forbid—others will be taken. I have not come here today to console you, I am not come to calm you but to reveal to you the full extent of

> your woe and suffering. Like a bandit I have come to tear the best from your hearts. [. . .]
>
> Before you stands a destroyed Jew. Do not envy me! This is the most difficult order I have ever had to follow. I am extending toward you my crushed, trembling hands and implore you: "Place your sacrifices in my hands so that further sacrifices can be prevented, so that I can save a group of one hundred thousand Jews." [The German word *Opfer* has the double meaning of "sacrifice" and "victim."]

12. Dawid Warschawski, the director of textile production in the ghetto.
13. Dr. Szaja-Stanislaw Jakobson, born 1906, a graduate of the Jagiellonian University in Cracow. He was deported to Auschwitz in August 1944 and was murdered there.
14. The Poznanskis were one of the great Jewish manufacturing families that built the textile industry in Łódź in the nineteenth century.
15. Vilma, sister of Oskar Rosenfeld; Erich, son of Rosenfeld's sister, Frieda Mandl.
16. At this point, eighty-nine thousand five hundred people were still living in the ghetto.

    Between September 7 and 12, 1942, about sixteen thousand people were deported from the ghetto, among them almost all children under ten as well as the sick and the old who could no longer be categorized as able-bodied. Since the Jewish Order Service was unable to round up the required number of people, the Gestapo stepped in with extreme brutality. The hunt for human beings surpassed anything that had taken place so far in the ghetto. At least sixty people were shot in the course of the hunt. The deportations went without exception to the extermination camp Kulmhof where the deportees were immediately murdered in gas trucks. The same fate was shared by at least seven hundred of the sick and the children, who had been dragged from hospitals and homes in the ghetto on September 1.
17. Dr. Josef Lamm, born 1891, deported from Prague to Łódź in the fall of 1941. Rosenfeld apparently discussed with him in the ghetto his planned novellas, cultural history, and essays.
18. Bazar Square, place of public executions.

19. It cannot be documented when the first reports of mass killings by poison gas reached the ghetto. The clothing transports had aroused great anxiety already in the spring. (See note 2 to Notebook E.) In the summer, the letter, dated January 19, 1942, from the rabbi of Grabów, a place northwest of Łódź, had reached the ghetto. The original letter is missing but its content has been preserved: "An eyewitness, who managed to flee the hell, came to me. [. . .] From him I heard everything. The place where all are being killed is named Chełmno. [. . .] People are being killed in one of two ways, either by being shot or by poison gas." (Cited from Lucian Dobroszycki, ed., *The Chronicle of the Łódź Ghetto, 1941–1944.* New Haven, Conn.: Yale University Press, 1984, xxi.)

The way in which the letter came into the ghetto and how widely distributed its message became is not clear from the various sources.

The willingness, or even ability, to believe such information varied considerably. Thus Jakub Poznanski, a factory manager in the ghetto, wrote in his diary on September 26, 1943: "Persistent rumors circulated in the ghetto about liquidation of the ghettos of various Polish towns. Even if excesses occurred in some towns, this doesn't mean by a long shot that the Jews are being murdered in masses" (Jakub Poznanski, *Pamietnik z getta Łódzkiego.* Łódź: Wydawnictwo Łódzkie, 1960, 102).

Notebook F

1. Notebook 11 contains a table of contents of the planned work:

> Outline of a Cultural History of the Ghetto (Archive Work and Statistics Department)
>
> I. Łódź: to the establishment of the ghetto: historical background of Łódź, share of the population—share of Jews in economic life—occupational hierarchy, and so on.—Social and political life—cultural life (education, theater, literature, press, film)—religious life (education, religious services, rabbinate, ritual)—internal Jewish life (orthodoxy, liberalism, Zionism, socialism, assimilation)—state of language (Yiddish, Polish, German,

Hebrew); population shifts—emigration—personalities of Łódź—map of Łódź, typography, historical data, etc.

II. Establishment of the ghetto: description of the ghetto area as it was before. Appointment and political position of the Eldest.—Beginning of the ghetto regime.—Organization of the ghetto.

III. Supplying the ghetto: rations—coupons—kitchens—collective nourishment—categories of supplies (colonial goods—bread—milk—vegetables—meat—wood—coal—clothing, etc.).

IV. Work in the ghetto: ressorts and all other types of work—salaries—deliveries—business (cooperatives, private businesses, black-market trading)—trade (of Jewish artisans); transportation (horse-drawn carts, electric streetcars, trucks).

V. Community administration: district—postal service—banking—ghetto currency—hygiene—lodging—housing administration.

VI. Population movement: deaths—births—outsettling—insettling.

VII. Health care: health department—hospitals—old-age homes and orphanages—rest and recuperation homes—clinics—pharmacies—physicians.

VIII. Judicial system: organization—courts—characteristic court cases.

IX. Cultural life: cultural center, concerts—literature—press—painting—schools—libraries—education.

X. Religious life: rabbinate—religious services—kashrut—education of the young—Talmud—study of Thora, etc.

XI. Miscellaneous: German language—contact with German authorities—Baluter Ring—public pronouncements—functions of the German authorities.

XII. Statistics department and archive: work done by these bureaus.

XIII. Curiosities: counterfeit foodstuff—new types of occupations, cemetery, burials, ghetto illnesses, individual human lots, prostitution, etc.

XIV. Index: group index—subject index—name index.

2. Zechariah 14:2 continues: "For I will gather all nations against Jerusalem to battle; And the city shall be taken, and the houses

rifled, and the women ravished. And half of the city shall go forth into captivity; But the residue of the people shall not be cut off from the city."

3. Boruch Praszkier, manager of the kitchen department of the Eldest of the Jews.
4. Moses Karo, director of education of the Eldest of the Jews (department for children's education and transfer).
5. As did the Wehrmacht, several department stores used the ghetto for the production of goods, among them Neckermann's. Josef Neckermann was in various ways involved in forced labor in the ghetto. As Reich commissioner for the supply of winter uniforms and other military textile wares, he supervised production in the ghettos of Łódź and Białystok.

Notebook G

1. Dr. Abraham Kamenetzky, born 1874 in Slonim, studied philosophy and philology in Heidelberg, Berlin, and Berne. The author of numerous scientific essays for *Zeitschrift für die Alttestamentarische Wissenschaft* [*Journal for Old Testament Study*] in Berlin, he was a coeditor of the *Jewish Encyclopedia* published in Russia. In the interwar period, he was active in the Jewish community in Łódź. In the ghetto, he worked in the archive and was one of the writers for the *Daily Chronicle.*
2. Tusia Eibuschütz, manager of the department for coupons.
3. The Balfour Declaration of 1917 promised the Jews a "national home" in Palestine.
4. Wife of Professor Wilhelm Caspari. Caspari, born in 1872 in Berlin, was a leading cancer researcher. In 1930 he took on a professorship at the Speyer-Clinic in Frankfurt am Main, from where he was deported to Łódź in October 1941. His wife was deported to Chełmno in September 1942. Caspari died in the ghetto on January 21, 1944, of exhaustion.
5. Dr. Oskar Singer, born 1883, writer and publicist. Singer wrote for numerous newspapers and magazines, among them the *Prager Tageblatt* (*Prague Daily*) and the Zionist publications *Selbstwehr: Jüdisches Volksblatt* (*Self-Defense: Jewish People's Gazette*) and *Jüdische Nachrichten* (*Jewish News Report*). Singer was also the author of an

antifascist play, *Herren der Welt* (*Lords of the World*), a contemporary play in three acts (Prague, Vienna, Zurich, 1935). Singer was deported from Prague to Łódź in the fall of 1941. In the ghetto he worked in the archive. In late 1942, he took over the editorship of the *Daily Chronicle* from Julian Cukier. In August 1944, Oskar Singer was deported to Auschwitz and murdered.

His essays and reports for the statistics department were recently published: Oskar Singer, "Im Eilschrittdurch den Gettotag . . ." *Reportagen und Essays aus dem Getto Lodz.* Sascha Feuchert, Erwin Leibfried, and Jörg Riecke, eds. Berlin: Philo, 2002.

6. Dr. Bernhard Heilig, born 1902 in Prostejov, Moravia, was a businessman and economic historian. He was particularly interested in Jewish economic history and made his mark with publications about the textile industry and the history of Czech and Austrian economic development. He contributed articles on economic subjects to numerous newspapers. Heilig died in the ghetto on June 29, 1943, of tuberculosis.
7. Dr. Karl Bondy, a physician from Prague, up to this time head of the so-called transport collective, which took care of the concerns of the "newly settled" from the German Reich (Altreich), Vienna, and Prague. The women's police division (Women's Order Service), which he set up, was dissolved in March 1943.
8. In the diary follow excerpts from *Meyers Konversationslexikon* (a popular German reference work): "The Jews proved themselves able and worthy during the War of Liberation through their willingness for sacrifice and courage to be recognized as German citizens. [. . .] Only in countries in Asia and Africa with despotic regimes are the Jews still living in bondage, so that oppression and excesses against them can be noted even in modern times."
9. Insertion in handwriting: "*Lyrik der Hebräer* (*Poetry of the Hebrews*) (*Meyers Konversationslexikon,* vol. 13, p. 2). 'Their imagery is simple but magnificent, hitting like lightning, their enthusiasm is sufficient, ecstatic, exuberant; their subject is the highest, the God of Israel and his guidance of the world.'"
10. Izrael Tabaksblat, representative of the party of labor Zionists (Poale Zion) in the ghetto. After the war, Tabaksblat published a book about the ghetto of Łódź, *Khurban Łódź* (*The Destruction of Łódź*), Buenos Aires: Union Central Israelita Polaca en la Argentina, 1946.
11. Luzer Najman, a confidant of Rumkowski from the prewar period,

until November 1942 member of the "Highest Control Chamber" of the Eldest of the Jews, which had been founded on December 6, 1940, as a supervisory agency over various work areas of production and nutrition in the ghetto. On November 2, 1942, the HCC was integrated into the Central Labor Bureau of the Eldest of the Jews as a business inspection agency.

12. This means pictorial tapestries with motifs like "outsettlement," "weaving mill," "rag sorting plant," "fortune hunter," "midday" (soup).
13. Israel Lejzerowicz, born 1902, painter, studied art in Berlin. Lejzerowicz worked, among other places, in the "scientific department" in the ghetto. See also Notebook H.
14. The reference is to the so-called Polish Youth Detention Camp that had been established on the grounds of Marysin, not far from the ghetto cemetery. This was preceded by an order from Reich Interior Minister Frick of December 3, 1942, to the Reich provincial governors and to the president of the government of Upper Silesia to incarcerate "underage alien youths" in camps. The children who were thus gathered were not only panhandling orphans and children whose parents were in concentration camps but also children who were kidnapped from their parents. Ten thousand children were incarcerated in the "Polish Youth Detention Camp" Litzmannstadt in the course of time and used for forced labor. Some of the children were "aryanized," that is, passed on to childless German couples. A large number of the children did not survive the camp.
15. From December 5 to 12, 1942, two thousand people were shot in the ghetto of Białystok and ten thousand were deported to Treblinka for extermination. Any resistance by the underground was brutally put down by the SS.
16. Here follows a curriculum vitae, that is, an outline of Rosenfeld's activities between 1900 and 1939.

Notebook 11

1. Rosenfeld apparently repeats here somebody else's report. During the transports in winter 1939–40, hundreds of people froze to

death, which is also noted in the files of the Reichssicherheitshauptamt (Reich Chief Security Bureau, headed by Himmler).

2. The reference is to the thicker soup on the bottom of the pot.
3. "It is known how I sought already early to penetrate the conditions of the primeval world as described in the book of Genesis. Since I sought to proceed in orderly and step-by-step fashion, I took up, after a long interruption, the book of Exodus. However, what a difference! Just as the childish plenitude had vanished from my life, I found this second book separated from the first by a tremendous divide. The total forgetting of the past is expressed in the few significant [words]: 'A new king arose in Egypt who did not know Joseph.' But the people, too, numerous as the stars in the heavens, had almost forgotten their forebear to whom Jehova had made this now fulfilled promise under the starry sky" (Johann Wolfgang von Goethe, *Dichtung und Wahrheit,* Werkausgabe, vol. 5. Frankfurt am Main: Insel Verlag, 1970, 462 [translation from the German by the present translator]).

Notebook H

1. Dr. Wiktor Miller, director of the health department of the Eldest of the Jews.
2. Dr. Ignacy Weinberg, deputy director of the health department.
3. Dr. Robert Ley (1890–1945), Reich director of the German Work Front.
4. Arthur Greiser (1897–1946), Reich governor and provincial chief of Wartheland with its seat in Poznan, where he was executed after the war.
5. Jews were "deployed" there for construction of the Reichsautobahn, which was equivalent to extermination through work.
6. *Kiddush HaShem* was understood in the Jewish history of persecution, especially by Christians, as the Jews' readiness to die rather than accept baptism (that is, to betray the name of God). Following the concept of Kiddush HaShem, many Jews in the Middle Ages and also during the Reconquista in Spain committed suicide either individually or collectively—sometimes entire Jewish communities. At the time of the Holocaust, heated debates took place

over whether the motive of Kiddush HaShem was not invalidated under the extreme exceptional circumstances of annihilation perpetuated by the Nazis simply for the sake of annihilation. While some rabbis believed to see in a martyr's death the applicable realization of Kiddush HaShem, Rabbi Isaak Nissenbaum, one of the most prominent Polish rabbis, sharply turned against this understanding that Kiddush HaShem was possible under the Nazis. In the Warsaw ghetto, he emphasized the contradiction of this concept by pointing out that only the sanctification of life, Kiddush HaChaim, counted for anything. As long as the enemies laid claim to souls of the Jews, it made sense to give one's life and refuse conversion. But since the enemy now sought to destroy the very existence of the Jews, the only response was to try to preserve it by all means possible. Another rabbi, Zamba, put it this way: "When baptism is no longer able to preserve life, then the martyr death of the Jews can no longer be seen as the sanctification of God's name . . . but . . . alone the will to survive." (Cited from Dan Diner, "Jenseits des Vorstellbaren: Der 'Judenrat' als Situation." In *Unser einziger Weg ist Arbeit. Das Getto Łódź 1940–1944*. Published by the Jewish Museum, Frankfurt am Main. Hanno Loewy and Gerhard Schoenberner, eds. Vienna: Löcker Verlag, 1990, 30.) See also Christoph Münz, "Der Welt ein Gedächtnis geben: Geschichtstheologisches Denken im Judentum nach Auschwitz und Jüdisches Gedächtnis (Ph.D. diss., University of Siegen, 1993).

7. The destination of the March 1943 deportation is unknown. Since the transport consisted mostly of sick and old people and those broken by murderous forced labor, it must be assumed that they were taken to an extermination camp.
8. Julian Cukier (pseudonym, Stanyslaw Cerksi), born 1900 in Łódź. Son of Ludwik Cukier, a Łódź industrialist and prominent representative of the Jewish community. Julian Cukier was a journalist and worked, among other places, for *Republika,* a prominent liberal daily newspaper. In the ghetto he worked for the archive. He initiated and directed the writing of the *Daily Chronicle.* He died in the ghetto on April 7, 1943, of tuberculosis.
9. See note 10 for Notebook E.
10. Marek Kliegier, deputy and later successor of Dawid Gertler, the head of the Special Division of the Jewish Order Service.

11. After the dissolution of the cultural center and its orchestras in September 1942, and the assignment of its artists to the various work ressorts, cultural activities developed on the level of the various departments and workplaces. Revue performances were especially frequent. Such revues were also performed by the Special Division (short, "Special") of the Jewish Order Service.
12. Rabbi Professor Emanuel Hirschberg, director of the "scientific department." The establishment of a "scientific department" in May 1942 coincided with a plan of the German ghetto administration for the establishment of a museum in Łódź as well as the branch of the Frankfurt "Institute for the Study of the Jewish Question," which was temporarily located in Łódź. The Łódź branch, for which Hirschberg apparently had to work at first, was headed by Professor Adolf Wendel, an Old Testament scholar at the University of Breslau. Little is known so far about the work of the Łódź branch. Concerning the work of the institute in Frankfurt am Main, see Dieter Schiefelbein, *Das Institut zur Erforschung der Judenfrage, Frankfurt am Main. Vorgeschichte und Gründung 1935 bis 1939.* Materials of the Fritz Bauer Institute, no. 9, Frankfurt am Main, 1993.

    Plans by the German ghetto administration in Łódź for a museum of the "Customs and Practices of the Eastern Jews" were apparently made as early as winter 1941–42. The museum was to present, besides cult objects, paintings, and photographs, a summary of the successes of the ghetto administration and the results of ghetto production. The "scientific department" in the ghetto was set up on order of the German ghetto administration, without consultation with the Eldest of the Jews and his archive, in June 1942 and was to report to Biebow directly. Meanwhile ensued a protracted controversy between the ghetto administration and Reich ministry of propaganda. The ministry rejected all plans for a "cultural exhibit." "People should be glad that the Jews have disappeared from their lives. It was hardly desirable to arouse any interest in them." In a reply dated August 27, 1942, to a decline of June 24, 1942, the ghetto administration tried to take the teeth out of the objections:

    > This exhibit is merely to be comprised of a few Thora scrolls, caftans, prayerbooks, a few pictures of Jewish types, as well as images of the

> Jewish communal life, such as the primitive manner of excrement disposal, the dilapidated housing, and so on. Such an exhibit is in no way meant to make an interesting impression on the viewer, rather, a repelling one. With regard to exhibiting cult objects I will, of course, abide by any regulations that you will issue to me. Otherwise, the ghetto administration and its director will guarantee that those who come into contact with [the exhibit] will see the Jews and current Jewish life represented in a form that will arouse in anybody a feeling of revulsion. [Gettoverwaltung an Reichspropagandaamt beim Reichsstatthalter in Posen am 27.8. 1942 (Ghetto administration to the Reich propaganda bureau at the Reich governor in Poznan on August 27, 1942), Polish State Archive.]

The "scientific department," meanwhile, was working on the creation of a folkloristic group of figures with themes like "Chassidic Wedding in Poland" and "Candle Lighting on Shabbat," or scenes in the synagogue as well as paintings and graphic prints (excrement transport, Jewish police, etc.).

Oskar Rosenfeld describes in Notebook 12, in carefully chosen words, the work of the "scientific department." He writes, among other things:

> The figures, or scenes, are mounted in glass cases that were made in the ghetto by trained experts, artisans. The cases are about 2 m wide, 80 cm high, 70 cm deep. The figures are the size of figures in a puppet theater. In part they have a caricature effect, in part they appear symbolic—depending on the kind of person they are supposed to represent and symbolize. The reasons for this are manifold:
>
> 1. Through the smaller scale, individual traits, like details in posture, are eliminated. Certain characteristics have to be left out, and others again, so that they still have some effect on the small scale, so that they are emphasized and made more coarse.
> 2. The massing of figures is due to the fact that one picture, one scene, has to exhaustively express the set theme. For example, the actors in a Chassidic wedding and their actions are represented in a small space.
> 3. The costumes—which in a normal figure are infused with life through the movements of the one wearing them, bending as the

person walks, struts, sits, etc.—remain rigid in their miniature representation. They appear doll-like, mummylike, annoying, comical, like caricatures.

4. The figures are crowded together. They form a collective not found in real life in this form, especially since they all have to be made to fit into a cramped space.
5. Figures that don't belong together, which are even socially totally different, are forced to touch each other, play with each other. Figures of opposite types are put together shoulder to shoulder, which, of course, can have a grotesque effect.
6. Even in real life, individual figures in and of themselves have a tendency to appear comical. Exaggerated accessories, penetrating colors, pathos of gestures—motions without words—bring unconsciously to mind puppet plays and their often maudlin and childish-dumb texts and plots.
7. The person responsible for these figure groups took into account, through overemphasis on objectivity, the taste and intention of those who are using this exhibit for their particular purposes.

In the end, the museum never materialized. Instead, a series of exhibits, with the participation of the statistics department of the Eldest of the Jews, were mounted for those particularly interested in ghetto production, customers such as businesspeople and army representatives as well as commissioners and political functionaries.

The "scientific department" was dissolved on June 24, 1943. It is possible that some of the figure groups that were in production were completed. What happened to them is unknown. A few of the figures were photographed. Contact prints are in the Polish State Archive of Łódź.

13. Hersz Szylis, a painter, worked in the ghetto with Israel Lejzerowicz, for the scientific department among other places.
14. During the first two years of the ghetto's existence, numerous youth groups and kibbutzim, agricultural cooperatives preparing for emigration to Palestine, still existed in Marysin. Since opposition to Rumkowski was rife within these groups, they were dissolved in the spring of 1941; they continued to work as youth groups, in part tolerated, in part secretly.
15. On April 19, 1943, on the eve of Passover, the SS began the final

destruction of the Warsaw ghetto. They met with unexpected strong resistance. Although the second deportation wave of January 18–22, 1943, had already been met with resistance by ghetto fighters, they had not been able to prevent the Nazis from deporting five to six thousand people. Now ensued a protracted, step-by-step annihilation action in the ghetto itself. At the start of the Warsaw ghetto uprising, the population in various areas of the ghetto was still fifty to sixty thousand. On May 16, 1943, the SS and Police General Jürgen Stroop announced: "Warsaw no longer has a Jewish residential district!"

16. Notebook 15 contains the following entry:

> **Tuesday, April 27.** Last day of Pesach. Minyan at Luzer Najman's, Dworska. From the window wood and coal center. Jews work there. Rain, storm. Gradually the room begins to fill.
>
> *Chazen* [Yidd., cantor], Praszkier, Schipper, Reingold, Schenschlini, Lublinksi, Wolkowicz, Caro, Überbaum, Freund, Rembelinski, Kleinmann, Kaufmann, Dr. Singer, and I.—*Shachris* [Yidd., morning prayer; Hebr., *shacharit*] and *mussaf* [additional prayer on Shabbat and festivals]. All in tallith, small Sefer Torah, an old treasure with *klej-kojdes* [Yidd., sacred objects], belongs to Boruch, who takes understandable pleasure in such things. Cantor Tafel sings beautifully [Moses Tafel was arrested on June 7, 1944, for illegally listening to the radio]. *Yizkor.* (Maskir [Hebr., memorial service] . . .) [Hebr., memory of the dead]. Wonderful atmosphere when Caro gives introduction to *Yizkor* and declares that they all passed away for Kiddush HaShem.
>
> Especially noteworthy: "Died, slain, starved, . . . etc." At the end together, "*Secher l'tzias Mizrajim* . . ." Only the Eastern Jews in Jewish life, magnificent how they celebrate such an improvised minyan.

17. B. I.—coupon (food ration for department chiefs and secretaries in the ghetto).
18. Dawid Gertler was arrested by the Gestapo on July 12, 1943. See also note 11 to Notebook E.
19. The note is to the dismissal of the mayor of Łódź, Werner Ventzki. His successor was Dr. Otto Bradfisch, born 1903, a lawyer and, since spring 1942, head of the Gestapo Litzmannstadt. Bradfisch was one of the chief organizers of the extermination deportations

in 1942. Prior to that he was active as an organizer of mass execution in the Ukraine by the Einsatzkommando 8 of the Einsatzgruppe B (mobile SS killing squads). Bradfisch had little interest in the economic exploitation of the ghetto population and pushed for a quick liquidation of the ghetto.

20. The reference is to the punitive assignment to excrement transports.

Notebook 15

Chapter title: Like Notebook 22, this notebook contains numerous abbreviations, which have been spelled out here to make them legible.

1. Shabbatai Zvi (1626–1676), a false messiah from Smyrna, leader of a widespread messianic movement. He converted to Islam in 1666.

Notebook 17

1. A longer version, written down on July 3, 1943, exists with the heading "The Face of the Ghetto, June 1943." It concludes with the sentence: "In the end nobody can escape the oppression of the ghetto. The June sun peers through the rain and the duskiness, people trot out to the ressorts, and barefoot children with pale cheeks and knowing, all too knowing, eyes sing the street melody: 'Sacharina originale finf a marek.'"

Notebook J

1. Insertion: Book of Judith 16:20. "Woe to the nations that rise against my people; the Lord Almighty will punish them on the day of judgment."
2. See note 4 to Notebook G.
3. Name for the workers in the ghetto who loaded and transported flour. Allusion to *wajze chevre* (Yidd., street urchin).

Notebook K

1. The "outsettlement" was in this case actually for "work" at the HASAG Works in Częstochowa, where comparatively bearable conditions prevailed. The majority of these workers survived.
2. Reference to the construction of temporary housing for those who were bombed out.
3. Reference to Kiddush HaChaim (sanctification of life). See note 6 for Notebook H. A similar formulation is found in Notebook 22. See note 1 to Notebook 22.
4. Jakob Wechsler and his brothers Shimon and Henoch were hiding a homemade radio receiver to which they listened regularly with friends, among these Oskar Rosenfeld. In the following, Rosenfeld alludes to it repeatedly.
5. Mendel Grosman, born 1912, an artist and photographer. At the behest of the Eldest of the Jews and with approval of the ghetto administration, Grosman took photographs for the scrapbooks and other documentation of the statistics department as well as for work permits in the ghetto. However, he also used the film material, which was put at his disposal for this purpose, for other, illegal photographs illustrating deportations and hunger. Grosman was deported to Oranienburg-Sachsenhausen on the last transport from Łódź. He died of exhaustion on one of the death marches shortly before liberation.
6. Coworker of the *Daily Chronicle.*
7. Reference presumably to a radio receiver.
8. Nahum Sokolow, born 1886 in Wishograd, Hebrew writer and journalist, president of the Zionist executive committee 1920–1931, president of the Jewish Agency and the Zionist Organization 1931–1935; died 1936 in London.
9. Reference presumably to the Allied landing in Normandy. The following day (June 7, 1944), the Wechsler brothers and others from the group of radio listeners were arrested in the ghetto, taken away, and executed. Several people were arrested on the same day at the barbershop Tatarka, where newspaper and copies of radio broadcasts were spread out and read aloud.

Notebook 20

Chapter title: Several of these entries appeared also as short articles in the *Daily Chronicle.*

1. The transports went without exception to the extermination camp Kulmhof (Chełmno). This was preceded by a protracted tug-of-war, concerning the liquidation of the ghetto, between the Reichssicherheitshauptamt and the Gauleitung (Germ., provincial government), the SS-Wirtschaftsverwaltungshaupamt (SS Chief Economic Administration Bureau), and army inspectors. An agreement had been reached back in February 1944 not to turn the ghetto into a concentration camp (and thereby put it under the auspices of the SS) as Himmler had originally ordered, but to "decrease its size step by step" and then evacuate it completely. "The decrease in size will be carried out by the Sonderkommando of SS-Hauptsturmführer Bormann, which has already been active earlier in the province," wrote Provincial Governor Greiser on February 14, 1944, to the head of the SS-Wirtschaftsverwaltungshaupamt Oswald Pohl. For this purpose the killing installation in Chełmno was reactivated already in April 1944.

   In early June, Reich Minister Speer made one more unsuccessful attempt to maintain the production capacity of the ghetto for the army. Likewise, without effect, was the intervention on the part of Biebow whose own career (and, before his being sent to the front, secure position) was closely connected with the continued existence of the ghetto.

   On June 15, 1944, Bradfisch ordered Rumkowski to hold three thousand men a week in reserve "for work deployment in the German cities during the removal of damage caused by bombing raids." Rumkowski issued an appeal on June 16, 1944, for "work deployment volunteers." By July 14, there were seven; one hundred ninety-six human beings were taken to Chełmno and gassed. Several of the victims were forced prior to their death to write postcards to relatives in the ghetto, "from Leipzig." The cards arrived in the ghetto on July 25 when none of the writers were alive anymore.

   Information about the fate of the deportees had reached the

ghetto before then. The diary of a young boy, which was later found in Auschwitz, contains the following entry dated July 16:

> It is pretty much certain that the seven thousand brothers who were outsettled this last month were also "treated in the well-known manner." . . . A letter was found in one of the railway cars that was being cleaned in the ghetto after the ride—a letter whose content made us shudder. It said that the outsettled were being taken to the area of Kolo! . . . The place of the "slaughterhouse" . . . rumors are penetrating the ghetto about four hundred thousand Hungarian Jews who were taken to Poland to be offered to Hitler. [The diary, which was written in Polish, Yiddish, English, and Hebrew, on the page of a French novel, is at Yad Vashem.]

The gassing at Chełmno was temporarily halted in mid-July. The action did not proceed fast enough in view of the approaching Russian army.

2. On July 30, 1944, the last, preserved *Daily Chronicle* was edited in the ghetto.

On August 2, Rumkowski announced that, on order of Bradfisch, the ghetto would have to be "moved to a different location."

At first the deportations got only slowly off the ground. People refused to appear at the collection points; many tried to go into hiding to escape the transports.

On August 7, Biebow made speeches at various places in the ghetto. The ghetto, just as the city "Litzmannstadt" itself, had to be evacuated because of the threat of bombing raids. The workshops of the ghetto would be moved to the German Reich.

> The relocation of the ghetto should proceed with calm, order, and benevolence. [. . .] I assure you that we will do our very best to continue to achieve the utmost and to save your life through the relocation of the ghetto. [. . .] I know you want to live and eat, and that's what you will do. I am not standing around here like a dumb schoolboy, making a speech that nobody follows. If you force me to use force, then we'll have dead and wounded. [. . .] The piggish mess and laxness must stop, that I'm telling you. I'm not an itinerant preacher who rushes through the ghetto. If you are not reasonable, the ghetto administration will resign and forcible measures will be taken. [. . .]

> There's room enough in the railway cars, the machinery is adequately relocated. Come with your families, take your pots, drinking vessels, and flatware; we don't have those in Germany since everything has been distributed to bombing victims . . . [The text of the speech is in the archive of the YIVO Institute for Jewish Research in New York.]

Biebow's speeches had their effect. By August 30, the entire population of the ghetto was rounded up by the SS and deported. Only about six hundred members of the "cleanup squad" and about two hundred seventy people who had managed to hold out in hiding places remained in the ghetto and were liberated by the Red Army on January 14, 1945. Another small group was directly deported to Oranienburg-Sachsenhausen in November. After the SS had erased the tracks of their murderous actions in Chełmno, Auschwitz-Birkenau became the new destination for deportations. About sixty-five thousand human beings were taken there from Łódź. Rumkowski himself was taken to Auschwitz on August 28 and, like most, was murdered shortly after his arrival. About one-third of the deportees were assigned to forced labor in various satellite camps. Several thousand were liberated.

Oskar Rosenfeld, who had turned sixty in May 1944, was murdered in the gas chambers of Auschwitz-Birkenau immediately upon his arrival.

About the Author

Oskar Rosenfeld was born on May 13, 1884, in Koryčany, Moravia. A founder of the Jewish Stage, the first Jewish theater in Vienna, he was a novelist, a playwright, a journalist, and an editor of the Zionist *Wiener Morgenzeitung* and the weekly *Die Neue Welt.* With the annexation of Austria to the German Reich in 1938, Rosenfeld fled with his wife to Prague, where he worked as a correspondent for the *Jewish Chronicle* in London, where he hoped to immigrate. Stranded by the outbreak of the war, he was deported to Łódź together with five thousand Jews in November 1941. When the ghetto was liquidated in August 1944, he was deported to Auschwitz, where he was murdered.